Johannes
BRAHMS

To my wife Anne

Johannes
BRAHMS

Ivor Keys

CHRISTOPHER HELM
LONDON

Christopher Helm (Publishers) Ltd
Imperial House, 21–25 North Street,
Bromley, Kent BR1 1SD
ISBN 0-7470-1805-7

A CIP catalogue record for this book is available from the British
Library.

Typeset by Paston Press, Loddon, Norfolk
Printed and bound in Great Britain
by Biddles, Guildford

Contents

Foreword and Acknowledgments

As his opus numbers approached the century mark Brahms was dismayed by a modest proposal from his publisher Fritz Simrock for a dated catalogue of his works. How much more would that elusive man have been repelled by the notion of a 'life and work' book, deeming the former irrelevant to the latter, and in any case nobody's business. As for the works we are on dangerous ground, and risk the wrath of his shade, in surmising by what promptings most of them came to be initiated. Concerning the actual processes of composition, which continue to fascinate in varying degrees all but the most superficial hearers, Brahms probably could not, and obviously would not, tell even his intimate circle how these 'heaven sent' formings of his materials came about. The finished work must be taken or left, must stand or fall. But if one has patience to read a surprisingly voluminous correspondence to and from fellow musicians, publishers and friends, there are precious points to be picked up, sometimes by implication, about compositional details (especially in the Joachim correspondence) and about details of the means by which the works came before the public, including the numbers and quality of the performers.

Two women who did not shrink from giving their reactions (greatly prized, as often as not) to Brahms's music were Clara Schumann and Elisabet von Herzogenberg, and the latter's husband, being a teacher of composition and a prolific but dull practitioner, added comments and queries, sometimes in the humble manner of Dr Watson seeking clarifications from Sherlock Holmes.

Brahms cannot have been unaware of posterity, and he built his works to last. In a rare, precious conversation recorded by the singer and aspiring composer George Henschel he said:

> One ought never to forget that by actually perfecting *one* piece one gains and learns more than by . . . half-finishing a dozen. Let it rest, let it rest, and keep going back to it over and over again, until it is . . . a finished work of art, until there is not a note too much or too little, not a bar you could improve upon. Whether it is *beautiful* also, is an entirely different matter, but perfect it *must* be.

You see, I am rather lazy, but I never cool down over a work once begun, until it is perfectly unassailable.

Nevertheless these 'unassailable' works were addressed to his fellow men then and there, and ran the inevitable gauntlet, which certainly did not prevent some of them being assailed.

Some biographers have subscribed to the notion of a fairly humdrum life only tangentially relevant to the corpus of music, and adjusted their 'life and works' proportions accordingly. Brahms's first biographer, Max Kalbeck, did not take this line. In a monumental four-volume work occupying a decade (1904–14) he put all the details of the life and the works in one large continuous narrative in, as far as possible, chronological order. One's instincts nearly a century later are to attempt this again. The life was clearly lived for the works, and the works were clearly addressed to the living (and by force of circumstance, to live performances, there being no other kind). Without anticipating what the book has to say, it is obvious that the quality of much of Brahms's music far transcends its period. Otherwise there would no longer be books about Brahms, as opposed to research documents. But his importance to music history lies in the persuasiveness of his achievements, in instrumental music and song particularly, in a world of centrifugal artistic forces. Wagner and Verdi were huge figures but specialists: the history of chamber music would have benefited very little in their hands. Berlioz's great masterpiece *Les Troyens* was an opera again, quite unknown except through false rumours.

Kalbeck tirelessly collected first-hand evidence about Brahms from every conceivable source while it was still available. When there is no evidence to the contrary, or any suggestion of improbability, we have no reason to dispute his facts. But the weakness consists in the number of surmises about the genesis of the music, and the various levels of analysis, again with surmises, which arise from its 'straight-through' embodiment in the biography.

To divide this book into 'narrative' (Chapters one to six) and 'catalogue' (Chapter seven) is, one hopes, not an evasion of the difficulty. The narrative includes all the important works, their dissemination, their audience and the current aesthetics and prejudices of the day; all of these are the life. The catalogue adds, for most of the works, particular observations. These may be details of the content of the songs—a key to Brahms much under-used in modern performance—or they may be of a more analytical kind, particularly pointing to Brahms's surprises in the matter of form and key structure. These are by no means intended for students alone. Most of the music examples have been arranged, so far as is consistent with a proper indication of the score, for two hands in the hopes that they will be heard rather than merely read.

It will be evident from the references which books and articles have been particularly consulted. Very large Brahms bibliographies can be found in reference dictionaries (e.g. *The New Grove Dictionary of Music and Musicians*). Two recent specialist books are: (for the choral music) Virginia Hancock, *Brahms's Choral Compositions and his Library of Early Music* (UMI Research Press, Ann Arbor, Michigan, 1983), and (for the songs) A. Craig Bell, *The Lieder of Brahms* Grian-Aig Press, Darley, 1979.

The pillars of the present work are:

(a) The 16 volumes of *Briefwechsel*, Deutsche Brahms Gesellschaft, Berlin, 1907–22 and reprinted by Schneider, Tutzing, 1974. These are in German and the translations are mine. Brahms frequently omitted dates, and the editors supplied them in brackets. To simplify matters, I have incorporated them without differentiation, unless they have been shown to be incorrect.

(b) *Letters of Clara Schumann and Johannes Brahms 1853–1896*, edited by Berthold Litzmann, published in English in two volumes, Arnold, London, 1927, reprinted in paperback by Vienna House, 1973.

(c) *The Herzogenberg Correspondence* edited by Max Kalbeck, Murray, London, 1909.

(d) Litzmann's *Clara Schumann, an Artist's Life*, two volumes, Macmillan, London, 1913.

(e) Kalbeck's *Johannes Brahms*, four volumes, Deutsche Brahms Gesellschaft, Berlin, 1904–14, reprinted Schneider, Tutzing, 1974.

(f) The indispensable Catalogue of his works, by Margit L. McCorkle and Donald M. McCorkle: *Johannes Brahms-Thematisch-Bibliographisches Werkverzeichnis*, Henle, Munich, 1984.

My acknowledgements are in alphabetical order: Mr Ian Ledsham and his staff at the Barber Institute Music Library, University of Birmingham for much patient help in the assembling of materials; Mrs Rosalind Lund for tireless and accurate work on a word-processor; Prof. Robert Pascall of Nottingham University for very prompt and unselfish assistance, particularly for a photostat of Schumann's 'Neue Bahnen' article; Dr Michael Robbins for prompt and detailed help with a number of queries on the European railways of Brahms's day; Mrs Christina Tebbutt of Boughton, Northampton, for the loan of an invaluable out-of-print source, George Henschel's *Musings and Memories of a Musician*; Prof. David Tunley (University of Western Australia) for facilitating my reading of Kalbeck in Perth; Richard Wigmore, for reading and perceptive comments; Emeritus Prof. R. Willetts (Birmingham University) for quick attention to a query on Zeus and Kronos, involving some abstruse information at his fingertips.

I.K.

The publishers would like to thank the Royal College of Music for granting permission to use photographs and engravings from their collection. Particular thanks are due to Paul Collen for all his help with picture research.

PART ONE

PART ONE

CHAPTER ONE

To the Accolade

On 7 May 1833, in a tenement apartment in a seamy district of Hamburg, Johannes Brahms was born—a name known by all who love music. But it might have been Brahms*t*, for this is how it figures on a certificate given to his father, Johann Jakob, and subsequently treasured by Johannes. Johann Jakob was born in Holstein in the marshy country north of the Elbe estuary on 1 June 1806,and he left the family trade in mixed grocery and second-hand goods (including pawnbroking) to make a living in music with practically nothing in his pocket. The father's escape might have been called an escapade, but it certainly saved Johannes from middle-class parental opposition to the notion of an 'itinerant musician', which title he was later to give himself with pride. Johann Jakob served a sort of musical apprenticeship ending in December 1825, and the certificate describes him as having had three years in the municipal music of Heide (in Holstein) and two years in learning instrumental music with Theodore Müller. When he arrived in Hamburg he played the horn in the town guard (*Bürgergewehr*) and in dance-music in the sailors' quarter; then he graduated as double bass to a sextet of superior musicians hiring themselves out for dances, serenades and celebrations. This settled position, such as it was, in the sextet seems to date from 1840, but ten years before that the bold young man married his landlady, Christiane Nissen (full name Johanna Henrika Christiane Nissen) born in Hamburg 17 years before himself. The first child of what was initially a happy and loving marriage was Elisabeth Wilhelmine Luise (*b*-1831), the second Johannes, and the third Friedrich (*b*-1835) who as the years proceeded got no pleasure from being called the 'other' Brahms, or even the 'wrong' Brahms. The proud father even used some of the scanty resources to announce the birth of Johannes in the local paper *Wochentliche Nachrichten* ('Weekly news').

Few hard facts survive about Brahms's early childhood. We owe to Kalbeck the justifiable surmise that Johannes gained his pronounced francophobia at his mother's knee from her horror stories of the French occupation of Hamburg, and the facts that he witnessed the two-day fire of Hamburg in 1842 which roared uncomfortably close to his family home before a change of wind, and that a year later he was run over by a *droshky* on the way to school, one wheel passing over his chest, which caused him a six-week convalescence.

It perhaps goes without saying that he was teased at school for practising the piano, but this does not figure among the 'Hamburg scars' which he adverted to later in life. It was natural that the father should recognise the son's great musical talent, first teaching him the elements himself, and in 1840 sending him for lessons to Otto Cossel, a pupil of the doyen of Hamburg music teachers Eduard Marxsen. From his own experience, Johann Jakob supposed that the only realistic way to earn money by music in their circumstances was through an orchestral instrument, so perhaps he was more disconcerted by the boy's obvious penchant for the piano. His precocious mastery soon brought him towards the limits of what Cossel could teach him, especially as he showed obvious creative gifts allied to that particularly acute aural memory usually called 'perfect pitch'. For a few years Cossel and Marxsen exercised an amicable condominium—in later life Johannes made unstinting acknowledgements to both—but from 1845 Marxsen took over the entire responsibility; vitally important to Johannes, Marxsen was a conscientious composer in both the small and large forms. As for using his talents in public, Johannes not only helped on the piano at his father's occasional engagements at dockside taverns and elsewhere, but got an early taste for out-of-town excursions: the opening in 1842 of the Hamburg-Bergedorf section of the Berlin line led to Sunday solos at the Gasthof 'zur schönen Aussicht' ('At the beautiful view').

In 1843 the father and his colleagues arranged for the son a semi-private subscription concert in aid of his future education. The calibre of the executants, and their superior tastes when circumstances allowed, is shown by the programme: the Beethoven Quintet op.16 for oboe, clarinet, bassoon, horn and piano, one of the Mozart piano quartets, and an étude for piano solo by Henri Herz with which no doubt Johannes brought the house down. The prodigy was not unremarked and the condominium resisted, with the father's perhaps wistful concurrence, a proposal from an agent that Johannes should tour the USA. The night-life of dockside bars cannot but have obtruded on the teenager, and shaped his disconcerting, fearful and chauvinistic notions of the female sex. We do not know whether Pastor Geffeken of the protestant St. Michael's church, who confirmed Johannes in 1848, was able to ameliorate or merely strengthen these prejudices, but we do know that, self-taught or not, Brahms throughout his life showed a thorough-going knowledge of the bible—and the apocrypha—and later had as a treasured possession a copy of Luther's bible of 1545.

Meanwhile, in 1847, Johannes had a respite from Hamburg in a long summer spent at Winsen in the countryside to the south-east on the way to Lüneburg. Here he was the guest of Herr and Frau Giesemann, friends of his father, a visit repeated the following spring. His first public concert was in November 1847, to which he contributed another barn-stormer, Sigismond

4

Thalberg's Fantasia and Variations on Themes from Bellini's *Norma*. However, an altogether greater moment was the experience of hearing Joseph Joachim play Beethoven's Violin Concerto on 11 March 1848. In early 1855, by which time the two were intimate friends, Johannes had confessed to Joachim:

> Always and always the concerto reminds me of our first acquaintanceship, of which you admittedly know nothing. You played it in Hamburg, it must be many years ago, and I was certainly your most enraptured listener. It was a time when quite chaotic emotions seethed in me, and it made no difference to me to confuse you with Beethoven. I reckoned the concerto to be your own.

He went on to say that the recollection brought to mind three most powerful impressions: the Symphony in C Minor (Beethoven's Fifth), this concerto, and *Don Giovanni*.

Another life-time interest has been remarked by Virginia Hancock:

> Brahms wrote his name and that date (1848) in an old copy of David Kellner's 1743 treatise *Treuliche Unterricht im General-Bass* ['Trustworthy treatise on general-bass'] which also had a copy of Johann Mattheson's *Die Kunst, das Clavier zu spielen* ['The art of keyboard playing'] bound in at the back. This is just the first of a number of eighteenth-century books of instruction in musical practice which are to be found in his collection.[1]

On 21 September 1848 Brahms's first own public concert took place; it netted a negligible amount, but its programme is worth reproducing as a reliable indication of public taste (Bach excluded) considering its purpose.

1. Adagio and Rondo from Pianoforte Concerto in A by Jacob Rosenhain [presumably without accompaniment], played by Brahms

2. Duet from Mozart's *Figaro* sung by Madame Cornet and Fräulein Cornet [Madame Cornet was the leading local singer-teacher, particularly of opera]

3. Variations for Violin by Alexandre Artôt, played by Risch [a friend of the Brahms household]

4. Song: 'Das Schwabenmädchen', sung by Madame Cornet

5. Fantasie on motifs from Rossini's *Guillaume Tell* by Theodore von Döhler, played by Brahms

Interval

6. Introduction and Variations for Clarinet by Johann Georg Herzog, played by Glade [a household friend]

7. Air from *Figaro*, sung by Fräulein Cornet

8. Fantasie for Cello, composed and played by d'Afrien [a household friend]

9. (*a*) 'Der Tanz'
   (*b*) 'Der Fischer auf dem Meer'
   (two Lieder by Marxsen, sung by Madame Cornet)

10. Fugue by Johann Sebastian Bach [which, is unknown]

11. Serenade (for the left hand alone) by Marxsen [a precedent for Brahms in the genre]

12. Etude by Henri Herz [perhaps the same one as in 1843]

Hereabouts, or a few years later, Brahms began a series of pocket-books—one can hardy call them 'commonplace books' in view of their huge range of quotations—which he entitled *Schatzkästlein des jungen Kreisler* ('Young Kreisler's little treasure-chest'). The 'Kreisler' was the fictitious creation of the novelist and music critic E.T.A. Hoffmann (he of the *Tales*), the fantastic and iconoclastic standard-bearer of all eager Romantics. He gave name and inspiration to Schumann's piano pieces *Kreisleriana* op.16 (1838), but Brahms probably knew nothing of this at the time. What the pocket-books' quotations do tell us (some 645 in all, but a few contributed by Joachim) is that Brahms was as red-blooded a romantic artist as any, but that he had a huge appetite for history—of mankind in general, not merely of Marxsen-induced Bach.

Kalbeck writes of another appearance at a speculative public concert on 1 March 1849, which makes piquant reading. The 'benefit' was shared with Theodor Wachtel, a *droshky*-driver turned singer. Brahms contributed as a solo Thalberg's Fantasie on Motifs from Don Juan, the placard called him Brahm*t*, and the belated concert notice praised the singer but did not mention the pianist. There was a second, better advertised, own-benefit soirée on 10 April in which Brahms played Beethoven's 'Waldstein' Sonata, re-peated Thalberg's *Don Juan*, and also played an 'Air Italien' by Karl Mayer and, as a first public hearing of one of his own compositions, a Fantasie on a Favourite Waltz. The latter was repeated, with more Thalberg, at another shared concert with a singer on 5 December, but did not survive the holocaust of juvenilia which the veteran composer looked back upon in his early twenties! At this time there was a large, and sentimentally acclaimed, colony of Hungarians in Hamburg, *en route* for the most part to the USA, having been made refugees by the drastic re-imposition of Viennese authority after the brief and heroic independence, under Kossuth and others, arising from the 1848 revolution. On 10 November in the municipal theatre of Hamburg a violinist, Eduard Reményi, contributed as announced 'some farewell-songs on the violin' to a Hungarian *pot-pourri* of songs and dances. Whether or not Brahms heard this actual concert—more likely than not—and whatever a modern ethnomusicologist might say about authenticity, the 'Hungarian-isms' of the day remained with Brahms for life, and this of course was etched into his mind before he had any inkling that he would live most of his adult life as a faithful resident in the capital of the Austro-Hungarian Empire.

The year 1850 could have been more significant than it turned out to be, for it was marked by a visit to Hamburg of Robert Schumann and his pianist-virtuoso wife Clara. It is hardly to be supposed that Johannes did not attend the Philharmonic concert on 16 March at which Robert conducted his *Genoveva* Overture and Clara played her husband's concerto. What is more, a few days later Clara shared two concerts with Jenny Lind, the soprano nicknamed 'the Swedish nightingale'. Johannes took the opportunity to send a parcel of compositions to Schumann, but Schumann did not take the opportunity to open it, probably being pre-occupied by worries as to a move from Dresden to Düsseldorf to succeed Ferdinand Hiller as municipal director of music, to which indeed he sent his agreement at the end of the month. 'Pre-occupied' is probably a mild word for one who had already suffered a severe nervous breakdown. What was in the unopened parcels is unknown. The first completed of the published works were the Scherzo op.4[2] and the song 'Heimkehr' op.7, no.6, but modern scholarship does not date them before 1851. Unknown to Johannes, fate was reserving for him a far more momentous encounter with the Schumanns, but an unwitting precursor down this road was his friend Louise Japha who went to Düsseldorf to study with Robert, but found herself mainly with Clara.

If it is the earliest survivor of Brahms's compositions, the Scherzo in E flat minor op.4 is quintessentially of his style, without longueurs or wasted notes. Its pounding passions are all the more forceful for the formal grip which deepens their channels. The main key of E flat minor reinforces visually the audibly spectacular. Another indelible finger-print is the climactic elongation of the

into

making a cross-rhythm known to all baroque composers, but given new life and indeed sledge-hammer force. If the piece were originally conceived as a sonata movement (for which there is no evidence) this is contradicted by its eventual shape, with two substantial 'trios', each with its lead-back into the main subject, which is extended at the final entry. To write a free-standing self-sufficient scherzo had its precedents in the four examples by Chopin. Indeed, the opening gestures with their intervening silences are bound to remind one of the beginning of Chopin's Scherzo in B flat minor op.31, as also the lyrical tune and its accompaniment in the second 'trio'. However, the very 'reminiscence' is in itself Brahmsian, evoking a defiant 'so what' that we shall encounter again in the first symphony.

As to 'Heimkehr', 21 *passionato* bars *allegro agitato* suffice for the home-coming, to Uhland's images: 'Break not, path . . . drop not, cliff . . . earth, dissolve not, heavens fall not, till I can be with my love'. This represents a better fate than many of Schubert's earth-tramping lovers attain, and Brahms pulls no punches in going from minor to major at the end. But note already the contrapuntal power that makes the left hand melodic, to imitate and urge on the voice. Song was the one genre of music that occupied Brahms all his life, and this one makes a memorable start.

To 1852 is assigned a piano sonata, subsequently op.2, the slow movement of the op.1 Sonata, and probably the andante and intermezzo of the op.5 Piano Sonata, though these may date from Brahms's 'Rhine journey' of the following summer. Certainly the rest of opp.1 and 5 were not written out before 1853, the former in spring, the latter in autumn. The works form a trilogy of the only extant piano sonatas—he never went back to the genre—and are discussed together in the second part.

While these works were coming to fruition, or perhaps merely lodging themselves in the brain, a crop of songs can be allotted to 1852, but first, dated 8 March (but not published until 1869) was a curiosity, Brahms's étude arrangement for the left hand, accompanied by the right, from the perpetual-motion rondo from Weber's C major Sonata for piano, op.24. This was a famous war-horse of the nineteenth-century virtuosi. To transfer its four minutes of continuous semiquavers from the right hand to the left was an indication of Brahms's technique, and a tribute to Marxsen's instigation of it—not forgetting the concert programme of 1848.

A body of some 200 songs, individually described, would exceed the scope of this book, and would be out of proportion to their general quality *vis-à-vis*, say, the chamber music. But this is not to say that the comparatively meagre number in general recital use is justifiable. The catalogue (Chapter 7) of works lists titles, poets, first lines and dates, with some analytical points, but this narrative also mentions points of historical or biographical interest. For instance, of the 1852 songs one is bound to notice that the *Spanisches Lied*, op.6. no.1, sets the same words, translated by P. Heyse ('In dem Schatten meiner Locken') as Hugo Wolf in his more famous version from his *Spanisches Liederbuch* published in 1891. Perhaps there is a more telling economy in Wolf, with the gently sighing 'Ach nein!' once at the end of each stanza instead of Brahms's thrice, but it is interesting to see Brahms first in the field with the castanet rhythm of

predominant in the piano's dextrous texture. Op.7, no.1, 'Treue Liebe', holds its own in anthologies with a vivid water-music on the piano and a memorable and folk song-like tune strikingly varied at the climax where the true love meets the beloved not on the shore but in the waters.

By far the most noteworthy of the 1853 songs is the one which Brahms chose to be the first published, 'Liebestreu', op.3, no.1. The poet, Robert

Reinick, had a connection with Schumann, for whom he began to make an opera libretto out of C.F. Hebbel's play *Genoveva*, before Schumann took it over himself, not much to the work's advantage. The song of passionate true love, with a large climax, is in E flat minor. More significant is the fact that the left-hand part is melodic, not just a harmony-prop but either a counterpoint to the theme or a close imitation or duplication of it. It also forms below the throbbing triplets a frequent two against three, another favourite textural idiom of Brahms.

Meanwhile Reményi had re-appeared on the Hamburg scene. He has had a bad press in Brahms's biographies, emerging as an opportunist musical charlatan of poor taste and wayward morals. However, he must have been a player of enough calibre and a companion of enough resourcefulness to make his proposal to share a short tour with Brahms an attractive proposition for a home-bound pianist with no travel resources. Reményi's repertoire included the Vieuxtemps Concerto in E major (op.10), the Beethoven 'Kreutzer' and C minor Sonatas. The tour began in April at Winsen, which, as one of the few places where Brahms's friends could help swell an audience, gave them a good start. At Celle occurred the well-known feat of Brahms, because of a low-pitched piano, transposing the Beethoven C minor Sonata into C sharp minor with great sang-froid. It is of course a good deal easier to do this than to modulate, with a different note-placing to imagine, into B minor, but it is a feat none-the-less. Brahms set no store by it, but it may have made Reményi more conscious of where the centre of the stage was, and of his own right to occupy it. After a concert in Lüneberg, the pair, presumably on foot most of the time, went at the end of May to Hanover, where Joachim, until recently one of the Liszt ménage at Weimar, was now *Konzertmeister* ('leading violinist') to the court of the King. Reményi's connection with Joachim rested on their having been fellow students at the Vienna Conservatoire. Brahms's henceforward life-long connection rested on his playing to Joachim the op.4 Scherzo, movements from op.1, and 'Liebestreu', with inevitable results. Joachim arranged for the pair to play to the King, and sent them on to Weimar with an introduction to Franz Liszt. However, he also wrote a glowing account of Brahms to Schumann at Düsseldorf. The first extant letter of the long Brahms–Joachim correspondence dates from the beginning of June. Joachim already calls him 'Mein geliebter Johannes' and suggests that he and Reményi bring to life in Göttingen Brahms's A minor Violin Sonata— alas, yet another work of which there is no trace.

Meanwhile the pair had gone on to Weimar. Kalbeck is very funny, or at least sardonic, about that ménage, where a new phase of genius is announced (as by a pope) '*urbi et orbi* at least once a month with solemn strokes of the tam-tam'. The luxury, the affectations of Liszt's metaphorical incense-burners at the Altenburg, and the general and easily observed insincerities surrounding the great man must have struck, to say the least, the provincial poet-and-peasant nature of Brahms. However, on the other hand there is nothing to show that Liszt himself was not completely urbane throughout the visit, even if the highly suspect story were true that Brahms nodded off during Liszt's performance of his recently completed B minor Piano Sonata. It seems that Brahms, at the crucial moment when a brilliant company had assembled to hear him, was too shy to play, and that Liszt himself played, from manuscript, the op.4 Scherzo, and some of the op.1. Whoever played what, two things were clear: that Brahms was a potential great composer and one to be viewed, naturally, as a splendid recruit to the 'music of the future' emanating from Weimar, and that Liszt was indeed a surpassing pianist, but to be viewed instinctively by Brahms, as the days went by, as a ramshackle composer.

The first extant letter from Brahms to Joachim comes from Weimar at the end of June and contains the words 'Reményi is leaving Weimar without me', which could have been expressed less disingenuously the other way round. Brahms felt he had been left in the lurch (which financially he undoubtedly had been) but Reményi, who had more notion than most as to which side his bread was buttered, would have been irked by Brahms's distancing of himself from a palpable centre of musical patronage. There is a young man's desperation as Brahms continues by confessing that he cannot go back to Hamburg with no achievement to show. Would Joachim back up Liszt's recommendation to Härtel in Leipzig to publish some of Brahms's music? The result was some two months under Joachim's protection in Göttingen, where he was summering. There is a charming and touching letter from Johann Jakob dated 1 August which acknowledges Joachim's goodness in befriending his son. 'May Heaven preserve for Johannes the purity [*Reinheit*] of his youthful spirit'. Refreshed in spirit by joining in student life, and in finances by a joint concert with Joachim, Brahms made his first journey to the Rhine, facilitated by a stay with a family named Deichmann at Mehlem near Godesberg; indeed it was through the Deichmanns' musical parties that Brahms had the pleasure of enlarging his experience of Schumann's music. What is more, Frau Deichmann gave him the pleasure and responsibility of taking her three sons on a walking and steamer trip. So by degrees Düsseldorf and the Schumanns came nearer, and on 30 September the great visit began.

Shyness, memories of unopened parcels, fears of an exalted milieu—all disappeared at Brahms's first touch of the piano (a piano, incidentally, that was to become his treasured possession). And what a touch it was, as the young eagle, as Schumann was to call him, fell upon his first two Sonatas and his Scherzo, before the astonished ears and eyes of the leading living German composer and his virtuoso pianist wife, herself also a composer—the pair, of all pairs, on whom the experience had the utmost effect. We are not talking of the craggy bear Brahms was to become, but of a golden youth with piercing blue eyes and with a lower lip apt to be pressed forwards in moments of emotion, of which there must have been plenty. With Mendelssohn now dead, the Schumanns had reason to remark on the absence of German-speaking composers of the first rank. There surely must come a musical Messiah, if not to save his people from their sins, at least to help consolidate, and build upon, the new realms won by the arch-Romantic Beethoven. That he should be German-speaking could hardly be doubted in view of the history of music from Bach onwards, and, especially if the 'young eagle' began by attacking his op.1, here indeed was Beethoven come again. With its hammer-and-tongs full-orchestra beginning and the abrupt silences of the "put-that-in-your-pipe-and-smoke-it" kind, they would be bound to think of Brahms as carrying on where Beethoven's 'Hammerklavier' Sonata op.106 led—at least to its beginning, as the rhythm of both shows.

(Beethoven)

(Brahms)

Beethoven's extra quaver at the beginning is only an apparent discrepancy as Brahms's left-handful of the first chord takes that amount of time to arpeggiate. It is extremely unlikely that Brahms flinched from the 'plagiarism', still less that he was unconscious of it. So the enraptured Schumann described his guest to Joachim as 'he that should come'. But this is as nothing compared to the famous article 'Neue Bahnen' ('New Paths') which he was to contribute (after a silence of some ten years) to the paper which he had co-founded and edited, the *Neue Zeitschrift für Musik*. The climax of it was:

> It seemed to me . . . that there would and indeed must suddenly appear one man who would be singled out to articulate and give the ideal expression to the tendencies of our time, one man who would show us his mastery, not through a gradual process, but, like Athene, springing fully armed from the head of Zeus. And he has come, a young man over whose cradle Graces and Heroes stood guard. His name is *Johannes Brahms* and he comes from Hamburg, where he has been working in quiet obscurity.

Translators of this famous passage use a variety of names of the two principals in this mythological birth. Schumann's original is, 'Wie Minerva, gleich vollkommen gepanzert aus dem Haupte des Kronien spränge.' Minerva is the Latin equivalent of Athene, but Kronos, if it is he, is certainly a mistake, as he was the father of Zeus (Latin, Jupiter) and thus Athene's grandfather. But Zeus was born in Crete, and a Cretan epithet of Zeus was Kronios (son of the Wizard). So, by letting the epithet stand for the name itself we can save Schumann's reputation. It would attribute to him, and presumably to his readers, an extent of classical knowledge that one cannot imagine in Beethoven or Schubert, even were they minded to write essays.[3] Schumann goes on to say, 'He made of the piano an orchestra of lamenting and exulting voices. There were sonatas—veiled symphonies rather.' 'Sonatas for violin and piano' and 'string quartets' are also mentioned. It tells us much to note

11

the plurals in this last sentence and also to realise that not even one such piece remains from this period. If they had survived previous self-criticism Schumann may have unwittingly killed them with his trumpet summons. There was of course no point at all in writing actual symphonies with no orchestra at beck and call, but Schumann goes on to say, 'Later, if he can wave his magic wand to where the massed forces of chorus and orchestra unite their strength, there lie before us still more glimpses in the secrets of the spirit world.' Brahms does not appear to have read this essay, at least in print, until he shared it with Joachim in Hanover in early November.

In the calm happiness of the Schumann house Brahms worked out most of the third Piano Sonata in F minor, that was to become op.5—that is to say its completion by adding movements 1, 3 and 5 to the already existing 2 and 4, these latter perhaps being products of Hamburg, or even of the 'Rhine journey'. But it was after he left Düsseldorf that all was written down, since it is recorded that he played the entire Sonata to the Schumanns on 2 November (his last night there) 'out of his head'.

An interesting curiosity, and a piece well worth the having, is Brahms's contribution to a sonata for violin and piano put together to welcome the arrival of Joachim on the happy scene. The first movement was by Albert Dietrich, a composition pupil of Schumann's, with whom Brahms struck up a lifelong friendship, and an intermezzo and the finale were by Schumann himself. Brahms's movement was published as an individual scherzo in 1906, well after his death. His chosen key was C minor which was by no means inevitable, with the outer movements in A minor and the intermezzo in D minor. But anyone who chooses C minor and elects to start on G unaccompanied to the rhythm

is intentionally evoking Beethoven's Fifth Symphony. This might not be of moment in a committee-sonata, were it not for the mightier confrontation, deliberately engineered, in Brahms's hard-won first symphony. The welcome-home sonata was called the 'F–A–E Sonata' because it used these notes as its motto, in allusion to Joachim's own motto, *frei aber einsam* (free but lonely) which is taken to be a reference to his then unmarried state. Biographers have assigned to Brahms, following Kalbeck, a counter-motto, *frei aber froh* (free but happy). Michael Musgrave[4] has voiced severe doubts about this, both as to the F–A–F motto's existence and as to its supposed musical expression; for instance, the combination of F–A–E and F–A–F which Kalbeck claimed to see in the opening bars of Brahms's String Quartet in A minor op.51 involves the sort of contortion only acceptable to fringe schools of twentieth-century thought. One might add that the two most usually quoted F–A–Fs, in the Ballade for piano op.10 no.2 and in the Third Symphony, have accidentals which not only alter the intervals but which would be spelt by Germans *Fis–*

A–Fis and *F–As–F* respectively. Furthermore the conjunction sounds wrong in Brahms's mouth; would he not be far more likely to proclaim himself 'free *and* happy'? The Scherzo is a fine rhetorical piece; its drastic galloping is in marked contrast to the slower intermezzo types that Brahms was apt to prefer later on. The trio uses the broader lyrical tune that Schubert brought into vogue at this place in the scheme, but Brahms uses typically asymmetrical lengths of phrase. The final *grandioso, sempre ff* asks too much of two instruments for too long a time. (Perhaps a trick played on the violinist dedicatee.)

Both Joachim and Schumann helped with the delightful but anxious task of finally deciding what Breitkopf and Härtel were to publish. Eventually put out of the reckoning (and out of existence as far as we can see) were a Phantasie for piano trio, another trio, the A minor Violin Sonata and a quartet in B minor, and the agreed first print was of the first four of the canon as it now stands, with the op.5 Sonata and the op.6 songs going to another publisher, Senff.

During the visit Schumann taught Brahms to play chess. In later life Brahms said Schumann had taught him nothing else! But this is perhaps not as brutal as it sounds. As far as composition goes Schumann never taught Brahms, nor purported to. The styles never met, except in reminiscence or homage. From the heart comes the acknowledgement of what the young man *did* learn at that family hearth: *wozu der Mensch auf der Welt sei* ('for what purpose man is in the world').

On 3 November Brahms went to Hanover—to Joachim, who had arrived there a few days before. There, if not before, he encountered the full force of 'Neue Bahnen', now in print for the musical world to see with the predictable emotions of awe, jealousy and fear. But now it was necessary to go to Leipzig to deliver the compositions both to the publishers and, if possible, to the public by performance. Brahms initially balked at this hurdle, calling the city, with a young man's idealistic intolerance, a 'giant counting-house'. But the hurdle, if there was one, fell at his approach. A bare month after he first arrived, he penetrated the august Gewandhaus Chamber Concerts and played, to acclaim, his Sonata op.1 and Scherzo op.4. In the audience were two eminences, Liszt and Berlioz, no less. Clearly the ever-generous Liszt did not allow himself to be affected by any cross-purposes there may have been in Weimar, and as for Berlioz, he had already, with an affable Reményi, met Brahms at a reception, and 'he praised me in such warm and heart-felt terms, that the others meekly agreed with him'. It was a pity that the German never fully reciprocated with the Frenchman, though two years later he went so far as to declare to Clara that a favourite piece was the 'Flight into Egypt' section of *The Childhood of Christ*: 'one is prone to stigmatise as affected and coquettish this sort of simplicity in a man like Berlioz who is inclined otherwise to bully the ears [*sonst so die Ohren mitnimmt*]. I have often heard it, and it has always enchanted me.' The memoirs of the singer George

Henschel contain a charmingly ambiguous side-light supplied by Brahms himself on his youthful playing and demeanour. The Hauptmann referred to is the German composer and music historian (1792–1868). Henschel writes:

> Taking up a volume of Hauptmann's letters I had lent him, he said, 'Just look; do you see these asterisks instead of a name?' I did, and read the whole sentence, which described a certain composer, indicated by asterisks, as a rather haughty young man. 'That's me', said Brahms amusedly. 'When I was a very young man I remember playing, at Göttingen, my Sonata in C to Hauptmann. He was not very complimentary about it; in fact, had much fault to find with it, which I, a very modest youth at the time, accepted in perfect silence.'[5]

Missions accomplished, Brahms left Leipzig on 20 December, in the company of Julius Otto Grimm, a pianist and composer and a life-time friend, then based in Göttingen. Such was the speed at which publishers moved, when they had a mind to, that Brahms, in a Christmas letter of thanks to the Schumanns, was able to send them copies of opp.1 and 3 (Breitkopf and Härtel) and the op.6 songs (Senff), calling them all in their new clean dress his 'foster-children'. Op.1 was dedicated to Joachim, op.3 to Bettina von Arnim, whom Brahms had met in Düsseldorf and then came on dedication terms with in Hanover, through Joachim. This was shrewd, since Bettina was the belle-lettrist widow of the poet Achim von Arnim and had been a friend of Goethe and Beethoven. Op.6 was dedicated to the two Japha sisters of Hamburg, now in Düsseldorf, Minna to study art and Louise music with the Schumanns.

Meanwhile Schumann had written to the delighted Brahms parents in the warmest tones. What a home-coming it must have been! Johannes had set out seven months before not so much to seek his fortune as to keep the wolf a little further from the door, but had returned acclaimed by great musical figures, and above all published. It was truly a happy Christmas, but it was to be a disconcerting New Year.

NOTES

1. V. Hancock, 'The growth of Brahms's interest in early music' in R. Pascall (ed.), *Brahms, biographical, documentary and analytical Studies* (Cambridge University Press, Cambridge, 1983). '

2. Details of the published works, in order by genre and opus no. and analysis of the larger of them, are to be found in Part Two.

3. In this matter I am indebted to two colleagues, Prof. Robert Pascall of Nottingham University for a prompt photocopy of the original, and Emeritus Prof. Ronald Willetts for the facts about Kronios. The reference is: R. Willetts, *Cretan Cults and Festivals* (Routledge and Kegan Paul, London 1962), p. 244 and references.

4.   Michael Musgrave *Frei aber Froh: A Reconsideration*, in *Nineteenth Century Music*, vol. 3 (1979–80), pp. 251ff. (University of California Press).

5.   George Henschel, *Musings and Memories of a Musician*, London 1918.

CHAPTER TWO

To the Requiem

The parental joys could not long detain in Hamburg the youth who had suddenly experienced the exhilaration of the friendship of great ones, like Joachim and the Schumanns, and in January 1854 he was off to stay with Joachim at Hanover, where he added to his circle of professional friends the already considerable figure, as a pianist at least, of Hans von Bülow. One of the effects of Schumann's tremendous introduction was a strengthening of Brahms's rigorous self-criticism in composition. The foster-children in their new clean clothes of publication had to satisfy both believers and disbelievers in the proposed new Messiah. The manuscript which most nearly survived—just possibly an accidental loss—was the Sonata for Violin and Piano in A minor which got as far as being offered to Senff as a proposed op.5. But Senff refused it on the grounds that they did not publish violin music. The F minor Piano Sonata took its place, and no more is heard or seen of the Violin Sonata.

However, one work, dated and signed by 'Kreisler jun.' was at any rate completed in those January days at Hanover: the Trio for Piano, Violin and Cello op.8 in the unusual key of B major. Note the primacy of the piano in the title, as with many other ensemble works of Brahms! This work, then, was the first published of the large body of his chamber music, which far outweighs in combined quality and quantity any rivals in the second half of the nineteenth century. Of course there was much chamber music played in 1854, both by professionals and amateurs, obviously enough for publishers to market. However, if we look at the contributions, if any, of Berlioz, Schumann, Liszt, Wagner and even the relatively prolific but fairly short-lived Mendelssohn, it is clear that chamber music was thin on the ground as far as post-Schubert great composers went, and that to some it was moribund. (This refers to the situation when Brahms was a very young man. Thanks in part to Brahms's encouragement, Dvořák made a signal contribution to 19th-century chamber music. An account of Dvořák's indebtedness is to be found in J. Clapham's 'Dvořák's Relations with Brahms and Hanslick' in *Musical Quarterly* lvii, 1971 (April), p. 241.) That it is alive and well in the twentieth century can properly be credited to the integrity and determination of Brahms, though he was hardly to know this in 1854. Even the op.8 Trio was subjected to drastic afterthoughts (to be discussed later), but not until 1889. Even then the very ambiguity of Brahms's words to Clara (from Ischl, 3 September 1889) show the affection for the 'child of nature':

> With what childish amusement I whiled away the beautiful summer days you will never guess. I have rewritten my B major Trio and can call it op.108 instead of op.8. It will not be as wild as it was before—but whether it will be better—?

The two versions are compared in the catalogue, but some of the 'wildnesses' have their place in a narrative. The signature of 'Kreisler jun.' is a key to some of those in the first movement, notably the whimsicalities, unexpected changes of texture and direction, and a tendency sometimes, but particularly at the end, to go to orchestral extremes of desired force. There are some 50 bars, without modulations, of ever-warmer song before these eruptions begin, but then we are treated to a fantastic patchwork of pseudo-fugues, canons, martial moments and bagpipe pastorals, not really welded by thematic cross-references.

Some of the soft-pedalled piano harmonies of the slow movement read like a more inspired elaboration of the song, 'Liebe und Frühling', from op.3, also in B major; the secondary theme is very reminiscent of Schubert's song, 'Am Meer' from the *Schwanengesang*. From what we know of Brahms, it seems very unlikely that this was accidental, but if it was a message of a secret significance shared for instance with the Schumanns we do not know it now. What is clear, however, is that the suave secondary theme announced by the cello in the last movement:

is a quotation of a quotation. The original is the last song of Beethoven's cycle *An die ferne Geliebte* ('To the distant beloved'): 'Nimm sie hin denn, diese Lieder' ('Take then these my songs'). But it is a phrase which haunts the first movement of Schumann's great C major Fantasy for Piano op.17, a movement which Schumann described to Clara Wieck in their anguished separation before their marriage as 'a deep lament for you'.

Drastically altered though the work was when Brahms was playing with the notion that his creative life was at an end, we should not forget that for eight years, until the appearance of the first String Sextet op.18 in 1862, it held its own as his only, and highly esteemed, published chamber work.

Though the happiness of Brahms's visit had stimulated Schumann to renewed composition, his last such period, in the background loomed not only his propensity to depression and delusions, but also (obvious to all but the Schumanns themselves), his deficiencies as a choral and orchestral conductor, which continued to lead to complaints and innuendoes which they found insulting. In this context their visit to Hanover at the end of January was a triumphant and happy interlude. Brahms had the pleasure of hearing Joachim play Schumann's recent Fantasy in C for Violin and Orchestra, op.131, and, with Joachim conducting, Schumann's Fourth Symphony, and Beethoven's 'Emperor' Concerto with Clara as soloist. The Schumanns went back to Düsseldorf, and shortly afterwards Robert complained of sounds in his ears, sometimes of beautiful music indeed, but more often devilish noises. At intervals he worked at variations for piano on a theme in E flat which he persuaded himself had been dictated to him by spirits. Then on 27 February he suddenly put down his pen, left the house and threw himself into the Rhine. He was rescued by the captain of the steamer *Viktoria*. He had already asked once to be committed to an institution; now his wish was perforce granted, and he was taken to an asylum clinic upstream at Endenich on 4 March.

Without another thought the horrified Brahms rushed to Düsseldorf to the aid of a distraught Clara. The faithful friend Grimm was also there, and like Brahms stayed there through 1854. Dietrich too was a frequent visitor. Joachim could not down tools at the court of Hanover, nor abandon promised engagements, but of course visited Endenich as well as Düsseldorf; he hardly needed telling—in Brahms's letter to him of 3 March—that 'it is an unending comfort to Frau Schumann to see dear well-known faces'. Youthful and inexperienced as he was, Brahms achieved perhaps all that could be hoped: the saving of Clara, with six young children already, and another to come (Felix, 11 June), from herself having a breakdown. Her own determination and capacity for clear and detailed thought must have had good practice for some years, to make good Robert's patchy abilities in this respect when it came to everyday business. She and Brahms used the solaces of music to the full, which in those days meant music-making. Mourning was real and irremediable, except for the remissions caused by false hopes of Robert's recovery. Until the end the doctors felt that the interests of both Robert and Clara were best served by not allowing them to see each other. The agonies still had two years to go. But no-one who subscribed to an early-Romantic creed about music could regard its practice as incompatible with the conventions of mourning. In March, for example, Brahms with two others played his op.8 to Clara[1], and she joined him in playing a two-piano sonata in D minor. Of this shadowy work Brahms wrote to Joachim on 19 June: 'I should like to be able to leave aside for some time my D minor sonata. I have often played the first three movements with Frau Schumann. Actually I have never been satisfied with two pianos.' The reference to three movements presumably implies a total of four (or more, see op.5), one of them being a scherzo or equivalent. If, as some have supposed, the scherzo movement became the three-time funeral march at the beginning of the second movement of the *German Requiem* it must have suffered a drastic alteration which is now

18

difficult to conceive, or it was a very remarkable and early example of the scherzo substitutes which figure so frequently in Brahms's later music. However, it is more likely that the third movement, scherzo or not, was abandoned, and that the slow movement was used in the *Requiem*.

In March the first of the anthology books *Schatzkästlein des jungen Kreisler* was full, and Brahms fired by Schumann's own collection called his *Dichtergarten* ('poets' garden'), began a second. Two characteristic tenets which the swift-maturing youth made his own occur there; from the poet Friedrich Novalis: 'Much is too sweet to be thought; yet more is too sweet to be spoken'; from Friedrich von Sallet: 'But yet there is an all holiest element in our spirit. What glows there in its inmost, hidden kernel is not for me to pull out and with childish vanity make to glitter in the common light of day.' Reticence is a virtue not helpful to a biographer, particularly at this stage of the story! Clara obviously recognised Brahms's collecting instincts by giving him for his birthday an anthology of Robert's writings, 'on music and musicians' (*Gesammelte Schriften über Musik und Musiker*, which came out in four volumes (Leipzig, 1854)).

Composition was not wholly interrupted, by any means. The Piano Variations on a Hungarian Song op.21 no.2 probably, and opp.9 and 10 certainly, date from this year. The former work is chiefly notable for the rhythm which attracted Brahms to the theme—alternating bars of three and four beats—and for some ideas of piano figuration which come to more secure fruition in the last movement of what became the first Piano Concerto op.15. That work still had some way to go before its painful birth, because in mid-1854, thanks to Brahms's dissatisfaction with the two-piano medium it had become a 'projected symphony'. Kalbeck sees in the key and subject matter of the first movement of the eventual concerto a reference to the first movement of Beethoven's Ninth Symphony, which Brahms heard in 1854 for the first time, at Cologne, conducted by Ferdinand Hiller. Kalbeck imaginatively ascribes the remarkable descending trills to the thrill of horror at the fatal leap from the Rhine bridge.

Opp.9 and 10 both have an overt reference to both Schumanns. The theme is the first 'Albumblatt' ('album-leaf') in the collection of pieces of various dates published by Schumann under the general title of *Bunte Blätter* op.99[2]. Clara herself had already written, as her op.20 in 1853, a set of variations on this theme, presenting them to Robert on his birthday, 8 June. On 24 May 1854 she played her work to Brahms, who responded by composing 16 variations on the same theme. Variations one to nine and 12–16 are dated 15 June in the autograph. Variations ten and eleven are on a separate inserted leaf dated 12 August, Clara's name-day, and are given the remarkable heading, 'Rose and Heliotrope have bloomed'. A truly Brahmsian paradox is enshrined in the tenth variation: the scent of rose and heliotrope must waft over a theme whose bass is itself turned upside-down two octaves and a third away; at the ninth bar that bass becomes the middle voice, no longer simultaneous with the tune but forming a canon at a bar's interval. As soon as one describes such a thing it becomes almost impossible to persuade a reader that this *poco adagio* is the emotional centre of the work. As this technical *tour de force* ends, it is 'signed off' with an inner voice quoting a Romance by Clara which is the theme of Robert's Variations (entitled Impromptus) op.5.

Among other allusions to Robert's music is variation 14, in which Brahms imitates Schumann imitating Chopin (as in *Carnaval*). A sight of the variations in June evoked an excited and fulsome comment from Joachim (in Berlin on a concert tour): 'Du junge Musik-Imperator!' However, perhaps even more pleasure was given by Schumann's lucid praise and obvious recognition of the work's private allusions when he was shown the publication in November by Breitkopf and Härtel, whom Brahms had also persuaded to publish Clara's set on the same theme.

Clara was not always at home in this fateful year. While she was away in mid-August at Oostende sea-bathing, 'for her nerves' according to Kalbeck, Brahms put together for her and himself a four-hand arrangement of Schumann's Piano Quintet—four-handed except for the Scherzo, that is, which he left for her to play alone. With and without Joachim she buckled down to her best (and financially most necessary) therapy, public concert-giving. Brahms was the gainer too, by her performance of the slow movement and Scherzo of op.5 in concerts in Leipzig (23 October) and Frankfurt, and of the whole Sonata in Magdeburg at the beginning of December.

Brahms paid a price for his quixotry in staying in Düsseldorf, in a tiny lodging, instead of following up the great opportunities of the previous year. We know from letters that he had to borrow from Joachim and Grimm, who of course obliged, and did not dun him either. But his name remained to some extent before the musical public because Breitkopf and Härtel also published in November the op.8 Trio, which they took on Clara's recommendation (one good turn deserving another).

Also written in 1854 was the other work with Schumannesque overtones, the four Ballades for Piano op.10. The first puts into music, which begins as a song without words but which stirs itself to an awesome trumpeting climax, the emotions of a blood-soaked Scottish Ballad 'Edward', in which a questioning mother draws out from Edward the confession that he has killed his father, and is cursed to hell for her pains. The writing for piano is terse, and more economical in its handfuls than the sonatas, but it is the more powerful for that, as well as being more accessible to lesser techniques. The second ballade is *andante*, but with interrupting fast passages, which, being sectional and hardly related at all to the main theme, disturb the unity of the piece. But the main theme itself is a beautiful example of a favourite trait of Brahmsian melody, an arpeggio with a gap in it, making successive intervals of a third and a sixth thus: ·

etc.

In a sense this music is a fulcrum, for the reprise of the above theme is in B major, and the opening D major never returns. Thus we have a bridge whereby the D minor and D major of the fierce first movement leads to the B minor and major of the two remaining movements. This kind of floating tonality disappears from Brahms's style from now onwards, to be resumed in Mahler's early works. Brahms would have been astonished and disgusted to be thought of as his precursor in any respect. Though none of the Ballades is in the sonata form the sense of the balanced shape of moods and length is enhanced by the third being called 'Intermezzo' and with its fast six-eight time, sudden silences and gossamer touch obviously performing the function of a scherzo. Very Schumannesque are the light but tart accented dissonances, evoking that very remarkable enigma of a piece 'Vogel als Prophet' ('Prophet bird') from *Waldscenen* op.82. The dreamy waltz-like fourth ballade, with its main theme using the minor/major alternation in its first two bars, breathes the spirit of Schumann too (compare for instance the A major theme from the seventh of his 'Novelletten' for Piano, op.21). The ballades were offered in the autumn to Senff, who refused them, and they were published by Breitkopf and Härtel in February 1856.

Walking together in the high places of art, and united in reverential love for Robert, Clara and Brahms present a puzzling picture, especially to those who do not believe overmuch in self-control. The power of shared music to generate and somehow validate shared feelings is notorious. As to Brahms, we owe to Artur Holde[3] the following passage omitted from the published Brahms–Joachim correspondence:

> I believe that I do not have more concern and admiration for her than that I love her and am under her spell. [The original reads, 'Ich . . . verehre sie doch nicht höher als ich sie liebe und in sie verliebt bin.'] I often must restrain myself forcibly from just quietly putting my arms around her and even . . . I do not know, it seems to me so natural that she could not misunderstand. I think I can no longer love an unmarried girl [original simply 'ein Mädchen']—at least, I have quite forgotten about them. They but promise heaven while Clara shows it revealed to us.

This is part of a long letter from Düsseldorf dated 19 June 1854, at a time when Brahms, at least, knew Schumann to be incurable, however much he dissembled for Clara's sake.

One of the communing and consolatory duets (four hands, one piano) was Robert's suite *Bilder aus Osten* ('Pictures from the East'—and not very oriental at that). A beautiful B flat minor movement bears the remarkable instructions *reuig, andächtig* ('with contrition and devotion'). One can imagine the pair in those circumstances coming nearest to obeying Robert's behest! Clara's diary of 24 May records their playing this suite, and adds: 'It is not easy to play with Brahms; he plays too arbitrarily, and cares nothing for a crotchet more or less'—a private remark affectionately made, but threatening a rift in the life of any married musicians.

We may point to two remarks both recorded on 12 September, the Schumanns' wedding day: from Brahms to Joachim, 'I do not think the perpetual excitement here is good for me'; from Clara to her diary, 'Brahms, dear fellow, whom I really love like a son . . . '

As the winter concert season drew on, Clara braced herself to tour and earn. In November she went to play in Hamburg and had the pleasure of dining with Brahms *en famille* there, and being shown among other things a parade of his prized tin soldiers. She thought the parents natural, salt-of-the-earth people, but perhaps with their disparity in ages in mind, she confided to her diary, 'Perhaps I am appointed to be a mother to him in her place.' At another parting from Brahms she promised to call him 'du' henceforth, with the repetition to her diary of 'for indeed I love him like a son'.

Left to home 'comforts' Brahms wrote on 15 December to Clara:

> How little peace I am given here . . . if ever I have free time I have to have four at a time in one room, with continual running in and out . . . Until now I was writing while five people had a lively conversation about my new coat . . . how I yearn at least to sit a proper long evening with him [Grimm] in the station bar . . .

Small wonder, perhaps, that Christmas found him again in Düsseldorf, where Clara gave him the complete works of Jean Paul. As for the mother–son relationship, propinquity would have changed that in a moment had either of them moved, and there was still more than a year of comforting to be done even before Robert's death. But it was March 1855 before Brahms even addressed Clara by her Christian name, and June before he wrote her the magic 'du'.

A fact which must have weighed on Clara's mind in her dealings with him was that the year 1855 shows no completed compositions, except for essays in pastiche: two gigues and two sarabandes for piano. One is always conscious that there may have been aborted or discarded ones, but the increasing freedom with which Brahms wrote to Joachim makes it unlikely that there should be no real documentary evidence. There is one curiosity: in a letter to Clara (7 February) he quotes, some nine years in advance, the adagio theme from the String Sextet in G sharp major, op.36, with its characteristic off-beat triplet accompaniment. With such long gestation periods as this, it could well be, as Peter Latham[4], among others, has surmised, that a pianoforte quartet in C sharp minor dates back to these emotionally turbu-lent times. It was remodelled in C minor and published by Simrock as op.60 some twenty years later (1875). Brahms then made a suggestion in the sardonic humour with which he had come to veil his intimate feelings: 'You may place a picture on the title-page, namely, a head—with a pistol in front of it. This will give you some idea of the music. I shall send a photograph of myself for the purpose.' Brahms also spoke, apropos this piece, of 'the man with a blue coat and yellow waistcoat'—that is, Werther, the young hero of Goethe's tear-jerker of 1774, which had threatened to make suicide for love fashionable.

The year 1855 had begun with the baptism, postponed in hopes of his father's recovery, of Felix Schumann with Brahms as a godfather. Professional life was resumed almost immediately. Brahms and Clara were in Hanover for 24 hours beginning on 3 January, attending a rehearsal of Joachim's 'Heinrich' Overture. At the end of the month, Clara left for a concert tour of Holland and Brahms impetuously rushed after her to Rotterdam, costing him his last *taler*, as he wrote to Joachim. Hence probably, in the same letter, his giving of lessons to 'a little miss and to Fräulein Wittgenstein (Ah, AAAhhh!) in Cramer's Studies, scales, etc'. In fact, according to Berthold Litzmann, the editor and translator of the Brahms–Clara letters, the fees were not bad for the time—about £1 for six hours. Although Brahms had complained in March of having only four hours a week and no prospects of more, by mid-August he was telling Clara of six hours at least: 'I'm becoming a rich man'.

At Whitsun Brahms greatly enjoyed the stimulation of the Lower Rhine Music Festival—held that year at Düsseldorf. Jenny Lind led the soloists. There was a choir of 654 and an orchestra of 165—including 65 violins and 14 double basses, commanded by Ferdinand Hiller. One can imagine the effect of 'And there was light' from Haydn's *Creation*, a work which Liszt attended and was bored by. Clara would not have been pleased to read Henry Chorley, who was reviewing the festival for *The Times*, who described Schumann's *Das Paradise und die Peri*, notwithstanding Jenny Lind's singing, as a 'Paradise Lost'. At the festival Brahms met the critic Eduard Hanslick, who later became a staunch friend and apostle.

Brahms's letters to Clara away on her frequent tours are ambiguous when seemingly least enigmatic. A 'du' creeps in at the end of a letter of 25 June. The sentence is, 'Please go on loving me as I shall go on loving you always and for ever. Wholly yours, Johannes.' But two days later it is 'Sie' again. On 4 December his words constitute a true love-letter to all appearances, yet using 'Sie'.

On 6 August Clara had moved in Düsseldorf from Bilkerstrasse to a quieter house at 135 Poststrasse in which 'a delightfully pleasant' room had been found for Brahms. But while Clara was away he had two admissions to make which gives us a side-light on him: on a visit from his friend, 'I am taking my meals with Joachim, until your return, in the taverns of Düsseldorf.' Clearly Clara had her uses! Secondly, 'Your letter found me still in bed at 7.30 am, and from this you can see that I do not get up early, but really very late.'

Not so much from necessity, but to find Brahms a few more *talers*, Joachim arranged for him to make a third artist in concerts in Danzig in mid-November. After playing in Berlin as well Brahms gave a concert of his own at Bremen, learning some of the facts of such life. His programme included the Schumann Piano Concerto, whose rehearsal consisted of the merest play-through, after the orchestra had already rehearsed other music for three hours. 'The piano', he wrote to Clara, 'had a dreadful touch and not a trace of strength or richness of tone in the middle.' He wrote to her again early the following morning that he had played Schumann's big C major Fantasy op.17, and 'came a cropper over the first run in the bass'. (Pianists would have thought the place for croppers was the end of the second movement—the march—where indeed the absence of them would be a matter for boasting.) Continuing his solo efforts he went back to Hamburg and played his first piano performance there with orchestra, Beethoven's 'Emperor' Concerto, though without much success. The enthusiasm, such as it was, was reserved for a Schubert march in C, probably the six-eight one from the *Marches caracteristiques* op.121, in his own arrangement whereby he played with two hands what was meant for four. However, such concerts kept the wolf from the door, and enabled him to insist on being a paying guest in his parents' house. He also used the December visit to play Bach's 'Goldberg' Variations to Marxsen and he even found his way to acquiring a precious manuscript, Beethoven's op.110 Piano Sonata in A flat. Christmas itself was again in Düsseldorf, giving Brahms the renewed joy of choosing presents for, and playing with, the Schumann children. His own blossoming antiquarian interests were also gratified. From a description of what the book contained we can be almost certain that Joachim gave him Mattheson's famous eighteenth-century vade-mecum on everything from dances to setting out an orchestra, *Der vollkommene Kapellmeister*, and Clara recognised and endorsed a life-long passion by placing in his hands the first volume—ten church cantatas—of the complete edition of the Bach Gesellschaft, writing in it, 'to my beloved friend Johannes Brahms as a beginning'. He did indeed follow up this beginning by subscribing to the edition until his death. (His name can be seen in the prefatory lists.)

An unusual step on the road to world fame was perhaps unknown to Brahms. The first public performance of the op.8 Trio took place in New York. The pianist was William Mason, son of the pioneer American educationist Lowell Mason. William was a pupil of Liszt and a member of the Weimar circle at the time of Brahms's visit with Reményi. Thus some purpose was served after all.

In 1856 Clara, clearly foreseeing the inevitable, had made increasing concert plans, even including a visit to England in April, which in itself ruled out a visit to Endenich at short notice. Joachim had dissuaded her the previous year, but now her own purposes were to be served, consciously or no, by a determination to continue and strengthen her career as a concert artist of the front rank, almost apart from the financial necessity of doing so. Brahms, having dipped his foot into the same water or whirlpool of concert life, returned to the Leipzig Gewandhaus on 10 January to play Beethoven's Fourth Concerto and two pieces by Schumann, the B minor Canon op.56 originally written for piano with a pedal attachment, and one of the Novellettes, op.21. He also contributed to the festival in Hamburg marking the centenary of Mozart's birth, by playing the D minor Concerto K466, with his own cadenzas, which the audience found 'too modern' according to Kalbeck. The Concerto had a moderate success, with a smallish audience. He went on to play at Kiel and Altona where the programme included the Beethoven 'Eroica' Variations and his own arrangement of Bach's organ Toccata in F. In Vienna Clara had a great success with the public and with Hanslick, and included in her concert of 12 February the andante from Brahms's op.5 piano sonata.

As for Robert's sufferings there is a long letter from Brahms to Joachim dated 25 April. It tells of a dispiriting visit to Endenich, with Robert's obvious deterioration bearing out the 'incurable' verdict of the doctors. He hardly understood anything Brahms said, and talked incessantly the while. Brahms in his turn could not understand what were sometimes mere babblings. In the letter he says that he and Joachim must get down to it; 'in one or two months it is seemingly just a matter of having Robert nursed, and it is thus *for us* [underlined] to consider what must happen'. (This seemingly means that in one or two months the necessity for continuous nursing was the best that could be expected.)

As a composer Brahms had obviously stepped back to look at his first ten opus numbers, and decided that his technique needed improving, particularly in counterpoint. Ordinary mortals might find it hard to credit this on seeing some of the variations in op.9 (Variations on a Theme by Schumann). But in a letter of 25 April to Joachim, who was himself a composer, he proposed a regular exchange of counterpoint exercises, on pain of forfeits to go towards buying books. One of the fruits of these studies is the austere but beautiful Organ Fugue in A flat minor—a key to outdo all young Brahms's efforts on the flat side of the spectrum, its seven flats being a *ne plus ultra*. We know it was finished by 5 June because it is then mentioned in a letter to Joachim; a prelude is also referred to, but if written it was never published. The Fugue is discussed in the catalogue among the works without opus numbers. It was published as a supplement to a music magazine, *Allgemeine musikalische Zeitung* no.29 in 1865, on which Joachim was moved to write 'Who except Johannes makes that sort of thing nowadays!' As a counterpoint colleague Joachim wrote at appreciative length from Heidelberg as soon as he received the original in June 1856. But he found some consecutive fifths at the end. Brahms said he had noticed them but found them correct in their context; he would look again, however. They are still there, between the top voice and the left hand in the penultimate bar. As part of the self-tuition, in the same month

Brahms finished copying out Palestrina's famous six-voice mass, the *Missa Papae Marcelli*, whose 'Crucifixus' he had written down in 1853, together with other items of Italian Renaissance-style counterpoint. One of these was an interesting and powerful eighteenth-century offshoot of the straight church style, the eight-voice 'Crucifixus' by Antonio Lotti, which had had sufficient vogue to have been copied out by Schumann in 1851 for a private singing-circle devoted to Bach motets and earlier music.

Variation technique also figured in the correspondence with Joachim in June. Brahms felt that variations in general ought to be stricter and cleaner, perhaps with a view to his own liberties taken in op.9. A remark apropos one of Joachim's variations goes to the heart of Brahms's aesthetics: 'It is quite correct that the notes of the melody lie within it. But in the key of D they now sound on other steps of the scale.' Now the warning to analysts comes: 'And we can only find them with our eyes!'

Meanwhile musical life had gone on. In May the Lower Rhine Festival was again at Düsseldorf and had brought friendships with Theodor Kirchner, a prolific minor composer and pupil of Mendelssohn, and with Julius Stockhausen, the celebrated bass singer with whom indeed Brahms shared some Rhineland concerts that summer, adding to his own public repertoire Bach's Chromatic Fantasia and Fugue and Beethoven's 32 Variations in C minor. He was excited enough to go to Antwerp on 4 July to welcome Clara back from England; the next day they went to Oostende for him to be shown the sea, and on 6 July they were back in Düsseldorf.

However, the final crisis was near. Schumann was fast failing. Clara was at last allowed to see him, to her infinite anguish, and on 29 July he died. Two days later he was buried at the cemetery in Bonn. Clara stayed praying and weeping in the chapel. Joachim, Dietrich and Brahms carried the laurel wreaths, members of the Singverein carried the coffin, and there was wind-music and singing.

On 14 August Clara and Brahms and his sister Elise (an imaginative and useful invitation on Clara's part) had arrived with the two youngest Schumann sons, Ludwig and Ferdinand, in Switzerland for a month's respite. The chosen resort was Gersau, a little port on an arm of Lake Lucerne below the dominating and beckoning height of the Rigi, some 15 years before it would have been possible to ascend it by mountain railway, but a short walk for Brahms, by his standards. Sometime in this period, or in Brahms's final month in Düsseldorf before he left for Hamburg on 21 October, must have come the resolution, for paramount practical purposes, of his future relationship with Clara. It was precipitated by Robert's death giving them the freedom to marry, to put it in the abrupt terms which one cannot imagine either of them so bluntly expressing. It is perhaps needless to say that there is no evidence in the matter. The most likely supposition is that Clara, at least, with her 14 years of seniority and her intimate knowledge of the two composers, saw even the sharing of future responsibility for herself and seven young children as involving a sacrifice she could not ask. Everything in the climate of her day (and in her subsequent career) pointed to her being, and remaining, a high priestess in the service of Art with a capital 'A'. Doubtless if resources permitted she would have been entitled to sacrifice her own 'Art' to his—in which she passionately believed; but the combined resources emphatically did *not* permit, then or for a foreseeable future. At the end of the day, whether she loved him maternally or sexually is immaterial to the decision. She loved him well enough to let him go, or gently to make him go. As for Brahms, his headstrong chivalry now seemed to have led to an unchivalrous position. Perhaps he felt like Aeneas leaving Dido. But Dido, who in any case had not originally commanded Aeneas to go, committed herself to the pyre; Clara, though she often groaned at the necessity, was basically just as determined to be a great pianist as Brahms was to be a great composer.

The horns of this dilemma are almost side-by-side in Clara's diary.

> Saturday 18 . . . Johannes . . . has composed a wonderfully beautiful adagio for his C sharp minor Quartet—full of tenderness.
> Tuesday 21st. Johannes left. I went to the station with him—as I came back I felt as if I were returning from a funeral.

Back in Hamburg the most notable event of the autumn season was the Schumann memorial concert on 22 November with the Hamburg Philharmonic, at which Brahms played Schumann's Piano Concerto and Joachim the op.131 Fantasy and the Bach Chaconne with the piano accompaniment which Schumann had supplied thinking this would ease the concert use of this Everest of a piece.

The main composing activity was the turning of the D minor 'Symphony'—recently a two-piano sonata—into its final form as the Piano Concerto, op.15. Over the year's end the work itself, and detailed letters about it, went to and fro to Joachim, who was urged (*c*11 December) to insult and buffet it (*schimpfe und streiche*). Joachim indeed made some strong criticisms, mainly of key structure. Evidently Brahms took some of this to heart (though we cannot of course make documentary comparisons) for on 22 April 1857 he wrote: 'Here comes the rondo for the second time. As with the first time I ask for a really *strict* critique. Much is completely different—for the better, I hope—much merely altered.' There are quite humble questions about the orchestration, and the candid tribute: 'Without you I couldn't have done it.' Nor do small details escape; Brahms suggested 'Perhaps we could strike out the piccolo; it has only eight notes in the first movement?' It was indeed left out. But correspondence about this protracted birth was still going on in early 1858.

For the four youngest children as much as for Clara, Brahms spent Christmas again at Düsseldorf, but Clara was there for only a few days, as she went on to Leipzig to give the elder daughters a second Christmas and to perform in the New Year's Day concert at the Gewandhaus. Her diary tells us that she performed Mozart's D minor Concerto for the first time in her life, but was not quite successful in Johannes's 'beautiful cadenzas, playing them too loudly and nervously'[6]. However, there was a storm of applause for Beethoven's 'Eroica' Variations such as she had seldom experienced. She also stayed to enjoy Robert's Fourth Symphony.

Clara left for another two-month concert tour in England on 23 April 1857. The previous day Brahms wrote thus to Joachim: 'I would truly howl, now that all the trees are so beautifully green, if I had to go to the land of fog [*Nebelland*].' At least he did not refer to England by the cliché of 'the land without music', which Joachim and indeed Clara herself had reason already to contradict. In the course of Brahms's lifetime England deserved to have overcome his anglophobia. In the end it amounted to little more than fear of sea-sickness.

This Whitsun the lower-Rhine Music festival was held at Aachen, with Liszt in charge, and Brahms did not attend, feeling an incurable antipathy to such items as Liszt's 'Festklänge' and E flat Piano Concerto. The latter's meretricious popularity must have particularly grated on him, as he continued his remorseless struggles with his own piano concerto. He must have felt his own conscience forcing him into compositional battles that Liszt's work evaded with impunity and applause.

In June Brahms laconically told Joachim: 'I was in Detmold and for twelve louisdors [a pretty low sum] played to their princelinesses [*Fürstlichkeiten*] morning and evening for eight days.' This was in fact to lead to a pleasant, if initially uncomfortable, way of buying composing time. For the next three autumns, from September until Christmas inclusive, he taught the Princess Friederike and other well-heeled pupils, played himself, and conducted the small choral society—which stimulated him to compose and arrange for them. Detmold was a small principality set in wooded country some 40 miles south-west of Hanover, living out its pleasant days with no foreshadowing of Bismarck's unification.

There is a real parting of the ways here. Brahms had now a professional reason, however short-lived, for residing in a particular place, and Clara, at the end of September, moved house from Düsseldorf to distant Berlin with a view to teaching there. In the last song of *Dichterliebe* op.48 (1840) Robert had set in unforgettable fashion Heine's clinching words in which the distraught poet of the title calls for 'a coffin bigger than the great barrel at Heidelberg, a bier longer than the bridge at Mainz, carried by twelve giants mightier than the St. Christopher in Cologne Cathedral, in which to drown his love and his sorrow'. Robert applied these words all too closely to himself 14 years later; now Clara was figuratively, by going to Berlin, burying all her sorrows in the fateful river.

Some time early in this year (1857) seems to be the date of completion of the Variations on an Original Theme op.21 no.1. This work shows with remarkable clarity the 'strictness' which Brahms had recommended to Joachim, and more details of the structure can be found in the catalogue. However, the piece, even though the fifth variation is an intricate canon, is quite free of pedantry. The fact that it is his only set of variations for piano which does not use a theme from elsewhere might not in itself amount to much, but the theme is a truly beautiful one, with lovely contours and a beguiling shape of two equal halves but of nine bars each caused by elongating each of the two cadences. The music is young but experienced, sometimes even complex, and has become more sparing of its storms. With or without Clara it shows a newly-refined sentiment. It is not often played in public; one must be attuned to a long and mainly quiet leave-taking. But it is a landmark in the piano music none the less.

A letter to Joachim of 5 December shows, with some mockery of himself and others, that Brahms had a number of happy and educative experiences in his first season at Detmold. There was an orchestra there, directed by August Kiel, a pupil of Louis Spohr: 'with Kiel I stand rather better than not at all'. With the leader of the orchestra (*Konzertmeister*), Carl Bargheer, a pupil of Joachim among others, Brahms was quickly on friendly terms, and the letter asks for the loan of the orchestral parts of Beethoven's Triple Concerto, so that Brahms, Bargheer and the leading cello can perform it. Brahms had rehearsed a variety of music with his choir: 'now we're at the Messiah'. But a typical *cri de coeur* is: 'How little practical knowledge I have! The choral practices showed me great gaps—they'll not be useless to me. My own pieces are extraordinarily unpractically written!' These latter were probably folk-song settings. Obviously one takes with a pinch of salt his claim that 'the serene highnesses' diversions (*Die durchlauchtigen Ergötzungen*) give me no time to think about myself'. It sounds like a happy and worth-while experience, particularly as it sowed the seeds of the two Serenades. However, the Piano Concerto still dogged him; on 22 December he tells Joachim: 'I have no judgement and no more power over the piece', and again on 16 January 1858: 'send me back my unhappy first movement, so incapable of being brought to birth'. However, at least he was now back with his parents, with red blancmange ready to welcome him.

Joachim did, in February, return the concerto, with words which bring home to us the debt Brahms owed to his friend:

> Here at last is your piece returned—I have looked it through again completely, and I must hope that the places with the altered orchestration please you. If that is not so, get hold of a good stick of india-rubber—which cannot be lacking in your Hamburg, proud ruler of sea and islands . . . But, man, I beg you for God's sake send it to the copyists; when shall I at last hear it?

However, another work must have been by then in some sort of readiness, the Serenade op.11, since a letter to Joachim of 24 February asked advice about sending both pieces to the Hamburg Philharmonic.

In the event a mooted public launch of the Concerto in Hamburg did not take place, rather to Brahms's relief. With good reason he feared for the Concerto at the hands of the listless Hamburg public, and he doubted the determination of G. D. Otten, the conductor. But the ostensible and, to Brahms, truly *Hamburgisch* reason was that Herr Cranz the owner of the one suitable piano, declined to have it used. Instead, there was a private rehearsal in March with Joachim conducting his Hanover orchestra. Clara managed to be there also, to her delight, and Brahms expressed heartfelt thanks for the experience. There was an amusing exchange in the letters arranging the rehearsal: Joachim to Brahms, 'Frau X, an enthusiastic friend of your artistry, is here and greets you.' Brahms to Joachim, 'Do not be seduced by the bosom of her dress; she herself hasn't got one.' The 'X' is the mark of Andreas Moser, editor of the letters. Now that it does not matter, the name is lost for ever.

For all its annoyances—and they were certainly to increase—Hamburg was clearly to be seen as Brahms's headquarters in his change of address to the second floor of the 74 Hohe Fuhlentwiete. But for most of April Brahms was in Berlin, to see how Clara fared in her new home. In this time they immersed themselves in Bach's Cantata in C minor, doubtless the great *Ich hatte viel Bekümmernis* ('My spirit was in heaviness'). But later there was a 'tiff' in their correspondence. Clara had praised him in unmeasured terms, and particularly over his settings, written this year, of 28 German folksongs (in manuscript; they were not published until 1926). Brahms, with a not untypical recoil that she took ill, warned her against idolatrous enthusiasm. The argument rumbled on. From Wiesbaden, where she was taking the waters, Clara wrote: 'Do not try to kill it all in me by your cold philosophising.' His hatred of lionising, or even timid flattery, grew stronger with the years, and led to many a seemingly uncouth, rebuffing remark, coming near to, or even overstepping the bounds of cruelty. He simply did not know how to comfort himself, especially in times of what should have been elation, towards those to whom he had given enormous happiness by his music, and who could not forbear to try to tell him so. Perhaps these words, a confession to the singer George Henschel, will explain him and perhaps excuse him.

> I am not ashamed to own that it gives me the keenest pleasure if a song, an adagio, or anything of mine, has turned out particularly good. How must those gods, Bach, Mozart, Beethoven have felt, whose daily bread it was to write things like the *St Matthew Passion, Don Giovanni, Fidelio*, Ninth Symphony! What I cannot understand is how people like myself can be vain. As much as we men, who walk upright, are above the creeping things of the earth, so these gods are above us. If it were not so ludicrous it would be loathsome to me to hear colleagues praise me to my face in such an exaggerated manner.[7]

Clara was not to know this, at this early stage, and even in November it still rankled:

> I am sorry I did not write to you about the Hungarian Dances, for you know

how I like to please you. I only refrained because I feared you might say
something unkind to me, as you have so often done in similar cases before.

(These dances were presumably the ones arranged for piano solo, which
Clara had introduced to the public on 14 October.) One can imagine the
anger, compounded of embarrassment and inhibition, caused to him by
Bülow's ridiculous formula of the three Bs—Bach, Beethoven, Brahms—
whose alliteration purports to put Brahms above Mozart, and whose longe-
vity has prevented the adoption of an alternative trinity such as Berlioz,
Bruckner and Bartók.

This was indeed a folksong year, for in addition to the 28 mentioned above
there were 14 dedicated to 'the children of Robert and Clara Schumann',
published this year. What is more, folksong texts and shapes are used in the
short songs comprising op.14, all of which were written in 1858.

Some of these latter, together with op.19, begun about this time, may have
been encouraged by the charming soprano voice and person of Agathe
Siebold at Göttingen, where Brahms after all went for a summer holiday
having cried off earlier. Göttingen was—indeed is—a charming old university
town some 50 miles south of Hanover on the River Leine. Clara was there,
staying in the same house as Julius Otto Grimm and his young wife. Agathe
was the daughter of a medical professor, and an attachment quickly blos-
somed. Clara did not stay to analyse her feelings. Brahms's return to Detmold
for the second season interrupted such love story as there was.

The Detmold choir were now put through two of the most satisfying Bach
Cantatas from the choral viewpoint, no.4, the splendid chorale variations on
Christ lag in Todesbanden, and no.21, *Ich hatte viel Bekümmernis*, which
Brahms and Clara had learnt in Berlin. In composition, the Serenade op.11
was the subject of anxious second thoughts. It had evidently been scored for
either single instruments, chamber-music-wise, or at any rate for a small
combination, and now Brahms wanted to use a complete orchestra. He wrote
to Joachim in 8 December requesting supplies of lined paper for scoring, and
explained: 'I need the paper to change my first serenade, now and finally, into
a symphony. I can see that it is not right to have it in this mongrel state.
[*Zwittergestalt*]. I had such a beautiful, big conception of my first symphony,
and now!—'. Brahms's 'mongrel', and helpless exclamation mark and dash,
point to his dilemma as a post-Beethovenian in his first encounters with the
idea of a symphony. How significant that he obviously felt that Schumann's
examples offered nothing to him, in spite of all! How sad for posterity that
Dvořák was still in his teens (born in 1841)! Had the two been true
contemporaries the world might not have had to wait for the 'beautiful, big
conception' and make do with only four Brahms symphonies. The far-sighted
Clara confirmed, even may have initiated, the decision about the Serenade
with her letter of 8 November, which we might think hard on Mozart:

The other day I heard for the first time a serenade of Mozart's for 13 wind instruments and realised clearly that it was specially planned for these 13 instruments, whereas yours needs a full orchestra. Another thing struck me—in spite of Mozart, I could not help longing for your serenade, which delights me in quite a different way. What struck me about Mozart was a great monotony of sound—I never like listening to several movements for wind instruments alone; the oboe in particular, otherwise so arresting, often becomes quite exhausting.

It was to be a further year (mid-December 1859) before Brahms sent the 'symphony' version to Joachim, and even then he was in some doubt about his instrumentation, especially as to some high trumpet notes; he had a sorrowful premonition that Joachim would strike out many of them. Brahms expected some rescoring of the brass in the trio of the first scherzo: 'Laugh away, I simply wanted to be able to make some noise with them.' As usual with altered works no musical traces remain of the 'mongrel' stages of the work. The work had a performance under Joachim at a concert in Hamburg (28 March 1859); to Brahms's query whether three each of first and second violins and two each of violas, cellos and double basses, or four and three were appropriate, Joachim answered: 'As many strings as you can get! At least four firsts and seconds. Otherwise better with single strings.' This is negative evidence of a sort, since in the final version single strings are out of the question both for balance and for the awkward double stops, with one paragraph actually marked *divisi*. The final form of the work was first performed, again under Joachim, at Hanover on 3 March 1860.

No such uncertainties occurred with the second Serenade in A major op.16, which always had its unusual layout of two of each woodwind, two horns, no trumpets and drums and no violins, but orchestral violas, cellos and double basses. At least the first movement of this must have been complete by December 1858, since Clara commented mainly enthusiastically on it in some detail in a letter of 20 December. Interestingly enough she was worried by a very individual stroke, the ushering in of the recapitulation not by a long E in the bass—standard classical practice for a work in A, but by a homing in on A itself for some time before the main theme returns—however, more of this in the catalogue. Clara also probably had all the five op.19 songs in front of her, since she mentioned two by name. It seems odd that she did not mention what has become the most well-known of the set, 'Der Schmied' ('The smith') with its hammer-and-sparks accompaniment. 'But I like all the songs! Leave me my joy in them and do not spoil it by your customary remarks.' Clara was nothing if not persistent.

To autumn 1858 can also be assigned two short choral works. The first, an 'Ave Maria' op.12 for four-part female chorus and small orchestra or organ, initiated a fairly large repertoire for such choirs. It was to Brahms a favourite genre with its sweet limpid sounds, and he enjoyed it all the more for the ease with which he could get the performers to dote on him. This piece, although apparently written in Göttingen, may have had its inspiration in a quartet of girls he had put together at Hamm, near Hamburg, from which grew the

Hamburg Ladies choir, for a few years his pride and joy. 'Ave Maria' is set as a sweet pastorale with muted violins, like the voices, weaving garlands of thirds, and with low divided violas, all above a frequently static bass and in six-eight time—the true pastoral recipe in fact. The wind instruments contribute sparing but characteristic sounds to one of the most euphonious scores in all Brahms's works.

'Begräbnisgesang' ('Burial song') for mixed choir and wind instruments, op.13, is quite another matter. It was not the first time that Brahms had succumbed to the charms of a funeral march (see the 'Rückblick' of op.5) but the solemnities are powerful, though simple enough for serene highnesses and their friends to sing. Though there are no trumpets there is assured writing for three trombones and tuba. It is already typical that there is less assurance and interest in the hymn's pledge of immortality, but there are a number of telling modulations, one of which Clara thought could have been improved. It appears she was right, but Brahms did nothing about it. His only afterthought was to remove the original cellos and basses. If one adds the probable composition of the first two of the op.20 duets it can be seen that in 1858 Brahms was emerging at an accelerating pace from the comparative hibernation of the Düsseldorf years.

There was, however, another tie to be broken—another deck to be cleared. As soon as Detmold released him in January 1859 Brahms was back in Göttingen, with Bargheer as his travelling companion. He was intent on renewing the delights of Agathe's love. But his friend Grimm opened Brahms's eyes to what the world of 1859 saw and expected of such situations. Not to put too fine a point on it, Brahms jilted Agathe, who thought of herself as engaged and broke the relationship off. When confronted with the realities the young man decided that he neither wanted to have his cake nor eat it. Brahms had written: 'I cannot wear fetters', and she obliged him by relieving him of such as there were. It did not palliate Agathe's sorrow and indeed anger to be subsequently immortalised by the spelling of her name in the G major Sextet, op.36:

(The English note B is H in the German spelling.)

However, the blows which together with his Schumann experiences made a man of Brahms were the successive failures of the slow-born Piano Concerto op.15. The first performance on 22 January, with Joachim conducting, might be called a lack of success—possibly even a *succès d'estime*. The manners of a royal court and the respect which Joachim had by then acquired could achieve that much, but no more. But Leipzig, with the brilliant reign of Mendelssohn behind it and a proud tradition, in its own eyes, of knowing what was what, was quite another matter. Schumann's accolade had inspired some, puzzled others, and antagonised not a few. There were after all other unmentioned claimants for the role of Messiah. And what, the Leipzigers could well ask, had the young man done since then? Quixotry in Düsseldorf, even if they knew of it, was not the way to get on in the world. The average Gewandhaus-goer would be used to having his piano concertos in a major key. True, Mendelssohn's ever-popular First Concerto began in G minor, but it offered an *affetuoso* of an enjoyable kind thanks to the immediate participation of the solo pianist. Beethoven's C minor was much less played than no.4 or the 'Emperor'. Mozart could offer a precedent in D minor itself, but its preliminary orchestral palpitations were fairly short, and one could hum the tune of the second movement. (The list is far from exhaustive, other examples being Schumann's, Mendelssohn's second, and some by Hummel. But only Mozart's C minor K491 stands a real comparison as far as form is concerned and although it was of course known to cognoscenti it was less to the romantic taste than the turbulent D minor. See also the cadenzas it evoked from Beethoven.) But Brahms's D minor, to the unprepared layman listener, began like thunder and continued like thunder, while the pianist did nothing at all for a long time until he played a quiet 'new' theme, to ineffectual punctuation on soft trumpets. In a letter to Joachim headed 'early Friday' (that is the next morning, 23 January) Brahms bravely wrote:

> My concerto here was a glittering, decided—fiasco. The first rehearsal evoked no feelings in performers or listeners. At the second there was no listener, and not a muscle moved on the musicians' faces. After the performance proper three hands started slowly to clap at the end, but a clear hissing from all sides forbade it.

The face he put on it was quite remarkable, even in the dawn after the hideous night: 'I believe this is for the best . . . After all I am still trying and feeling my way. All the same the hissing was rather too much.' The performance was a good one, under Julius Rietz.

The most alarming upshot of this debacle was that Breitkopf and Härtel refused the work's publication altogether. The Swiss firm of Rieter-Biedermann[8] took it 'at a very modest fee' and printed the piano part in 1861, and the orchestral material in 1862 but no printed full score was available until 1874, and these dozen years or so reflect the time that the work took to establish any real popularity.

Often though Brahms had occasion to rail at Hamburg, he achieved some consolation there in March. On the 24 March at a Philharmonic concert he played the Concerto with some public appreciation at last. The whole programme is an indication of the stamina of both principals and audience.

   1.   'Wasserträger' Overture by Cherubini

   2.   'Gesangsszene' for Violin and Orchestra by Spohr, played by Joachim

3. Arias by Handel, sung by Stockhausen

4. Piano Concerto by Brahms, played by Brahms

5. Praeludium, Menuet and Gavotte from Partita for Solo Violin in F major by Bach

6. Three spring songs,
    (a) 'Frühlingsglaube' by Schubert
    (b) 'Frühlingslied' by Mendelssohn
    (c) 'Frühlingsnacht' by Schumann

7. Symphony no.8 by Beethoven

Brahms accompanied the songs and Joachim conducted the Concerto. On 28 March at a concert additional to the subscription series Brahms's First Serenade was played; not yet in full orchestral dress, it was billed as 'serenade for string and wind instruments' to a very full house, including all the Brahms family. Brahms wrote excitedly to Clara:

> Yesterday, the Serenade was played to nearly 1200 people, and you were not there, you could not enjoy it with me, and I had to think of you far away and alone . . . The rehearsals were crowded, and people seemed to like it even then. At the concert, yesterday, it made its mark. They worked away with their hands until I came down and went in front . . . You would never have recognised the people of Hamburg.

The resilience of Brahms as man and composer shows through in a letter of 1 April to Joachim in which he details the large nett receipts due to the three artists and even plays with the idea of performing the Serenade in Leipzig, of all places. By the beginning of May Joachim was in London, together with Clara; for a birthday greeting he wishes Brahms 'above all, for you and for us musicians many new Brahms scores. Get rid of your swollen cheeks by dieting, and let's hear from you.'

The summer saw the regular establishment of Brahms's ladies' choir in Hamburg, it having grown from a quartet to an *ad hoc* body, and finally to a formal body (though a select one) with a regular conductor and rules enshrining that conductor's not negligible discipline. As to composition, the correspondence with Clara in 1859 shows at least the following to have been written from the combined choral experiences of Detmold and Hamburg: Psalm 13 for female voices and organ op.27; three Sacred Choruses for female voices op.37; *Marienlieder* for four-part mixed voices op.22. In particular Clara gives discerning and detailed references to the psalm, which is mentioned twice by Brahms:

> Hamburg, Sunday afternoon, Goethe's birthday, 28 August. Tomorrow my girls are rehearsing a psalm which I have composed for them. I wrote it in the evening a week ago last Sunday, and it kept me happy till midnight; as it has an organ accompaniment we shall sing it again in the church, this and my Ave Maria . . . I have at least 40 girls now.

Later from Detmold (9 November) he quotes the last verse and refers it to the upsurge of his powers: 'How beautiful to create with fresh strength.' The church he refers to is the Petrikirche; at the choir's last performance before Brahms left for Detmold they all wore black.

As part of a birthday offering to Clara, Brahms must have sent her the whole, or most, of the Second Serenade, and there is a detailed and heartfelt appreciation of its beauties in a letter of 18 September, which includes a quotation in staff notation of a sighing phrase in the adagio, which she says she always plays *pp*:

(A very Clara-ish liberty to take with a passage clearly marked *f*!)

From Detmold Brahms took a few days leave to go back to Hamburg for a concert, performing his 'Ave Maria' and 'Begräbnisgesang' and Schumann's Piano Concerto. He repaid these leave days by staying on in Detmold for a while in January 1860, and did not return. He was invited for the next autumn as usual but he gracefully refused, pleading works to correct and publish. The very quietude and beauty of Detmold had served him in good stead when he sorely needed them

Early in January 1860 Joachim and Brahms stayed for a short time in Berlin with Clara, and then the three went their ways. But Brahms's way was only back home to Hamburg, whereas for the other two the world was their oyster. Clara's tour took her by way of Cassel and Düsseldorf to Holland. In a letter to Brahms from Amsterdam dated 5 February there is a slight twist of the knife, perhaps, in a gentle reproach.

> I was very miserable in Cassel. I could not get poor Agathe, and many other things, out of my head. I kept on seeing the poor lonely girl, and I felt all her grief. Ah, dear Johannes, if only you had not allowed it to go so far! But I did actually see her in person, that is, I saw her in the distance at the theatre where she had come with Frau Grimm, Fräulein Wagner, Bargheer, etc., for the concert. I admired her strength in being able to do it.

Both Serenades had concert hearings, the A major in Hamburg under Brahms's direction on 10 February, and the D major, at last for full orchestra, under Joachim at Hanover on 3 March. On 21 March Clara tried to forward the cause by programming the second and third of the Ballades op.10 in a recital in Vienna. As she told her diary that night, 'I played some of Johannes's ballades very well, but in spite of this they were a complete failure, which I felt very much.'

Much time and energy in early 1860 went into the preparation of another fiasco, the manifesto protesting about the so-called 'New German' school in music, and their assumption that their theories about the future of the art were accepted by all musicians of any importance. Joachim had long seen the necessity to distance himself, both as composer and conductor, from the activities whose headquarters were in Weimar, and indeed had made this clear in a firm but not belligerent letter to Liszt as far back as 1857. If anything, it was Brahms who now took the lead in persuading Joachim to put pen to paper in protest, and between them they canvassed many musicians for promises of support. Schumann, who had founded the *Neue Zeitschrift für Musik* in 1834 as an organ for fighting the Philistines, gave up its editorship after ten years, and was succeeded by Paul Brendel, whereupon the paper became an outright supporter of the new school. The nub of the manifesto reads:

> The above journal continually spreads the view that musicians of more serious endeavour are fundamentally in accord with the tendencies it represents, that they recognise in the compositions by the leaders of this group works of artistic value and that altogether, and especially in north Germany, the contentions for and against the so-called music of the future are concluded, and the dispute settled in its favour . . . The undersigned . . . declare that . . . the principles stated by Brendel's journal are not recognised, and that they regard the productions of the leaders and pupils of the so-called 'New German' school . . . as contrary to the innermost spirit of music, strongly to be deplored and condemned.[9]

Contrary to the whole purpose of the efforts of Brahms and Joachim, 'the undersigned', by an unexplained premature printing in the Berlin *Echo* of 6 May, turned out to be only four in all: the two principals, J.O. Grimm and Bernhard Scholz, a pianist, conductor and minor composer who was two years younger than Brahms. When one considers the well-tuned, well-nurtured propaganda machine of the other side, and measures the public renown already achieved in composition by Liszt and Wagner, the puny ineffectiveness of the four is laughable. The only extended work of Brahms that was, in a sense, mature had been hissed off the stage of the only musical metropolis outside Berlin, and even Joachim's most noteworthy work, the Hungarian Concerto, had not yet been published. There were indeed very few colours to nail to the mast. Liszt serenely disdained a reply; this could be left to Wagner. By his foolishness, Brahms had only himself to blame for being thrust, for the rest of his life, into the position of an anti-Wagner figure-head by faction-loving controversialists, of whom there were quite as many in Germany as ever there were in France.

The main plank in the manifesto's platform and the main reason for it, was that the compositions of the 'new Germans' lacked integrity. The fuss forced Brahms, to his detriment and our loss, to be fiercely circumspect about his own forms, and about the audible logic of every bar. He was brimming with new wine and there was now a public expectation that he would put it into old bottles. The irony of the Leipzigers hissing the Concerto partly lay in the fact that the work sounded new and cataclysmic, not that it reverted to antiquated structures. This is hardly surprising, since Brahms was probably the only one in the hall who thoroughly knew what Beethoven's structures were—and what is more, had learnt by costly trial and error how to use them and how to alter them for his own purposes. Sir Donald Tovey mentions the work's vicissitudes and asserts: 'The final result was inevitably a classical concerto . . . Everything that happens in this gigantic work is as much a *locus classicus* as anything in the last two pianoforte concertos and the Violin Concerto of Beethoven.'[10]

From Clara's diary there is a description of life in Hamburg, not always quite idyllic, beginning on 7 May, Brahms's twenty-seventh birthday. In fact she had arrived the previous day but had hidden in the hotel to give him an early surprise.

> I stayed in Hamburg from May 7 to 24, and spent the time very pleasantly on the whole. I tried to teach myself to be indifferent to Johannes's fits of ill humour, and sometimes I succeeded . . . We had a great deal of music together, the Serenades (both of which I like equally), the Harfenlieder (several times) [op.17] and to my constant joy, the *Marienlieder* [op.22] and *Volkslieder* given by the Ladies' Choral Society . . . On Sunday, the 20th, a party of us including some of the Society, went for a delightful expedition in the steamer to Blankenese. When we got there, we sought out the most beautiful trees in the garden and sang under them, Johannes sitting on a branch to conduct.

They left Hamburg for Bonn, where Brahms stayed on with Joachim, while Clara went upstream to stay with her children at Kreuznach, on a Rhine tributary called the Nahe, south of Bingen. There she acknowledged a 'magnificent surprise' for her birthday, a packet of compositions: the D minor Variations that were incorporated into the Sextet op.18, a double-canon piece, 'Geistliches Lied' op.30, which she contemplated 'with more amazement than comfort', and the two Motets op.29. Amusingly enough, Clara was quite willing not only to suggest improvements, but to advise him how to set about them. For instance, apropos op.29 no.2,

> the last allegro leaves one nothing to wish except that it were longer . . . The magnificent *crescendo* at the end seems only to accentuate the shortness of the piece, and it even closes too abruptly—please, dear Johannes, work it out; everything necessary is there: a fresh, vigorous *motif* and many beautiful combinations of sound, for example the passage on the last page but one, where the tenors go above the altos, which one wants to hear more than once, and other similar places.

The published work shows no evidence that Brahms took any notice. Indeed there must have been a cheeky reaction, since Clara's letter of 5 October says, among other things, 'Only a mincing little pedant would think of such a thing. You are a regular good-for-nothing; first one is to say all that one thinks, and then if one does, one gets a rap over the knuckles.'

The complete String Sextet op.18 was sent to Joachim in September. 'Send it back if the piece does not appeal to you.' It certainly did appeal, and had its first performance, by Joachim and his colleagues, in Hanover the following month, with Brahms and Clara present. It had another private performance at Joachim's home for the pleasure (which indeed was great) of the Hanoverian ambassador to Vienna, Excellency von Stockhausen, the father of the beautiful Elisabet von Herzogenberg. On 26 November Joachim and Brahms were together in another assault on Leipzig, this time with Joachim playing his Hungarian Concerto (dedicated to Brahms, and to be published the following year) and with Brahms conducting his Second Serenade. Clara attended, and her diary tells us:

> The Serenade is wonderfully poetic; in spite of occasional lack of strength, and the weaknesses of the performance, I was quite carried away. I should have liked to throw myself on Johannes's neck, I was so moved by it, and the coldness with which the audience received it made my heart bleed. Joachim's Hungarian concerto raised a genuine *furore* . . . I was torn between joy and sorrow for my two dearest friends, and my feelings were indescribable. I was somewhat calmed on the morning of the 27th when Johannes's Sextet was exquisitely played by Joachim at the Conservatoire, and roused decided enthusiasm.

There is some detail of op.18 in the catalogue, but here the significance of the choice of medium should be noted. Brahms does not court comparisons with his great forerunners by using the string quartet, the classical chamber music vehicle *par excellence*. This consideration weighs just as heavily as the way the extra viola and cello serve his predilection for richer, deeper sounds. Indeed the first ten bars were added at Joachim's suggestion, so that the main theme is adumbrated twice, and first by the cello.

Joachim's Christmas present to Brahms was a score of Mozart's *Idomeneo*. In return Brahms was at last able to send printed scores of the First Serenade before Christmas, and the Second afterwards. He was really in business again.

The score of that post-Christmas present was the first piece of Brahms to be published by Simrock (then in Bonn), beginning an association that led, without much delay or any regrets, to mutual profit, financial trust on Brahms's part and a long-standing personal friendship with Fritz Simrock. At the time of the second Serenade Fritz's father, Peter Josef, was still head of the firm, and he needed a good deal of persuasion from Fritz because of the work's unusual instrumentation. Clearly not all potential customers would be willing to expose their violas as the top of the string texture. That Simrocks had the chance to step in was because of Breitkopf's refusal not only of the Concerto but, as Brahms writes to Joachim (13 September 1860): 'other things sent back without a word'. The vocal music comprising opp.12–14 was published by Rieter-Biedermann either in December 1860 or early in the New Year. Simrock brought out the op.17 harp-songs (but printed so that a piano accompaniment was possible) at about the same time, and opp.19 and 20 in 1862.

Thus the log-jam of publication, partly caused by Brahms's own hesitations, was breaking, and his professional friends were rallying to give him public hearings. For instance on 15 January 1861 both Clara and Joachim, artists who habitually performed for an evening at a time in individual recitals, came to Hamburg, and the next evening to Altona, to perform at a concert shared with Brahms and his Hamburg Ladies Choir. The programme included Clara and Joachim playing Beethoven's 'Kreutzer' Sonata, Clara and Brahms playing Schumann's Variations for two pianos op.46, and Brahms conducting the ladies in the whole of op.17 and the first two of op.44. Interestingly, though there was not one suitable piano available in Hamburg for the Piano Concerto, now there were two. At last there was thorough-going praise from the critic of the *Hamburger Nachrichten*, Robert Heller. Hamburg also heard Brahms as a concert pianist in Beethoven's Triple Concerto, in the eminent company of Ferdinand David (violin) and Karl Davidoff (cello), and as an exceptionally artistic partner of Stockhausen in three song-cycles: Beethoven's *An die ferne Geliebte*, Schumann's *Dichterliebe* and Schubert's 'Die Schöne Müllerin'. Fired by these experiences, Brahms wrote in the summer the first six songs of his own cycle, op.33, which he called *Romanzen aus Tiecks Magelone* and dedicated to Stockhausen.

After the excitements, excursions, tragedies and fiascos of the recent years one could call most of the rest of 1861 uneventful, were it not for the events on paper. In the summer and autumn Brahms composed three major works: two piano quartets, op.25 in G minor and op.26 in A, and the monumental Piano Variations and Fugue on a Theme of Handel op.24. If we add the Variations for Piano Duet on a Theme of Schumann op.23 and, in all probability, some vocal duets and part-songs, we can see a marked acceleration born of the peace of congenial surroundings, and increased confidence in his powers. The peaceful surroundings, away—but not too far—from the noise and distractions of Fuhlentwiete, were supplied by Dr Elisabeth Rösing in what was then a country retreat outside Hamburg named Hamm, a 'composing house' in Schwarze Strasse. Hamm was a favourite summer rendezvous of the Ladies Choir, which was the link, inasmuch as Dr Rösing's two nieces were the sisters Betty and Marie Völckers who with Laura Garbe and Marie Reuter comprised the quartet out of which grew the choir. Brahms was so delighted with his lodgings at Hamm that he stayed for the entire summer and beyond, for as late as 11 October he wrote to Clara: 'I pay ridiculously little here and it is only as a great favour that Dr Rösing accepts any money from me at all for the room she kindly lets me have.' There was a repayment of the most handsome kind, the dedication to her of the Piano Quartet op.26, one of the sunniest and most overtly charming of all his chamber works.

One should perhaps qualify the 'increased confidence' in one respect: Brahms looked to Joachim in some matters of string technique. Joachim acceded generously and promptly. For instance Brahms sent him in mid-October the fair copy from which op.18 was to be printed, and Joachim replied: 'Your sextet has gone immediately off to Simrock the day after it arrived, having been fingered and bowed.' Brahms put himself in his friend's hands and did not even want to see what he had done before publication. Joachim acknowledged most enthusiastically both the piano quartets, but ventured to say of the former:

> The *invention* in the first movement is not so pregnant as I am used to getting from you, but is often quite wonderful what you make of the themes! Altogether your second parts [i.e. developments and recapitulations] with all their multi-plicity of counterpoint and fantasy come out as a unified whole.

Brahms, typically, shied away from the praise, and disregarded the rest: 'Your letter is far too friendly, I have continually shaken my head over it.' What would he have said to Schoenberg's vehement approval, to say nothing of his orchestration of the quartet! There is a wistful element in Brahms's final committal of op.18 to print: 'You could well make a sigh or two at seeing my sextet already printed. True, if I had waited even longer, it could perhaps have been better, but waiting has its own evils.'

Apart from Clara and Joachim, Brahms's summer visitors included Dietrich and a young conductor (six years younger than Brahms), Hermann Levi, who is for a while to play a part in this narrative. By 1861 Levi had worked his way up to being *Kapellmeister* of the German Opera at Rotterdam. For part of the time of his visit Levi slept in Brahms's room in the family house in Hamburg, and was honoured by being shown by Frau Brahms the lead soldiers which her son was to keep in his desk in Vienna.

Clara worked hard for him in the autumn; on 16 November she played in Hamburg the taxing piano part of the G minor Quartet, with its exuberant 'Hungarian' last movement, and Brahms played second piano to her first in Mozart's two-piano Sonata in D. On 3 December, also in Hamburg, she played, for the first time and under Brahms's own baton, the D minor Concerto. 'The public,' according to her diary, 'understood nothing and felt nothing.' She was also energetic—the right word for such a prolonged piece of pianism—in performing the Handel Variations in both Hamburg and Leipzig in December, but with almost nothing to show for it in critical acclaim. Brahms evidently meant them for Clara's repertoire as well as his own. He wrote to her from Hamm on 11 October: 'I composed the variations for your birthday [13th September] and you have not heard them yet [because she was supposed to have visited Hamm for the purpose] although you ought long ago to have been practising them for your concerts.' It is an indication of her powers that two months after this letter she was indeed introducing them to the Hamburg public. It is fitting that the 'public' man Handel supplied the theme for these decidedly public, concert-hall variations. The importance of Handel to Brahms is proved not only by what he caused choral societies to sing, but also by his being a subscriber from the beginning to Chrysander's edition published by the Händelgesellschaft; see his letter to Clara of 27 January 1858: 'The Händelgesellschaft is now under way; I am waiting for the first volume.' Like all German writers he used the double-dot (*Umlaut*) in the surname, ignoring Handel's deletion of it upon becoming a naturalised Englishman.

At the end of the Handel Variations there is Brahms's first published full-dress fugue. Precedents for this are Beethoven's examples, in his 'Eroica' Variations op.35 and in his monumental Thirty-three Variations on a Waltz by Diabelli op.120, but in neither of these cases is the fugue pursued right to the end of the piece. Brahms's last pages, however, are designed to bring the house down while driving the fugue home to its integrated, climactic conclusion, replete with cascades of octaves and thirds in either hand—if one can have such a thing as an upward cascade. As far as strictness is concerned, only once in the 25 variations does he alter Handel's basic shape of two repeated eight-bar phrases. Far from constricting the imagination, this leaves both composer and audience to revel in a very large range of colour, harmony and pianistic resource. The work was published by Breitkopf in 1862 after they had beaten Brahms down over his honorarium.

The year 1861 ended with some momentary discords. The toughness of Clara's will and ambition can be felt in a letter to her daughter Marie from Hamburg on 3 November in which she turned down royal employment in Hanover, an offer doubtless engineered for her sake by Joachim: 'I cannot yet accept such a position, I am conscious of too much power and vigour, too much capability for performing in public; and then the position is too dependent.'

Some of the vexations with the Hamburgers' coldness must have carried over from the Concerto to the Handel Variations. Clara wrote in her diary:

> I was in agonies of nervousness, but I played them well all the same, and they were much applauded. Johannes, however, hurt me very much by his indifference. He declared that he could not longer bear to hear the variations, it was altogether dreadful to him to listen to anything of his own and to have to sit by and do nothing. Although I can well understand this feeling I cannot help finding it hard when one has devoted all one's powers to a work, and the composer himself has not a kind word for it.

The indomitable lady, unabashed, invaded Leipzig and played the variations again on 14 December. Brahms joined her, Joachim, and her children between Christmas and New Year, but spoilt things by ill-humour.

Early in 1862 Brahms paid a visit to Hanover mainly for revising compositions, with Joachim's expert help lovingly available as to string technique. In March he was invited by his friend Dietrich to Oldenburg, at that time a grand duchy in Lower Saxony, west of Bremen. This was the connection with the dedication of the G minor Piano Quartet op.25 to Baron Reinhard von Dalwigk, who was Intendant of the court which Dietrich served as principal musician. Brahms greatly enjoyed the completely unbuttoned atmosphere and the evident appreciation of his playing of Beethoven's Fourth Piano Concerto. Clara, away on a concert tour, wrote from Paris (6 April) commiserating on an accident to Brahms's mother: 'I am extremely sorry about your mother's trouble. I am so much afraid it will leave her weak. it is always rather serious when old people break a bone.' However, she follows this with a reproach from Brussels on 1st May: 'I shall not ask you any more to tell me what you are working at—alas! I hear nothing more about these matters nor about your inner life in general.'

In answer to this a bomb-shell dropped into Clara's lap in June, the first movement, in draft, of the First Symphony, beginning at the allegro. She lost no time in quoting the first four bars to Joachim (still in England) with the comment 'That is rather strong, but I have become used to it.' She unerringly recognised the mastery 'which is becoming more and more characteristic of him. It is all interwoven in a most interesting fashion, and at the same time it bursts forth absolutely spontaneously.' With this glimpse his friends had to be content, because not for almost another 14 years could he bring himself to be satisfied with the whole. However, at the end of September Brahms wrote from Vienna to Joachim enclosing for his sincerely requested criticism a string quintet (with two cellos as in Schubert, not two violas as in Mozart and Beethoven), commanding him that the world is not to see it. The world indeed cannot see it in this form, for like the Piano Concerto it suffered a change of medium: first to a two-piano work, finally to the Piano Quintet op.34.

Meanwhile he had attended the Lower Rhine Festival in June, this year at Cologne, where he heard the Choral Symphony, the 'Sanctus' and 'Osanna' from Bach's B-minor Mass, and Handel's *Solomon*. The beautiful soprano voice of Frau Louise Dustmann-Meyer captivated him, as indeed it captivated Wagner. After the festival Brahms stayed on nearby in the valley of the Nahe (not far from Clara and her children). The regime was composing mornings, eating and drinking and walking afternoons, and musical evenings with Clara. To Joachim Brahms wrote on 20 June: 'Now I am sitting in a tavern by the Nahe, under the Ebernburg . . . Dietrich is in the next room where he is belabouring his bride [*seine Braut bearbeitet*].' Before Joachim had time to wonder what *that* meant, he goes on: 'This Bride is, namely, a ballade for choir and orchestra. Unfortunately I'm not thinking out notes, but fully enjoying fresh air and freedom.'

Back to Hamm in mid-July, Brahms showed in letters to Joachim that even that favourite spot could not deflect him from gloomy and unsettling thoughts about the future. One of Dr Rösing's nieces, 'his' Betty Völckers, had become engaged to a violinist from the Cologne Conservatoire, Otto von Königslöw 'but he played very boringly, absolutely not like an enraptured bridegroom'.

Further clarion calls in the *Neue Zeitschrift für Musik* of 21 March and 18 April might have raised Brahms's spirits—or more likely caused yet more introspection. By now the policy of the editor, since 1844 Brendel, had long since made the periodical the mouthpiece of the 'Music of the Future'. But in a more general sense Schumann had founded it to help the new Davids against the old Philistines, hence the 'new' in its title. If only for circulation reasons Brendel could not afford a complete anathema of Schumann whom many could still regard as the founder of modern romantic music, especially in his youthful works. Thus it came about that a series of articles, witty and well-researched, were accepted from a passionate and learned jurist from the small court of Dessau, named Adolf Schubring. His learning included Latin, Greek, Hebrew and Sanskrit. The main articles were called 'Schumanniana'[11]. The ensuing essays were on his followers, either actual pupils or those following his general direction. More than a century later, Brahms may not appear to us to be in either of those categories, but Schubring is unbridled in his homage:

> But why should I trouble myself about Brahms? His genius will safely lead him on the right path in the future, just as it has up to now. For a while longer he can take pleasure in waking the echo of the valleys with his idyllic reed (*Schalmei*); soon, rest assured, the young eagle, once he is certain his wings are fully grown, will swing himself up to the highest domes of the mountains, on which the paltry Myrmidons can only gape from afar.[12]

Obviously Schubring can unleash classical allusions and mix metaphors just as well as Schumann, and perhaps more accurately. Schubring leaves his readers to put names to the 'paltry Myrmidons', but continues almost to out-Schumann Schumann:

> Brahms blows with equal virtuosity the battle trumpet and the shepherd's reed, and he has the gift of expressing in music, with equal power, truth and beauty, sadness and joy, hate and love, mourning and rapture.

We can shorten the panegyric by going straight to his climax: 'it is given to him . . . to arrive in music at the same stand-point as Goethe holds in poetry'.

Brahms had for some time wished to breathe the less stuffy air, as it seemed to him, of Vienna, the seat of an emperor and the only German-speaking city which a musician with a sense of history could regard as a metropolis. He left home on 8 September. His filial sense comes out in the oft-told story, well vouched for, of his advising his father, if in trouble, to take a look at his son's old score of Handel's *Saul*. When that rainy day came, Johann Jakob opened the score and found a store of bank-notes in it. It was as well that what Brahms called to Simrock the 'merry Emperor-city' (*lustige Kaiser-stadt*) turned out to be a happy and invigorating place, as he had to get over what he was bound to feel as an insulting disappointment. Friedrich Grund, who had founded the Singakademie in his native town of Hamburg and had been director of the Philharmonic concerts, at last retired. Brahms had good reason to be hopeful of succeeding him, but instead the post went to the singer Stockhausen. On 18 November Brahms was moved to a literary figure of speech which he would have been taught was an oxymoron in parading his feelings to Clara: 'I am as much attracted to my native town as I might be to my mother . . . and now this hostile friend comes and ousts me.' The oxymoron seems contrived, and is literally false. Stockhausen, an enthusiastic and persuasive interpreter of Brahms's songs, was not hostile to him, nor was Brahms to Stockhausen, to whom, as far as we know, he never spoke of the matter, much less complained. The uncharacteristic self-pity of the letter could have been brought about by the comparative failure two days before of the G minor Piano Quartet, given with members of the Hellmesberger Quartet at one of their soirées. Hellmesberger himself having heard both quartets, was overjoyed by the new talent. But it was the usual story of apathy and incomprehension from critics and public, so that Brahms may well have wondered why he had left home, even if home didn't particularly want him. 'Out of the frying-pan into the fire' would not describe his predicament; coldness was the problem. Nevertheless he soldiered on, as he had to, and made a debut on his own account on 29 November, playing the A major Quartet with the Hellmesbergers, his transcription of Bach's Organ Toccata in F, Schumann's big C major Fantasy op.17, and his own Handel Variations and Fugue.

One of the friends Brahms made in Vienna was the virtuoso pianist Carl Tausig, a pupil and a lifetime disciple of Liszt. Clara must have bristled at the very thought, and it is amusing to see Brahms calming her down by letter. On 6 January 1863 Brahms gave a recital as a piano soloist, playing his op.5 Sonata, to whose andante the hitherto ambivalent critic Hanslick gave high praise: 'it belongs to the most inward experiences that recent piano music has to offer'. A big programme added Beethoven's 'Eroica' Variations, Bach's Chromatic Fantasy and Fugue, Schumann's Concerto sans orchestre, and Frau Marie Wilt singing four Brahms songs. Great applause calling for an encore, Brahms produced his war-horse, Schubert's Characteristic March with the four-hands-worth of music played by his large two. Kalbeck says that this concert was attended by Wagner, then in Vienna trying to organise a *Tristan* performance. Brahms reciprocated and eventually visited Wagner. Politeness reigned, and evidently the silly manifesto was not mentioned. As for the Schubring essay, one cannot imagine Wagner thinking of himself as a Myrmidon. But a home-made war-horse was about to emerge as one of the fruits of this winter, the most virtuosic, and yet controlled as to form, of all the piano repertoire: the Variations on a Theme of Paganini op.35. (In fact Brahms initially called them Studies.) They were probably written for Tausig[13], but Brahms could also play them—at least at this date. Clara on 18 October acknowledged them and was evidently not going to be defeated, though she rightly called them 'witches' variations' (*Hexenvariationen*). 'I have started practising them most eagerly.'

In February came an event which first altered, then all but destroyed—in its consequences—the relationship between Brahms and Joachim. His friend got engaged to Amalie Schneeweiss, literally snow-white but nick-named 'Ursi', from Styria—the district round Graz—in Austria. Joachim told Brahms (19 February) 'she has an alto voice, and you only have to hear it to know the depth and purity of her being.' She was now 23 years old, to Joachim's 32, and had been on the stage since her sixteenth year. 'But, dearest Johannes, do not let yourself be deceived by the usual ideas that are unfortunately associated with our debased opera world. You will not see anything like that; her mind and her appearance have remained so simple and pure.'

A letter to Schubring in March is eloquent of what Vienna could mean for a creative musical artist, with its daily reminders of the great ones. Of these the experience of handling Schubert manuscripts, thanks mainly to the publisher Spina, made the greatest impact, especially the unfinished oratorio *Lazarus*. Brahms even mentioned blowing the ink-drying sand off the manuscript; Kalbeck says Brahms kept the sand!

But the future was not yet secured, and Brahms left Vienna on 1 May to go in the first instance to visit Hanover and see Amalie for himself. He was charmed, but sensed immediately that the days of Joachim and himself being in each other's pockets must end, to accommodate her. Perhaps this in itself increased the inclination to Vienna. But meanwhile there was opportunity to hear op.34 rehearsed in its string quintet form. Joachim had already (letter of 1 April) voiced his doubts; in sum, the piece as scored for strings alone was at once too thin for the emotional climaxes, and also in places too thick! He seems to have reached the root of the matter when he said that the work lacked charm of sound (*Klangreiz*). We cannot judge this for ourselves because, as ever, once a version was jettisoned it was destroyed. Whether Brahms had himself sensed this, or whether it took the Hanover rehearsal to convince him, the result was the same. He quickly set to work to turn it into a two-piano duet, which Clara found inexplicable, having seen the work herself. 'Could you not have altered it quite easily and yet left it as a quintet?' Brahms was not pleased with the new version either, and two years later the work found its final form as the Quintet for Piano and String Quartet. It is interesting how, in the case both of this piece and of the first Piano Concerto, the 'big' emotional style of parts of the music led to the participation of the pianist. The symphonist was not ready yet.

Brahms was in Hamburg in time for his thirtieth birthday, but this time the visit was clouded by the animosities between his father and fast-ageing mother. His sister took the mother's side and his brother Fritz did nothing and contributed nothing. He was able to patch things up after a fashion, but moved out to Blankenese, where he began work, at least, on the cantata *Rinaldo* op.50, to Goethe's words. There was enough of it written for Joachim to comment enthusiastically on it at the beginning of August, and for Brahms later in the year to toy with sending it as a late entry for the prize offered by the Liedertafel of Aachen.

But now the balance was to be emphatically tipped, and, in effect, for the rest of his life, to living in Vienna. Brahms's sturdy persistence before the public there, and the friendships he had quickly made with its outgoing people had borne fruit, though the offer was a modest one. He was invited to take charge of the rehearsals and concerts of the Singakademie. This was not even Vienna's best choir, which all but the most partisan would say was the Singverein, under Johann Herbeck, but he accepted it with far less shilly-shallying than later invitations sometimes caused, and Clara approved, adding from her hard-worn worldly wisdom something which Brahms's career abundantly validated: 'There is scarcely a city in Germany in which you would so easily find recognition as in Vienna' (letter of 10 July).

Clara had by now bought a small house, for a country seat and retreat, in Baden-Baden, in the suburb of Lichtenthal. Baden-Baden was a resort and spa of high fashion and lively society. Berlioz had the previous year opened the new theatre with his opera *Beatrice and Benedict*, and summers there were enlivened by such figures as Ivan Turgeniev, Anton Rubinstein, and the waltz-king himself, Johann Strauss, the object of life-long hero-worship by Brahms.

On 28 September came Brahms's first rehearsal with the Singakademie. The most taxing piece which he put before them was Bach's large Church Cantata no.21, *Ich hatte viel Bekümmernis*, unusual among these works in having four sizeable choruses. The missionary zeal involved in persuading choristers to learn these difficult Protestant notes in a mainly Catholic milieu can easily be underestimated, together with the energy and time Brahms had to expend on writing out every single note that the court organist, Rudolf Bibl, had to play, since continuo-playing was a skill forgotten for nearly a century. The other works in the first concert were Beethoven's 'Opferlied', Schumann's 'Requiem for Mignon' and some German folksongs, which were actually in Brahms's own arrangements, though he did not allow himself to be credited with them on the programme. As this concert took place as early as 15 November the wear and tear on singers and conductor must have been considerable. The choir had been at a low ebb and were evidently willing to do their best for their exigent 'saviour' (*Retter*) as they openly called him. Needless to say with a comparatively esoteric programme the folksongs scored most with public and critics. However, there was a true success to end the year, achieved by the Hellmesberger Quartet, with two colleagues, in the B flat Sextet op.18 (27 December).

For the rehearsals for the next concert, due on 6 January 1864, what should be put into the singers' hands but more Bach (Church Cantata no.8), moreover with the title *Liebster Gott, wann werd' ich sterben* ('Dearest God, when shall I die?'). One does not need to be a choirmaster to know the likely comments from the singers and ultimately from the public. Funds did not permit of an orchestra as such for this concert, and there was unaccompanied music by Mendelssohn and Johannes Eccard among others, the very remarkable 'Saul, Saul' by Schütz, and yet more death in an 'Elegischer Gesang' by Beethoven. This concert was bedevilled with technical slips and had a poor reception.

For the third concert the Singakademie tackled yet more Bach, Cantatas 1, 2, 4 and 6 of the *Christmas Oratorio*, an unusual item to be given in March. Brahms was disappointed of his hopes of getting Amalie Joachim as the alto soloist, not because he could not afford to give her a fee but as Joachim so delicately put it: 'My Ursi will not in any case be able to sing, because for the last two weeks there have been symptoms, gradually leading to certainty, that she has to set her sights wholly on the serious-but-beautiful thoughts of a mother's duties.'

The evening with Wagner had taken place at the house of Baron von Voclow in Penzing, near Schönbrunn. Brahms played his Handel Variations and Wagner listened with attention and admiration, as to some expert archaeologist. It led to nothing. How could it? But another enterprise was abandoned without explanation, presumably because Brahms feared it *could* lead to something. At this time he gave lessons to a beautiful golden-haired pianist who later in life was to have more influence on Brahms than even Clara had. She was, in 1864, only 16, but of great musical gifts. She was Elisabet, the daughter of that Hanoverian ambassador von Stockhausen for whom Joachim had arranged the private hearing of the op.18 Sextet. She was later to marry a prolific but dull composer, Heinrich von Herzogenberg, enabling Brahms to have the pleasure of a longing, but safe, relationship with her.

The committee of the Singakademie, perhaps to save themselves from yet more Bach, and to play a final card in the competition for esteem and audiences, persuaded their conductor that their next concert, on 17 April, should be an all-Brahms affair. The aura of Bach was not quite dispelled, for one of the items was the first of the two Motets op.29, a chorale and fugue on the sixteenth-century hymn 'Es ist das Heil uns kommen her' ('A saving health to us is brought') whose words amount to a Protestant manifesto on salvation. Other items were the 'Ave Maria' of op.12 and two of the *Marienlieder* of op.22. Then with a leap into the secular Brahms included the six-part song 'Vineta' op.42 which with its beautiful melody and melting harmonies has been a favourite piece from that day to this, and another of his folksong arrangements, 'In stiller Nacht'. Four soloists sang the first two songs of op.31, 'Wechsellied zum Tanze', and 'Neckereien', the first opus in the cosy genre of quartets with piano which was to peak in the 'Liebeslieder' Waltzes. There is a piquant symmetry about the publication of op.29: the pieces were refused by Simrock and printed by Breitkopf and Härtel. The instrumental part of the very ample concert was a repeat by the Hellmesbergers of the op.18 Sextet, and Brahms and Tausig playing as a two-piano sonata what was to become the Piano Quintet. Although Brahms was obviously not satisfied with it as a two-piano duet either it is interesting that he did not destroy this version. Indeed he allowed it to be published as op.34b in 1871 and presented the autographed score of it to the dedicatee of both versions, Princess Anna of Hesse. He reckoned her gift in return as enormously more precious, an autograph manuscript of Mozart's Symphony no.40 in G minor.

Clara thought it foolhardy, but Brahms resigned his post at the end of the first concert season. He felt that some of the all-too-obvious mistakes in performance were attributable to failures of his own conducting technique, but he also felt the lack of any real help in the administration. In truth he was hoping for loads to be taken off him which are bound to be laid for the most part on the conductor of an amateur organisation. There are many time-consuming consequences of his programme choices, of which the provision of a continuo part is one example. However, usually even more time is consumed in delegating chores in such matters as *ad hoc* orchestral accompaniments of miscellaneous pieces, and the assembling and marking of materials. Brahms could of course do this work; few others were better equipped to do so. However, the composer in him felt time's chariot hurrying near.

Even so, there was composition in 1864 apart from the works already mentioned, notably the nine songs of op.32, the last of which, 'Wie bist du, meine Königin' is one of the most famous of all his songs. However, hardly less so is the rapt setting of Hölty's 'Die Mainacht' op.43 no.2, though all these, together with the first three movements of the second Sextet, op.36, may have been products of the summer, after his resignation.

Brahms resigned his post indeed, but showed no signs of leaving Vienna permanently. His visit to Hamburg in June was saddened by the parting of his father and mother; his previous patching-up of their quarrel had failed. One of the causes, and a substantial one to frayed nerves at close quarters, was Johann Jakob's practice on the double bass, renewed and intensified by his at last achieving a permanent position, at Stockhausen's invitation, in the Hamburg Philharmonic Orchestra. It fell to Brahms, and his purse, to sustain the now inevitable parting. The family house could not be afforded, and the father went to lodge in one room at no.80 Grosse Bleichen and the mother and daughter in two in the Lange Reihe. Fritz had no part in the proceedings.

The way back to Vienna went via Göttingen of all places. If Agathe was still in his heart she had to remain enshrined in the second Sextet, for Grimm had told him that her professor father was dead, and that she was a governess to an English family residing in Ireland. On 31 July Brahms paid a surprise visit to Clara at Baden. She therefore postponed for ten days a visit she was to pay to Switzerland. Brahms did not stay in her little house but at the 'Bear' in

Lichtenthal, where he busily composed, and re-composed. He went for four days to Karlsruhe to a gathering of composers (*Tonkünstlerversammlung*) and hated it. Baden on the other hand was most congenial, with firmer friendship with Levi. By the end of October he was in Vienna again, telling Clara 'I have three quite small rooms at 7 Singerstrasse, up seven flights of stairs, on the fourth floor.' His main immediate task was op.34; he told Clara at the end of October: 'For the last few days I have spent every quiet moment at my quintet in order to be able to send it to you. But I am never allowed an hour's peace.' His frequent references to Viennese *bonhomie* make it difficult to regard this last sentence as a real complaint. By the beginning of November op.34 was in its final form in score, since Clara paints a picture of excited and comradely preparation in the making of parts: 'Levi and David [the assistant conductor at Karlsruhe] are sitting copying as if they were riveted to their seats, and Levi tells me how wonderful the instrumentation is . . . we intend to try it on Sunday at Levi's.'

The upshot was a verdict of 'masterly' but with some doubts about passages in the last movement. Clara, on 10 November issued characteristic instructions: 'You must alter a few things in the last movement; there are passages which seem cold and dry to a warm heart.' Joachim's telling word is 'gemacht', literally 'made'. If the function of art, according to the classical tag, is to conceal art, woe to the artist who lets his artifice show! If the criticism that certain passages, or even whole movements in Brahms, seem 'made', one must concede that one is only able to impugn them because of his transparent logic. Totally laughable to Brahms and his circle would be the twentieth century's unspoken insult to its own intelligence: 'I understand this; therefore it is somehow suspect.'

There is a rich crop of completed compositions in 1865, though as usual it is difficult to give dates to the actual process. Brahms's love affair with the carefree side of Viennese life found an expression in the Waltzes for Piano Duet op.39, dedicated to the critic and now enthusiastic friend, Hanslick. They were sent to Elise Schumann, for her to play with the Princess von Hesse. But the other major achievements of the year—the first Cello Sonata, op.38, the Trio for Horn, Violin and Piano op.40, and the G major Sextet op.36—ought to be viewed in the context of a varied and energetic life, whose variety of joys, sorrows, distractions and relaxations can perhaps best be revealed in chronological order.

Early in February Brahms received a telegram from his brother Fritz summoning him to their mother's bedside. By the time he had made the long journey from Vienna to Hamburg, arriving on 4 February, he was too late, as a stroke had killed her. Brahms's sister was with her at the end. They buried her on Sunday 5 February, and Brahms achieved what he alone could have done: at his prompting Johann Jakob went to the funeral. Brahms's grief was real, but impotent, though we need not resist the supposition that his feelings at least re-inforced his work on the *German Requiem*.

Schubert, never far from Brahms's mind, twice in this year took up his time and missionary energies. In February he made a determined effort with his friend Levi to get *Fierrabas* accepted for stage performance at Karlsruhe, saying it would be a comparatively easy matter to alter the text and note the cuts required. Perhaps not surprisingly, this came to nothing.

On 8 February Clara wrote from Cologne telling him of a grotesque treatment for an injury to her right hand which she had sustained in January while walking in the Berlin Zoo with a Professor Lazarus. She was having *Tierbäder* for it, that is, plunging the hand into the warm body of a recently-slaughtered animal. Clara delivers this, as ever, with a straight face. Brahms reacts with a sympathetic sermon, which confirms much that we could otherwise deduce about his own stoicism; his letter of 6 March begins:

Dearest Clara

I send a sigh as big as that to begin with! [This is because she has had to cancel a visit on which he claims to have spent several days of preparation.] I had ordered new coffee-cups, had the plate cleaned, and bought fireworks! preserves! in short had done all that impatience and loving expectation could do . . . I hope you will take the matter . . . not in the spirit befitting a Christian who has to regard all crosses great and small as a luxury, but as becomes a human being who (like yourself) has always done her duty, and who has a right to expect something from Providence—and who, after all, did not lay out the Berlin Zoo . . . The world is round, and it must turn; what God does, is well done[14]; consider the lilies, etc.; or better still, do not think at all, for things cannot be altered, and a wise man repents of nothing.

On 23 March Clara told Brahms that at Joachim's instigation she had committed herself to an England tour from mid-April to the end of May. Considering how many pieces Brahms had already sent for the pair of them to comment on, it is noteworthy that in April he sent her the E-flat chorus from the *Requiem*, 'How lovely are Thy Dwellings': ('Wie lieblich sind deine Wohnungen'), begging her not to show it to Joachim. 'In any case it is probably the weakest part in the said *Deutches Requiem*.' He also quoted the words he had chosen himself for the first chorus 'in F major without violins but accompanied by a harp and other beautiful things. The second is in C minor [sic] and is in march time.' As to 'How lovely . . .' Clara gave her reactions from London on 1 May, putting her finger, with music quotation, on the weakness, which others may have felt, when the lyricism gives way to the continuous quavers of praise:

51

Brahms's letter raises two unanswered questions about the second move-ment: how did it come to drop to B flat minor, and when did the march time turn out to be triple time? The latter was surely paradoxical enough for him to have mentioned if it was already the case?

By May Brahms was already back in Baden-Baden. Clara's address was no.14 Lichtenthal; Brahms was at no.136, having the 'blue room' for his own living-room. He described to his Vienna friends the Fabers the delights of his secluded lodging with its beautiful mountain views. On this visit he met, and instantly liked, the painter Anselm Feuerbach. His increased certainties are marked by the unhesitating way he begins to negotiate over concert perform-ances and publications of the new works. In two successive letters to Simrock (6 September and 2 October) he describes the Cello Sonata as 'not difficult for either instrument'. Duos, and especially the pianists, who have struggled with the last movement will think this a disingenuous claim! The slow public headway made with the op.18 Sextet also casts doubt on the claims made for the new one. 'It is in G major, is for the same instruments and is written to display the same happy character. That is a favour that one is not often in a position to offer to the public.' Nevertheless, in common with most of Brahms's second works in a similar genre, it *is* more relaxed because the trail has been blazed, so to speak.

October found Brahms still enjoying the delights of Lichtenthal when his father surprised him by announcing that he was marrying again. He would be redressing the balance of the years in a way more advantageous to a widower, by marrying not only a restaurant-keeper but a widow 18 years his junior. The lady's name was Caroline Schnack. Brahms rejoiced with his father, and encouraged him, the more so after he had met Caroline.

As if his own compositions were not enough, by October he supplied Rieter-Biedermann, as part of his Schubert propaganda, with a vocal score he had made of Schubert's last Mass, no.6 in E flat. Here may be found a direct relevance to the *German Requiem*. Schubert's first movement, in E flat and in triple time, must have inspired 'How lovely . . .' with the sweetness of line and harmony, and Brahms might even have been stirred to emulate Schu-bert's set-piece choral fugues with his own two examples (at least) in the Requiem. There was a long-standing tradition, in orchestrally accompanied church music, of set-piece fugues, for example in Haydn, Mozart and Beethoven as well.

As the winter concert season began he exerted himself as pianist and executant spokesman for his music. In November and December he visited Karlsruhe, Basle, Winterthur, Zürich, Mannheim and Cologne. He played his own Concerto twice and unleashed his Paganini Variations on the Swiss. He played in the first public performance of the Horn Trio on 28 November 1865 at Zürich. The programme of a concert in the casino at Basle (11 November) gives some idea of the stamina with which money's-worth was supplied: as a colleague-pianist, the A major Piano Quartet; as soloist, Beethoven's Thirty-two Variations, Schumann's Fantasy in C op.17, Bach's Chromatic Fantasy and Fugue, two impromptus by Schubert and the war-horse Characteristic March, and as conductor his own harp-songs op.17. Ferdinand Hiller, the municipal director of music at Cologne and virtual musical king of the Lower Rhine, had arranged a concert which included Brahms playing his Concerto and conducting his D major Serenade, evoking a claque complaining about 90 minutes being given over to a stranger, speaking a strange musical language. But esteem was recouped by the success shortly afterwards of a chamber concert in which Brahms had the tact to have Hiller as partner in the piano-duet Variations on a Schumann Theme op.23, and by an acclaimed performance of the G minor Piano Quartet.

The Swiss part of this tour brought two new friends: Professor Theodor Billroth, an eminent surgeon and enthusiastic viola player, who shortly moved to Vienna and was to be the dedicatee of the op.51 String Quartets, and Victor Widmann, a poet and man of letters living in Berne, one of the few others to whom Brahms sometimes bared his soul.

Detmold made a fuss of Brahms at Christmas (and of the Horn Trio) but there were two surprise outings from there. Clara's diary tells of her visit to Fräulein Rosalie Leser at Düsseldorf, where sad memories must have persisted.

> On Christmas Eve we all sat very quietly together, I might almost say in deep melancholy, and not until eight o'clock could be make up our minds to light up the Christmas tree. But lo! Hardly had Marie lighted the tree, when who should come in but Johannes from Detmold, where he had just been giving a concert . . . I had previously been trying to dissuade him from coming, as it was a journey of seven hours, but he had undertaken it and I was very pleased and excited.

On 30 December Amalie Joachim wrote to Clara:

> I was particularly sorry that Brahms again failed to come. I am firmly convinced that it was on my account he did not come; not that I am in his way—I am not so vain as to think that—but he thinks he takes Jo away from me, and that I resent it . . . It would have been delightful if Brahms had kept his promise, and I would have thanked him for every hour during which he took my Jo away from me . . . Only think, dear Frau Schumann, who has just interrupted me!? Brahms has just come. Is that not splendid! I am so delighted—although he says he must go away again tomorrow!

The first entirely free-lance year had ended with Brahms inevitably going where circumstances and finances led him. The business of being a pianist and the compulsions of being a composer had yet to be organised as an effective sharing-out of his energies. The ambivalence can be illustrated in two letters. On returning to the Rhineland after Switzerland he wrote to Clara:

> What has pleased me most is that I really have the gifts of the virtuoso. I am entirely dependent upon the kind of piano I have. If it is good I play with the

greatest calm and ease. The bigger the pieces, the better. I played [Schumann's] Fantasy op.17 twice and also the Paganini Variations . . .

Yet inside twelve months he was writing to Joachim who had invited him to do a concert tour: 'I can no longer feel myself at ease in a virtuoso's skin.' As a player, in contrast to the insistent practising of Clara, it is evident that he was to some extent living on the pianistic capital he had acquired under Cossell and Marxsen. But if this still ran to public performances of his Paganini Variations there was little cause to fear, and if the public was not mentally comparing him with Tausig by coming only to *hear* him, he was already achieving a reputation which induced them to come to *see* him.

The year 1866 began with a Brahms week in Oldenburg organised by Dietrich, the reason for the one-night stay at the Joachims. Then he went to Hamburg on 11 January to more than reassure himself about his father's new wife, with whom he kept up a caring filial relationship until death. He also liked the look of his new step-brother, another Fritz, who reciprocated the friendship. Johann Jakob and Caroline were married on 22 March.

There is a notable falling-off in concert work until the autumn, and the main reason is the continuing work on the *Requiem*, first at Karlsruhe, as the guest of the distinguished engraver Julius Allgeyer, then in the spring in Switzerland again. He began that visit at Winterthur, but then went into a hilly retreat above Zürich called Fluntern, now a suburb, renewing ties with Billroth, who was then living in Zürich. But he did not neglect to go back for a while to beloved Lichtenthal; he arrived on 17 August and Clara's diary records: 'Johannes has played me some magnificent numbers from a German Requiem, and also a string quartet in C minor.' The dating of the latter work is even more shadowy than usual. There is a letter from Joachim to Brahms from Hanover dated as early as 26 December 1865 enquiring whether it is ready, and whether Brahms would entrust it to the Joachim Quartet for 18th January 1866.[15]. However, the piece was not finally sent for publication until 1873, when Brahms at last permitted himself to confront Beethoven in the chamber-music genre *par excellence*. Amid her musical delight in the visit, Clara voices indignation about Brahms's having grown a beard which 'quite spoils the refinement of his face'. It is not to be supposed that she confined such a remark to her diary.

At the beginning of the concert season in the autumn they went their ways: Clara was in Leipzig in December and did her bit for the new Horn Trio.

> We had studied your trio (I had begged it from Simrock) very well and the horn player was excellent. I do not think he spluttered once, though it is true that he played on a *Ventil-horn* [valve horn]; he would not be induced to try a *Wald-horn* [the natural instrument for which Brahms had specified a preference].

Brahms was entitled to know his own mind in this, since he had learnt the instrument from his father.

In spite of his lack of a virtuoso's skin, Brahms did go on a concert tour of Switzerland with Joachim. Here is an interesting side-light for Joachim, writing to his wife from Zürich on 29 October:

> In spite of Brahms I would really rather be with you. But I have to go to Winterthur now, where we are giving a concert this evening. Brahms went on by an earlier train, says he is going to *practise*, believe it who may! He makes a new resolution to do so every day.

Brahms had promised Clara a vocal score of the *Requiem* for Christmas, that is to say the whole work except the soprano solo movement which was not finished till 24 May 1868. The manuscript of the full score of what Brahms then regarded as the complete work is marked 'Baden-Baden 1866'. But even in acknowledging the 'beautiful promise' Clara uncovered two gaffes which, if they were teases, certainly misfired: 'Is it kind . . . to say, as you did, that a fortnight ago the idea of giving me the pleasure of having your Requiem seemed quite right and natural to you, but that now it strikes you as unnecessary . . . . You wrote the other day that you liked it more when you played it to Joachim in Switzerland for the second time. Why?' Of course this last statement may have been no more than the simple truth, but it is like Clara to make it refer to herself personally. Nevertheless she did receive the vocal score, and writes from Düsseldorf on 30 December: 'The pianoforte arrangement of your Requiem has given me unspeakable joy'—as how could it not?

Brahms, spending Christmas in Vienna with his old friends the Fabers could look back on rising fame mirrored in the publication of a substantial crop of works: the Paganini Variations, the second Sextet, the Sacred Choruses for female voices op.37, the Cello Sonata and the Horn Trio. To have achieved 40 opus numbers and the *Requiem* before the age of 34 was an achievement that could not be gainsaid.

He had done what the 'Neue Bahnen' article had hoped for; he had 'waved his magic wand to where the massed forces, in the chorus and orchestra, lend their strength', but now confronted the question of finding these forces and getting them to exert themselves in a difficult piece quite outside the terrain which he had hitherto cultivated. His previous compositions had been for himself to play, for his doting small choirs to sing, or for chamber ensembles led by such stalwarts as Joachim and Hellmesberger. In the *Requiem* he must have known what a great thing he had done, yet typically he tries to protect himself from disappointment by pretended uncertainties about the work itself. What a tribute it is to Clara that she bears the brunt of this self-questioning and, it seems, never fails to rise to his slightest word, even to his imagined word at a distance.

Early in 1867 Clara was again in England embracing Edinburgh and Torquay as well as London, and deliberately having far less concerts and social life than Joachim who was also there. On 2 February she transmitted a message from Joachim:

> An Englishman [a Mr Behrens of Glasgow—but an Englishman to Clara]-
> . . . whom Joachim met in France and to whom he spoke about your Requiem,
> asked whether you would allow him to subscribe 1000 francs towards defraying the expenses of its production.

This came to nothing, but it shows how much British interest (and of a practical kind) there was in a composer who never stirred an inch in their direction! Then on 26 February Clara wrote: 'I had a most unpleasant surprise when I heard you had given up all serious thoughts of producing your Requiem.' In telling Brahms about England she is unwittingly two-faced. 'People take up music in order to make money . . . I really believe I should die if I had to stay here.' This from an artist who went there, and frequently, to make money, and comparatively painlessly and quickly, what is more!

While Clara was in England Brahms gave concerts in Vienna, Graz, Klagenfurt and Budapest, performing his Handel and Paganini Variations. He proudly sent money from the takings to his father and sister, particularly asking his father to spend it on 'unnecessaries'. However, Hamburg dealt his pride another blow. Stockhausen having resigned the conductorships—of the Philharmonic Concerts and of the Singakademie—which Brahms had persuaded himself he yearned for, he was again passed over, the posts falling to Julius von Bernuth from Leipzig. This evoked a passionate protest from Joachim, but to no avail.

In the summer Brahms persuaded his father to meet him in Vienna and go on a trip to the Austrian mountains. The cellist Josef Gänsbacher, the dedicatee of the E minor Sonata op.38, was the third of the party for part of the way. But what is truly touching is the letter to Johann Jakob about getting to Vienna, making every detail clear, with alternatives. From his frequent requests for up-to-date railway time-tables, it is evident that Brahms was a railway buff. What sort of ticket to get, what times of trains, where to sleep *en route*—all is meticulously laid out. The unpolished old man was introduced to the metropolitan friends and then, to his delight, introduced to the sort of mountains he had never seen, and in the case of the Schafberg at any rate seeing the view from the top,[16] going up, with much cajoling, on a donkey while his son, needless to say, went in his harum-scarum way on two feet. The journey could hardly have been more spectacular nor more taxing. But there was at any rate a railway through the Semmering Pass[17] to Mürzzuschlag (of subsequent composing fame), then a coach to Mariazell and Wilalpen. By some means they arrived at Bad Aussee where they stayed with a Hofrat Lumpe, the father of one of Brahms's singing girls. Having said goodbye to Gänsbacher the intrepid Brahmses made their way to Bad Ischl (even more famous for composition ultimately) then past the Wolfgangsee to Salzburg where they both made a pious visit—as who would not?—to Mozart's birthplace. There followed excursions to Berchtesgaden and Königssee, whence Johann Jakob made his way home to Hamburg, spending a few hours in Hanover with Joachim, but being by then so intent on returning home as to refuse the visit to Kassel which his son had recommended. But he told Joachim with tears in his eyes about his courtship.

In the autumn Joachim joined Brahms for a concert tour, starting in Vienna but going as far afield as Budapest. One interesting sentence from the preparatory letters catches the eye: Brahms to Joachim, 24 September, 'Unless your wife is coming [she didn't] I think we should spare ourselves the boredom and vexation of songstresses?'

On 1 December Herbeck presented the first three movements of the *Requiem* with his Vienna forces at a Gesellschaft der Musikfreunde Sunday concert. Joachim writing to his wife the same evening made no bones about it being an imperfect performance. 'Who knows how long Brahms will have to wait before he hears it played as it ought to be played.' After the performance 'a few cads who hissed met with no success, Brahms was loudly called for, and the applause kept on although it took him five minutes to come from the hall up the steps to the orchestra.' Joachim thus puts the matter kindly when there was no need to pull his punches in a private letter. His sense of the greatness of the piece was paramount; 'Oh Uzzi, if only I could produce the work as I feel it and you could listen!' But Brahms may have taken his five minutes debating with himself whether he should acknowledge a travesty. There is a choral fugue at the end of the third movement, the last piece performed on this occasion. To symbolise the 'everlasting arms' sustaining us there is a most unusual device: the keynote of the fugue is sustained below for its whole length on the lower strings and drum. At the concert the timpanist ignored the dynamic markings and thundered out his D, more or less obliterating the fugue and making a noise, as Hanslick put it in his critique, like a train in a tunnel. This raises some unanswerable questions: was there no orchestral rehearsal of the fugue? Was the timpanist not there? If there were a rehearsal it seems inconceivable that the mistake was not rectified then. If so, was it sabotage on the part of the timpanist? Or who put him up to it? Luckily the desolated and angry composer did not have long to wait for redress.

Two months before the Vienna performance the conductor-composer, Karl Reinthaler, of Bremen had taken the initiative in offering a first performance of the *Requiem* for the following Good Friday (1868). Brahms was uncertain what to say, except that the work was difficult and that 'in Bremen they are more chary of top A than in Vienna'; but he was won over by Reinthaler's selfless enthusiasm abetted by Dietrich as intermediary. Indeed Brahms went much further and undertook himself to attend as many weekly rehearsals as his engagements permitted. Thus he could be found travelling in January and February weather from Hamburg to Bremen and back for the sole purpose of attending a choir practice. The sensible voice of experience can be heard later in the letter: 'here is a full score of the first three movements—I earnestly wish and hope that you can have the strings take part in the choral rehearsals.' When there was a clash of dates at this period it arose from concerts with Stockhausen in northern Germany and in Copenhagen. There, as far as Brahms was concerned, the tour came to an abrupt end because of a gaffe of the first order. At the time Danish feelings were strong against Prussia because of the perennial quarrels as to the political 'ownership' of the two provinces of Schleswig and Holstein. However, this did not affect the esteem in which cultivated Danes held German artists of calibre, until the moment, in a musical party, at which the conversation turned to the Thorwaldsen Museum in Copenhagen and Brahms was asked whether he had seen it. He acknowledged its outstanding interest, and voiced his thought, without regard to where he was, that it was a pity the collection was not in Berlin! The remark, like many more of Brahms's later, was as innocent of malice as it was of tact, but it ensured him much time for further choir practices in Bremen.

The performance conducted by Brahms and thoroughly well-prepared and delivered in an electric atmosphere in a packed cathedral, was an overwhelming success, and overnight made Brahms into a great composer acknowledged throughout Europe. We may include England in Europe for this purpose for in that huge audience was John Farmer, a music educationist currently engaged in bringing musical life to Harrow School; for Farmer the experience of the *Requiem* was like that of Paul on the way to Damascus. Dietrich was there, and, to Brahms's great delight, Clara. Stockhausen sang the bass solos—the soprano one had yet to be written. Both Joachims were there, and according to Kalbeck took part in the performance. The church authorities felt that although Brahms's words were all biblical there was too little reference to Christ and Redemption, indeed none at all except by implication for those who wanted to imply it. Therefore, to add a touch of personalised piety there was performed, by Amalie with Joseph's obligato, the beautiful B minor air, 'Erbarme dich' from the *St. Matthew Passion*, and Handel's 'I know that my Redeemer liveth', though how this soprano air was sung by Amalie's contralto is not explained (if indeed it was sung by her). There was supper afterwards in the Ratskeller at which everyone was jubilant. Clara's diary records: 'Reinthaler made a speech about Johannes that so moved me that (unfortunately!!!) I burst into tears.'

The details of the forces used in Bremen may be partly deduced from a letter to the publisher Rieter dated 24 May in which Brahms showed what parts he had prepared, namely three piano scores, twelve copies of each string part (i.e. making possible 24 players of each!) and 200 vocal parts (*Singstimmen*, almost certainly individual voice parts, not choral *scores*). In the same letter Brahms wrote: 'There is still no organ part [the organist probably played from one of the vocal scores] and I am doubtful whether it ought to be included in the score.' But at any rate the organ part *was* published; see the first sentence of a letter from Brahms to Reinthaler (March 1871).

There can be no doubt that the organ was thought desirable, although 'organ ad lib.' is printed. For instance, on 26 April, by overwhelming request, there was a second performance in Bremen, but in the concert hall, not in the cathedral; Clara writes of it (5 May) 'you will probably have missed the organ sadly at times.' In 1871 Levi, hoping to lure Brahms to a performance in Karlsruhe, writes: 'There is a beautiful organ and wonderful acoustic.'

Johann Jakob was in Bremen cathedral for his son's triumph, but nonetheless at the end of the month (30 April) Johannes in a long, loving but conclusive letter, explained that he had determined he must henceforth live in Vienna, not continuing to pay double, that is, by retaining a *pied-à-terre* for himself at Hamburg. Thus the long-awaited giant step forward of the far-seeing son spells the irrevocable end of his Hamburg family life.

Perhaps the soprano-solo movement, for many the most beautiful piece in the whole work, is a memorial to this vanished past. Its words speak of a mother's love, but are not the end of the matter. It was added almost immediately, in May, a quick out-pouring from what must have been a joyful heart, rather than one needing comforting.

NOTES

1. There is an interesting sidelight on this in Clara's diary:

> I cannot quite get used to the constant change of tempo in his works, and besides, he plays them so entirely according to his own fancy that today, for example, although I was reading the music, I could not follow him, and it was very difficult for his fellow-players to keep their places . . . Brahms was not very polite; it seems to me that he will be spoiled by the tremendous idolatry with which he is treated by the younger generation . . . I am afraid that he will often put his foot in it . . . I am very sorry for this, but I should not have the courage to tell him of it. (Clara's diary is extensively quoted in Litzmann's *Clara Schumann, ein Kunstler-leben*, published in German in three volumes (Leipzig, I 1902, II 1905, III 1908) and in English, edited and abridged by Grace E. Hadow, with a preface by W. H. Hadow (two volumes, Macmillan, London and Breitkopf and Härtel, Leipzig, 1913).

2. A detailed list of all the Schumann references is to be found in O. Neighbour, 'Brahms and Schumann. Two Opus Nines and Beyond', in *Nineteenth Century Music*, Vol. 7, 1983–4, pp. 266ff. (University of California Press).

3. A. Holde, 'Suppressed passages in the Brahms-Joachim correspondence published for the first time, *Musical Quarterly*, vol. 45, no. 3 (1959), p. 312.

4. P. Latham, *Brahms*, Master Musician Series (Dent, London, 1948).

5. Berthold Litzmann, *Letters of Clara Schumann and Johannes Brahms 1853–1896* (English edition, vol. 1, footnote to page 44).

6. However, the cadenzas were if anything hers rather than his. See G. S. Bozarth, 'Brahms's posthumous compositions . . .' in M. Musgrave (ed.), *Brahms, 2* (Cambridge University Press, Cambridge, 1987), pp.92–4.

7.   Henschel, George, *Musings and Memories of a Musician* (London 1918), p. 118.

8.   The firm began in Winterthur in 1849 as a retailing business. It published music from 1856 onwards, and in 1862 set up a Leipzig branch which eventually became its headquarters.

9.   Translation by E. Blom, quoted in Latham, *Brahms*, p. 31.

10.   D. Tovey, *Essays in Musical Analysis*, vol.3 (Oxford University Press, London, 1935–9), p. 114. There is a thorough-going essay relevant to our purposes in the same volume on Joachim's 'Hungarian' Concerto.

11.   The gist of them can be seen in Kalbeck's introduction to the Brahms–Schubring correspondence in *Johannes Brahms: Briefwechsel*, vol. viii (original publisher Deutsche Brahmsgesellschaft, Berlin, 1915. Reprinted Hans Schneider, Tuking, 1974), pp. 172ff.

12.   At the risk of insulting the present readers, Myrmidons are defined as human beings made out of ants.

13.   Carl Tausig, of Polish birth, was a favourite piano pupil of Liszt, and a modern-minded conductor of some distinction.

14.   This quotes the first line of a well-known eighteenth-century hymn: 'Was Gott thut, das ist wohlgetan'.

15.   This assumes that the work was, in some form, op.51 no.1.

16.   At least, this is what Kalbeck says. If it is literally true, it is an even greater tribute to the old man and the donkey.

17.   The railway, completed and opened to public traffic on 17 July 1854, was the first to cross the Alps. The one-mile tunnel at the summit was just less than 3000 feet above sea-level. By this means one could travel from Vienna to Trieste. Mürzzuschlag was on the far side of the tunnel from Vienna.

CHAPTER THREE

To the First Symphony

It was as a man of far more consequence that Brahms attended the Golden Jubilee Lower Rhine Festival held at Cologne at Whitsun, although no works of his figured on the programme. Fired by his experiences of vocal sound, he threw himself into a renewed burst of song, completing most of the set of the *Magelone Romances* (op.33) and adding the very substantial last chorus to the cantata *Rinaldo* (op.50). The songs and part-songs to complete opp.46–9 also flowed from his pen, and some time this year the sketching of the 'Liebeslieder' Waltzes op.52 and perhaps 'Schicksalslied' op.54. One of the op.49 songs was perhaps the most famous of all, from the moment of publication, the 'Wiegenlied' ('cradle song'). This was sent in July 1868 to Frau Faber to mark the birth of a second child but indeed, Brahms said, 'for every happy occasion, male or female.' As Bertha Porubsky, a brunette Viennese recruit to the Ladies Choir, she had certainly taken Brahms's fancy, but now he was a trusty family friend—the life and soul of the Fabers' Christmases. This year most of the summer composition was done at or near Bonn, in what Brahms told Joachim was a charming garden dwelling. The new number of the *Requiem* went, as ever, to Joachim for his views, and in September it was tried out in Zürich at a private performance arranged by friends. Johann Jakob was an attender at these precious days, having been persuaded by his son to join him in an expedition up the Rhine, beginning with a meeting in Heidelberg.

In spite of Bremen, 1868 brought several roughnesses into the friendship with Clara; her daughter Julie's precarious physical state was a constant worry to Clara, and at the end of May it was borne in on her that her son Ludwig was mentally ill, an ever-present hereditary nightmare come true. However, Brahms must have earned most of her sharp reproaches for his sulks and a rough manner which wounded her and frightened the children. As early as 2 February he was unwise enough to suggest she eased herself out of her nomadic concert life, without thinking out the implication that she was no longer up to it—indeed that is what he almost said—and of course he got a dusty answer. However, what she wrote, returning to the fray on 15 October, rings very true, as a conclusive reason why they could not throw their lots together:

> You regard them [the tours] merely as a means of making money. I don't! I feel I have a mission to reproduce beautiful works, and particularly those of Robert, so long as I have the strength to do so . . . The practice of my art is an important part of my ego, it is the very breath of my nostrils.

There could not be clearer evidence that one obsession was matched by another. Her ego was no more negotiable than his.

However, it is not all recrimination. There was a greeting-card sent from Switzerland containing the famous horn-call from the First Symphony (see the catalogue—music example p. 175) and there were times when her diary records him as having been charming from beginning to end.

The first performance of the final seven-movement version of the *Requiem* took place in a Leipzig Gewandhaus concert on 18 February 1869, conducted by Carl Reinecke. The reception was cool, as though the Leipzigers were determined to show that the verdicts of Bremen counted for nothing in their post-Mendelssohn judgement. Be that as it may, the work had no fewer than 20 subsequent performances in that same year (1869) notable absentees from the list being Vienna where it was first heard on 5 February 1871, and Berlin (26 March 1872). The first foreign performances were in St Petersburg (May 1872), Utrecht (June 1872) and London (April 1873, at a Philharmonic concert at St James's Hall). Paris had to wait until March 1875 but this delay can be sufficiently explained by the Franco-Prussian War, especially as the composer had celebrated the French downfall (and earned a good deal) with his 'Triumphlied' op.55.

Brahms himself conducted in Vienna the first performance of his cantata *Rinaldo* op.50 on 28 February. Gustav Walter was the tenor soloist and the male choir was the Akademische Männergesangverein, basically university singers. Brahms told Simrock of his pleasure in their young fresh voices which he numbered at no less than 300. The senior male choir, the 'Wiener' had too much to do. Brahms's request for vocal parts does not tally with the 300—30 first tenor, 42 second tenor, 50 first bass, 40 second bass—but even if there was no sharing these are still impressive numbers by today's standards, especially when remembering that this was Vienna's second male choir. Brahms was also anxious that the audience would expect another 'Venusberg'. Typically, instead of *presenting* Armida's magic love garden—an opportunity such distinguished theatrical gentlemen as Lully, Gluck, and Handel vividly seized—Brahms *ruminates* on it, thereby, to many critics, showing himself disqualified from consideration as an opera composer *manqué*. For instance, Ernest Walker with typically elegant disdain, calls it

> with its purely theatrical situations under concert-hall conditions . . . his most notable failure . . . The most ardent Brahmsian may indeed, as he turns the last

page, bid a justifiably cool farewell to Rinaldo and his companions, without caring in the least degree whether or not they will find Godfrey at Jerusalem.[1]

Perhaps something more can be done for the work in the catalogue, but this is perhaps the place to anticipate 1870 with a frank sentence from Brahms to Clara evoked by his attendances at the *Meistersinger*: 'In all else that I try my hand at, I tread on the heels of my predecessors, whom I feel in my way—but I could write an opera with the greatest pleasure without feeling Wagner in the least in my way.'

Stockhausen arrived in February 1869 for a Vienna concert with Brahms, followed by a tour going as far afield as Budapest, though neither performed much of Brahms's music. But before they left Vienna he had to give his opinion about a St Luke Passion which existed in Bach's handwriting. Here the composer is able to help the historian, and he writes to Allgeyer (27 February) 'Certainly, if the authenticity of a Bach manuscript can be shown beyond doubt, then whatever the circumstances it ought to be printed', but as to this work 'I do not know why Levi wants to maltreat his choirs with it.' He rams the opinion home to Levi the following month: 'If our Bach could have written it, it could only have been while he was still at the bed-wetting stage.' (Curiously enough, the Committee of the Bachgesellschaft printed it in 1898. Brahms had only just reached his grave in time to turn in it.)

On 12 May, after eloquent persuasions from Levi, Brahms conducted the *Requiem* at Karlsruhe. A story about a rehearsal in April, told by Levi to Brahms, rings very true a century and more later to anyone who has had connections with an amateur choir:

> Yesterday evening after the rehearsal, when most of them had already gone away, I was still sitting lost in my thoughts at the piano, and without any real intention I began to play the first bars of the Requiem. Immediately the girls who were already at the door turned round, their cloaks flew off, they arranged themselves round the piano, and began to sing, with beaming faces, until we eventually got stuck in the third movement.

A good few choralists could guess, too, exactly where they got stuck.

In July there is a tantalising glimpse of Brahms in Clara's diary, written in the little house at Baden-Baden. Clara was at home awaiting the formal proposal for the hand of her daughter Julie from an Italian count, Marmorito by name.

> Julie bears the uncertainty of her fate with extraordinary patience, she is always sweet and attentive to me . . . At last on Saturday the 10th, came Marmorito's formal proposal for Julie, and on Sunday I wrote him my consent—But God knows my heart bled as I wrote . . . On that Sunday, the 11th, we told our acquaintances of Julie's engagement. Of course I told Johannes first of all; he seemed not to have expected anything of the sort, and to be quite upset.
>
> July 16th. Johannes is quite altered, he seldom comes to the house and speaks only in monosyllables when he does. And he treats even Julie in the same

manner, though he always used to be so specially nice to her. Did he really love her? But he has never thought of marrying, and Julie has never had any inclination towards him . . .

Julie died just over a year later, on 10th November 1871.

The 'Liebeslieder' Waltzes, still in manuscript, gave great joy both in Clara's house as duets and at Levi's in Karlsruhe with singers also. Sending them to Simrock at the end of August for printing, Brahms was still uncertain what to put on the title-page, raising the difficulty of calling them love-songs when the singers were optional. Brahms was able to tell Simrock in October of the pleasure with which he put a printed proof copy in Clara's hands and thus saved her from the anxiety of playing from manuscript.

In this same autumn Levi gave an unofficial private première to a deeply-felt work, the Rhapsody for alto solo, male choir and orchestra op.53, to words from Goethe's 'Harzreise im Winter'. Just as sometimes Brahms deliberately mis-described his happy works as funereal, so too this work, ranging from troubled dissonance to hard-won serenity—with the former more striking than the latter—he gave misleading descriptions, describing it to Simrock as a postscript to the 'Liebeslieder' and to Julie Schumann as a 'bridal song' at the time of her wedding at the Catholic church in Baden-Baden. It was not dedicated to the happy pair—indeed it was not dedicated to anyone at all. Perhaps he in a sense dedicated it to himself. Dietrich said Brahms so loved the piece that he kept it under his pillow.

It was harder going on the professional orchestra front, where apart from the Piano Concerto there was still only the D major Serenade to go on as a 'symphony orchestra' piece. Otto Dessoff, the organiser and conductor of the Vienna Philharmonic Society's Sunday concerts, was a determined friend. After to-ing and fro-ing and his threatened resignation, some orchestral dissidents were brought to heel, and there was a thoroughly successful performance on 12 December of the Serenade with Brahms conducting. Clara was in Vienna to hear it, and the dissidents doubtless developed instant amnesia.

However, another metropolitan venue for the hearing of Brahms was obviously going to emerge. The Joachims had moved to Berlin in the autumn, Joseph having accepted an appointment as the first Director of the new Hochschule für Musik.

In January 1870 the Alto Rhapsody op.53 was published by Simrock and almost immediately had its first performance, at Jena on 3 March, with Ernst Naumann conducting. The alto soloist was the celebrated Pauline Viardot-Garcia, the re-creator of Gluck's *Orpheus and Alceste*. Her lively hospitality at her home at Baden-Baden was most gratefully experienced by Brahms ever since his first visit there. History had one of its inconsequential revenges on the innocent Pauline. Jena, on the river Saale some twelve miles south-east of Weimar, was principally known as the site of the battle in 1805 when Napoleon decisively defeated the Prussian army. The Franco-Prussian war, starting a few months after the Rhapsody's première, forced Pauline as the wife of a Frenchman to give up living in Germany and made the Alto Rhapsody the last occasion of importance in her life as a singer. Brahms as good as told Amalie Joachim that he though of *her* as his Rhapsody singer in a letter of March 1872.

In the spring of 1870 Clara and Brahms had been discussing by letter the rumours (which Brahms in a lost letter must have asked her about) of a rift between Joachim and Amalie. Clara in a letter from Brussels of 5 May was wrong, or rather not yet right:

> From what I know of Joachim I do not think he would take such a step even if he were unhappy, because of the children whom he loves so tenderly . . . All the same I do not believe I am far wrong in thinking that Joachim is not happy, and I am frightfully sorry for him.

On 30 April Herbeck conducted his last concert before resigning as director of the concerts of the Gesellschaft der Musikfreunde in Vienna. Brahms was indeed offered the post, but not without consideration, to say the least, of other equally 'public' figures such as Rubinstein, Dessoff and Richter. As is usual in such situations, some could not and most would not keep quiet about the names. Very characteristically, Brahms having persuaded himself he wanted the post vacillated for an unconscionable time when it was within his grasp. Joachim and Clara both gave dispassionate advice, but it is the conductor Levi who expresses himself in the most perceptive terms, hitting Brahms's nail on the head in mid-July:

> You are not the man to drive yourself to victory over the thousand petty obstacles which are inseparable from every public post. I am afraid you would succumb to them in a short time, and then, embittered and damaged, you would retreat into apathy.

However, the world suddenly became hostile to explorations of any kind. After revisiting Mürzzuschlag (through the Semmering Pass) in May, partly for composition, partly to distance himself from the ever more public discussion of Herbeck's post, Brahms went with Artur Faber to Munich to attend performances of *Das Rheingold* and *Die Walküre* in mid-July. He had also intended to go to the Passion Play at Oberammergau but 'Christ' had been called up with a view to the Franco-Prussian War. On 19 July the French declared a war for which Bismarck and the Prussian army, thanks also to the organisational genius of Count Helmuth von Moltke, were entirely ready. Part cause of the German victory, as quick as it was complete, was the mobilisation of three armies within three weeks. This was done by the taking over for military purposes of all the relevant railway transport. Thus it was that Brahms was unable to keep his promise of coming to Clara's aid at Baden-Baden where a French invasion could have been imminent, but never materialised. She wisely decided to stay to protect the house, if not from the French, and the dreaded Algerians in their army who went by the nickname of

Turcos, at least from being taken over as billets. Her worries were not only material ones. Her son Ferdinand had been called up and she was naturally in terror for him. But her feelings were not entirely one-sided, though she intended to get flags to bedeck the house. Having to go to sleep while hearing the bombardment of Strasbourg, she felt for the French mothers, the more so as the French contribution to the society of Baden-Baden had been so recent and pleasurable. Peter Latham[2] has remarked that 'Brahms, who had taken little interest in the Austro-Prussian War of 1866, developed a violent fit of patriotism over the events of 1870, and even considered joining the Prussian forces.' The crucial difference between the two wars was that the second was against the French! This was not a mere chauvinism-in-reverse. Brahms had a mistrust, sometimes amounting to resentment, of what he regarded as French flippancy in artistic matters. For instance, in a letter of March 1887 to Elisabet von Herzogenberg he wrote, 'Do you really believe they would play one note of my music in Berlin if French composers of today had a shade more talent?' This is not so reprehensible a blind spot when one reflects that so great a masterpiece as Berlioz's Les Troyens to all intents and purposes could not be heard in Brahms's lifetime, nor even seen on stage or in score.

The shortness of the war took all Europe by surprise. The armistice-cum-capitulation was signed on 28 January 1871 and even this was delayed by the heroic but fruitless resistance to the siege of Paris. The French were spared nothing: William, King of Prussia, was proclaimed German Kaiser (emperor) on 18 January 1871, not in Berlin but in the Hall of Mirrors at the palace of Versailles[3]. These considerations are not irrelevant, for we have to explain not exactly a pot-boiler, but a tub-thumper, the 'Triumphlied' ('Song of triumph') op.55. Brahms's dedication of this piece to the Emperor William I was quite without qualms. As Professor J.A.S. Grenville commented:

> Steadfast and honourable men [of the liberal opposition] turned themselves practically into a government party . . . they placed the 'national question' first. Not for the last time experienced and intelligent men believed they could make a distinction between the 'good leader' and the 'bad leader'[3].

At the end of the year there are two pictures. From combatant Berlin Clara writes to her friend Rosalie Leser:

> God knows how Christmas Eve weighs on my heart this year. I would far rather have no Christmas tree, but Felix and Eugenie are still too young to be asked to give themselves up entirely, as we do, to the terrible seriousness of the time . . . Our hearts are out there with our dear ones who are freezing tonight, God knows where, as they have frozen so often.

From non-combatant Vienna Brahms gave friendly advice to a pianist-composer Friedrich Gernsheim who was coming to play his own piano concerto with the Philharmonic:

> Above all do not go to any hotel in the inner city. I can recommend the 'Crown Prince' on the Aspenbridge. I lived there myself two years ago . . . The horse

tram [*Pferdeisenbahn*] goes past the hotel, and will take you to the concert hall, to Dessoff's, to the opera without your having to walk twenty steps. What about a piano? I could also order this for you if I knew whether you wanted a Streicher or a Bösendorfer . . . Frau Schumann, Hiller, and your humble servant [*meine Wenigkeit*] play Streichers.

The most characteristic part of this letter is his detailed and money-saving knowledge of public transport.

Although the year 1871 began with two important events in Vienna—his playing of the Piano Concerto, Dessoff conducting, on 22 January, and his conducting of the complete *Requiem* for the first time there—April saw Brahms back for a while in Hamburg, impelled by a German's wish to be German at the end of the war. The newly-found national consciousness was the impulse towards another great and moving occasion, of both mourning for the dead and joy in the victory, in the scene of his former triumph, Bremen cathedral, on 7 April (Good Friday again). Of perhaps the greatest significance to our story is the evidence it affords of Brahms's election in the popular mind to an unofficial laureateship of the new nation. The *Requiem* was followed by the first movement of the 'Triumphlied' in its full panoply of massed voices in an eight-part choir. It owes not a little to Handel's example, and indeed Brahms felt able to recommend it to Reintaler in lieu of the 'Hallelujah Chorus'. On 25 April he played his Piano Concerto, then retired to his beloved Lichtenthal, in particular to complete the 'Triumphlied' and the 'Schicksalslied' ('Song of destiny'). As usual, this latter piece was in his mind earlier—May 1870 according to the composer himself, who speaks of it in a letter to Grimm as being a companion piece to the Alto Rhapsody. But it would be a mistake to think of him in any sort of purdah in this situation. On 2 August Brahms acknowledged a present of a case of champagne from Simrock, now in Berlin: 'How happily it smokes and bubbles for me! The concerts of our—Viennese—Strauss go on until 15 August. That is no light inducement for a Berliner!' One can hardly go higher than to be on champagne-receiving terms with one's publisher, and to invite him to Strauss from Berlin!

One of the first fruits of the summer's work was the first performance of the 'Schicksalslied' on 18 October at Karlsruhe. Clara attended this distinguished affair. Brahms conducted his own work, and his orchestrations of some Schubert songs performed by Stockhausen, and Levi also conducted items from Schumann's *Faust*. The year also saw the publication of the songs, 16 in all, comprising opp.57 and 58. What is more, Brahms exerted his editorial skills on behalf of his musicological friend Friedrich Chrysander, who had inaugurated a series of scholarly publications called *Denkmäler der Tonkunst* ('Monuments of music'). The first volume in the series was a book of Palestrina's motets, the second a selection of Carissimi's oratorios, the third an edition of some Corelli works by Joachim and the fourth Brahms's edition of some of Couperin's harpsichord suites, which remained a model into this century. The purposes of the series, at least as far as German music was concerned, were taken over in 1892 by the far-reaching and government-subsidised *Denkmäler deutscher Tonkunst* ('Monuments of German music') with Brahms, Joachim and Chrysander on its distinguished editorial committee. This cultivation of the past can be seen as an offshoot of romanticism, and indeed would now be regarded as an obvious feature of nineteenth-century musical history. However, the calibre of Brahms did much to ensure that the 'monuments' and collected editions came to such fruition.

On the domestic front, in October Brahms's sister Elise married a watch-maker named Grund, a widower with six children. Brahms could hardly be blamed for thinking this most unpromising, but it seems to have turned out well, and in any case his family feeling, and by now his finances, enabled him to give her an annuity which he continued until her death in 1892. By the end of October he was back in Vienna, where the conductorship post was still simmering with no-one seemingly able to bring it to the boil. Levi's was now the counsel carrying greatest weight. In October Brahms wrote:

> Now for the third time the conducting of the Gesellschaft der Musikfreunde is being offered to me, and I am really taking it up. I do not know how to escape, since everything that I can specify is being arranged according to my wish. I shall have at least 32 colleagues of the opera orchestra for the concerts, and in general everything possible.

Brahms having at last brought himself thus far, it is Levi who puts on the brakes, writing from Karlsruhe on 30 November: 'Just wait for the winter! Now less than ever do I want to feel that you are a sitting target for the caprice of a metropolitan public and the pens of stupid or malicious writers.'

Levi was one of the friends who took seriously Brahms's search for an opera libretto, and over the year-end proposed *Schulamith*, based partly on the *Song of Songs*. Brahms more acutely than graciously replied that he could not make a symphony out of a duet for two flutes, and could not see how to make modern drama out of a biblical love-song.

But there was one decision made, and it turned out to be a life-long one. After various Vienna lodgings his address was now in the district called the Wieden; the house was no.4 Karlsgasse, and he lived on the third staircase in flat no.8. He kept a picture of Bach over the bed. There was a bust of Beethoven, a head of Bismarck, and a Mona Lisa. There he continually made his own coffee, and rolled his own cigarettes.

On New Year's Day 1872 Clara wrote to Brahms to send him the first postmark of the German Empire. She was offered a post in Joachim's new Berlin school. She shilly-shallied, making provisos that she hoped were unacceptable, and was rather disconcerted when it looked as though they were not being rejected out of hand! But eventually she did indeed refuse, from which it is difficult to escape the conclusion that an assured income and a fixed headquarters were not as important to her (even with family responsibilities) as a travelling virtuoso's life, so long as she had it in her. At any rate she was as usual in England for the early part of the year. One of her 'lollipop' pieces was a Gavotte from Gluck's *Paris and Helen* which Brahms had prettily arranged for her. She sold the English rights of publication to Novello for £20.

On 1 February Brahms rushed back to Hamburg to the death-bed of his father suffering cancer of the liver. On 11 February the old man died, but his death had brought about a reconciliation of Brahms and his brother Fritz. Brahms was back in Vienna by 22 February with professional life going on: on that day his letter to publisher Rieter asks for the organ part of the *Requiem* to be sent to Wüllner in Munich. The work received an excellent performance there on 24 March, but did not make much impact on that Wagner-devoted city.

On 4 March Brahms wrote a loving letter to his step-mother Caroline, sending money and promising more on her request—without ever seeking details about its purpose.

Swinging back to the annoyances of professional life we may note that a performance of the 'Schicksalslied' went very badly. As Brahms wrote to Levi: 'Rubinstein is certainly a middling conductor, and as he did not offer me the direction, I consequently let the thing take its course' (*folglich liess ich das Ding laufen*). This very Brahmsian upshot was followed by more Rubinstein trouble. Negotiations for the inclusion of the 'Triumphlied' in the festival at Düsseldorf fell through. Brahms was insistent that while the work was still in manuscript he should conduct it. The conductor of the festival, Rubinstein, felt diminished by this, and so Brahms withdrew the work. Dr Franz Gehring, the music critic of the *Deutsche Zeitung* told the story in his paper, and Rubinstein attributed what he called this 'polemic' to Brahms, and was thereafter irreconcilable.

The manuscript state of the materials of 'Triumphlied'—not printed until November 1872—by no means prevented Brahms from entrusting its first complete performance to Levi, in Karlsruhe on 5 June. This was a great occasion not only for Brahms, where what he sometimes called his Bismarck-song had a great triumph, but also because it marked Levi's farewell to Karlsruhe after an outstanding reign, before he migrated to Munich to be conductor at the Court Theatre, where perhaps inevitably he grew nearer to Wagner, and consequently (what a pity it had to follow!) further from Brahms. On the other hand, the conductor-pianist Bülow came much nearer at this time to Brahms and further away from Wagner; the latter having stolen Bülow's wife, Cosima née Liszt. Bülow evidently felt that not everything could be grist to the Wagnerian mill.

For the summer Brahms went again to 'my pretty hill in Baden', that is, the house rented from Frau Dr Becker at the top end of the Lichtenthaler Allee. No specific composition can be pinned down to this time, though struggles with the forthcoming pair of string quartets seem likely. But there would have been programmes and materials to get together, because at long last Brahms took on the conductorship (in place of Rubinstein!) of the performing arm of the Gesellschaft der Musikfreunde. He returned to Vienna in mid-September, for the first of three seasons with them.

The 'Triumphlied' was published by Simrock in November. There is some acidulated merriment in Brahms's suggestions for an English edition; Simrock should devise a new title-page so as not to disturb England's nice neutral feeling. 'Perhaps they would find more appropriate a picture of a cannon with a Hindu at its mouth.'

The first concert in the new post was a typical one: The Dettingen 'Te Deum' by Handel, a Mozart concert-aria sung by Marie Wilt, a proper obeisance to older polyphony in two choruses by Eccard and Isaak, and Joachim's orchestration of Schubert's Grand Duo. The Schubert Duo's only extant form is as a piano duet, but it was usually thought in the nineteenth century to be a boiling down of an otherwise lost symphony. This concert took place on 10 November. However, Brahms scheduled an extra-curricular concert for 8 December, of which the choral works were the 'Triumphlied'— panic-stricken letters to Simrock because the chorus parts were late for rehearsals—and the large orchestrally-accompanied offertorium for eight-part choir, 'Venite populi' by Mozart, K260. That the choir could do this concert, with the Brahms materials late, so soon after the first, and be ready again on 5 January, is a tribute to its skill, and Brahms described them to Simrock as enormously well-tempered and industrious.

Four monthly concerts in January to April certainly kept Brahms busy, but not unhappy, in early 1873: on 5 January the main items were Schumann's 'Des Sängers Fluch' ('The singer's curse')—ribaldry from the choir is not recorded—and Mendelssohn's 'Die erste Walpurgisnacht' ('The first Walpurgis night'); on 28 February came Handel's *Saul*; on 23 March Bach's Cantata no.4 *Christ lag in Todesbanden*, some Brahms arrangements of folksongs and of Schubert's 'Ellens Gesang' for three-part women's choir, four horns and two bassoons. Finally on 6 April, Bach's Cantata no.8, *Liebster Gott, wann werd' ich sterben* ('Dearest God when shall I die') followed by Cherubini's *Requiem*, of which event Hanslick was moved to complain about being buried twice in one concert, once by Protestants, once by Catholics.

The middle of the year was clouded by an occasion which should have united in harmony and common purpose Joachim, Clara and Brahms, namely the first Schumann Memorial Festival proposed for Bonn, with Joachim as the chief conductor and organiser. As to Brahms, it is a typical tale of too thin a skin and too vague a literary style. The festival dates were 16 to 18 August; Brahms had been invited to contribute a choral piece, and in January he wrote to Friedrich Heimsoeth, the chairman of the committee, declining this, first on the grounds that he could not find a suitable text, then shifting his position somewhat, asking 'why should I do it when he who speaks my language better should do it—in a word, use something of Schumann'. This could well have seemed a specious reply (Schumann assuredly did not speak Brahms's language), using a false modesty to cover a fear of being suborned into a *pièce d'occasion*, with composing time at a premium. The ball now fell into Joachim's court, and he wrote from London on 31 March proposing that on the first day of the festival there should be heard Schumann's C major Symphony and Brahms's *Requiem*, that is, if Brahms truly would not compose a new piece, notwithstanding his letter to Heimsoeth. To the *Requiem* proposal, though the immediate necessity for some definite decisions ought to have been obvious, Brahms replied: 'As to your wanting to put my Requiem on—yet—I can indeed not tell you my reasons against it—so further [*also weiter*].' Make of this what one will, it is certainly not an encouragement, and this is to a life-long friend bound just as much as Brahms to Schumann's memory. The questions then arose of whether Schumann's *Das Paradies und die Peri* should be on the programme as well as, or instead of, the *Requiem* given the rehearsal time available, and if the *Requiem* were to be done, who was to conduct it (a matter which was probably the nub, and one which ought to have been settled from the outset). The long and short of it was that the *Requiem* was dropped from the festival altogether, and that Brahms claimed, probably correctly, to have heard of this first from the newspapers. To Brahms's brusque complaints about this, Joachim countered with complaints about his noteworthy cooling-off in his general attitude not just in their personal relations but even in musical matters where largeness of heart ought to be combined with a businesslike approach. No wonder that Clara, seeing that Brahms had now no official reason to attend at all, mused on the possible outcome to Joachim (letter from Baden-Baden, 8 July): 'I wonder if he will come to it? If he stays away he will be blamed, and if he comes I am afraid he will be in a bad temper, and then he will be blamed for that.' He did come, and he was initially in a bad temper, but the touching euphoria of the overwhelming reception given to Clara—massed handkerchief wavings initiated by Joachim, brass fanfares from the orchestra—brought about a reconciliation of all three of them.

Before the festival the estrangements had meant that Brahms had not gone to Lichtenthal for his composing holiday, but to Tutzing on the Starnberger lake south of Munich, where a rich crop was to be reaped. As early as July he was able to announce himself to Billroth as in the act of writing, not his first quartets, but of the first to be delivered. With these he was able to give Clara an 'extra festival' in Baden-Baden at the end of August, as she described it: 'Two string quartets which seem to me of the greatest importance, several marvellous songs, and the Variations which I think *very* beautiful.' These last were the Haydn Variations in both versions, for two pianos and for orchestra, based on a wind-band movement headed 'Chorale St. Antoni' in a Divertimento then ascribed to Haydn. Brahms had copied it in 1870 in the library of the music historian C.F. Pohl in Vienna. The songs were probably the eight published that year (1893) as op.59 which included the famous 'Regenlied' ('Song of the rain'). The orchestral Variations quickly made their way. At last there was a genuine furore at the first hearing. They were done, from manuscript, at the first concert of the new season of the Vienna Philharmonic on 2 November, and Kalbeck tells us that even at the rehearsals Brahms was still altering details of the orchestration. However, it is easy to forget that he was already 40 years old when he at last showed the world his mastery of straight orchestral writing with this accessible and colourful piece. The quartets, thanks to Levi, had try-outs in Munich, and the first of them featured in a Hellmesberger soirée on 11 December. Meanwhile Brahms's Gesellschaft concerts had begun their second season with Handel and Bach, but not excluding modern works such as Volkmann's Concertstück for Piano and Orchestra.

After the triumph of the Variations Brahms encouraged Simrock by writing that they 'passed off quite well' (*ganz gut passierten*). On the other hand he was beside himself because Simrock had printed the two-piano version in two separate piano parts, not in score. There was also a complaint about Simrock's chorus parts for Mozart's *Davide Penitente* due at the January concert, in one number of which only the first choir was printed.

Thus the year showed various degrees of roughness with the all-compensating smoothnesses of creative satisfaction. Levi and Brahms are sufficiently at one in November to share some pretty deplorable sentiments. From Brahms:

> if you need a woman pianist, I can strongly recommend Fräulein Leschetitsky, née Annette Essipoff. She is intent on making some noise here [*Spektakel*]. She is as unmusical as all female pianists, but she plays properly and she is a woman you could well bear with without a piano. No, seriously she can be recommended.

From Levi,

> We absolutely cannot use female pianists here. I spend half my free time withstanding concert announcements [life does not change!] . . . I rejoice over every triumph of a pianistess so long as it is celebrated on the far side of Madrid.

The next year (1874) both the Herzogenbergs of Leipzig were going to enter into Brahms's life, to make quite soon a large extra dimension. In a sense Clara was leaving his visiting card there by mastering and playing his Piano Concerto at a Gewandhaus concert in December, to Reinecke's carefully conducted accompaniment. 'The audience behaved at least respectfully . . . I ought to play it every year for three or four years, and then the public too would become intimate with it. Who knows if I shall ever be able to play it again, for the pain in my arm is very bad . . . ' Brahms's First Concerto is not the piece for muscular rheumatism.

For Christmas, we can guess what Brahms means to Simrock when he acknowledges presents 'from the Rhine and from Havana'. For Clara, or rather for her poet son Felix, Brahms had a Christmas surprise, a setting of his words 'Meine Liebe ist grün'. The song was published as the first of two *Junge Lieder* to Felix's words in the second set of op.63.

New Year's Day 1874 was marked by the conferring on Brahms of the Order of Maximilian by King Ludwig II of Bavaria, the music-obsessed friend of Wagner, who was declared insane (though not solely on that account) and committed suicide in 1886. If we may allow a political interlude before concerts and composing get under way, a letter from Levi (Munich, 13 January) makes interesting reading, as he evidently supposes Brahms would sympathise with its sentiments:

> Now if you sit, as I have done, for a whole day as a general-election supervisor, and see what depraved, sozzled and stupid faces come up to the urn and deliver their votes, just the same as each educated person, you are tempted to think of universal suffrage as Bismarck's double-edged gift [*Danaer-Geschenk*] and to want to return to the three-class system.

Sticking to his policy of a wide choice of historical masterworks, Brahms gave Mozart's *Davide Penitente* K469 at the Gesellschaft concert on 25 January. The cantata is Mozart's own salvage operation on the torso of his Mass in C minor, and is well suited to a large choir capable of eight-part singing. Simrock's materials must have arrived in time. A few days later he was off, not without misgivings, to a Brahms week arranged in Leipzig by two idolators, Heinrich and Elisabet von Herzogenberg. Two and a half years had to pass before the precious and intimate exchange of letters began, but we can see a more pleasant view of Brahms than some of Clara's recent ones in the letter Elisabet sent to their mutual friend in Vienna, Frau Bertha Faber:

> I must tell you how much we liked your Johannes this time. He was not like the same person . . . So many people suffer shipwreck on that dangerous rock called Fame; but we all felt it had mellowed him . . . He does not wear a halo of infallibility *à la* Richard Wagner, but has a quiet air of having achieved what he set out to accomplish, and is content to live and let live.

The programme included chamber music concerts with himself as pianist and listener and the orchestral and choral works *Rinaldo*, Alto Rhapsody (with Amalie Joachim) and the Haydn Variations as well as the three orchestrations Brahms had himself made of his settings of Hungarian Dances, nos.1, 3 and 10. Reinecke, the Leipzig conductor, joined Brahms in some of the 'Liebeslieder' Waltzes. At a Gewandhaus concert Brahms played the piano part of his G minor Quartet, and also the Handel Variations. The Simrocks and Clara were at all the concerts, and of course the Herzogenbergs.

A proposed concert in Munich in mid-March involves interesting insights into details of professional life, some of which ring true to twentieth-century musical administrators. But first, in January, Brahms regaled Levi with a long list of 'Triumphlied' performances in Germany and Switzerland he was supposed to be attending, and asked whether it did not amount to a 'devil take it' (*zum Teufelholen!*). From Levi it is clear that a month before a season-ticket concert due in mid-March the programme and even the date were not settled. Obviously such risks involved a healthy belief in the drawing-power of Brahms and in the skills of one's own orchestra. Even on 12 February Levi was still considering adding Berlioz's notoriously tricky *Harold in Italy* to a programme which was to include Brahms playing his own Concerto, Levi himself conducting the Haydn Variations, and rounding it all off with the three Hungarian Dances. The latter, however, Brahms declared go better if not prepared before his arrival! There is another practical difficulty mentioned on 22 February. There was no contra-fagotto to hand. 'Because of cholera and financial constraints [the German is *Krach-Rückwirkungen* and could betoken reactions to anything from severe controversy to a stock-exchange crash] we are completely bankrupt.' If Brahms really needed the instrument they would get one in from somewhere and raid the box-office takings. (For some, life has not much changed.) In fact there were two successful concerts, the orchestral on 13 March and on the next day a chamber concert at which one of the sextets was proposed, and Brahms played in one of the piano quartets. Then Brahms had to gird himself up for a big operation, but one close to his heart, in Vienna on 31 March: a Gesellschaft concert given over to Handel's *Solomon*.

Through a letter of Clara's from Berlin on 11 April we hear of another honour:

> the day before yesterday they elected you an honorary member of the Academy of Arts and Science here. I don't know whether you are pleased about it [he was, as his next letter shows] but be that as it may. I wished to be the first to tell you, before it is announced officially.

They evidently did not ask the honorand whether he wished to be honoured.

After a Gesellschaft concert on 19 April featuring his friend Dietrich's Violin Concerto Brahms began his summer travels with a conducting engagement out of the common run. By way of contribution to the Lower Rhine Music Festival at Cologne on 24 May he conducted a choir of no less than 500 voices in the 'Triumphlied'. Here he met, on terms of mutual admiration, the singer Georg Henschel, born in Breslau in 1850, and later to pursue a career in the USA and in England, where he became Sir George. To Henschel's memoirs we owe independent, though possibly rose-tinted views of Brahms. This is how Brahms struck Henschel in Cologne in 1874:

> He was broad-chested, of somewhat short stature, with a tendency to stoutness. His face was clean-shaven [he must have heeded Clara's exclamations] revealing a rather thick, genial underlip; the healthy and ruddy colour of his skin indicated a love of nature and a habit of being in the open air in all kinds of weather; his thick straight hair of brownish colour came nearly down to his shoulders. His clothes and boots were not exactly of the latest pattern, nor did they fit particularly well, but his linen was spotless. What, however, struck me

most was the kindliness of his eyes. They were of a light blue; wonderfully keen and bright, with now and then a roguish twinkle in them, and yet at times of almost childlike tenderness. Soon I was to find out that the roguish twinkle in his eyes corresponded to a quality in his nature which would perhaps be best described as good-natured sarcasm.

Switzerland claimed him for performances of the 'Triumphlied' at Basle in June and at Zürich in July. The latter was a particularly important affair, marking a festival of all Switzerland, inaugurated by Brahms conducting his own piece. On an impulse Brahms stayed on in Switzerland for the summer, taking rooms above Rüschlikon on the lake of Zürich. Here he cemented a friendship with the theologian and man of letters J.V. Widmann, a favourite companion on tours involving geography and history. The compositional fruits of this time in Switzerland were certainly the completion of opp.61–4, all vocal works published this year, and probably the final form of the Piano Quartet in C minor op.60, published the following year. The precise dating of the genesis of this work is even more difficult than usual because only the autographed manuscript of the last movement survives. Brahms had given his manuscript of the eventual slow movement to Elisabet von Herzogenberg, and this is now lost. We do know from Brahms's own little catalogue that the first two movements are early, going back to the days of the Schumann crisis—when the work was envisaged in C sharp minor—and that the andante and finale are later, as can be seen from the music.[4] The 'early' first two movements, and particularly the pounding passions of the almost unrelenting scherzo, are well epitomised by Brahms to Billroth: 'This quartet is only communicated as a curiosity, say as an illustration to the last chapter of the Man with the Blue Jacket and Yellow Vest', that is Goethe's 'hero' Werther. Of these works, opp.63 and 64 were given to Peters to publish, probably by way of following up the Brahms week in Leipzig. Another sequel to the success of the 'Liebeslieder' Waltzes, was another set probably completed this year (1874) of 'New Liebeslieder' op.65, for the same medium of vocal quartet and piano duet. The words of the 14 waltzes proper are again by Daumer, but the final movement is a quieter leave-taking to words by Goethe. The music presents the ultimate in triplicity, not three but nine crotchets in the bar, and the piano's bass for most of its length repeats the consolatory tune of the last section of the Alto Rhapsody. But another composition found its way to Clara, her diary of July in Baden-Baden recording: 'Johannes sent me one of Felix's songs, as a pleasant surprise from Rüschlikon.' The dates make it almost certain that this was op.63 no.6, Felix's previous two having already been delivered.

Apart from Swiss friends and visitors the pressing English made themselves felt in Rüschlikon. Joachim wrote from Berlin on 5 June following up an enquiry from a Mr Peyton of Birmingham. (Mr Peyton was a most persistent and enthusiastic man; it was through him that the chair of music was founded at Birmingham University and that Elgar first sat in it.) His request was for

Brahms to write or at least conduct something for the Birmingham Festival. Another letter, from Brahms to Joachim, still from Rüschlikon in early September, referred also to proposals from Sir Augustus Manns, the director of the Crystal Palace concerts in London. Brahms was obviously mindful of the honour, but simply did not want to go to England:

> I have already written to Manns; I really can't spare fourteen days for journeying in winter-time . . . Mr Peyton has thoroughly plagued me with letters . . . Can you help me out with a lie for Birmingham, a practical excuse?

Brahms's next letter to Joachim, from Vienna in October, opens abruptly: 'Cuckoo take the Englishman and his music festival!' Peyton kept sending what Brahms called 'book-sized letters' (*Briefbücher*) and furthermore asked him to continue the correspondence in Latin script (that is, not German). 'They want the rights of the composition for England, Ireland and Scotland, and offer £200 for an oratorio, or £125 for a 'smaller' cantata that takes about 1½ hours(!)', and for that Brahms was to conduct as well. None of this came to anything, more is the pity.

Perhaps Brahms had determined to make his third winter season of Gesellschaft concerts his last, even before it started. Certainly it was to contain a climactic array of great music. The first, on 8 November, included three of his own part-songs for unaccompanied mixed voices op.62, Berlioz's *Harold in Italy* and his own performance of Beethoven's 'Emperor' Concerto, and the second, on 6 December, was devoted to no less a piece than Beethoven's *Missa Solemnis*.

Christmas was lubricated by a present of Rhine wines from his friends Laura and Rudolf Beckerath of Rüdesheim, and Brahms ended the year with a happy trip to Breslau, organised by the fourth manifesto-signer Bernhard Scholz, at which he played his Piano Concerto.

However, we can end the year by thinking of Levi on a lonely, cold Christmas expedition to Tegernsee. He writes to Brahms:

> The B major melody, 'Wenn zu der Regenwand' [that is the poem of Goethe, 'Phänomen', which Brahms had just set as a duet in op.61 no.3] is so plaguing me that I must reach for writing-paper as the last means of getting rid of it. Could I but tell you how this song has seized and touched me! Would that you were once again lying in my bed, and I could be sitting in front of you and stroking your brow . . . I have a terrible longing to see you again. It is Christmas Eve; I am sitting alone in the tavern at the Tegernsee, half frozen after a long sledging journey. It is a magical evening; from my room I can look out over the whole lake, that is as light as day; tomorrow I go further into the mountains.

The intermezzo at Breslau continued with a soirée on 2 January 1875 at which Brahms played the piano part of his G minor Quartet op.25, and one of his Bach war-horses, the big Toccata in F, originally for organ with its big pedal solos getting the full treatment from his left hand, and with Scholz as his partner, some of the 'Liebeslieder' op.52. The programme is worth detailing, as soon as one asks what other contemporary composer-pianist could match it for variety and musical worth. Brahms rarely allows such commitments to become a matter of routine, being luckily able to make his way; but in congenial company, as here, the effect on him was rejuvenating.

However, he had to hurry back to Vienna for a particular jewel in the concert-giving crown, the Gesellschaft concert on 10 January, graced by both Joachims. Joseph played his own 'Hungarian' Concerto and the Schumann Fantasy, and Amalie sang the solo in the Alto Rhapsody, and in the Bach Cantata no.34, O ewiges Feuer, whose A major solo with its accompaniment for flutes and muted strings is one of the prettiest of all Bach's enchantments—and of course a tribute to Brahms's missionary knowledge.

Scholz figures in the next Gesellschaft concert (28 February) as the orchestrator of Bach's Organ Prelude and Fugue in E flat, from the Clavierübung Book III, which preceded Brahms's Requiem. The concert of 23 March was devoted to Bach's St Matthew Passion and the last of all, on 18 April, to Max Bruch's Odysseus with Henschel in the title role. Thus ended Brahms's final season as a salaried conductor. However, there were no recriminations or hints of failure. Brahms took a courteous leave of his directors and was made an honorary member of the Gesellschaft der Musikfreunde. He eased himself out of Vienna quickly. He had no thought of living elsewhere, but only to avoid complications with Herbeck, his successor. As he put it in a jaundiced way to Levi: 'I do not want either to wrangle with him, or to wait until he eases me out.' Thus it was that Brahms sent a post card to his friend Levi (26 April) inviting himself to a Munich visit. The visit came shortly to an abrupt end, and one can deduce the reason from Levi's long and dignified letter, undated but presumably from the end of April or beginning of May:

> the fact that I shun even the most distant intercourse with the Futurists' band, and that I am thoroughly hated by them, ought to make you consider whether I really deserve your truly harsh words.

Levi was to become a renowned conductor of Wagner, whose very mention brought the hot-heads to a state which no brow-stroking could remove.

Brahms's first thought, when he was free of times and places, was for a visit to Italy, and Florence in particular. But he eventually went to Karlsruhe on 8 May and Mannheim on 10 May to play, with Dessoff, the duet accompaniment of his 'New Liebeslieder'. Dessoff was now the municipal director of music at Karlsruhe. Brahms also accepted Joachim's invitation to the Lower Rhine Festival at Düsseldorf from 16–18 May, though not before making clear that he liked solitude in a hotel using a truly small room. Joachim and Julius Tausch shared the conducting, and although Joachim was willing to hand the baton to Brahms for his 'Schicksalslied' Brahms was more than content for Joachim, who had borne the burden and heat of the rehearsals, to conduct it himself. We learn from Clara's diary how it went, though not at first hand since she was prevented from attending by a severe attack of neuralgia in her arm.

> I cried like a child all day. I had been so looking forward to the Musical Festival at Düsseldorf, with Joachim conducting . . . Later, I heard that it had not been as satisfactory as had been expected; the choirs from the various towns had not studied their parts properly and both the Beethoven Mass and Brahms's 'Schicksalslied' were uncertain; Johannes himself told me that he never wanted to hear it so wretchedly performed again.

After much indecision he chose for his summer haunt Ziegelhausen on the River Neckar near Heidelberg. As he put it in an invitation to Simrock, Ziegelhausen was a very pretty place, five minutes by train from Heidelberg, 30 minutes by skiff. The sunniest composition of this time was the third String Quartet op.67 in B flat, completed in time for Joachim to try it out, and enthuse about it, in Berlin towards the end of October. As usual there is a veil over closer details but a little light comes from his reply to Franz Wüllner, gracefully refusing an invitation in July:

> Such a long time to get a 'No' out of me! You know how greatly I admire your choral performances, and it must be a pleasure to hear the *Requiem* performed by the young people. Your letter was a great temptation to leave my pretty house here . . . but all the same I stay sitting here, and write from time to time highly useless pieces in order not to have to look into the stern face of a symphony.

He had a visit from Clara in July, when he played to her the Piano Quartet op.60 before it was sent to Simrock for publication. She wrote shortly afterwards to thank him with

> heartfelt content for our pleasant afternoon . . . I have been thinking about the quartet a great deal, and the last three movements have quite taken hold of me, but—if I may say so—the first does not seem to me to be on the same level, it has not the same freshness—though there is freshness in the first theme.

She goes on, characteristically, to wonder whether he couldn't rewrite it, but adds: 'Forgive me, perhaps all this is quite stupid.' There could be two answers to this, first that it might not be the function of this particular movement to be 'fresh', and that it embodies a striking formal experiment which may have passed Clara by—see the catalogue. Brahms decided (letter of August to Simrock on holiday in Switzerland) not to send the final manuscript to him in Bönigen at the Interlaken end of the lake of Brienz because 'it would make the bluest day turn cloudy'. But he does not fail to go into details again about the 'Werther' on the front cover, for which he will supply a photograph of himself.

Autumn saw Brahms back in Vienna, to receive grateful acknowledgement and plaudits from Joachim, to whom he had sent the new String Quartet, which Joachim had tried out in Berlin to his own and Clara's pleasure. On the other hand Clara's pleasure was emphatically not served by seeing *Tristan* in Munich:

> I cannot remember ever having heard or seen anything more odious than this opera . . . Anyone who can listen to it or see it with pleasure must lack all moral feeling . . . but even to think about it makes me boil with indignation, so let us say no more about it.

She would obviously have subscribed to the English nineteenth-century criticism: 'adultery with drums and trumpets'.

The first performance of the op.60 Piano Quartet was given in Vienna on 18 November, by Brahms with members of the Hellmesberger Quartet, and the year was rounded off, as it had begun, with a happy occasion at Breslau, a performance under Scholz of the A major Serenade, announced by Simrock as being in a new edition revised by the composer. Some of the revision, as far as the strings were concerned, consisted of minor revisions by Joachim. There is interesting evidence in a letter to Scholz of the forces Brahms envisaged for this eventual quasi-symphonic form: 'eight violas or more, six cellos, four basses—or thereabouts' (*oder so was*).

The interaction of fame and ready publication—the one feeding the other—aroused many demands for Brahms's presence as conductor or player or even as president of the musical feast with no duties but to shed lustre. He was too level-headed not to see the necessity of cherishing the magic well spring within him. The fierce jealousy with which he guarded the solitude of his creative life could lead him into refusals so abrupt as to wound, or even to silences for which he had to apologise occasionally—to friends that is, for breaking silence to others in itself took time! He could wryly amuse himself over this. For instance, to the conductor Otto Dessoff: 'I even have a secret passion for writing letters, but it is very secret indeed, and completely vanishes in front of the writing-paper.'

However, early in 1876 he made a Dutch tour, helping to nurse the great regard that country showed him. There were two upshots: a love affair with Schnapps from Amsterdam, and the dedication to his genial Utrecht host Prof. Engelmann of the String Quartet in B flat op.67 written the previous year. Brahms acknowledged to Joachim a dozen years later (1889) that this string quartet was his favourite of the three, probably because of its happy freedom after the severities of the preceding two, which had to stand some sort of comparison in the classical chamber medium *par excellence* with the towering corpus of Beethoven's 16 examples. Engelmann with his pianist wife kept open house for Brahms, Joachim and their friends, and in acknowledging the dedication, wrote 'I have now less reason to worry about my immortality.' He was a professor of physiology.

For some charming vignettes of Brahms at this time we return to Henschel, the singer whose professional and personal qualities led Brahms to break with his all-too-practised reticence. In February 1876 he and Brahms were together in Koblenz as soloists.

> On the day before the concert there was, as usual, the final full rehearsal to which in most places in Germany the public are admitted. Brahms had played Schumann's Concerto and missed a good many notes. So in the morning of the day of the concert he went to the concert hall to practise. He had asked me to follow him thither a little later and to rehearse with him the songs—his, of course—he was to accompany for me in the evening. When I arrived at the hall I found him quite alone, seated at the piano and working away for all he was worth, on Beethoven's Choral Fantasia and Schumann's Concerto. He was quite red in the face, and, interrupting himself on seeing me stand beside him, said with that childlike, confiding expression in his eyes: 'Really this is too bad. These people here tonight expect to hear something especially good, and here I am likely to give them a hoggish mess (*Schweinerei*). I assure you, I could play today, with the greatest ease, far more difficult things, with wider stretches for the fingers, my own concerto for example, but these simple diatonic runs are exasperating. I keep saying to myself: "But, Johannes, pull yourself together,—Do play decently" but no use; it's really horrid.' After our little private rehearsal of the songs, Brahms, Maszkowski [the conductor] and I repaired to Councillor Wegeler's, Brahms's host . . . to inspect the celebrated and really wonderful wine-cellars of his firm, and to partake of a little luncheon in the sample room afterwards. Towards the end of the repast, which turned out to be rather a sumptuous affair, relished by Brahms as much as by any of us, a bottle of old Rauenthaler of the year '65 was opened, with due ceremony, by our host. It proved indeed to be a rare drop, and we all sat in almost reverential silence, bent over the high, light-green goblets, which we held in close proximity to our respective noses. Wegeler at last broke the silence with the solemn words: 'Yes, gentlemen, what Brahms is among the composers, this Rauenthaler is among the wines.' Quick as lightning Brahms exclaimed: 'Ah, then let's have a bottle of Bach now!'

Curiously enough, after these preliminaries, Henschel goes on to say 'The concert went off well, as did the supper afterwards . . . and Brahms went so far as to make a speech—a very rare thing with him.'[5]

In the train to Wiesbaden Henschel had the happiness of finding Brahms (alone in the compartment) more communicative than ever before:

> There is no real *creating* without hard work. That which you would call invention, that is to say, a thought, an idea, is simply an inspiration from above, for which I am not responsible, which is no merit of mine. Yes, it is a present, a gift, which I ought even to despise until I have made it my own by right of hard work. And there is no hurry about that, either . . . When I, for instance, have found the first phrase of a song, say,

When the sil — very moon

80

I might shut the book there and then, go for a walk, do some other work, and perhaps not think of it again for months . . . If afterward I approach the subject again, it is sure to have taken shape; I can now really begin to work at it. But there are composers who sit at the piano with a poem before them, putting music to it from A to Z until it is done. They write themselves into a state of enthusiasm which makes them see something finished, something important, in every bar.'[6]

For more than a decade, Joachim had been an annual concert-giver in England. In April he wrote to Brahms from London conveying the news that both of them were to be invited to Cambridge for honorary Doctorates in Music. The Cambridge Professor of Music, George Macfarren, wrote to Brahms in most honorific terms with the invitation, saying *inter alia*: 'This is the only country in which the Faculty of Music is represented in its Universities', and thus offering some counterweight to German jibes about *Das Land ohne Musik* ('the land without music'). Joachim had pointed out, what is more, that this would be 'the first time the degree was given to foreigners for their free compositions' (that is, as opposed to offering, like Haydn, a specific work as a form of singing for one's supper—an exercise, in university parlance). But, as became clear, the degree could not be given without Brahms's personal presence. In July Joachim tried to bring the matter to a head, but rightly feared a first-sentence 'No'. Footling though it might now seem, there is every reason to suppose that Brahms feared sea-sickness, but one can easily suppose that a greater fear would be lionisation in a foreign language.

Meanwhile one of the 'highly useless things', the String Quartet in B flat, was taking its first audible steps towards the world at large. In May the Joachim Quartet had rehearsed it in Clara's hearing and both she and Joachim had enthusiastically greeted it in letters to Brahms, Joachim going so far as to say: 'Even you have hardly written more beautiful chamber music than in the D minor movement and in the finale, the former full of magical romanticism, the latter full of inwardness [*Innigkeit*] and grace in a form rich in artistry.' The form was that of variations, on which Brahms would shortly have occasion to express himself without mincing words. (Did he ever mince them on compositional matters?)

Henschel had taken upon himself to advise Brahms on a new haven for summer composing, the port of Sassnitz on the Baltic island of Rügen off the Pomeranian coast. The two of them met there at the end of June, taking care to keep out of each other's way in working hours but sharing relaxing hours in conversations of which Henschel kept a valuable record in his Rügen diary. The precious outcome as far as the history of the symphony is concerned—the history might otherwise have been much shorter—was the bringing to fruition there of most of the score of Brahms's First Symphony. It cannot have been quite finished there, because on signing the score he dated it September 1876 and recorded the place as Lichtenthal, Clara's retreat near

Baden. Henschel's vignette of Brahms on 8 July reads:

> His solid frame, the healthy dark-brown colour of his face, the full hair, just a
> little sprinkled with grey, all make him appear the very image of strength and
> vigour. He walks about here just as he pleases, with his waistcoat unbuttoned
> and his hat in his hand, always with clean linen, but without collar or necktie.
> These he dons at *table d'hôte* only. His whole appearance vividly recalls some of
> the portraits of Beethoven . . . He eats with great gusto and in the evening
> regularly drinks his three glasses of beer, never omitting, however, to finish off
> with his beloved 'Kaffee'.

Some of the Rügen conversations were carried on by the two friends in one
hammock. 'We both managed to climb into it simultaneously, am amusing,
though by no means easy task to accomplish.' The summer being marked by
the first complete *Ring* at Bayreuth, some talk turned to Wagner. Brahms
found some things admirable, but not moving, blaming the remote myths and
the 'stilted, bombastic language . . . What really happens with the ring? Do
you know? And those endless and tedious duets! . . . ' Again, from 15 July:
'Today I read out from a Berlin paper, the news of the death, at Bayreuth, of a
member of the Wagner orchestra. "The first corpse", said Brahms, dryly. On
marriage, Brahms said "I sometimes regret that I did not marry. I ought to
have a boy of ten now; that *would* be nice. But when I was of the right age for
marrying I lacked the position to do so, and now it is too late."' One can only
observe that a girl child seemed of no consequence, and that at the age of 43 in
his burly prime it was 'too late'. The rub, of course, was that it was the
beginning of a true compositional prime, and we might leave the conversations with the counsel he gave his would-be-composer friend:

> Let is rest, let it rest, and keep going back to it and working at it over and over
> again, until it is completed as a finished work of art, until there is not a note too
> much or too little, not a bar you could improve upon. Whether it is *beautiful*
> also, is an entirely different matter, but perfect it *must* be.

England continued to impinge on this single-mindedness; on 28 July the
publishers Novello offered Brahms a large sum for a full-scale oratorio such
as Mendelssohn's *Elijah*. It is difficult to imagine Brahms assenting to this,
and impossible to imagine what sort of work might have eventuated had
Brahms ever got himself into an English-oratorio frame of mind.

On 1 August the correspondence with Heinrich and Elisabet von Herzogenberg began. At this time they were not only ornaments but driving forces
of musical society in Leipzig. He was a composer, of high ideals and much
theoretical knowledge, but he achieved little that was distinctive. Brahms had
embarrassingly little to say to him on this score. The safer, congenial ground
was Heinrich's deep love of Bach, and his efforts with a choral society in
bringing the works before the public, in which he was heartily seconded by his
wife. She was a true musician. Brahms had earlier given her some piano
lessons and she had not only a fluent technique but an excellent memory and a

capacity to read a score, which meant that Brahms soon began to send her nearly all his works before they were published, and sometimes indeed took serious account of what she had to say about them. As if these were not gifts enough she had looks and charm which Brahms was the more able to enjoy as she was safely and happily married.

We can see Elisabet as she appeared to a young woman's eyes a year later. The writer is Ethel Smyth, feminist and composer, who, going to Leipzig in a determined search for tuition at the age of 19, found the post-Mendelssohn Conservatoire wanting and was rescued as to lessons by Heinrich and protected and loved by Elisabet.

> At the time I first met her she.was 29, not really beautiful but better than beautiful, at once dazzling and bewitching: the fairest of skins, fine-spun, wavy golden hair, curious arresting greenish-brown eyes and a very noble, rather low forehead, behind which you knew there must be an exceptional brain. I never saw a more beautiful neck and shoulders; so marvellously white were they, that on the very rare occasions on which the world had a chance of viewing them it was apt to stare—thereby greatly disconcerting their owner, whose modesty was of the type that used to be called maidenly.

Ethel goes on to note in her playing a fundamental coldness at the bottom of all that tender warmth and enthusiasm, and linked it with the life-long cosseting and anxiety brought about by a weak heart. The sharp eyes of Ethel also saw what a man perhaps could not: 'I used to tell her that when talking to men she became a different woman—a difference which though slight was perceptible—but this mild accusation did not fit in with her scheme of things and was eagerly repudiated.'[7]

The Herzogenbergs wrote their first surviving letters to Brahms each on the same day unknown to each other and each sending him a copy of the same piece, Heinrich's piano duet Variations on a Theme of Johannes Brahms op.23. (The theme is from one of the op.7 songs, 'Mei Mutter mag mi net'.) Heinrich's letter speaks of his work with humility and then talks of Bach. Elisabet has a more individual contribution: 'I remember hearing that, at Sassnitz, they give you nothing to eat but pale grey beef and indescribable, wobbly puddings, made of starch and vanilla.' In his reply to them both Brahms is able to reassure her about his menus. As to the variations he does not commit himself but gracefully and flirtatiously evades them thus: 'How can I be disinterested, when, as I open the duet and play it in imagination, I have a distinct vision of a slender, golden-haired figure in blue velvet seated on my right.' But he goes on to show where he stands in the general matter:

> I could wish people would distinguish variations from *fantasia-variations*, or whatever we may choose to call the great number of modern writings in this form. I have a peculiar affection for the variation form, and consider that it offers great scope to our talents and energies. Beethoven treats it with extraordinary severity and rightly calls his variations 'alterations' [*Veränderungen*]. All

the later ones by Schumann, H [=Heinrich] or Nottebohm are very different. I am of course, objecting neither to the form nor the music. I only wish for some distinction in the name to denote the distinctive character of each.

However, Elisabet at this stage could not have priority over Clara, to whom in September Brahms played the outer movements of the Symphony—the first movement four years after she had first seen it (or most of it, without its introduction). In October he played her the whole. Even now it was not quite in its final form—see the catalogue. But his other musical life went on. A composer is never exempt from the laborious notation of his music or the close checking of copyists' work. Somehow this year Brahms had edited for Breitkopf and Härtel's complete Mozart edition the unfinished *Requiem*, distinguishing carefully between Mozart's and Süssmayer's hands. On the 24 October he had sent to Simrock the fair copy for printing (*Stichvorlage*) of his string quartet in B flat, which had its first performance on the 30 October by the Joachim Quartet at the Berlin Singakademie. Sometime thereafter he made the arrangement for piano four hands which was published the following April. Anyone who has done it will know the slow physical labour of getting the notes accurately on to paper, let alone deciding what they should be. In the age before discs and tapes piano duets were the usual means of disseminating concerted music—which says much for the sight-reading and domestic playing skills of the audience Brahms served. The score and parts of the quartet were published in November.

However, the great event of this month was the Symphony's first performance under Dessoff in Karlsruhe (4 November). It was wise and typical of Brahms that the work's career began in a non-metropolitan way—but with a devoted conductor and good orchestra. Performances followed quickly, not with a travelling orchestra, as might nowadays be the case, but freshly learnt by the local musicians—at Mannheim (7 November), Munich (15 November), Vienna (17 December) and the following year under Brahms's own baton at Leipzig (18 January) and Breslau (23 January).

In a letter to the Viennese conductor Reinecke Brahms displays his wry, common-sensical self:

> Now I would like to acquaint you with news that you may find very surprising: my symphony is long and not straight-forwardly lovable. So I would not like it at the end of the concert; it would be better at the beginning and still better thus: 1. Overture 2. Aria 3. 'Symphony' 4. 5. 6. etc. But Henschel will be sensible and sing a beautiful aria; afterwards, if the symphony fails, he will sing my most lovable song!

Before the end of the momentous year Brahms, to the honour and joy of the Herzogenbergs, had pledged himself to stay with them for his visit to Leipzig to conduct the Symphony at the Gewandhaus. To get him away from his usual hotel Elisabet, who added wonderful cooking to all her other enticements, had offered him 'a bed at least as good, much better coffee, no very large room but two decent-sized ones, a silken bed-cover, any number of ash-trays, and, above all, peace and quiet.'

For the first Vienna performance of the first Symphony Brahms was back, also as a conductor, to his old stamping-ground, a Gesellschaft concert (17 December), though now under the aegis of Herbeck. But none of these early performances could honestly be described as a public success; how could it be? To go no further, there is surely a contradiction between the traditional expectation of applause at the end of each movement (with even a possible encore) and the experience, which we take for granted, of the dramatic cumulation which was surely, by now, the composer's intention?

The end of the year saw Brahms immersed again in a question which honoured as well as plagued him. He had been offered the municipal directorship of music at Düsseldorf (sacred name!) which would also involve the command of a new music school, which could look forward to a government subsidy, but only if Brahms took the post. The long delays and the frustrated hopes of the organisers caused inevitable annoyance all round, and Clara's hesitations re-inforced Brahms's delays.

Thus the year of his greatest compositional achievement so far could still exact the price of being a free-lance. Could the passing of the age of patronage have been a calamity in disguise?

NOTES

1. E. Walkter, 'Goethe and some composers', *Musical Times*, vol. 73 (1932), pp. 172ff.

2. P. Latham, *Brahms*, Master Musician Series (Dent, London, 1948), p. 55.

3. These details and comments are in J. A. S. Grenville, *Europe Reshaped 1848–1878* (Fontana, London, 1976), *passim*.

4. The music is further discussed in the catalogue, and there is a detailed consideration of its evolution in J. Webster, 'The C sharp minor version of Brahms's op.60', *Musical Times*, vol. 121 (1980), pp. 89–93.

5. These and the next quotations are from G. Henschel, *Musings and Memories of a Musician* (Macmillan, London, 1918), by which date he had long been a naturalised Briton.

6. From 'Die Mainacht', op.43.

7. R. Crichton (ed.), *The Memoirs of Ethel Smyth* (Viking, London, 1987), p. 88.

CHAPTER FOUR

The Years of Maturity

The Leipzig première of the First Symphony, in a Gewandhaus concert on 18 January 1877, was the occasion of Brahms's first stay with the Herzogenbergs. He conducted both the symphony and the Haydn variations, and accompanied some of his own songs sung by Henschel. Clara thought his conducting 'most inspiring—a rare exhibition of artistic skill . . . The Leipzig audience behaved as it always does—respectfully: enthusiasm was shown by only a few.' This is at odds with the note by Kalbeck, the editor of the Herzogenberg correspondence, which says the work was 'very favourably received'. Perhaps he meant to add 'for Leipzig'. However that may be, after a Gewandhaus chamber concert in which he played in his C minor Piano Quartet op.60, Brahms secured himself a better performance of the Symphony at Breslau on 23 January. He was frank to the Herzogenbergs about it, stressing the advantages of someone else taking the first rehearsals, in this case a young man named Julius Buths (b1851) deputising for the indisposed Scholz: he also indirectly criticised himself: 'The introduction to the last movement was just as I like it: that is to say, different from what it was in Leipzig. Unfortunately, I am inclined to allow such important matters to slide.'

Although Brahms definitively wrote to Clara in January: 'I have refused the Düsseldorf post', the affair still rumbled on, as is evident from a letter from Brahms to Simrock of 24 May, but more important is the light the letter sheds on the intentions as to the presentation of the printed Symphony. 'Please do not allow the usual practice nowadays of putting numbers (I, II, III, IV) above the individual movements. That is hateful [hässlich].' Such very strong words over a detail must surely be a pointer to the conception of the work as a 'straight-through' drama?

Meanwhile Dr Joachim (for he had accepted Cambridge's honour) was doing splendid work for the new Symphony in England. Brahms had agreed to the work being played in Cambridge by way of compensation for his non-attendance. Joachim had heard Brahms conduct the Leipzig performance and asked for the score and parts, still of course in manuscript, to be sent to him. The proposed conductor was Charles Villiers Stanford, whom Joachim described as a zealous (*strebsamer*), aimiable or even dapper (*netter*) musician and seemingly quite acceptable as a conductor. But Joachim explained that to send the parts in advance to Stanford would serve no purpose, as the orchestra would be exclusively Londoners–doubtless a surprise to Germans enjoying their multiplicity of orchestral life. Almost needless to say, Cambridge had no contra-bassoon, but Joachim was reassuring: 'I have already taken steps about it: I cannot stand the hollow tone of the bass tuba.' But he begged the score quickly so that Macfarren could provide the customary extended analysis, with quotations of leading themes, 'usually amounting to a small book'. It is amusing to see English conductors through an experienced foreign eye. First Brahms was warned off the London Philharmonic Society whose conductor, William Cusins, wanted to do the Symphony.

> Cusins is a mediocre conductor who unfortunately has neither the authority, such as Bennett had, nor the necessary baton technique for dealing with an orchestra. I would like it if you could entrust the symphony, for London, to the brave Manns in Crystal Palace. He is no refined or important musician, but he is an enthusiastic friend of music; his excellent orchestra follows his every gesture, and plays with the greatest care, since he has the wind and part of the strings at his disposal *daily*.

Joachim reported from London in mid-March—that is, after the Cambridge and before the London performances:-

> Your symphony went very well, and was received with enthusiasm, particularly the adagio and the last movement. I have after all promised the symphony to the Philharmonic. I couldn't do otherwise, . . . but nor did I wish to, having found out that it would first be done by Manns, and that the Philharmonic orchestra consists almost entirely of the same people(!) . . . What is more, since Cambridge the fate of the work is secure in England, the principal papers are all *very* warm, and the oftener it is heard, the better for its understanding.

The Cambridge programme is worth noting for its memorable content: 1. Overture 'Woodnymphs' by Joachim; 2. Beethoven's Violin Concerto played by Joachim; 3. Brahms's 'Schicksalslied'; 4. another overture by Joachim; 5. Brahms's Symphony.

The early part of the year saw the harvesting, if not also the sowing, of a large crop of songs, the 23 in all that comprised opp.69–72 all of which were published in 1877. Kalbeck even says that 18 of them can be ascribed to the month of March. The new intimacy with the Herzogenbergs is reflected in Brahms giving to them a first look, but almost in the same breath he insists on their sending them on to Frau Schumann 'without losing a day' (23 April). As Clara made short, but trenchant comments on all of them (2 May) it is possible to compare the reactions to some extent, and there is unanimity of praise for 'Des Liebsten Schwur' op.64 no.4, 'An dem Mond' op.71 no.2, 'Geheimnis' op.71 no.3 and 'Alte Liebe' op.72 no.1. On the other hand both ladies were bold enough to disapprove 'Klage I' op.69 no.1, 'Tambourlied' op.69 no.5 and 'Willst du, dass ich geh' op.71 no.4. There is an amusing discrepancy about 'Geheimnis'. Herzogenberg confessed how they had revelled in the sentiment of every left-hand suspension, then guiltily read the inscription *sehr lebhaft* ('very lively'). Was there some mistake? Brahms replied that he set the tempo mark down in desperation, 'thinking the song very dull'. This was one of the double-firsts, of course.

Brahms's birthday was this year marked in two unusual ways, first, by his sending to Simrock a greeting *from* himself, second, by Joachim's youngest son Paul choosing that day (7 May) to be born. In reply to Joachim's greetings and the news he writes, 'One can hardly in the event wish for him the best of all wishes, not to be born at all', but softens this with 'May the new world-citizen never think such a thing, but for long years take joy in 7 May and in his life.'

A distinction born of experience, no doubt, but not otherwise immediately clear, is the subject of a letter to Simrock (16 June). Brahms wanted the main body of the finale of the Symphony marked *allegro non troppo ma con brio* instead of *allegro moderato ma con brio*. Perhaps with the long-awaited onset of 'the' tune, the time for explicit moderation is at an end. In the same letter Brahms refers to the innumerable but money-making arrangements of the already famous 'Wiegenlied' and suggests a minor-key arrangement for naughty or sickly children.

On 6 June Brahms arrived for the summer at Pörtschach on the lake of Wörth near Klagenfurt in Carinthia. The recommendation must have been through his friends the Fabers who had a country retreat there. One learns from a letter to Faber that Brahms brought his own piano from Vienna, but could not get it into his lodgings in the castle. It therefore had to be exchanged with one in the villa of a Dr Karl Kupelwieser, and *he* was the son of Schubert's friend Kupelwieser, making a connection that charmed Brahms. The compositions of the summer must have included most of the opp.85 and 86 songs, but above all the fruits both of the countryside and of the bringing to life of the First Symphony was the sketching of the second. Even 'sketching' may be too precise a word, for Clara writes from Baden-Baden to Levi—again a friend—on 24 September: 'Brahms is in a happy mood, very delighted with his summer resort, and he has finished—at all events in his head—a new symphony in D major . . . he has written out the first movement.' Whatever its state then, he set himself to write down the whole when he left Pörtschach for Lichtenthal on 17 September, since it had its first performance in the same year (30 December).

A visitor to Lichtenthal in September was Bülow, who got Brahms to play through the First Symphony to him. Bülow conducted it in Hanover on 20 October, *en route* to Edinburgh where a performance on 10 December inaugurated a long attachment there to Brahms's music. A truly grateful and friendly letter to Simrock acknowledged the receipt of a beautifully bound special copy for the composer of the First Symphony in full score. In the same letter is an interesting note of the requirements, that is the size, of the Gesellschaft orchestra for the Second Symphony: seven desks of first violins, seven desks of seconds, five of violas, cellos and basses (the latter is ambiguous, but probably means nine or ten players of each, though the basses might have one copy each). Brahms also mentions *einfache Harmonie*, that is one printed copy of each wind part. Simrock had to bear Brahms's laboured joke about the character of the Second Symphony: 'it is so melancholy that you will not be able to bear it . . . the score will need a black edging'. To Elisabet he wrote on 22 November:

> I do not need to play it to you beforehand. You have only to sit down at the piano, put your small feet on the two pedals in turn, and strike the chord of F minor several times in succession, first in the treble, then in the bass (*ff* and *pp*) and you will gradually gain a vivid impression of my 'latest'.

The first performance of the new symphony took place in Vienna on 30 December, conducted by Richter. Billroth sent a telegram to Clara in Berlin that same day to assure her of its great success. We have confirmation of this from an eyewitness, C.F. Pohl the music historian, who wrote to Simrock:

> Exemplary performance, very warm reception, third movement encored, repeated calls to the composer for applause. Timings of the movements: 19, eleven, five, eight minutes. The adagio was not applauded in proportion to its deep contents, but it remains the most valuable movement musically. And now: prosit New Year.[1]

Thus the year ended with the publication of the First Symphony crowning a gestation of some 20 years, and the success of the Second after barely one year, as far as we can see. It is also significant that a conductor other than Brahms produced it even in Vienna. The days of personal evangelism were beginning to be over. Brahms in 1877 was established enough to be on a committee advising the Austrian government for the awarding of grants to assist composers. He had no reservations about his successful candidate for the year: Antonin Dvořák.

However, one work and one city still seemed to need missionary work, the Piano Concerto and Leipzig. Thus Brahms invited himself again to the Herzogenbergs, to their great pleasure and pride, and played the concerto in the Gewandhaus on New Year's Day, 1878. He followed this up with the new symphony on 10 January. This was the occasion of Brahms meeting a young English composition student in her twentieth year named Ethel Smyth, who had come to the Leipzig Conservatoire to study. Heinrich and Elisabet von Herzogenberg were shortly to rescue her both from unsuitable lodgings and from scandalously poor teaching, and when she knew Brahms better she had penetrating and not very complimentary things to say.

From Henschel I gathered that at the extra rehearsal . . . there had been a good deal of friction . . . The Gewandhaus musicians were inclined to be antagonistic . . . Brahms, accustomed to the brilliant quality of Vienese orchestras . . . found his own race, the north Germans, cold and sticky, and let them feel it . . . At that time I only remember a strong alarming face, very penetrating blue eyes, and my own desire to sink through the floor when he said, as I then thought by way of a compliment, but as I now know in a spirit of scathing irony, 'So this is the young lady who writes sonatas and doesn't know counterpoint!'[2]

Brahms left a night-shirt at the Herzogenbergs, and Elisabet sent it on to Utrecht, 'laundered a snowy white'. However, his first stop was Hamburg for the First Symphony on 18 January. His native city continued its propensity for letting him down. Writing to Herzogenberg on the day of the concert he congratulated himself that he is 'not entertaining you here, for the weather is vile as only Hamburg weather can be—and is, on 360 days a year. (It is difficult enough to hit the other five.)' 'However, the orchestra are so enthusiastic that I am really looking forward to this evening'. Be that as it may, Clara wrote from Berlin a week later: 'I am sorry to hear that you were not pleased with Hamburg.' However, the object of the tour (via Bremen) was to perform the symphonies in Holland, the First in Utrecht (26 January) and the Second twice in Amsterdam (4 and 8 February) with a performance in between at The Hague (6 February), a schedule in which the elations far outweighed what were negligible exertions to Brahms's physique. On the other side of the scale, Levi having failed to get Brahms to let him put the new symphony down on his Lent season's programme at Munich, reverted to the First Symphony, which according to Leopold Schmidt, the editor of Levi's letters, did not come off well, and again set back the Brahms cause in that city.

After another performance of the new Symphony at the other end of Germany (at the Royal Opera House, Dresden, 6 March) which gave the Herzogenbergs much happiness Brahms stirred himself on other people's account. Together with Levi he counselled Clara most firmly to accept an offer—very much on her own terms in any case—to teach in Frankfurt for the Conservatoire there. Clearly not liking the new Director, Joachim Raff, as a composer—he had youthful connections with Weimar—she mistrusted him as a man, needlessly as it turned out. Dvořák was the other beneficiary. Brahms sent him a very friendly letter offering to help him to place two string quartets with Simrock, one of them, op.34 in D minor, being dedicated to Brahms. But he warned Dvořák to correct the many wrong and missing accidentals!

On 8 April a long-cherished dream came true. He set out on his first trip to Italy—what he called a rehearsal journey (*Probefahrt*), travelling with the composer Karl Goldmark as far as Rome, and with Billroth for the entire trip. Simrock received such news as there was, namely a note from Florence on the way home: 'This is the last of my greetings [i.e. the first]. I hope you have kept, and read well, my earlier, better and longer letters [i.e. none].' But he was he was obviously bowled over. Back in Pörtschach in May he told Simrock, 'I saw Venice, Florence, Rome etc. in fullest spring—they were magic days.' There was no music in the Sistine Chapel, and terrible music in St Peter's. The choice of Pörtschach again, in spite of a pressing invitation to Switzerland from Widmann, tells its own tale, as does the principal work of this year—the sunny D major triple time of the Second Symphony being succeeded by the sunny D major triple time of the Violin Concerto. But dates drive us to suppose that the happy fecundity amounted to more than that; in all probability 1878 saw the beginning of the Second Piano Concerto, as well as some of the piano pieces op.76—published the next year—and some more songs. No wonder that Brahms could not bring himself to leave for an appearance at the Lower Rhine Festival at Düsseldorf, even though Joachim was conducting the Second Symphony there. He explained to Simrock (15 June) that he had been expecting the cancellation of the festival because of an attempt on the Kaiser's life only a week before it was due to begin, after which it was 'too late'—a most implausible reason. Of course Joachim was the beneficiary of the additional composing days, and on 24 August Brahms sent him the solo part (only) of the first movement of the Violin Concerto for technical comment while assuring him that there would be four. Naturally there was an immediate and joyful reply.

At the end of September Brahms attended the festival marking the fiftieth anniversary of the Hamburg Philharmonic. He told Joachim he was going 'in spite of all possible misunderstandings and forgetfulnesses'. What is more, he conducted the new symphony and Joachim did the honours by leading the orchestra. At last there was a great reception. Most of the autumn was devoted to shaping the Violin Concerto, with an interlude at Breslau where Brahms conducted the new Symphony and the Alto Rhapsody on 22 October. A postcard to Joachim on the following day shows that the concerto was still a four-movement work as late as that, as the composer admitted to having stumbled (*gestolpert*) in the adagio and scherzo. It is not until the next month that Joachim hears that 'The middle movements have fallen out—naturally they were the best! I am having them replaced by a poor adagio.' 'Poor' is a typically deprecatory adjective for a wonderful last-minute inspiration. It would be easy—and perhaps correct—to surmise that the difficulty was caused by the length and elaboration of the first movement. But the Second Piano Concerto (almost certainly somewhere in that fecund head already) has a first movement which yields nothing to that of the Violin Concerto in length and elaboration and has two large interior movements. The difference might lie in the unsuitability of the violin as an instrument for the kind of scherzo that should come after the long, lyrical stretches of the first movement. Perhaps all these suppositions are a warning not to make them.

Nothing illustrates better Joachim's enthusiasm and trust both in Brahms and in his own technique than his willingness to programme the Concerto for

New Year's Day at the Leipzig Gewandhaus in spite of not receiving the definitive solo part until 12 December—and even then not the score, or a keyboard reduction, as far as the evidence goes.

If the two great Pörtschach pieces, the Second Symphony and the Violin Concerto, bring to mind Milton's 'linked sweetness long drawn out' there is a notable contrast in the two Motets for Mixed Chorus op.74, published that year, of which the first 'Warum ist das Licht gegeben?' was given its first performance, on 8 December, by the senior Vienna choir—the Singakademie—under Eduard Kremser, their conductor. These are learned, extended and austere essays in choral technique, especially in counterpoint of all kinds. Brahms at one stage hesitated about dedicating them to the great Bach historian and Buxtehude editor Philipp Spitta fearing that the works might be thought to be courting a comparison with Spitta's beloved Bach— which is of course exactly what they do. A few days later (15 December) there was a Viennese performance of the First Symphony which Brahms described to Simrock as 'inept' (*mies*). However, it does have an interest for conductors in that Brahms makes explicit that the *poco sostenuto* at the end of the first movement does *not* mean going back to the tempo of the introduction. He wants instead an outright *meno allegro*.

For the last precious days of piano rehearsal, before going to Lepzig with Joachim, Brahms went to Berlin, inviting himself to the Simrocks, whom he sometimes teasingly called Erler.

> If my old time-table is still right I leave here at 8.40 pm and am at Erler's at mid-day, 12.43 . . . I hear that at Erler's they sleep on manuscripts. Now that is all right by me, as he does not print spiky motets but only gentle sweet Hoffmanns.

It is clearly nothing to Brahms for vital rehearsals to be preceded by a night in the train.

In one respect Brahms made an irreversible—or at least not reversed— decision in 1878. Clean-shaven he may have been in January in Leipzig but, says Henschel:

> In 1878 Brahms had considerably changed his outward appearance by the growth of the long and flowing beard in the frame of which his face has become familiar to the last and present generations . . . At the end of a concert in Vienna Brüll and I were receiving, in the artists' room, the congratulations of friends, when suddenly I saw a man unknown to me, rather stout, of middle height, with long hair and a full beard, coming up toward me. In a very deep and hoarse voice he introduced himself 'Musik-Direktor Müller', making a very stiff and formal bow, which I was on the point of returning with equal gravity, when, an instant later, we all found outselves laughing heartily at the perfect success of Brahms's disguise.[3]

Dessoff wanted his share of the spoils in a letter of 19 October: 'In case you have already had yourself photographed in full beard to satisfy the wishes of your countless female admirers, please send me a copy.'

Leipzig received the first performance of the Violin Concerto with respect but not acclaim. The size of the orchestra on this occasion is fixed by a letter from Herzogenberg beforehand detailing the number of copies of the string parts required: 'five first-violin parts, five seconds, three violas, and eight basses (if copied separately, five cello parts and three double bass parts).' That is to say, a maximum of 42 strings *vis-à-vis* the wind and brass. There is some evidence of greater success in the next performance, in Vienna on 14 January, though ironically it was for that part of the work by which Brahms particularly honoured Joachim: the cadenza which Brahms left him to supply. Brahms wrote to Elisabet from Vienna: 'The cadenza went so magnificently at our concert here that the people clapped right on into my coda'—thereby, to our ears, defiling a piece of holy ground.

Delighted with the Concerto's supreme tribute to his powers, Joachim gained Brahms's quick permission to use it on his visit to England. In sending him a score and parts for the purpose (24 January 1879) the composer's human touches are illuminating and ring very true:

> If you had anyone to hand who had the goodwill and time to go through the parts yet again, and put into them what has been added in *red* in the score, it would be as well, but not of the utmost importance. Most of what I missed [in the performance] or did not hear in the manner I wanted, I find stands there on the paper and is sufficiently marked . . . Above all, and this I noted particularly in Vienna, the players wanted rather to hear you than play their own notes. At their desks they are looking sideways; very fatal, but understandable.

However the collaboration with Joachim aroused in Brahms the desire for further concert-giving, 'I would like to get my fingers more into order, and make some music with you.' This did indeed happen later in the year. In his letter from London of 22 February Joachim was able to report a decided success at the first concert, at Crystal Palace, though the accompaniment was not always delicate enough (*zart*).

> I am to do it again at the Philharmonic concert, I think by heart, which I could not risk this first time because I have been truly suffering these last weeks from the horribly wet and cold climate—coughing and lumbago are a lowering combination!

This Philharmonic concert went better orchestrally, with mostly the same players, probably, and the success was so decided that a second Crystal Palace performance was requested, to which Brahms agreed.

Meanwhile Clara, now living at Frankfurt because of her Conservatoire commitments, had suffered for a year the misery of knowing that her youngest son Felix had incurable consumption. He died at home during the night of 15–16 February, and Brahms, true to form, rushed to Frankfurt to comfort Clara as best he could, and to distract her with joint work, desultory in the previous year, on a new comprehensive edition of Schumann's works for Breitkopf and Härtel.

In March the University of Breslau offered, and Brahms accepted, its honorary degree of Doctor of Philosophy, the citation referring to him as 'a most illustrious man, now the leader of the more severe art of music in Germany'. However as Latin does not possess either a definite or indefinite article, a possible translation of the phrase might be *a* leader, or prince (*principi*). At all events, Dr Brahms found he had to sing for his supper with composition, which is the origin of the Academic Festival Overture composed a year later.

In the spring the piquant possibility of Brahms being a successor of Bach as Cantor of St Thomas's Leipzig momentarily opened up when he was offered the post. He asked Elisabet about it (29 April) but she dissuaded him—if indeed it was really required—using the sort of words he must have used to himself:

> What would become of your delightful summer holiday, your beloved Pörtschach, with its lake from whose waves there rise D major symphonies and violin concertos, beautiful as any foam-born goddess! No, we cannot imagine you here, however desirable it may be for us and for Leipzig to have you descend on us like a whirlwind.

For fully half the year Joachim and Brahms were engaged in a patient and friendly collaboration to get every last note of the Concerto ready for printing. A letter from Brahms in March asked 'is the piece now good enough and practicable enough for printing'? But it was not until the end of June that all was sent to Simrock. Joachim's suggestions were partly of orchestration but mainly of details of arpeggios, to ease their fingering or, more important, to help the carrying power of the principal notes of their harmonies. A comparison of the suggestions with the ultimate score shows that even in such technical matters Brahms often stuck to his guns. One unresolved problem— which remains largely unresolved today due to notational insufficiencies— was the meaning of *staccato* dots under a slur, which to a pianist means *semi-staccato*, but to a string player means *staccato* but within one bow-stroke. How exactly this *staccato* is to be played, and with what part of the bow, remains a matter for discussion at rehearsal between the leader of the orchestra and the conductor. If the composer is in attendance, or even on the rostrum, he cannot always be credited with knowing exactly what he wants, let alone how to achieve it! At all events, it took Simrock only four months to publish the score, a piano-accompanied version, and all the parts (October 1879).

On 23 May Brahms set out again for Pörtschach, booking all seven available rooms in the lodging to ensure his privacy. If it was wholly written there, the Violin Sonata in G op.78, must have come easily, because in July he sent a manuscript copy of it to Clara who could not help bursting into tears of joy. In August he took it to Aigen, near Salzburg, where Joachim was staying, to play it through, with the Herzogenbergs (from Berchtesgaden) for audience, completing the inner circle of the elect of his musical family. In this connection there is a Brahms-made mystery which cannot now be solved. In a subsequent letter to Elisabet (from Vienna in 1879) he says apropos a dedication to her:

> I want to see your beautiful name on the most beautiful possible piece, but at the crucial moment it never seems to be just that! I did think of the sonata, but you remember we were none of us quite satisfied with it at Salzburg.

It is hard to suppose that the published version of this euphonious and melodious piece is what failed quite to satisfy such an audience. The last movement, pattering away in the minor key before the final rainbow, is partly based on the 'Regenlied' ('Song of the rain') published as op.59 no.3 by Rieter-Biedermann. Brahms jokingly wonders to Simrock whether Rieter-Biedermann will sue them for republishing two copyright bars–'or is eight the legal minimum?'

However, the other works to be ascribed to this summer are certainly not of the 'sweetness and light' variety; they mark a momentary return to the more extended forms of the piano solo—the two Rhapsodies op.79. Brahms had evidently thought of dedicating to Elisabet the four Ballades and Romances for vocal duet and piano op.75, but then not deeming them perfectly suitable in spite of her great and detailed enthusiasm for them he dedicated them instead to the painter and engraver Julius Allgeyer, biographer of the painter Anselm Feuerbach. If, as has been surmised, the words of one of the duets are too explicit a love-song they are very small beer in comparison with the wordless vehemence of the Rhapsodies, especially the second, which appears in any case to hint at the bloodthirsty 'Edward', the first of the duets (see the catalogue).

The autumn tour with Joachim did come off, and took them as far afield as Arad and Temesvar, both now in westen Romania, and the latter now called Timişoara. The repertoire pulls no punches: Beethoven's G major Violin Sonata op.30; Bach's Chaconne for unaccompanied violin; Gluck's *Paris and Helen* Gavotte arranged by Brahms for piano, and some Scarlatti sonatas, which Brahms called 'Caprices'; a Spohr Adagio; Schubert piano pieces, offered by Brahms as 'Andante, Scherzo and March' and the Brahms Violin Concerto with piano accompaniment. It is notable that the out-of-practice Brahms also offers Beethoven's last Sonata op.111, no less—without of course knowing what sort of piano to expect. The pieces were carefully timed in advance by Joachim, and it must interest posterity to observe that the timing of the concerto including of course Joachim's cadenza was 35 minutes.[4]

How much more than a mere publisher Simrock had become is shown by two letters from Brahms in October. In the first he wants the entire honorarium (1000 *talers*) for op.78 by some means deposited into Clara's account, by making it an anonymous contribution to a supportive fund organised by Director Bendemann in Düsseldorf. The second letter is a tease, describing the Rotunda Festival in Vienna and reproaching Simrock for not being there to sell his wares. Kalbeck's note to the correspondence says that the tight-rope artist Blondin was the main attraction, and that the whole scene was bathed in the new electric light.

Brahms's newly-disciplined fingers had to assist him at an energetic concert in Budapest on 10 December, when he conducted his Second Symphony, and played his First Piano Concerto. A further impetus to his pianism could have been the publication by Senff as *Studies for the Pianoforte* of a collection, from various dates, of Brahms's idiosyncratic arrangements: a posthumous Chopin étude in F minor with its right hand in perpetual motion (sufficiently difficult in single notes for most mortals) playing two notes at a time; the Weber Moto-Perpetuo, now for the left hand; and the left-hand version of Bach's D minor Chaconne. One cannot imagine what size of market Senff can have envisaged!

Christmas was spent as usual with the Fabers, and New Year with Clara at Frankfurt, mainly working on the Schumann edition. Clara evidently found this an uncomfortable partnership, though reading her diary for 28 December one cannot help wondering whether Brahms was not wilfully teasing her to some extent:

> He always says that proof-correcting is unnecessary, the compositors always make fresh mistakes. If that is a matter of course, it really does seem hopeless. He is not in favour of pushing it on rapidly . . . Am I to go dragging on for six or seven years with work which I could get done in two? It would make my life a burden, if I were always to see proof-sheets, which I had no time to correct, lying on the piano . . .

The next year, 1880, began with a flurry of concert-giving. Brahms was his own master, and indeed his own agent, in these matters. So though he complained from time to time, he can hardly have done so much unless he enjoyed it. The schedule on leaving Clara at Frankfurt took him to Hanover to conduct the *Requiem* on 3 January. Having sought it in vain in shops and offices he was driven to ask Simrock to send him an all-Germany railway timetable (letter from Münster, 6 January). Then he conducted the *Requiem* and the Second Symphony in Cologne (13 January), the Second Symphony again in Krefeld (20 January) where he also played op.79. The next day he was in Bonn, again for the concerto/symphony double-bill, and this concert he repeated on another visit to Hanover on 24 January. By way of a rest cure he conducted the Violin Concerto in Vienna on 3 February with Joachim as soloist, then went with him on a concert tour to Poland and Prague, where he visited Dvořák.

The appetite for concert-giving not yet sated, Brahms performed twice more his double act of playing the Piano Concerto and conducting the Second Symphony, at Schwerin on 10 April and at Königsberg (then in East Prussia, but now Kaliningrad in the USSR) on 13 April. A momentous event on 2–4 May in Bonn was the unveiling of the Schumann memorial sculpted by Donndorf. Clara told her diary that 'we could not get to like the relief; the likeness is not bad, but it lacks the spiritual expression. The rest is poetically, tenderly, charmingly designed.' Joachim and Bonn's municipal director of music Joseph Wasielewsky were jointly responsible for the musical arrangements but the latter fell ill (to the relief of Clara, who could not abide him) and thus Brahms came to share the conducting, both the Bach and Mendelssohn Choruses at the unveiling, and Schumann's 'Rhenish' Symphony and his own Violin Concerto (with of course Joachim) among the concert items. At the chamber music matinee Brahms played the piano part in Schumann's E flat Quartet so badly that, to quote Clara, 'I felt as though I were sitting on thorns, and so did Joachim, who kept on casting despairing glances at me.'

Simrock published the Rhapsodies in July, and a delighted and proud Elisabet was at last able to see herself immortalised in print. Another publication was more likely to make the pot boil, a further 11 Hungarian Dances in two books. An ethnomusicologist would doubt the authenticity of their origins (a matter which, in comparison with their interest as music, weighed very little if anything with Brahms), and in respect of numbers 11, 14 and 16 he would be entirely right since they are of Brahms's own invention. However, Brahms describes them all, as in the previous collection published in 1869, merely as 'set' (*gesetzt*) by himself for piano four-hands. He envisaged arrangements of several kinds: for piano solo both normal and simplified, for violin and piano, with Joachim's help, and even for orchestra. Interestingly it was Dvořák who orchestrated nos.17–21, having shown his fitness for the task by his orchestrations of his own first set, by then equally famous, of Slavonic Dances, which were published by Simrock, to the financial content of all concerned. On the other hand, Brahms's arrangements with Joachim encountered a bolt from the blue. In a letter from Berlin (11 July) Joachim told Brahms that he had cut off all relations with Simrock, and at the same time asked Brahms, where possible, to avoid speaking to the publisher about Joachim or any of his family. After one early reference to his wife the rest of the letter pointedly omitted her from all the proposed domestic arrangements about the children—the end of their holidays and the getting back to school. This filled Brahms with foreboding (letter of 27 July):

> I had hoped your letter would be more consoling and hopeful . . . You two had
> so much in common, which gave promise of a long and happy life together. And
> now—! I find it hard to believe there is any serious cause for it.

However, the serious cause was the, to Brahms, quite unfounded suspicions, amounting eventually to an unreasoning, devastating jealousy, about his wife's faithfulness. Later in the same letter Brahms wrote 'And added to that, there is the dissonance of a broken friendship! I imagine you will not be in the mood now either for my work or your own.' Joachim nevertheless did complete the violin and piano arrangements of the second set, numbers 11–21, of the Hungarian Dances—as he had done for the first set in 1871. There was a dissonance, but not an outright break at this stage. How much further matters had gone was evident in early November, when Joachim was moved, or moved himself, to write thus to Brahms: 'You know, dear friend, what great weight I attach to your judgement in matters of common humanity, that I reckon you as shrewd and upright, but . . . ' At this stage Andreas Moser, the editor of the correspondence, indicates an omission from the letter which is made good by Artur Holde[5]:

> in my experiences with this Simrock person I can go only on what I have found myself to be true—and the result is infinitely depressing. He has acted towards me like the most crafty scoundrel; through him, my life is night. I must learn to bear my fate like a man; but the poor, poor children!—that grieves me unutterably.

By December Brahms felt impelled to write at length to Amalie Joachim, assuring her that he considered Joachim to be completely in the wrong. One can read Brahms's uprightness but also his feeling for self-preservation in the letter, again as filled out by Holde:

> It may have occurred to you that despite a 30-year friendship, despite all my love and admiration for Joachim, despite all our artistic interests which have bound me to him, I am very careful in my association with him . . . and would never think of wishing to live in the same city in collaboration . . . Friendship and love I will breathe simply and freely . . . I beg to be excused when fine feeling strikes me as complicated . . . when it is maintained and increased by morbidly painful excitement.

There is a mystery in Holde's addition to the following sentence, shown in italics: 'Dear friend, after all this I do not need to acknowledge that you are in the right about the detail you have told me of—*as, for instance, in the case of the rehearsal.*' In a further letter towards the end of the year Brahms in an open-hearted but incautious letter gave Amalie permission to use his written support in any way she needed to. When the affair came the following year to the divorce court she did so, to Brahms's perturbation. The affair broke Joachim's friendship, such as it was, and though it was resumed up to a point from 1883, it never regained its previous strength, let alone resumed the heady days of the counterpoint exchanges.

But the sad narrative has out-run the chronology. At the end of May Brahms went for his summer 'holiday' to Ischl, a spa and holiday resort in Salzkammergut on the Traun River, because Pörtschach had become too full of prying people. Elisabet thought this an odd decision: 'I thought half Vienna disported itself there', to which Brahms replied 'I have positively no objection to all Vienna. I should probably flee from half Berlin or even half Leipzig, I admit; but half Vienna is quite pretty, and will bear looking at.' Among the friends he particularly enjoyed at Ischl were Johann Strauss and the distinguished and enlivening pianist Ignaz Brüll who was often called in by Brahms to use his sight-reading skills. The lodging was at 51 Salzburgerstrasse, the food and drink, as often as not, at the Café Walter on the Esplanade. The compositions this year were the Academic Festival Overture (op.80) and the 'Tragic' Overture (op.81), the beginning of *Nänie* (elegy or dirge) op.82, evoked by the death of the artist Feuerbach, and at least the first movements of two Piano Trios, the one in C which became op.87 and one in E flat of which no trace remains. Clara's birthday (13 September), was celebrated at Berchtesgaden and turned out frightfully wet, but it was graced by the presence of both Joachim and Brahms, who played the first movement of the Concerto as a birthday present. Brahms also played the first movements of both Trios, and morning and evening played with Clara the duet versions of both Overtures, an experience she called 'magnificent', but making for an exhausting day. The Academic Festival Overture with its quiet C minor opening and threatening touches of the bass drum puts one in mind of the 'more severe art of music' in Dr Brahms's citation, but throws into brighter relief the final student song 'Gaudeamus igitur' rendered in full blaze at the end. Perhaps Brahms took a leaf out of Weber's 'Jubel' Overture of 1818 which does the same for 'God save the King'. With this overture he paid his dues to Breslau. What gave him the notion of providing in the same breath, as it were, a sister overture, the 'Tragic', is unknown. It is certainly not an overture to anything, nor, characteristically, does he invite our imaginations to any particular contemplation, such as Berlioz does with King Lear. Kalbeck surmises that it arose from a study of Goethe's *Faust*, and that what became the two middle movements of the Third Symphony were intended, with the Overture, for a production at the Vienna Burgtheatre which never transpired.

This is the place for two vivid vignettes of the composer at Ischl, retailed by Kalbeck, and according with the view surely by now forced on us of a passionately compulsive composer, allowing neither friend nor foe to deflect him. As to proof or disproof, all one can say is that rebuttals by the composer's contemporaries are conspicuously lacking. Kalbeck was taking an early country walk near Ischl on a warm July morning.

I suddenly saw a man running from the wood across the meadow towards me; I took him for a farmer. I was afraid I had been trespassing and was already reckoning on all sorts of unpleasant eventualities, when to my joy I recognised Brahms in the supposed farmer. But in what a condition—what a sight! Bareheaded, and in shirt-sleeves, no waistcoat, no shirt-collar, he brandished his hat in one hand, with the other dragged his cast-off coat in the grass behind him, and ran on quickly as though hunted by an unseen pursuer. Already from far off I heard him snorting and groaning. When he came nearer I saw how the sweat was streaming over his hot cheeks from the hair which hung about his face. His eyes were staring ahead into empty space and shone like those of a beast of prey; he appeared like one possessed. Before I recovered from my shock he had shot past me, so close that we almost collided; I immediately realised it was inadvisable to call to him. He was glowing with creative fire. I shall never forget the harrowing impression of elemental force.

The twentieth-century reader may well be surprised at Kalbeck's remarking the absence of waistcoat and collar on a summer-holiday walk in the Austrian countryside. The second vignette takes us gradually indoors:

Paying a morning visit to the house in the Salzburgerstrasse I went up the outside steps intending to come in by the wide-open back door, when I saw that the door of the music room was also open. At that moment bewitching sounds came from the piano which held me entranced on the doorstep. It sounded like free extemporisation, but from the frequent repetitions of certain passages I realised that Brahms was going through and improving and refining a new composition already complete in his head. He repeated the piece several times in individual sections, and eventually played it straight through . . . The solo changed into an extraordinary duet. The richer the shaping of the work became, and the more passionately its delivery arose, so the more strongly could be heard a strange growling, whining and moaning [Kalbeck here uses the wonderful onomatopoeias only German can supply: *Knurren*, *Winseln* and *Stohnen*] that at the peak of the musical ecstasy became sheer howling. Could Brahms, quite contrary to his inclination, have got himself a dog? . . . After about half an hour the playing and the howling stopped together, the piano stool was drawn back and I entered the room; not a trace of a dog.

There was a short-lived but very alarming interruption early in July. Brahms suddenly began to go deaf. He rushed back to Vienna having wired Billroth to meet him at the station. Billroth reassured him but also took him to a specialist. The aural catarrh cleared up in a few days, but somehow word got out that Brahms was ill. Elisabet and Clara both flew to their pens and the latter upbraided him (on hearsay) for lying in a meadow. The replies to a gratifying avalanche of letters took some composing time.

Stimulated by a project of Clara's to supply for teaching purposes selected parts of Czerny's keyboard studies, Brahms also about this time wrote out his 51 exercises for the pianoforte. They were not music, so have no opus number. Clara acknowledged them in a letter of 7 August. They were in fact published long afterwards, by Simrock in 1893.

What ignites the creative spark, and when, is in the case of Brahms almost always a matter of surmise. An exchange of letters with Elisabet in July 1880, at any rate establishes what Brahms was *not* intending to write. In the same letter (11 July) that anxiously enquires after his health, Elisabet (speaking for her choir-training husband also) writes:

Ever since the Pörtschach Motet [op.74 no.1, 'Warum?'] I have been longing for you to write more choral things; and when I think of you with your pockets full of good things, like a child's St Nicholas, it is always a vision of motets, or the like, which dazzles my greedy eyes.

Brahms's immediate reply was:

> I am quite willing to write motets, or anything for chorus (I am heartily sick of
> everything else!); but won't you try and find me some words? . . . They are not
> heathenish enough for me in the Bible. I have bought the Koran but can find
> nothing there either.

This does not wash with Elisabet, who quickly rejoins:

> I refuse to believe there is nothing else to be found for you in the Bible. There is
> still plenty of material in Job, which you read with such happy results before,
> and in the Psalms . . . Surely such words have more depth and immortality than
> many a Heine poem which has been done a hundred times over?

She had to wait ten years before Brahms published any more biblical settings
(opp.109 and 110) and was dead before the Four Serious Songs appeared in
1896 (op.121).

However tenuous the personal relationship had become,[6] Joachim now, as
always, showed himself a continuing champion of Brahms's music. Not only
had he set down the *Requiem* for his Hochschule's large Christmas-term
concert on 4 December, but he had also offered his orchestra for Brahms to
try out the two overtures on 6 December. Not only did Brahms accept this,
but he also felt he should stay at Joachim's although the Simrocks lived in
Berlin. The rightness of this decision hardly needs explaining, and Brahms
consoled the publisher by pointing out he need not polish the furniture nor
clean the windows. The materials for both overtures were in the printing
process in the autumn and in November Brahms asked Simrock for advance
copies of the string parts to go to Joachim. The numbers required point to a
large student orchestra: ten parts for first violins, ten for seconds, (that is, up
to 40 violins in all), seven for violas and twelve for combined cellos and
double basses. The try-out may have resulted in some alterations—which as
usual cannot be traced back—in that on 14 December Brahms wrote to
Simrock that 'Unfortunately I found that I must copy out the second overture
completely again.' The score of the 'Tragic' Overture was in any case in
manuscript for the first performance, in Vienna on 26 December with Richter
conducting, which had a cool reception. Its sombre colouring, with the
trombones eschewed for the final *forte*, together with the natural puzzlement
of an average audience as to what stage work may have lain behind it, ensured
the coolness, which might have been out-weighed if the other overture had
also been played, but this had to be reserved for a first performance in Breslau.
Brahms not only denied that the word 'Tragic' related to any particular
tragedy, but also was in doubt as to what to call the overture. He toyed with
'Dramatic', but this led straight to another difficulty which lay at the heart of
the musical aesthetics of his time, since to him all symphonic allegro
movements were essentially dramatic, in the sense that they were 'actions'
and led to dénouements.[7] To suppose that dramatic music could only be

allied to the stage, or to imagined stage action, as many did—perhaps the majority—would have undermined most of what Brahms stood for.

Before the end of the year Joachim had performed the Violin Concerto at a Gewandhaus concert together with variations of his own composing, for violin and orchestra, about which Elisabet enthused to Brahms (14 December). Brahms's Christmas presents both to her and Clara were Simrock's printed four-hand arrangements, made by Brahms as usual, of the Academic Festival Overture. He also sent to Heinrich Herzogenberg his editions of some Handel chamber duets, originally in Italian, which he had made for Chrysander, and which, as he had to confess to Simrock, would also be published by Peters as well as in the big Händelgesellschaft complete edition. Though Elisabet did little more than acknowledge these, being full of the overture, the work is important as showing the sort of keyboard realisation of a figured bass that Brahms felt was appropriate, at least in secular works. He asked for comment on the 'piano embellishments, and still more the German words' presumably done by himself.

Brahms began 1881, as he had three years before, with a concert trip taking him as far as Holland, with concerts at Münster, Krefeld and Amsterdam at the end of January, and at The Hague and Haarlem in February. *En route* he presented both Overtures on 4 January at Breslau, and called at Leipzig on the 13 January, to refuel the fires of the Herzogenberg's devotion. In answer to Elisabet's request on behalf of impecunious friends Brahms made a spring-clean of unwanted duplicates of his works, and by this means their 'Miss' (that is, Ethel Smyth) came into possession of a vocal score of the *Requiem*. 'She received the German edition after all . . . She scorns the English one!' This young lady of pronounced feminist opinions, and a trenchant way of expressing them later, yielded to no-one in her veneration of Brahms's music, but saw him with a cooler eye than the acolytes of Leipzig, and since Brahms was preparing himself for two months' absence in Italy we may give her the floor for a moment.[8]

> When I became practically the adopted child of the Herzogenbergs I got to know Brahms very well, and owing, no doubt, to his profound affection and admiration for 'Frau Lisl', as he called her, he was extraordinarily kind and fatherly to me . . . A salient trait of his was the greediness I consider one of the hallmarks of the true artist, and the Herzogenbergs not being at all well off, all they could manage by way of a cook was a series of moderately gifted practitioners . . . This, however, was of no consequence, for Lisl was not only a superb cook but practised the art with exactly the same sort of passion she brought to bear on disentangling the parts of a Bach motet . . . I think what chiefly angered me was his views on women, which after all were the views prevalent in Germany, only I had not realised the fact . . . Brahms, as artist and bachelor, was free to adopt what may be called the poetical variant of the 'Kinder, Kirche, Küche' axiom ['children, church, kitchen'], namely that women are playthings. He made one or two exceptions, as such men will, and chief among these was Lisl, to whom his attitude was perfect . . . reverential,

admiring and affectionate, without a tinge of amorousness . . . His ways with other womenfolk—or to use the detestable word for ever on his lips, 'Weibesbilder'—was less admirable. If they did not appeal to him he was incredibly awkward and ungracious; if they were pretty he had an unpleasant way of leaning back in his chair, pouting out his lips, stroking his moustache, and staring at them as a greedy boy stares at jam tartlets.

The Vienna Philharmonic orchestra, under Richter, had such a success with the Academic Festival Overture on 20 March that a repeat performance was called for on 10 April. However, by this time Brahms was delighting in his second visit to Italy, having as companions the 64-year-old Beethoven scholar Gustav Nottebohm as far as Venice, and Billroth and a Vienna jurist, Adolf Exner, as far as Rome. Brahms's route was Venice, Florence, Siena, Orvieto, Rome, Naples, Sicily, returning by Florence and Pisa, and arriving back in Vienna on 7 May, his forty-eighth birthday. He had had some Italian lessons before he left, and his letters, especially to Clara, show how impressed he was. He tried to insist that she took a gentle trip there also. For instance, he writes from Rome in April:

> If you stood for only one hour in front of the façade of the cathedral at Siena you would be beside yourself with joy and agree that this alone made the journey worth while . . . On the following day at Orvieto you would be found to acknowledge that its cathedral is even more beautiful, and after all this to plunge into Rome is an indescribable joy.

On his return through Rome he writes: 'In Sicily too, particularly at Taormina and Girgenti, it was indescribably beautiful.' Thus he was gripped by the timeless classical temples, set in the unchanged ambience of Mediterranean skies and warmth, and received the strongest reinforcement of the feelings evoked by that world, previously known through reading Goethe, and soon to evoke the setting of the 'Gesang der Parzen' ('Song of the Fates') from his *Iphigenie auf Tauris*. However, it is curious that he does not seem to set store on *pictures*, as far as mention goes. He does not protect himself from childlike joy in writing from Rome to Simrock on 25 April:

> Why do not I stay here until driven out by heat and insects? It is the most lovely spring; I enjoyed the first spring in Sicily, the second here, and in Vienna I shall have my third!

This year Brahms had a dedication made to him which 'tickled him not a little [*nicht wenig Spass gemacht*] more than a sonata or suite' (letter to Simrock 28 June). This was a set of 46 etchings on the subject of Amor and Psyche by Max Klinger, a copy of which Brahms asked Simrock to get and send to Clara (16 May). Klinger had made a sensation in Berlin at the Academy's exhibition in 1878 with two series of pen-and-ink drawings, one on 'Christ' and one called 'Fantasias on the finding of a Glove', which had evoked criticisms like 'eccentric' or even 'insane'.

Brahms's summer retreat was this year to Pressbaum in the country to the west of the city known as the Wienerwald, an hour from Vienna on the railway line to Linz, 'and when it rains'—he writes in an invitation to Simrock—'I shall stroll with you on the Ring or in the Prater'. At Pressbaum he completed *Nänie* and also a far larger work, the Second Piano Concerto, with its four movements including a full-blown scherzo. Typically, he wrote to Elisabet on 7 July: 'I do not mind telling you that I have written a tiny, tiny piano concerto with a tiny, tiny wisp of a scherzo.' Kalbeck in his note to Elisabet's reply says that *Scherzl* is the name given in Vienna to the crusty ends of a long roll of bread. This great work is dedicated to Marxsen, but there is no glimmer of hard evidence about what stirred Brahms to write it, and when, for it cannot be supposed that he wrote it all at Pressbaum in time for it to be sent to Billroth on 11 July.

In July an invitation came to Brahms out of the blue, or rather from Meiningen where Bülow had been the court's music director since the previous autumn. Would Brahms like to come and use the court orchestra for trying out any new works? Brahms, not knowing quite how the orchestra and the place itself would be suitable, replied that of new things he had 'only' the Piano Concerto. Bülow instantly agreed to making this work the main rehearsal study. What ambitious conductor-pianist would not? Thus Brahms came to Meiningen in mid-October having called at Frankfurt *en route* to play the Concerto and the *Nänie* to Clara. At Meiningen he was courteously and kindly received by Duke Georg II and Helene von Heldburg, and left more than satisfied, and with a promise to return late in November when a real Brahms night was planned. Elisabet had more than once been critical, almost to the point of, for her, vituperation, about Bülow's conducting—his dissections 'stripping an antique statue of its lovely flesh, and forcing me to worship the workings of bone and muscle', his affected pauses and arbitrary dynamics, and his scoreless playing to the gallery. Although she was too stretched for funds, after a convalescent holiday and a visit to her mother in Venice, to travel to Meiningen herself, (she sent Heinrich) she was shortly to change her tune. For his part Brahms assured her that 'these fellows play quite excellently, and they have no conception of such rehearsing, such practising, at Leipzig'. The Meiningen experience brought Brahms such reassurance about the new Concerto that he allowed its first performance, with himself as soloist, on 9 November at Budapest, where the slightly Hungarian references in the last movement were particularly appropriate. Within a short period, in another of his self-organised bursts of rail travel, he had introduced the concerto to Stuttgart, Switzerland,[9] Holland, and the principal German centres. But the high point was the Meiningen celebration with excellent performances of the 'Tragic' Overture, the new Concerto, the Haydn Variations, the Academic Festival Overture and the C minor Symphony, a feast at which the conducting was shared. Simrock was in the audience. Christmas hardly interrupted the round of performances; there was one in Vienna on 26 December and on 28 December he was off to the Herzogenbergs at Leipzig in readiness for performing the new Concerto and 'her' Rhapsodies at the New Year's Day Gewandhaus concert.

A cloud on the eventful and happy year was Joachim's visit to Pressbaum in September. He came to talk over his marriage difficulties but left angrily when Brahms made it clear that Joachim lacked reason, in both senses of the word. For Joachim the heavens were falling; from Brahms we may deduce a shrug of the shoulders as the door was slammed.

The Leipzig audience ran true to form on 1 January 1882. Fritzsch in the *Musikalisches Wochenblatt* (but note how music rated a *weekly* news-sheet) said 'One can hardly say that the Gewandhäusler showed any particular appreciation of their guest's importance in general, or of his new work in particular.'Elisabet had to forward the notices to Brahms who had already left to play the Concerto in Hamburg on 6 January, but comforted him and herself with the recollection of Hanslick's 'cordial words' on the Vienna performance. She relished his

> intuitive sympathy, which not only provides an outlet for his own feelings but helps others who have no command of words to express theirs . . . How often do we stand dumb before you, seeking comfort in the thought that you must know whether we have the right sounding-board for your music in our hearts . . . But it does seem sometimes as if you were hardly conscious of it . . . Your clumsy friends have their worst moments then.

He that hath ears to hear, let him hear this elegant and charming rebuke!

In the early part of the year Brahms again exerted himself in the concert world, mainly on behalf of the new Concerto, which he played in Hamburg on 6 January. This was followed by a conspicuous triumph in Berlin, brought about mainly by Bülow and the Meiningen orchestra, now allowed to tour, and incidentally to open the public ears to quite new standards of orchestral discipline and skill, in spite of its fairly modest numbers. On 8 January the Berliners heard the 'Tragic', the new Piano Concerto played by Brahms, and the C minor Symphony. On the next evening Brahms took the baton and Bülow played Brahms's First Concerto. Notwithstanding a potentially competitive situation a public embrace of the two heroes sealed the great occasion. There were more shared concerts, with the Meiningen orchestra at Kiel (13 January) and Hamburg (14 and 15 January), before Brahms went his own way to Münster for a benefit concert for his friend J.O. Grimm, then to Holland, to be made a fuss of again with concerts in Utrecht, The Hague, Rotterdam, Amsterdam and Arnhem—six Dutch concerts in ten days!

No sooner was he back in Vienna than he attended further exertions on his behalf by Bülow, this time as a concert pianist in an all-Brahms programme on 2 February. Liszt also attended, with generous enthusiasm. The biggest items were the early Piano Sonata op.2 and the Handel Variations op.24, which brought the house down at the end of the programme. To stop the never-ending applause Bülow threatened to play the fugue again, a joke which Brahms may not have felt was very funny. The very next day Brahms wrote to Simrock asking him to send two copies of the concerto to Liszt in Budapest, to gratify a polite request for him to study it.

Clara sitting in Frankfurt did not hear any of this, but wrote in her diary:

> Brahms is celebrating such triumphs everywhere as seldom fall to the lot of a composer. This is partly due to the performance of his works by the Meiningen orchestra as conducted by Bülow . . . It did not seem to me that this tour with Bülow was worthy of Brahms's high position as a creative artist, but now that it has at last made the world realise his full importance I am very glad and pleased for his sake, for however great a composer's gift may be, recognition does help him to surpass himself.

The shape of the paragraph, and the almost grudging conviction at the end bespeaks a high-minded snobbery on behalf of Brahms, which had it communicated itself to him would have brought about a damaging quarrel between the two men then and there (there was one later which was Brahms's fault). No doubt up to a point Bülow was 'using' Brahms in this crusade greatly to enhance his own reputation, but it is certain that he greatly enhanced Brahms's reputation as well. He was probably a better pianist than Brahms—certainly so inasmuch as he still offered a recitalist's repertoire—and certainly a better conductor than Brahms, whom one cannot imagine rehearsing an orchestra day by day till it became the best in Germany. Some composers are obviously poor conductors of their own works. It seems that Brahms was sometimes, on his own admission, disheartened and therefore lackadaisical, but when he was fired he could carry everyone into a higher realm.[10]

After taking momentary breath in Vienna Brahms was off again to Frankfurt where he played the new concerto on 17 February. Then at Dresden he found that his friend there, the conductor Wüllner, had crammed a veritable festival for him into the brief visit. On 22 February there was the new Concerto and *Nänie*. Then on 24 February a choral concert which included, at Brahms's request, the motet 'Warum ist das Licht gegeben' and some choral folksong settings by him. Then by way of surprise the A major Serenade op.16 was played, together with the Violin Sonata op.78. At the post-concert party Brahms played both the Rhapsodies op.79 and at 1 am boarded the Vienna train.

On 14 March Bülow at last brought the First Symphony to a triumph in Leipzig, and was also successful with the D minor Concerto. Because of a misapprehension of dates Brahms was not there, but Elisabet wrote at length the following day:

> Do you know, they quite lost their heads at the end of the C minor! The din was so great that we had to ask ourselves if that were really the Gewandhaus with the same people sitting there . . . As the allegretto in A flat [that is, the third movement] received comparatively little applause, Bülow promptly repeated it.

Then came the deluge . . . We made a heathenish noise, my brother shouting
encore at the finish like one possessed . . . When the horn first rang out in the
last movement, it seemed as if you were sending us a glorious greeting from afar.
You, poor thing, can never be a mere listener to music. You are really to be
pitied.

On Good Friday, 7 April, Brahms conducted a good performance of the
Requiem in the theatre in Hamburg, and was at last able to turn his thoughts
away from performances. But one performance which he did not attend
might be mentioned for a view of Bülow as a pianist, who one feels never gets
quite a fair report from Brahms's intimates like Elisabet. The Whitsuntide
Lower Rhine Festival was this year at Aachen with Franz Wüllner, from
Dresden, as conductor, At it Bülow played the D minor Concerto, in spite of
Brahms's ironically wondering why Bülow was bringing the accursed piece
(*verrufenes Stück*) to a festival. On his return Wüllner wrote to Brahms:

Bülow played your concerto extraordinarily well . . . he was in excellent
humour, played with great calmness, with great warmth and wonderfully
beautiful tone. The applause was unusually great, after each movement—at the
end with drums and trumpets.

However, by this time Brahms was back at Ischl and what is more at the
same house as in 1880, no.51 Salzburgerstrasse. One of his first duties there
was to send, at Elisabet's request, his autograph to Ethel Smyth

with my kindest regards, but I must really see the name [that is, Ethel's] printed
on a title-page, or how am I to remember it? I am at Ischl, and the weather is
horrible—appalling! It rains (or snows) incessantly. There is a stove in this
room (lighted, too) and I must have one put in the other. And this is Ischl—on
the 15th May!

Driven in to face the manuscript paper, Brahms completed three large works
in three months, that is, the remainder of the Piano Trio in C op.87, the String
Quintet in F op.88 and the Gesang der Parzen (Song of the Fates), op.89, a
setting of Goethe—the song Iphigenia remembers from her childhood in the
fourth act of his play *Iphigenia in Tauris*. Here at any rate there was a
recognisable impetus towards composition in that Brahms had recently seen
the play at the Burg theatre in Vienna. The sombre work uses some of
Brahms's most enigmatic and abrupt modulations, and characteristically the
tender and sustained quiet passage in the major key offers to mortals not
consolation but a description of the bliss from which they are excluded,
encouraging one to guess that the enigmatic 'consolatory' end of the Schicksalslied (Song of Destiny) means no more than that same thing. Brahms neatly
referred to the Fates' dealings with the threads of mortal life in sending the
piece to the surgeon Billroth on 31 July: 'the work has a particular connection
with you; it is a scissors and thread job.' The pessimism, amounting to
nihilism, of this piece is counter-balanced by the other two. Both have their

moments of ghostly shade—for instance, the fleeting scherzo of the trio—but in both the mood of happy ebullience carried the day. As early as 13 July Brahms was able to send the Trio and the Quintet to Simrock, not with a self-mocking or perverse recommendation: 'I tell you, you have not ever had anything so good from me, nor perhaps published in the last ten years!!!' Years later, in 1890, Brahms was to describe this quintet as probably one of his finest works. He sent it to Elisabet also, describing it as a 'little ditty' (27 July) and she repaid him with a *tour de force* of detailed comment, but apparently without irony says of the first movement: 'It is refreshing to see the framework exposed in such a bald prosaic fashion'—exactly the remark, without the 'refreshing', which an adverse critic might make! The middle movement of the Quintet, a slow-fast sandwich, makes use of a sarabande and a gavotte, written as baroque-style exercises for keyboard and dating as far back as 1854–5.

An enthusiasm which one could not guess from any of his own music was for Bizet's *Carmen*, a copy of which he requested Simrock to try to get from Choudens in Paris as from one publisher to another, not, as Brahms says in his letter of 25 June, for theatre use but 'for my own quite exceptional plea-sure . . . I love it better than any title from your editions'!

Another letter to Simrock (8 July) shows Brahms thinking of going to northern Italy with Billroth, perhaps via Bayreuth. The Italian journey did take place in mid-September. Simrock could not accept the invitation to join them. Brahms did not manage to go to Bayreuth. He made it clear that he twice had tickets he could not use, and he expressed himself thus to Simrock on 30 July to the extent of an underlining: 'If you really wanted to go to Bayreuth I would go with you *very happily*!' Wagner was one thing; meeting Wagnerians unprotected was another. We could contrast Clara's experience as related to her diary of a performance (not at Bayreuth!) on 26 April.

> I determined to go to *Rheingold*. The whole evening I felt as though I were wading about in a swamp . . . The boredom one has to endure is dreadful. Every scene leaves the people on the stage in a condition of catalepsy in which they remain until one cannot bear to look at them any longer. The women have hardly a bar to sing in the whole opera, they simply stand about, and the gods altogether are a flabby and villainous set. How posterity will marvel at an aberration like this spreading all over the world.

For a 'run-through' of opp.87 and 88 Brahms used one of the summer gatherings of musicians organised by a Professor Ladislaus Wagner at a villa at Altaussee, up the river Traun from Ischl, with its own small lake facing a mountain called Schönberg. The works were heard at a semi-private concert there on 25 August. In September, leaving an Ischl with boats in the streets, Brahms joined Billroth on a short Italian trip. They met at 'The Swan', a hostelry in Lucerne and then went by train (the railway being just then opened) through the St Gotthard tunnel to Milan, then to Brescia, Bergamo, Vicenza and some ten days in Venice. An intended visit to Verona was prevented by floods. This we learn from a letter to Simrock from Vienna on 11 October, which contains a notification of *Gesang der Parzen*, and also a spoof contract with Peters for complete rights to opp.83–86 (the Second Piano Concerto and three sets of songs) unless Simrock pays 1000 Marks to the poverty-stricken composer.

The autumn was clouded by the loss of Gustav Nottebohm. Brahms was at the bedside in Graz on 29 October, when he died, and indeed it was he who paid the funeral expenses. Brahms turned to Switzerland for the first performances of the *Gesang der Parzen*, the first of all being at Basle on 10 December, with Brahms also conducting the Second Symphony. Although the choral piece is only some 14 minutes in performance, the choral parts were sufficiently demanding for Brahms to be alarmed at an oversight whereby the performance materials had not arrived by mid-November (letter to Simrock, 17 November). However, it is interesting to note that Brahms, for all his experience as a composer, wanted Switzerland to have only chorus parts, orchestral parts and vocal scores for their rehearsals—but not the score, which Brahms wanted to keep so as to have a chance to correct it *after* hearing it. The work was repeated at Zürich on 17 December and Strasbourg on 20 December.

The next day Brahms made a surprise visit to Clara at Frankfurt. He found her trying through his new Trio with friends, and he was so surprised and touched that he impulsively invited himself there for Christmas. From Clara's diary we know that there was music and champagne for Christmas Eve, 'the festival made all the nicer by Brahms's friendly humour'. There were evidently other musicians available, and competent ones too, because the new Quintet figured in the domestic festival. Clara, incidentally, was not wholly satisfied with either piece. Perhaps only her diary knew her opinion that 'it is a pity that he does not always polish his work nor cut out dull passages'.

There was a public performance in Frankfurt on 29 December. Clara had obviously come to better terms with the Quintet which was

> enthusiastically received—it really is a magnificent work. The trio did not take so well, but the audience . . . applauded this vigorously too. The pity is that Brahms plays more and more abominably—it is now nothing but thump, bang and scrabble. Dec. 30. Brahms left. We felt certain that he had enjoyed the week with us, but we felt too that our intercourse had been purely superficial . . .

It sounds as though each of them had one too few skins, and that Brahms felt himself under emotional duress, the circumstance which inevitably and invariably stultified any spontaneity in his relationships. However, unless we can believe that the Third Symphony was entirely written in the next year's 'composing summer' one can sense the nagging pre-occupation this caused beforehand, especially as Brahms had imposed on himself what had become the usual round of concerts early in 1883. In a letter to Simrock from Vienna on 15 January Brahms listed some of them:

until 18 January, Bonn; until 23 Krefeld; until 30 Cologne . . . Later I go to Hanover, Schwerin, Meiningen; it evaporates [*verduftet*] so gradually, and I do not rightly know where my obligations stop. I and my second symphony are invited to Cologne for Whitsun,

that is for the Lower Rhine Music Festival. Later, from Schwerin on 10 February, he wrote 'So I go tomorrow to Meiningen . . . When shall I at last get home!' and he signs himself: 'Your poor traveller.' Perhaps the most interesting of these letters to Simrock comes from Meiningen on 15 February:

> I must still be here on Friday, but intend to travel to Nuremberg on Saturday, then by the night-train to Vienna where on Sunday at 12.30—that is, midday— there is in addition to the Dvořák symphony which you might well be thinking of travelling to, the 'Schicksalslied' to be done.

One notes the irony, making Dvořák's D-major Symphony the object of Simrock's journey, and the physical strength and self-organisation involved in such a schedule. The Symphony had both Brahms and Simrock to thank for its introduction to Vienna. Simrock was in fact at the concert (18 February), but Brahms did not realise it, and a letter of 25 February shows Brahms's sorrow at missing his friend, and also at the poor reception of the 'Schicksals-lied': ' we can still survive the catastrophe—, but meanwhile we are founding Bohemian schools in Vienna'. This is not a reference to Dvořák's admired music, but to the carrot-and-stick politics, mainly the former, involved in Count Taafe's attempts to hold Vienna's ramshackle empire together. The disappointing performance was conducted by Wilhelm Gericke as part of the season of the Gesellschaft der Musikfreunde. On the other hand the faithful Hellmesberger organised good performances of the new Quintet and of the new Trio, with Brüll as the pianist, on 15 February and 15 March respect-ively. Among all these activities came the news of the death of Wagner in Venice (13 February). Brahms did not hesitate to close a rehearsal and to send a wreath to Bayreuth.

On 1 April Brahms was in Meiningen, conducting the 'Schicksalslied', dedicated to Duke George II of Saxe-Meiningen, as a prelude to the Duke's birthday celebrations of the following day. On 6 April he was in Hamburg, where Julius Spengel had arranged a little festival as the fiftieth birthday approached. Brahms here conducted, in honorific circumstances, the 'Schick-salslied', and played his Second Piano Concerto. He had few of the quiet days he had promised himself there, since he decided to conduct the *Requiem* in Schwerin on 8th April. While he was there he had a good view of a fire, standing on a roof-top near a fire-pump. After yet one more concert, in Wiesbaden on 13 April, he returned to Vienna, and as his fiftieth birthday approached he wrote to Simrock as though his creative powers were fast ebbing. 'I shall leave you all in peace and ruining yourselves on my [works] hitherto'.[11] Kalbeck says Brahms celebrated his birthday 'quietly' in Vienna—not perhaps the right word if we note that he had a 'bachelor supper' with Billroth, Hanslick and Faber. He did not of course lack birthday greetings from Elisabet, who also described a performance of the 'Schicksalslied' that they had heard in Leipzig. Elisabet herself being a pillar of a smaller rival choir, her husband's Bach-Verein, there is an amusingly natural cattiness in her description.

> Nikisch [the famous conductor] took a lot of trouble, and did all that anyone could do at Leipzig, where the ladies of the chorus are not much concerned as to whether they sing flat or sharp, although they can look languishing, and sing from memory with their arms folded. Certain passages always sound out of tune, and just that heavenly passage 'And wait in vain' did certainly wait in vain for purity of intonation.

On 9 May Brahms was off again to the Sixtieth Lower Rhine Festival at Cologne where he both played his B flat Concerto and conducted his Second Symphony. Then at last he was free and decided on Wiesbaden for his summer retreat, enlivened by visits to his friends the Beckeraths and by visits from the mezzo-soprano singer Hermine Spies, with whom he began an agreeable flirtation.

Through the insistence of Andreas Moser, later the editor of the Joachim–Brahms letters, Brahms went down-stream to meet Joachim at a music festival at Coblenz (15–16 July) but there insisted, by word of mouth, on his position on the rift with Amalie, which he put into writing on 30 October:

> In the sad business of your wife I could never be on your side; I always had to deplore most profoundly the way you proceeded in this matter . . . I can never regret having written that letter . . . The fact that my opinion was made public, that the letter was even produced in court, disconcerted me at the time . . . But what a mess was brought out at the trial![12] In short, despite this occurrence which I regret, but for which I cannot ask forgiveness—if you can permit a tolerable relationship to far as we are concerned, I would like to offer you my hand . . .

Joachim 'touched to the inmost' accepted the hand in a letter of 9 November, just before he was to play Brahms's Concerto. What was proffered with the hand was the Third Symphony for Joachim to conduct after the first performance in Vienna on 2 December.

We can leave until January 1884 Joachim's reactions to the great work when he had studied the score and performed it in Berlin, and it is discussed in some detail in the catalogue. The fact that it had been completed was now a matter of immediate excitement throughout Germany, with requests for it from Leipzig, for example, urgently transmitted by the Herzogenbergs before anyone had seen or heard the score. The Dresden conductor Wüllner saw at any rate some of the work on a visit to Wiesbaden at the end of August, and it must have been as good as finished by mid-September. Clara's diary of 13 September records a birthday entry:

111

> Brahms came over from Wiesbaden yesterday and spent the day with us today . . . He was in good humour, when once he had got over the birthday congratulations as fast as possible. He said he meant to have brought me a bouquet, but the shop lay out of his way . . . The conversation was always general, and the fact that he has written a third symphony only slipped out in the course of conversation . . .

If he could tease Clara he could also tease Simrock, writing to him from Wiesbaden on 15 September:

> I do not have another penny. But now I am reckoning on the recognition and gratitude of yourself and all your colleagues. You will arrange a collection and send an eminent reward my way—because I am so kindly leaving you in peace, and you need not risk anything for me! [Again!] . . . God should reward you, and if I were after all to find you some pages of music from my youth I would also send them to you.

The 'music from my youth' ought to refer to the Quintet, but dates rule this out. If Brahms was referring to his own music, it could be to the Symphony's frequent use, on various starting notes, of the gapped arpeggio as a principal motif:

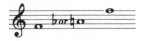

Perhaps the intermezzo-like third movement originated in a work now lost; it reads in places like an ingeniously orchestrated piano piece. Otherwise one is driven back to generalisations like the close proximity in the first movement of impetuous, even heroic, strides and country-side delights.

The dedication of the Second Piano Concerto was not the limit of Brahms's tribute to Marxsen. In recognition of his teacher's golden jubilee in the profession he paid for Simrock to publish Marxsen's 100 (sic) Variations for Piano on a Folktune, never a likely best-seller, or even likely to be published at all. Another generous act was his nominating to Simrock of his sister (Frau Elise Grund) as the first beneficiary of the honorarium for the new Symphony. One thousand Marks were to be sent direct to her, and it was left to Simrock to suggest what was to come Brahms's way—'the usual' (whatever that was), 'the half' or 'the double'.

The first performance of the Symphony, on 2 December conducted by Richter in Vienna, was a great triumph, the applause precipitated by, and obliterating, organised hissing after each movement. It is striking that Brahms writing to Simrock on 7 November says that they needed the parts eight days(!) before the performance, though preferably before. The numbers 'for here' of string parts needed were: nine first violin, nine second violin, six viola, five cello and five double bass. Dvořák's Violin Concerto was also on the programme, and he joined the festive dinner at the Fabers afterwards.

True to form Brahms found the paeans of praise, especially those in print, thoroughly embarrasing and distasteful, writing to Herzogenberg on 11 January 1884: 'In about a week I hope to send you the too, too famous F major, in a two-piano arrangement . . . The reputation it has acquired makes me want to cancel all my engagements.' The two-piano arrangement was made by himself and published just before the score and parts.

Joachim conducted the new Symphony in Berlin on 4 January 1884, and was moved to write thus to Brahms (27 January):

> The last movement struck me most forcibly. I usually have no time for poetic fantasising in music, yet in this piece (as in few others in the whole realm of music) I cannot rid myself a particular poetic picture: Hero and Leander! When I think of the second subject in C major [that is, this horn and cellos theme]:

> I cannot help imagining the bold, brave swimmer, his breast borne up by the waves and by the mighty passion before his eyes, heartily, heroically swinging on, to the end, to the end, in spite of the elements which storm around him! Poor mortal—but how beautiful and reconciling is the apotheosis, the redemption in his downfall.

Brahms made absolutely no sign that he had read this, let alone agreed with it. The proffered hand did not reach far, for when Brahms was in Berlin at the end of January for the repetition of the Symphony, at a popular concert first under Wüllner, then with himself conducting, he did not even meet Joachim, pleading a mass of correspondence on his one free day!

As in previous years the first months of 1884 were largely devoted to helping the launch of the latest crop of composition, usually still by conducting but sometimes simply by attendance. Brahms went back to Wiesbaden, birthplace of the Symphony, to conduct it there on 18 January. This is where Clara heard it. She called it a masterpiece but rather surprisingly it struck her as 'elegaic from beginning to end'. This was an immediate judgement confided to her diary, but in a letter to Brahms (11 February) she used the sort of poetic images that Robert had indulged in; for instance:

> the second movement is a pure idyll; I can see the worshippers kneeling about the little forest shrine, I hear the babbling brook and the buzz of insects . . . The third movement is a pearl, but it is a grey one dipped in a tear of woe, and at the end the modulation is quite wonderful.

Brahms was too kind, or too busy, to demolish any of this. Before he conducted the symphony he had played the B flat Concerto, making it indeed a big evening's work. An interesting piece of programming took place at

Meiningen on 3 February: 1. the new Symphony; 2. Beethoven's Grosse Fugue played by all the orchestral strings; 3. the Symphony again. At the Leipzig Gewandhaus the Symphony shared the stage with Hermine Spies, who sang two Schubert songs, 'Memnon' and 'Geheimes', to Brahms's orchestrations, and also a group of Brahms songs to his devoted accompaniment. The previous day he had played in his Violin Sonata in a chamber concert—the first appearance of the Brodsky Quartet which was to become famous throughout Germany. The missionary journeys took Brahms as far as Amsterdam where on 27 February he handed over the B flat Concerto to Julius Röntgen, now living there, the son of a distinguished Gewandhaus *Konzertmeister*, Engelbert Röntgen—the family being well known to the Herzogenbergs.

The visit to Dresden in March was a three-concert Brahms festival. Here the Symphony was conducted by Wüllner so that Brahms could hear it. Other items during the festival were the Alto Rhapsody (with Hermine Spies, who also sang Brahms songs), the D minor Concerto played by the composer and the last chorus of the cantata *Rinaldo*. Bülow came to play the F minor Sonata op.5. On 14 March Brahms conducted the Symphony in the Museum at Frankfurt, visited with longing by Clara in her imagination, for she was away on her sixteenth concert-tour in England.

In April increasing ill-health caused the resignation of Ferdinand Hiller from his posts as municipal director of music and head of the Conservatorium of Cologne. Brahms unhesitatingly but politely refused the offer to succeed him, and as unhesitatingly recommended Wüllner, having been particularly impressed with him not only as an inspirer, but also for his very marked achievements among young people as a choral conductor. Wüllner moved there in September.

Brahms left Vienna on 8 May for his fourth Italian tour, this time with a friend from Krefeld, Rudolf von der Leyen, as his companion. This time he restricted himself to northern Italy going outwards through the Brenner Pass to Trento and Lake Garda, and staying as the guest of the Duke of Meiningen at his Villa Carlotta on Lake Como. The stay had to be fairly short as he had promised to attend the Whitsun Lower Rhine Music Festival, this year at Düsseldorf, where he conducted the Third Symphony and the 'Schicksalslied'. Thus it was rather late in the year (the end of June) that he went into summer retreat at Mürzzuschlag, at the southern end of the Semmering Pass, a place resonant with happy memories of the tour with his father.

As to what he was doing there Simrock received two very oblique indications. On 25 June Brahms sent him a newspaper cutting which announced the new summer retreat, and said that Brahms was working there 'on a major piece'; and in a postscript to a letter of 19 August Brahms listed a large amount of writing-out which his copyist was doing for Simrock (by their descriptions they were opp.91 and 95) but he adds 'I appear to be taking better paper with more staves on it'. As doubtless Simrock guessed at the time, this refers to a start being made on the Fourth Symphony. This autumn or winter saw the publication in the Bachgesellschaft edition of Cantata 150, from which, with a significant added chromaticism, the passacaglia basis of the last movement was to be taken. It is ironic that modern scholarship has doubted whether this cantata is by Bach at all.

On 16 October he returned from Mürzzuschlag to Vienna, but was not long at home, because he was at Hamburg on 24 October to attend the first performance there of the new Symphony, given by the Philharmonic under Julius von Bernuth; this was so successful as to encourage a second performance there early in December, this time conducted by Brahms, at the Cecilienverein, to great success again. But meanwhile he had joined Bülow and the Meiningen orchestra on one of their exemplary and ear-opening tours, covering Budapest, Graz, and three large concerts in Vienna. The programmes shared the two Concertos, Bülow playing the First—without a conductor—and Brahms the Second, Bülow conducting. This reflects the difference between the two works, the first more difficult technically but more straight-forward in tempi, the second (just) easier but requiring, especially in the first movement, exacting ensemble work. The orchestra also played, under Bülow, the F major Symphony and the Haydn Variations. These concerts occupied the end of November and the beginning of December.

Leipzig had a three-day inauguration of the new Gewandhaus from 11 to 13 December which Brahms could not attend because it clashed with his Hamburg concert. Telling him of the plans, Elisabet still has a little dagger for the choir: 'The third evening is bound to be good, but it is a question whether Händel's *Messiah* and the Choral Symphony will go much better than usual.' However, Brahms gave them pleasure by a surprise visit at Christmas, in spite of their new house, to which they had moved in the summer, still being in Elisabet's eyes barely habitable: (24 December)

> Let me add a word of special thanks for your angelic patience when the whole house was upset, the spare room crammed so full of Christmas things that there was hardly room for the good Brahms, and you had to make shift with that treacherous sofa the first evening.

The letters of the year show at least two kindnesses of the 'angelic' man. On 11 December he asked Simrock to send four-hand arrangements of the three Symphonies to Maria Cossel, the daughter of his first piano teacher, and on 26 December he wanted a song sent to Amalie Joachim that he thought would be suitable and significant for her, namely op.91 no.2 for contralto and viola, published in 1884 but first thought of in 1863/4, when he indeed sent it to the then happy pair, but withdrew it, not being satisfied with it. It is based on an old carol tune, and the suitability lies in the words:

Jo - sef lieber Jo - sef mein

'Joseph, dear Joseph mine, help me rock my little babe.' Mary's words fit Joseph's name, but Brahms's gesture was in vain.

In the editorial field the edition of Schütz's works under Spitta aroused Brahms's passionate interest, but his undertaking to get Schubert's symphonies ready for Breitkopf and Härtel's complete edition caused two years of intermittent trouble and begrudged time.

The beginning of 1885 was marked for the Herzogenbergs by the impact on the Leipzig public of a 'Bruckner crusade' before and after a performance conducted by Arthur Nikisch of the Seventh Symphony, then in manuscript. Given the Herzogenbergs' aesthetics it is no surprise that they disapproved, but Elisabet's nice turn of invective makes two sentences of her letter of 14 January to Brahms worth quoting:

> In this world of so-called culture, there are many, many people ready to be imposed on by any inflated windbag, if its appearance is made with due pomp. One or two not impossible motifs, like grease-spots swimming on the top of weak soup, and there you have *Meister* Bruckner's whole stock-in-trade, while those who do not make immediate obeisance are stamped as unbelieving Thomases, who want signs and wonders to convince them.

Both she and Heinrich begged Brahms to back them up, and surprisingly, in view of his distanced, but real, appreciation of Wagner, he did so, showing a human but not creditable antipathy. Later in the year (in a letter to Wüllner in October which mainly deals with his own Fourth Symphony) he is not far off being a fuddy-duddy:

> All these first performances and the whole modern hunt for novelties interest me very little indeed . . . it is a case of novelty above all, and whether it stands approximately as high in the currency exchange as say Bruckner today. Forgive me, but it *is* the case.

But for all that Brahms possessed scores of the Seventh and Eighth Symphonies and of the *Te Deum*.

The year began with personal relations quite broken off with Joachim. There are no letters at all in the published correspondence between 29 January 1884 and 3 November 1885. However, the editor of the letters, Andreas Moser, in his introduction tells how he spent several weeks early in 1885 at Joachim's in Berlin to give him comfort in his wifeless loneliness. Joachim, having denounced Brahms's faithlessness, two hours later put all his soul into a performance of the Trio op.87 with Barth (pianist) and Robert Hausmann, the cellist of the Joachim Quartet. Moser, greatly moved, could not forbear to ask Joachim how he reconciled the anger in his heart with such a performance. Joachim replied:

> Yes, dear friend, but artist and man are two different things . . . I can do no other than feel this music with my whole being . . . it works on me like a force of Nature.

For Brahms himself there was conviviality at Krefeld at the end of January when he went to the golden jubilee of the Singverein there. He accompanied and took them through ('conducted' seems too strong a word) a piece he wrote for the occasion called *Tafel-Lied* (op.93b) for six-part chorus and piano. 'Six-part' gives perhaps a grander impression than the facts, since it really uses alternations of three-part women and three-part men until the *bonhomie* of the last verse. Even so Elisabet who had seen the music envied the Krefeld singers who could apparently toss this sort of thing off round the table. However, while he was there Brahms took part in the first performance of the Two Songs with Viola and Piano op.91.

At about this time Simrock was pressing the claims of the artist Max Klinger to make cover designs and frontispieces for Brahms's works. Brahms shared Simrock's admiration, but demurred at the proposal (19 February):

> That would be nice if I write pieces with titles such as 'Kreisleriana', 'Humoreske', 'Phantasiestücke', 'Novelleten', 'Karneval'! [All of them by Schumann!] But I doubt whether the simple Sonata title can specially arouse him, or that the innovation would please us!

However, he was still interested, particularly as Klinger was starting on the series, which ocupied him until 1894, of engravings and etchings, 41 in all, to which he gave the title *Brahms-Phantasie*.

With no new major work ready to disseminate, Brahms for the most part stayed in Vienna until the summer. An artist to make a particular impression on him was a violinist, only 21 years old, named Marie Soldat. She was Austrian, but a product of Joachim's Berlin Hochschule. She so captivated Brahms by her playing of his Violin Concerto at a Gesellschaft concert that doubtless to her surprise he took her out to the Prater in the next afternoon (with carousel rides and refreshments) and to *Macbeth* in the evening. What is more, he gave her his de-luxe-bound copy of the score of the Concerto, and did much to further her subsequent career.

A touching evidence of kindness within the family is a detailed and solicitous letter to the ever-faithful Simrock (25 April). Brahms's sister and her clock-maker husband Grund wanted to make a trip to visit Grund's home town (Neubrandenburg):

> I have advised her to go by way of Berlin to see the sights for a few days . . . Would you now be so very friendly as to help (only with advice) Herr Grund when he calls? Even to write out for him in which order to see the appropriate things, Museum, Panoptikum, Zoo etc. Do not encourage them to do too much at once, my sister suffers headaches and does not hold out for long. If you know a nice small hotel, would you perhaps be so good as·to let them know on a postcard? . . . If you would see to the hotel bill being paid, that would be one little joy more.

Simrock, foreseeing an imminent century of opus numbers, proposed to publish a proper dated catalogue of Brahms's works. The reply came from

Mürzzuschlag, which Brahms had chosen again, on 16 June, and reveals his shyness and lack of feeling for historical consequence (at least his own):

> I am completely against the 'historical dates' that you and Herr Keller [Simrock's editor-in-chief] have in mind. I find them quite unnecessary, but also unseemly. It looks disgracefully vain on my part, and no-one will believe I have not had a hand in it.

His feelings in the matter were greatly reinforced by hearing the B minor Mass by Bach conducted by Richter on 1 April. He related the overwhelming experience to Billroth thus:

> You have never yet had such an impression of greatness and sublimity. What is more, one could not credit any work of man with such a capacity to exalt and shatter one.

The immediate task in the eyrie at Mürzzuschlag 'where the cherries never ripen' was the completion of the Fourth Symphony. There was enough written for Brahms to send the first movement, and part of the second, to Elisabet on 4 September with the request to 'pass it on to Frau Schumann—that is, play it to her'. It was in score, and it was a tribute to Elisabet's musicianship that the symphony came first to her, and not to Clara with the request the other way round. Elisabet did not find it easy—who could?

> Unfortunately—and to Heinz's great disgust—I still have difficulty in reading the horn parts, and have to wrestle miserably with those three wicked lines in the score: horn in E, horn in C and trumpet in E. All the same, I have gained a fair idea of it.

The latter was certainly true, as can be seen in her detailed comments in a letter of 1 October. Brahms must have finished the entire composition by early October because on 10 October, to ease the difficulties of score-reading, he sent to Elisabet an arrangement for two pianos with a request to hand it on to Clara by 1 November at the latest. By a postal delay Clara did not get this in time to see it before a performance at Frankfurt on 3 November, causing vexation to her and Brahms, and great embarrassment to Elisabet, who had held on to it till the last moment so that Joachim could hear it.

Brahms's anxieties that his friends should comment, and his readiness to suspect the worst when, through accidents or the difficulties of coming to terms with its daring complexity and above all with its unprecedented last movement, they were slow to respond, made him edgy indeed. A remark to Elisabet: 'I question whether you will have the patience to sit through the finale' is not fishing for a compliment but a genuine worry at having unleashed an unprecedented symphonic movement, a theme (or succession of eight chords) with no fewer than 30 continuously varied statements and a coda in which the music at last breaks away from the rhythmic shape of the theme. The coda does not bring the curtain down in a triumphant major key, but rather hammers home a tragic feeling. Such major-key 'consolations' as there are occupy the sarabande-like middle of the movement. One must call this unprecedented; Beethoven for one never wrote a tragic symphony, and Schubert's C minor Symphony does not deserve the name. How curious that the composer, with this boiling within him, should be inveighing about novelty!

The spirit of Brahms knew what it had achieved, but the human being was ready to withdraw if the Meiningen rehearsals and two performances did not convince even pre-disposed listeners. However, his reputation now meant that conductors were vying with each other to put it into their immediate programmes before anyone had heard it. In a letter to Elisabet from Vienna dated 10 October just before he set out for Meiningen Brahms mentions that 'Bülow would like to begin with it at Frankfurt straight away on 3 November. They [that is, Richter and the Vienna Philharmonic] choose to announce it here, too, at their own risk', and of course Joachim was straining at the leash.

Bülow not only offered the orchestra as before, but saw to it that the orchestral parts were prepared. Brahms conducted the first performance in Meiningen, on 25 October and Bülow the second, on 1 November. The Symphony won its way—perhaps one might say that after the first two movements it bludgeoned its way—and was not withdrawn. As with the Third Symphony, Brahms, Bülow and the orchestra took it on tour, to Essen, Elberfeld, Utrecht, Amsterdam, The Hague, Krefeld, Cologne and Wiesbaden. However, the inbuilt rivalries which were always a danger in such an arrangement, and the differing temperaments of the two men, and Brahms's increasing tactlessness with his sometimes thin skinned colleague caused a rift of over a year, and Bülow's precipitate resignation from Meiningen.

Clara wrote in some detail to Brahms about the new Symphony on 15 December. While not hesitating to tell him about some things she did not like, she put her finger unerringly on a beautiful modulation towards the end of the slow movement. But she too had encountered Bruckner: 'There is nothing new here [that is, Frankfurt], unless it is that I have heard Bruckner's amazing symphony, and feel greatly relieved, for I know now where I am.' With this Delphic utterance we can dismiss the unfortunate Bruckner, as our three central figures have now done.

The first big event for Brahms in 1886 was the performance by the Vienna Philharmonic of the Fourth Symphony conducted by Richter on 17 January. Brahms wrote of it briefly but with great content to Simrock the next day, being specially pleased with the happy time afterwards at Sacher's restaurant 'under the direction of Billroth'. This determined Richter to introduce it to London, which he did with Brahms's ready agreement on 10 May. On 1 February Joachim gave a meticulous performance with the Berlin Philharmonic. The Herzogenbergs had moved to Berlin from Leipzig the previous autumn, on Heinrich's appointment as professor of composition at the Hochschule, and so Elisabet was able to report on the concert that the playing of the Symphony

> was not good, but simply perfection . . . The effect was *overpowering* . . . I was moved to tears—happy tears—by the andante . . . Both Joachim and his orchestra were roused to the highest pitch of excitement in the last movement . . . nothing in the whole symphony went wrong—a rare achievement in the case of a new work!

Another missionary tour with the Symphony now fell to Brahms. It began at Cologne on 9 February when he also conducted the 'Schicksalslied' and played the D minor Concerto—quite a night's work. After that there were concerts in most major German cities (with Munich again a conspicuous exception). One of these was at Leipzig on 18 February, attended by the Herzogenbergs from Berlin, at which Adolf Brodsky, the Russian-born professor at the Leipzig Conservatory, played Brahms's Violin Concerto. Elisabet returned to Berlin 'in a fit of the dumps in spite of all the E minor glamour', for two reasons: she now remembered the musical riches of the good old days at Leipzig (at which she had often railed before exile to Berlin), and she felt she had quite failed—as so many had done—to convey in Brahms's presence, by 'penetrating his defences' to express her thanks for the enrichment of their lives, with 'no possibility of looking after him at home, or making his coffee, or having him all to one's self for a cosy chat'. In the same letter (26 February) Bruckner still looms: 'We played Joachim a page or two of Bruckner's E major—[that is, the Seventh Symphony] by request—but soon had to stop out of compassion.' Two snorting Herzogenbergs on a piano is hardly the right medium.

On 14 May Clara made a compact with Brahms that they should return each other's letters with a view to destroying them. Luckily for biographers the proposed amount of destruction did not happen. Clara destroyed her letters up to 1858, but kept most thereafter at the request of her daughter Marie. Brahms destroyed some of his—but they agreed he should keep intact the most important ones. There is a gap in Elisabet's (but not Heinrich's) correspondence from March till the beginning of December, caused by false and malicious gossip (an unnamed male being the culprit). Nevertheless Brahms sent to them, without covering letter, his newly-composed Second Cello Sonata op.99, and the clouds must have cleared as Elisabet wrote him a long letter on 2 December, full of her characteristic mixture of comment and chat.

At the end of May, Brahms had cause to congratulate himself on finding a summer lodging in Switzerland at Thun, or rather nearby at Hofstetten where the river Aare flows into the lake. The lodging, he told Simrock, was the most beautiful he had yet had, seeing on the one hand the ancient town and castle, and the Hotel Bellevue so convenient for visitors, and on the other the incomparable array of the mountains of the Bernese Oberland, from right to left the Stockhorn, the great triangular mass of the Niesen, the Blümlisalp—and by walking a few steps from the house, the Jungfrau and the Mönch. Posterity, however, can view Thun as the birthplace of beautiful chamber-music and songs, some of the latter inspired by the voice and perhaps the person of a longed-for visitor Hermine Spies—'Hermione without the O', as Brahms called her to his Swiss friend Widmann.[13] In mid-June the Lower Rhine Music Festival was held in Cologne, so it fell to the lot of Wüllner to conduct it, and he included the Fourth Symphony. Brahms made careful arrangements with Simrock about the materials, but did not go to Cologne himself, typically saying that he could not drag himself away from his beautiful scenery, without any hint of composition. The chief fruits of this summer were the Second Cello Sonata in F op.99, the Second Violin Sonata in A op.100, and the Piano Trio in C minor op.101. For two of them the initial impulse is, unusually, pretty clear. Brahms had heard in Vienna the cellist of the Joachim Quartet, Robert Hausmann, introducing himself as a soloist, and was greatly struck by him, and specially gratified by his performance of the First Cello Sonata op.38. We can tell the upshot from Heinrich's letter to Brahms of 26 October:

> Hausmann, dear fellow, came back from Vienna in a just-after-confirmation frame of mind. You must have shown him some beautiful things. He raves most about the whole of the cello sonata and an intermezzo in the violin sonata.

The intermezzo must be the *andante tranquillo* alternating with *vivace* which forms the second movement. The Violin Sonata is firmly linked with Hermine Spies, since it uses three Brahms songs, two of which she sang at sight to him. They are two of his best and were published (later than the Sonata) as the first two of op.105: 'Wie Melodien zieht es' and 'Immer leiser wird mein Schlummer'. The climax of the second song is at the words 'Komm', O komme bald' ('Come soon') which epitomises the pleasurable pain which Brahms managed to give himself from these sporadic longings. Another song entwined in the first movement is actually called 'Komm bald' (op.97 no.6) and puts the request tenderly: 'Why wait from day to day: All the garden is blooming for you', and this can certainly apply to the bower-like Thun garden, shaded by the giant redwood sequoia (*Wellingtonia*). Brahms brought Hermine to sing the first two songs, among others, to the Widmanns, and gave her copies of them which Elisabet confessed to making copies of when Hermine showed them to her.

Amid these idylls the terse and turbulent first movement of the C minor Piano Trio might seem out of place; but there are many examples in Brahms of the major-minor balance being kept, for instance in the two Overtures, and a sufficient and unsentimental reason for the Trio in that Brahms enjoys writing gruff music in the minor, especially in C minor. It is possible that even at this date the A major Violin Sonata was being balanced by the D minor one op.108. However, programming could be a consideration with these three chamber works, making two plus two to equal three. This was indeed the case in Budapest where, before conducting the Fourth Symphony on 22 December, he joined Jenö Hubay (violin) and David Popper (cello) in the respective Sonatas and ended with the first public performance there of the Trio (20th December). Typically Brahms only left Vienna for Budapest the day before, and never told Simrock his purpose.

Brahms often ended the week's work in Thun by going over to Berne on Saturdays, so as to spend Sundays with the Widmanns. There was also a happy foursome—Brahms, Widmann, Simrock and the portraitist Fedor Encke—to Kandersteg, just below the Lötschberg Pass. (However, even if they had wanted to they could not have continued through the Lötschberg by train as the tunnel was not started till 1906.) At the end of the stay, Brahms's thank-you letters were heartfelt as to friendly people—and special mention was made of potatoes, and cognac, and Frau Widmann's damson tarts.

Relations with Clara were turbulent, if they existed at all, between August and December. She writes from Obersalzburg on 24 August:

> When in one of your bad moments you wrote that you thought you have very often been a nuisance to me with your compositions you must have forgotten that as an artist I am never able to send you superficial criticism of your work . . . a speedy judgement is not always possible, as for instance when one only receives a manuscript score and is as little skilled as I am at reading it . . . I am not always mistress of my own time and strength and cannot, like Frau von Herzogenberg [there's the rub] bury myself in a work for whole days at a time.

The complaints were renewed from Frankfurt on 4 November:

> Why are you sending me nothing more? Do you wish to leave your old friend quite out in the cold? . . . The new sonatas I should be able to play almost immediately [with Joachim and Becker respectively] and in any case I would be able to start practising them at once.

Worse follows on 7 December:

> Not only did you definitely refuse my request but the very tone in which you did so was offensive. But I see from your last letter that you yourself felt you had hurt me, and after such kind words I cannot keep up the quarrel with my old friend any longer.

Hermine Spies gave concerts in Vienna in the autumn, including songs by Brahms, and he and Billroth gave a party for her to reinforce her efforts. Elisabet, her less impressionable eyes leading to a cooler judgement, asked in a postscript (2 December):

> How did Spies sing in Vienna? . . . When I think of Frau Joachim and the way her voice grew steadily fuller, it seems to me that concert work and tearing about is, on the contrary, making this one more casual. She sings so many things as if she were reading at sight, and I do wish someone like you would warn her . . . It would have to be put very plainly.

Brahms had actually already put it, if not plainly then playfully, on 4 November: 'I actually dreamt that I heard you skip half a bar's rest and sing a crotchet instead of a quaver.' Her reply could hardly have been more disarming: 'It was very kind of you only to dream that I am unmusical. I have not only dreamt it, but known it for ages.'

Brahms's brother Fritz died on 5 November, leaving him 10,000 *talers*, most of which he spent, but not on himself. Vienna heard the first performances of both this year's Sonatas, with Brahms at the piano, the cellist being, inevitably, Hausmann on 24 November and the violinist the faithful and enthusiastic Hellmesberger on 2 December.

In January 1887 the Prussian order 'Pour le mérite', founded by Frederick the Great, was conferred on Brahms, an exceptional recognition for a musician which pleased Brahms's friends. Still all was not smooth with Clara, who on 13 January was still smouldering: 'It was not only your words that offended me but your deeds.' It was not so much deeds but the lack of them, such as not sending the Sonatas for very feeble reasons, and not proceeding with a Brahms evening at Frankfurt which he himself had requested. But he did achieve a reconciliation with Bülow, now a free-lance. Early in February Bülow gave a series of piano recitals, constituting a Beethoven cycle, and after the concert of 6 February Brahms went to the Imperial Hotel to see him, and finding him not there, left him a card with a phrase from *Die Zauberflöte* quoted on it, to which the words were Pamina's question 'Dear one, shall I nevermore see thee?' This in Brahms's language amounted to an apology, and Bülow accepted the renewal of their friendship with alacrity. Indeed Brahms went so far as to go to Budapest with him, and thanked him by a public speech from the podium for his performance in the Brahms Piano Quintet. On 25 February Brahms played op.101 in Vienna with the Cologne players Heckmann (violin) and Bellmann (cello) but was not pleased with them— although others seemed to be.

By this time in his career Brahms's works were being performed independently throughout continental Europe, with England more than compensating for shortfalls in France and Italy. His children were thus making their own way, for his financial comfort, and to an extent which forbids their listing here. But mention should be made of the First Symphony, conducted by Wüllner on 1 February, not only for the excitement it generated in conductor, orchestra and public, but because it emboldened Wüllner to persuade Brahms to a new and more important reconciliation. Both he and Brahms were members of an organisation called the Tonkünstler-Versammlung ('Composers' Union') which met periodically for mutual support and to give concerts representative of members' works. This year the four-day meeting was to be at Cologne from 26–29 June, and Wüllner was thus willy-nilly the host by virture of geography, if nothing else. The Union had been almost from the beginning a vehicle for 'Music of the Future', but now with Liszt and Wagner dead the centre of gravity was changing. Wüllner and other members sensed this and wished to consolidate the Union in more senses than one. Brahms for his part must have seen it as a duty to reconcile the feuds between 'new' and 'conservative' sustained to music's detriment. Thus it was a triumph of Wüllner to get Brahms to interrupt his summer at Thun, but it was also a triumph for Brahms; he acknowledged to Wüllner how his foreboding had changed to delight; he played the piano part in his new C minor Trio at the Choral concert, but otherwise all he had to do was to be there and show himself no bogeyman. He had been anxious lest 'the other side' should say he had waited for Liszt's death before attending, but Wüllner would have none of it. He had to sit through the long and rather ramshackle oratorio *The Legend of Saint Elisabeth* performed in memory of Liszt at the first concert, but his own works to compensate him were two of the songs for six-part choir op.42 ('Darthulas Grabgesang' and 'Vineta'), the 'Triumphlied' and the Violin Concerto played by Brodsky.

Leaving Vienna on 25 April Brahms had made his fifth visit to Italy. His companions were Simrock and the composer and teacher Theodor Kirchner. Kirchner's early career had been in Switzerland—Winterthur and Zürich—but he was currently teaching at the Dresden Conservatoire. Now in his sixty-fourth year he was perhaps rather old to be immersed for the first time in the delights of Italy, but he was a quiet and rather sad figure, having outlived the days when he was a favourite composer for the piano—taken up by Clara among others—and he was impecunious as well. Brahms readily agreed with Simrock's proposal to take him with them as a guest. The letters from Brahms to Simrock beforehand about where they should start, the route and the amount of days to be spent in each place, even the kind of train tickets to be bought, amount to far more words than he ever put on paper to describe the actual trip. He was obviously in his element, and it is amusing to see how detailed is the advice he gives to his publisher-businessman friend, who could be supposed to be quite capable of fending for himself. For instance, as to clothing

> We shall be sweating from time to time. So, light clothing, but an overcoat and travelling rug. In the mornings it is cold in the churches and galleries; we shall not have opportunities for excursions on foot, so we shall often be sitting in an open carriage afternoons and evenings.

However, perhaps the most striking and clever advice is about poste-restante letters:

> have them addressed 'Simrock' in Latin letters [i.e. not German script]; otherwise they will be put in the F-box. If you put 'Fritz' [in front] they will not think it the equivalent of Frederigo, but treat it as the surname.

The route, after many changes of plan, was: Innsbruck, Verona, Vicenza, Venice, Bologna, Florence, then back via Pisa, Milan, St Gotthard, to (as far as Brahms was concerned) his beloved Thun, where he arrived on 15 May. To put Italy and Switzerland end to end like this is clear evidence of less concert commitments.

The composers' gathering at Cologne has already been described, but Brahms did not immediately rush back to Thun. Instead he went up-stream to Rüdesheim, well and truly in hock country where he spent some beautiful days with his friends the Beckeraths. For a surprise they arranged for Hermine and her sister to be there. But if an engagement was hoped for, or even expected, nothing came about. If it had come anywhere near a casting vote, uncertainty of rhythm and unevenness of timbre must have decided the matter.

The main work of this composing season was the Concerto for Violin, Cello and Orchestra which Brahms announced to Simrock as 'my latest [or last] folly'. This was offered to Joachim, clearly as a gesture of reconciliation, and accepted eagerly as such; but though their letters used 'du' they did not use Christian names any more. The Concerto was again a quick piece of work, since it was ready for rehearsal with orchestra in mid-September. The other work dating from this time was *Zigeunerlieder* ('Gipsy songs') for vocal quartet with piano op.103. In this connection it is amusing to look back to the letter Brahms sent to Heinrich before he left Vienna for southern parts:

> As I shall be making no music myself, you might send me your new things to look at there. They will sound very beautiful with the ripple of the river coming through the open window.

Apart from welcome friends such as Hanslick and his wife, there were other interruptions. On the way to Cologne Brahms called at Frankfurt on 24 June to play to Clara and an invited company (not invited by himself!). Clara's diary records that he played the A major Violin Sonata (with Hugo Heermann) beautifully, his new cello sonata (with Hugo Becker) less so . . . and the trio at the end was awful (*entsetzlich*). 'How is it possible for a composer to maltreat his own work so?' The proposed 'suicide pact' of letters ran into reservations and afterthoughts; Brahms had given back Clara's letters to him, and as to his letters to her she herself suggested (23 July) that he ought to make a diary from them, covering as they did almost all his career as well as containing interesting remarks and opinions invaluable for a biographer. Brahms did not carry out his original intention of throwing them into the Rhine.

Domestic affairs also intruded. Brahms's housekeeper in Vienna Fräulein Vogl having died, he was at a loss how to handle the matter from Thun. He even thought he might have to move; it never struck him to install a wife there instead. The matter was eventually solved through the solicitous efforts of his friends Richard and Maria Fellinger. Dr Richard Fellinger was the general manager for Austria of the firm of Siemens and Halske. Maria was a self-taught drawer and painter with a good voice. Her father was a professor at Tübingen who under the name of Christian Reinhold wrote the words of some of Brahms's late songs. Incidentally, the cellist Hausmann was at this time the Fellinger's lodger. Their house in Vienna, as one can gather from the tone of Brahms's letters to them, was a place he could be completely 'unbuttoned' in, and he loved their children Richard and Robert. Brahms would drop in without ceremony for Sunday lunch, and he spent the last seven Christmases of his life there. The editor of the letters to them, Leopold Schmidt, tells how at one of Brahms's first appearances Frau Fellinger supposing his ring at the door was that of an old deaf tailor she sometimes fed, called to the maid to take him straight to the kitchen. Largely through the Fellingers' efforts Brahms did not need to move, but had the good fortune to appoint a widow, Celestine Truxa, who took him and his lodging over and faithfully served him for the rest of his life.

The Double Concerto finished, Brahms travelled to Baden-Baden to meet Joachim and Hausmann and to rehearse it first with piano and then with the Spa's orchestra which they found 'animating and pleasant'. If indeed the orchestra was anything like the Baden orchestra for which Berlioz wrote his brilliant score of *Beatrice and Benedict* there was every reason to be confident that Brahms's far less taxing orchestration would succeed even on such an *ad hoc* occasion. Clara heard the piece in its proper orchestral clothing with joy, although she was beginning to be deaf on occasion: 'for some time I have not been able to distinguish harmonies which follow each other in quick succession, if I do not know them'. Almost worse than deafness, 'I often hear quite different notes from those which are being played.' From Baden-Baden Brahms wrote to the Widmanns to thank them for hospitality and for the many excursions he enjoyed with them. The family had been staying at Merlingen, half-way along the lake of Thun on the north side, from which the steamer runs across to Spiez. He sent greetings to the 'Touching Argos', and the editor, Kalbeck, explains the allusion with a dog-story. Argos had been lost on the Grindelwald glacier, north of the Eiger. He was presumed to have fallen into a crevasse, but after four days, totally exhausted, turned up at the Widmanns' house in *Berne*, Brahms being one of the joyful and astonished witnesses.

After the Baden rehearsals the orchestral parts went to Wüllner at Cologne, when the first performance was scheduled for 18 October. Even now the rehearsal had the same use for the conductor-composer as it would have done years before, for when Wüllner also received the score he was asked to ensure that the copyist put into the parts the alterations made in red on the score. As usual Joachim had a say in the final layout of the violin part, but Brahms also asked Hausmann to do the same for the cello part. There is now no evidence as to whether he did. Joachim's ideas had their usual mixed reception! But Brahms had written on the score 'to him, for whom it was written' and he must have been a happy man as he went back to Vienna between Baden rehearsals and Cologne performance. His pleasure was all the greater to be at home; Frau Truxa having put the place in order (always a venturesome thing to do) he described, again to Widmann (11 October) how it was 'extremely pleasantly arranged', and what is more there were lovely walks in the most pleasant weather.

> I eat midday and evening in the open air and the chestnuts are luxuriantly blooming for the second time . . . How is Argos, and would he not like, by way of sweet greeting from me, a nice piece of meat instead of rusks?

The Concerto quickly began its public life, at Wiesbaden, Frankfurt and Basle before the end of the year, and was soon out of Brahms's hands. His friend the singer Georg Henschel was by now a teacher at the Royal College of Music in London, and conducted two performances, on 17 and 21 February 1888. Brahms's Christmas Day concert at Meiningen was a busy and memorable one; he shared the conducting with Bülow's successor Fritz Steinbach. Steinbach (and the Grand Duke who paid for it all) contributed greatly to Brahms's posthumous fame by taking the whole Meiningen orchestra on a tour of England in 1902 at which exemplary performances of all four symphonies were given. At Christmas the concert comprised: the Haydn Variations, the Third Symphony, and the Second Piano Concerto played, not for the first time, by the young virtuoso Eugen d'Albert who was speedily making the concerto his own. Brahms's other Christmas fare at Meiningen was a performance of Ibsen's *Ghosts* and a meeting with Ibsen himself.

With the New Year's Day concert at the Leipzig Gewandhaus, 1888 began as might many another year, but it is evident that Brahms by now has less inclination to concert work. The mere fact of not being able to hear the Double Concerto in her old haunt drew from Elisabet a truly woebegone letter. Heinrich had a wasting disease in his legs which caused much pain and near paralysis, and a deformation of the right leg which ultimately necessitated surgery. Elisabet, herself fragile with a weak heart, nursed him for months on end. The cold and damp of Berlin were not to be risked, and they were living in Munich. She expressed herself as though by the waters of Babylon.

> Now we live by hope only, with patience and resignation for our daily bread. Sometimes I think it never will be the same again, and down goes my head into my hands, while the tears—which I can generally control—trickle down.

However, Brahms did give them solace in the course of the year, by sending them in March the *Zigeunerlieder*, written the previous summer, and in October the Third Violin Sonata in D minor op.108 which dates back to 1886 for its inception, but which was still in manuscript. (It was published in 1889, with a dedication to Bülow.) The Herzogenbergs also saw in manuscript the four sets of songs which were to become opp.104–107. These were 'reviewed' by Elisabet in detail (not all complimentary) in quite her old style in a long letter of 28 October from Nice, where they had gone for Heinrich's convalescence in which he had painstakingly to learn to walk again. There is an amusing air of panic about the Violin Sonata. Brahms writes to Elisabet on 3 November, with underlining: 'I have just written to Frau Schumann. In case she should want the sonata, please send it her at once. We can see about a copy afterwards.' Three days later he is yet more urgent: 'Frau Schumann asks me to request you to send her the sonata immediately, which I now do, with a *sffz* by way of emphasis. She is going to Berlin very soon, and would like to play it with Joachim.' Four days later again: 'I hope you really sent off the sonata on the spot? You know Frau Schumann is very touchy!' She was not only touchy but often incapacitated with rheumatic pains at this time. Her diary notes:

> Nov. 22 As my arm was very bad I let Elise [her pianist daughter] and Koning play me Brahms's new sonata in D minor, which he has just sent me. I was very sad that I could not play it myself . . . The sonata is magnificent; just like the first–ravishing.

A letter from Brahms to Widmann of 7 January also marks, or at least confirms, a number of turning points. Widmann had down the years fairly persistently tried to interest his friend in opera libretti which Brahms equally persistently turned down without perhaps giving himself or Widmann the real reason. Now Brahms writes:

> I had a happy Christmas in Meiningen and a happy New Year in Leipzig . . . for the rest however your letter should have come 20 years earlier. Have I never spoken of my two fine principles? . . . No opera, and no marriage . . . Imagine how much money I have to spare for an Italian trip if I do not marry this summer nor buy an opera libretto for 1000 francs.

The Italian trip, Brahms's sixth, did come off, with Widmann as his learned and exhilarating companion, in May. The preliminary instructions contained:

> I want you to bring with you something very important for a journey in Italy. You are thinking of Burckhardt or Gregovius [as travel guides]. Ah no, I am asking for two or three little blue packets of French tobacco, 'Caporal'; stick them in your travelling bag, and in your coat pocket when you cross the frontier.

However, until the last moment there were still hesitations on Brahms's part. If he had not eventually gone, would there have been a Fifth Symphony? Their route was Verona, Bologna, Rimini, San Marino, Ancona, Loreto (in the footsteps of Mozart and many others), Rome, Florence, then through the St Gotthard tunnel. But instead of going straight on to Thun, they made a 'beautiful finale' by getting out at Göschenen, staying the night at Andermatt above the tunnel, and then, 'for six or seven hours in the morning, walking down the gorgeous valley of the Reuss to Erstfeld'. Brahms arrived at Thun at the end of May. Among other visitors was Hermine again, staying with the

Widmanns in Berne. But this time she is shocked, and writes to Frau Fellinger in Vienna about Brahms's sudden white hair. 'Were it not for his youthful blue eyes he would be an old man.' Nevertheless he was known to achieve in a morning six or seven hours of walking, even if downhill. The summer saw two more acts of generosity. He told Simrock to make a gift of the manuscript of the Double Concerto to Hausmann, and at the second attempt he got Clara to accept from Simrock a fund from his unneeded composition money. Clara had confessed to Brahms her great worries about how she could look to the future of three grandchildren in particular, the sons of the fatally ill Ferdinand. The urgency of the admission of the proud woman was underlined by the letter (11 July) being sent from a hydro at Franzensbad where she was trying to cure a rheumatism which threatened her very career, as at least she saw it, as a concert artist. The sum was the then equivalent of £750, more than enough to keep the wolf from Brahms's door for several years.

The autumn brought the first public performance of the *Zigeunerlieder*, at the Berlin Singakademie concert on 31 October. Brahms had already described them to Clara, perhaps with a teasing glint in the youthful eyes (April 1888): 'They are a kind of Hungarian love-song, and beautifully sung as they were [at Billroth's with Brahms at the piano] you would have found listening to them a delight. Otherwise they might seem to you a little too rollicking.' The words are Hungarian folksongs made into German rhyme by Hugo Conrat. The music could be described as domesticised Hungarian, but happy the domestic life in Europe that could guarantee Simrock a public to buy *Zigeunerlieder*. However, the accompaniment for two hands rather than four at one piano is rich and taxing. It is one of the many examples of Brahms's piano music which offers an exhilaration in the physical process of getting the notes played. One can imagine the rollicking in Billroth's music-room being enhanced by wrong notes and snortings from the elated pianist.

At the end of November the Duke and Duchess called on Brahms on the way back to Meiningen from Berchtesgaden, but this year he had to refuse their Christmas invitation having committed himself to the first performance of the D minor Sonata (still in manuscript) with Hubay in Budapest on 21 December and to conduct the first Vienna performance of the Double Concerto, with Joachim, Hausmann and the Vienna Philharmonic, on 23 December. These dates would not have precluded him, as a younger man, from a dash to Meiningen, and even a concert on arrival.

Nevertheless Brahms did go to Meiningen at the beginning of 1889. At a concert there d'Albert played the D minor Piano Concerto and Joachim and Hausmann the Double Concerto, all to Brahms's great satisfaction. Joachim also played, at a rehearsal amounting to a private concert, both Beethoven's and Brahms's Violin Concertos, and also the new Sonata, and joined Hausmann and Brahms in the C minor Trio. On the way back to Vienna Brahms spent six good-tempered days with Clara at Frankfurt, playing the Sonata with Heermann and surprising Clara with the slowness of the adagio.

Clara 'once more thanked heaven for sending so strong and healthy a genius into the world in the midst of the Wagner mania' (diary entry of 10 January).

Vienna heard for the first time in public concerts the *Zigeunerlieder* on 18 January, sung, with Brahms at the piano, by a quartet arranged by the tenor singer Gustav Walter, who thus crowned a very successful series of recitals featuring Brahms's newest songs. Then on 13 February Brahms gave with Joachim the first Viennese performance of the D minor Violin Sonata. Relations with Joachim were further cemented at the beginning of March, when he attended the celebration of Joachim's 50 years of public artistic life at the Hochschule in Berlin. Brahms told Clara on 19 March that Joachim was 'more affable and friendly than usual'. The festival was very dignified and beautiful but as a musical occasion was nothing out of the way, except for an interesting sacred vocal concert of three cantatas by Bach and one by Schütz. On 9 March he went for some days to Hamburg to cheer his sister who was ill. Things may already have been brewing there which led to the event which 'made' this year. On arriving back in Vienna in mid-March Brahms spent much time on letter-writing on plans for another Italian journey, this time as far as Sicily. Billroth and two other university colleagues urged Brahms and he in turn urged Widmann. But Widmann decided he was not fit enough, and Brahms, having said that he did not care where he went so long as it was south, had an attack of what he called his 'usual perversity' (*die gewohnte Trägheit*). The upshot was that in April he went by himself instead for a few weeks at Villa Carlotta on Lake Como, as before. What is more, he decided to give up Thun. A new riverside promenade had been built giving all-too-close access to the beloved house to sightseers, the English being specifically mentioned. The choice fell upon Ischl and did not waver again, in spite of there being, as he regretfully admitted to Widmann, no train to Berne from there. Clara with her two daughters did visit Italy from mid-April to mid-May, staying mainly at Pisa and Florence. But the Herzogenbergs, who met her there, confirmed Brahms's suspicion that she no longer had the resilience to cope with the dirt, noise, and distractions of Italy, or even with the overwhelming number of artistic impressions on every hand.

Brahms went to Ischl in May. If he now put himself out of reach of friends in 'republican Switzerland', as he took to calling it, he could enjoy others near at hand, notably the circle of Johann Strauss, Bösendorfer (he of the pianos and the Hall), and the beautiful pianist Ilona Eibenschütz, who according to Kalbeck is enshrined in some of the last piano pieces, and the composer Goldmark. Not far away at St Gilgen, at the Salzburg end of the Wolfgangsee, was the summer villa which Billroth had built for himself, or rather for his family when he died—which event he had succeeded in postponing. At Ischl Brahms had accepted honorary membership of the Beethoven-Verein of Bonn, of which body Joachim was the honorary life-president. However, a much greater honour was almost immediately notified, by telegram in May, by official letter in June: the Freedom (honorary citizenship) of Hamburg.

This was accepted with joy, and was of course the subject of congratulations the world over. This was an occasion for choral music enshrining in its words the Germany of his allegiance by birth rather than the Austria of his residence. As is often the case the original manuscript bears neither title, date or signature, so that we cannot be sure when the work, a set of three eight-part unaccompanied choruses entitled *Fest- und Gedenksprüche* op.109, was originally conceived. Kalbeck gives reason to believe that it was begun in the summer of 1888 or even earlier. There is a letter to Simrock of 7th June requesting the chorus parts to be run off for rehearsals beginning on 25 June. The title, about which Brahms was uncertain, means roughly 'festal and commemorative mottoes'. Brahms at one stage favoured the adjective 'German' in front of it, with 'national' as an alternative for the English and other markets! Certainly the biblical words, chosen by himself, link God in no uncertain way with national aspirations. There is little doubt who His people are in 1889, and there are vocal trumpet calls befitting the strongly-armed man guarding his palace (*St Luke* 11:21)[14]. The work, printed in score the following year, is 'respectfully dedicated to His Magnificence the Herr Bürgermeister of Hamburg Dr Carl Petersen'.

Dating from this year are the last works in the genre, the Three Motets for eight- and four-part unaccompanied choir op.110. Here the words are much more conscious of sin and a longing for personal peace. They begin with the psalm verse (Ps. 69:29) 'But I am poor, and sorrowful' and end with four stanzas of a hymn written in about 1550 by Paul Eber and set by Bach in the *Little Organ Book* ('Orgelbüchlein') among other places—'Wenn wir in höchsten Nöthen sein' ('When we are in deepest need'). There is something of the technique of Schütz's German psalm settings in the first motet, but with a beautiful and striking modernism in the first bar (see page 260). The death-bed words of the last motet naturally evoke an opening phrase like a chorale but soon lead to a truly Brahmsian proud submission.

However, before he went to Hamburg his host country also honoured him On 6 June the Emperor of Austria decreed for him the 'Komturkreuz' of the Order of Leopold, which meant going straight to the top of the order, without using the intermediate grades. Frau Truxa had to exert guile and authority to get him and his dress into a fit state for the Emperor to receive him with clean (or nearly clean) white gloves and clean boots, involving going to the palace, with much grumbling, by carriage.

The Hamburgers received him, and he them, with mutual joy at the beginning of September. The ceremonies and concerts were timed to mark and enhance a great industrial exhibition there and the Cecilia choir was augmented to some 400 singers. Brahms was represented not only by the new 'Mottoes' but also by the Alto Rhapsody and the Violin Concerto played by Brodsky. Instead of returning straight home he went to Baden-Baden, to his old beloved hostelry, the 'Bear' in Lichtenthaler Allee. There his friend Widmann visited him, to partly compensate for the loss of Thun, and the two of them visited Clara, who made a most favourable impression on Widmann. The Hamburg festivities meant that Brahms had missed her seventieth birthday, but at this visit (20 September) he made her some distinguished, slightly late, birthday presents: the 'Mottoes', the Three Motets op.110 and the reworked Trio op.8. At this time a complete edition of Brahms's works was 'in the air', and indeed Simrock was about to take steps to buy out from their publishers the early works not in his catalogue. Brahms had a soft spot for the Trio, his first published chamber work, but he also had an experienced and remorseless eye for its weaknesses as a composition, and he was clearly not willing for it to be simply reprinted. In a letter to Clara from Ischl dated 3 September he wrote:

> You will never guess with what childish amusement I whiled away the beautiful summer days. I have re-written my B major trio and can call it op.108 instead of op.8. It will not be so wild as it was before—but whether it will be better—?

This last sentence truly illustrates the paradoxical indecision. A side-by-side study of both versions is a lesson no composition student should do without, and non-specialists can find a discussion in the catalogue. With a lifetime's experience behind him Brahms is able to put his finger on every weakness— inconsequential and merely episodic ideas, unnecessary and otiose details, especially 'effects' for their own sake—and instead has vastly improved the coherence of the work, and incidentally made it shorter in the process. Brahms played Clara the 'new' Trio on 20 September. The directors of the Museum Concerts at Frankfurt, according to Clara on 2 November, would like to ask Brahms to put his new Trio in their programme 'but dare not'. (Brahms had given a rather terse refusal to conduct his Fourth Symphony there.) Brahms replied to Clara: 'How gladly would I play my trio there, for it would be a sign that it still pleased me a little. Unfortunately, however, it does not please me at all—not in the least.' We had best finish the tale by going into the next year to observe how the 'usual perversity' worked itself out. Brahms wrote to Clara from Vienna on 23 February 1890:

> Yesterday there was a rehearsal and performance of my B major trio. I had already thrown the piece to the dogs and did not want to play it. The fact that it seemed inadequate to me and did not please me, means little. When it came to be discussed, however, no curiosity was expressed, but everybody, including even Joachim and Wüllner, for instance, started off by saying how much pleasure they had had in playing the old piece quite recently, and had found it full of sentiment, and romantic and heaven knows what else. And now I am glad that I did play it after all . . . I only feel sorry that I have not played it to you also, that is to say that I did not accept the chamber music evening. I suppose it is too late now?

At the year's end came a small disturbance. Brahms's body, grown bulkier in recent years, fell at last to illness—what was thought to be influenza. The new version of the op.8 Trio was given its first public performance, by

132

Brahms, Hubay and Popper, in Budapest on 10 January 1890. If we are to take Brahms seriously, between this performance and the next he had already mentally 'thrown it to the dogs', feeling that the graft had not taken. His reaction to a second performance, in Vienna on 22 February with Arnold Rosé (violin) and Hummer (cello) has already been recorded. His ambivalence carries on into the question of publication. There is no hesitation about wanting the new version published, but the corollary is not a veto on the earlier version, and Simrock, by now its owner, is allowed to do what he likes about it. Our own most likely attitude nevertheless is to regard the second version as definitive, and to hear the first, if at all, as a historical curiosity. But the sort of audience for whom Brahms's chamber music was written had admitted op.8 to their families and it had lived with them for almost 46 years, having been published in November 1854. Elisabet's detailed reactions, delayed by a prolonged and frightening bout of asthma, began from the standpoint that 'you had no right to intrude your master-touch on this lovable, if sometimes vague, production of your youth'. However, she concludes with a touch of her old vigour that 'it is *beautiful* in its present form, and I gladly leave it to the musical philologues to remonstrate with you. They are more concerned with the date of a thing than the thing itself—by which I mean no allusion to our quite unpetrified Spitta!'

The Joachim Quartet from Berlin gave a series of concerts in Vienna from 19 to 23 January, including Brahms's B Flat Quartet, which he himself liked the best of his three. (Though when Joachim asked him about the programmes in general he typically suggested having six Haydns and then going home.) However, the playing of the artists, on their mettle in a foreign capital, certainly remained in Brahms's mind when it was coming to grips with the summer's chamber work.

His faithful friend Wüllner got Brahms to Cologne again in mid-March for rehearsals and a performance, on 13 March, of the new Trio with the composer at the piano and Heermann and Becker for colleagues. But what really drew Brahms was the opportunity to hear the whole of the 'Mottoes' and Motets, opp.109 and 110, sung by a top-rate choir under their unsurpassed director.

The Trio then moved on to Frankfurt for a concert in the Museum on 21 March. Clara heard some rehearsals as well as her fitful hearing would allow, and after the concert she told her diary:

> The whole trio strikes me as better proportioned than it was, but I do not altogether like it . . . the second subject of the last movement is quite horrible. The first subject of the same movement is heavenly, and then the second with iron hand suddenly hurls one down from the skies.

It certainly is rather galumphing.

However, by now Brahms's thoughts were again turning to beloved Italy. As early as 28 February he had agreed in principle to go with Widmann, and the preliminary arrangements had again included packets of 'Caporal'. However, he told his Swiss friend that withstanding the seductions of Thun it would be Ischl again for the summer. They met at Riva at the top end of Lake Garda. On their return Brahms wrote to Clara on 1 May from Vienna:

> We walked in the most delightful spring weather with everything in our favour along Lakes Garda and Como, and through a whole number of delightful little towns—Bergamo, Brescia, Piacenza, Como, Parma, Cremona, Padua, Vicenza, Verona—I am mentioning the names just as they occur to me . . . My umbrella flew into Lake Como, but throughout the tour we did not have a drop of rain.

Later in the same letter thoughts emerge which underlie some of the kind prevarications in the Herzogenberg correspondence:

> You have probably received and are still receiving a whole series of new Herzogenbergs. How pleased one would be to feel greater pleasure at the ever-increasing bulk of these works, but it is impossible! For however much one might over-estimate the industry, amongst other things—a little drop of blood!

Brahms was in Ischl from May until the beginning of October. Although the only substantial work to be attributed to this period is the Second String Quintet in G op.111, it is difficult to be sure whether even now Brahms was slowing down as a composer. There are two enigmatic remarks to Simrock. There is a characteristic self-deprecation on 2 July; the reference to symphonies is probably to proof-correction of keyboard arrangements. 'Tell me when I *must* send the symphonies back; there is surely no hurry. I really like having them here; they hold me back so nicely from composing—!' Back in Vienna he wrote (12 October): 'My copyist is writing out the B major Trio and has also got a string quintet to cope with. For the rest on leaving Ischl I have thrown a lot of torn-up music paper into the Traun.' He covers himself as to the quality of the new quintet by telling Clara as early as August that 'it is certainly a misfortune that my first quintet (F major) is probably one of my finest works'. However, again Elisabet echoes, or rather pre-echoes, what most people would think in language as lively as it is clear-sighted (9 October):

> The 'old' quintet, the F major, affected me so powerfully again recently that the new one only found a footing with difficulty; but my heart soon surrendered to the newcomer, and is prepared to admit its possibly greater beauty and benignity, its riper, sweeter vintage. Yet why compare them, when they are so eminently worthy to stand side by side!

Her summing-up is deft: 'The person who invented it all must have felt very light-hearted. One feels you must have been celebrating—say, your thirtieth birthday!'

In November there was a silly contretemps about the score, then with the Herzogenbergs, going to Joachim, caused either by an off-hand remark of Brahms, or the lack of a remark at a crucial juncture. The thought that

Brahms could remotely have wanted to hold the work back from Joachim, of all people, caused a massive reproof from Clara, and an energetic smoothing operation from Brahms to Joachim. Nevertheless it was the Viennese violinist Arnold Rosé who arranged its first performance for Brahms on 11 November. Joachim and his colleagues performed it in a chamber concert in Berlin on 10 December. This was attended by the Herzogenbergs and evoked more details, mainly enthusiastic, from Elisabet. However, she had to comment that the cello had to fight to be heard sometimes in the first movement: 'the instrument itself gives signs of protest about the exorbitant demands made on it'. This particularly refers to the start of the piece—'all wood and no strings' is her remark on the cello sounds—and the balance, with four colleagues above the one cello trying to announce the main subject, caused anxious consultations within the ensemble and with the composer. At the end of the day Brahms left it to the players to sort out after all, retaining a simple *forte* mark for each part in the score. He obviously wanted to discourage sophistication and pulled punches. Pianists in the chamber works (especially the Cello Sonatas) must get used to appearing to make a noise without actually doing so, and now it is the turn of the upper strings.

As early as November Brahms had the Italian spring on his mind, and wrote to Widmann broaching it. (It did not happen in 1891 because of Widmann's breaking his leg while climbing the stairs of an underground wine restaurant in Nuremburg.) A beaker full of the warm south never lost its imperative attractions, and as Brahms occasionally hinted after op.111 that he had had his say as a composer he could feel that he had earned it, as he had his happy Christmas with the Fellingers. It might seem odd that Brahms, only 57 years old and in good health and encouraged by the highest possible public esteem, should have told Simrock and hinted to others that he felt he had run his course as a composer. As we cannot explain how the copious springs began and continued to flow, so it is probably otiose to surmise why Brahms felt them to be drying up. He was such a prolific and quick worker that a momentary 'writing block' might have had a disproportionate effect. He may have thought that the double concerto had not had its due reward, and therefore that the public and himself had lost interest in each other. This might appear ludicrously wrong-headed in view of his subsequent music, but what a composer feels, wrong or not, is decisively true for him. Two, at least, great 20th-century composers outlived the era of their creative powers—Sibelius and Elgar.

NOTES

1. C.F. Pohl, *Briefwechsel* (Brahms-Simrock, vol. 2, p. 66), ed. Kalbeck
2. R. Crichton (ed.), *The Memoirs of Ethel Smyth* (Viking, London, 1987), p. 79.
3. G. Henschel, *Musings and Memories of a Musician* (Macmillan, London, 1918), p. 123.

4.   Distinctly less than (e.g.) the 38½ minutes given in Aronowsky, *Performing Times of Orchestral Works* (Ernest Benn, London, 1959), p. 114. By courtesy of the BBC I have learnt that their records show only one performance in the last five years marginally shorter than 35 minutes, and an average length of not less than 38 minutes.

5.   A. Holde, 'Suppressed passages in the Brahms–Joachim correspondence published for the first time', *Musical Quarterly*, vol. 45, no. 3 (1959), pp. 318–19.

6.   On 17 September Joachim wrote Brahms's Christian name at the head of a letter—'Lieber Johannes'—for the last time, except for a solitary occasion in 1892.

7.   See the discussion of the First Symphony in the catalogue.

8.   The quotations are all from Crichton, *The Memoirs of Ethel Smyth*, *passim*.

9.   In Zürich on 6 December Brahms conducted the first performance of *Nänie*.

10.   Perhaps one relevant personal reminiscence may be allowed. I thrice heard Elgar 'conduct' *The Dream of Gerontius* at Three Choirs Festivals in the 1930s. It never occurred to me, or anyone else in the deeply-moved audience, to wonder whether he was a good conductor.

11.   The Third Symphony could well have been struggling within him at the very moment he wrote this.

12.   Holde, 'Suppressed passages in the Brahms–Joachim correspondence published for the first time', p. 318–9.

13.   It is better in German: 'HermioneohneO'.

14.   Brahms admits in a letter to the theologian Widmann (19 March 1890) that the quotation is outside the context of St Luke.

CHAPTER FIVE

The Last Years

In January 1891 Brahms was in Budapest for, among other things, a performance of the Horn Trio op.40, and while he was there he was delighted to receive an invitation to Meiningen to a week-long arts festival due in March. In February he dropped his defences about portraiture and wrote to Clara from Vienna:

> At the present moment I am lending my head to a sculptor and an engraver at the same time. I thought I should be rid of them when I told them I could not sit more than once. But it was no good. They came to an agreement and now etch and mould together.

Brahms was stirred to unwonted eloquence on a postcard to Clara by a performance by a young English pianist just coming up to his twenty-third birthday. He was Leonard Borwick, playing Brahms's D minor Concerto with the Vienna Philharmonic, conducted by Richter. Clara had taught him for some six years, and the Concerto marked a decisive step forward in his career.

> Borwick played quite excellently, with the most perfect freedom, warmth, energy, passion, in short everything that one could desire. I, of course, thought as well of all the beauty and goodness for which he has to thank his teacher!!! Really one could not have wished for anything better or more beautiful, and you may readily believe everything that your lady friends will tell you about it.

It was truly an extravagant and gratifying accolade for Clara as well—and Brahms was not extravagant.

At Meiningen Brahms heard his First and Fourth Symphonies beautifully presented by Steinbach, but one of the highlights of the week was the staging of Widmann's play *Oenone*, which the author, to the composer's delight, had swallowed his republicanism to attend. But posterity must thank the other highlight of the festival, the playing of a Weber Concerto and Mozart's Clarinet Quintet by the orchestra's first clarinettist and conductor's assistant, Richard Mühlfeld. Brahms was so enchanted by the tonal beauty of what he heard that he was fired to return to an 'Indian summer' of composition, the first two works, dating from this summer is Ischl, being the Clarinet Trio op.114 and the Clarinet Quintet op.115.

137

After Meiningen Brahms went to Frankfurt to visit Clara. It was a disaster. Clara was worried about Ferdinand far away in Gera (he died on 6 June); and she was also depressed by her uncertain hearing. She confessed to her diary on 20 March, the day Brahms came, that 'my hearing is so bad that I . . . cannot follow the working out of any piece, as the harmonies are all blurred . . . I often have to play the bass in the treble register before I can make out the harmonies.' We are brought up short by this bold sentence: 'Brahms came, but I at once fell into a violent altercation with him.' In the same entry she writes: 'His new quintet is exquisite.' On 27 March 'Brahms left. It was a release, but a melancholy one. The last eight days have been like a nightmare.' She wrote to Brahms for his birthday, 'but with a heavy heart, for I cannot forget what happened'.

Brahms went to Ischl in mid-May, and soon thereafter sent Simrock what purported to be his 'will', subsequently declared to be invalid for imprecision. One of his requests was to be cremated. Another, typically, ordered all letters and unfinished work found in his house to be destroyed. There was almost nothing for an executor to do about compositions, and the will as to the letters was not carried out by the executor, Dr Joseph Reitze of Vienna, who decided, with the approval of many, that it was in the public interest to keep almost all of them. Apart from the Clarinet Trio and Quintet, there were other works in this period of newly-found creativity. As early as June Brahms was writing to Clara:

> It is wonderfully beautiful and pleasant here, and, as I have often said before, I am made most happy by the charming people about me. Of the many and sundry musical fancies that flit through my brain not much will survive, though a little may. And if, for example, in a week or so six solo quartets, including one piano part, should lie in fair copy before me I shall be tempted to send them to you, as I believe they might give you pleasure . . .

This refers to op.112. In the next month he tells her that he has 'enriched life with another crop of summer fruit (which incidentally includes quite a pleasant collection of canons for women's voices).' Thus we can date op.113 as well, at least as to completion. Clara's son, Ferdinand, as we have seen, died on 6 June, and accentuated her sense of powerlessness, both in her art and her life.

> The doctors declared that his constitution had been so much undermined by his constant use of narcotics, that had he lived longer, his life would have been even more miserable than it had been before.

Well might the poor lady ask why she had to bring children into the world to watch them die. Recuperating at Berchtesgaden in August she is able to tell Brahms:

> Frau Herzogenberg is much better. How glad I am! Her doctor, who is here now, declared that she was so bad that for a while she was at death's door. I am

not sure that the unbridled ambition of this good lady [that is, for her husband] does not do her a lot of harm by keeping her in a constant state of agitation.

Doubtless most wives have always had ambitions for their husbands down the ages, but Brahms's milieu, and, by and large, his public, seems peopled to a remarkable degree by knowledgeable, socially adept, idealistic, assured female arbitrators, equating the morally acceptable with the artistically acceptable. If Wagner and Bruckner are deemed outsiders they are outside, and so much the worse for them. To serve a large middle class which knows and practises music and is passionate about it, stood Brahms in excellent stead all his life, but when Clara and Elisabet make no bones about saying what they like and dislike about the works of a composer who has a century of publications to his credit, it is no wonder that there are occasional altercations. One cannot imagine Frau Mozart or Frau Haydn ever behaving in such a way, or wishing to.

Brahms must have composed with his usual speed, because as early as July he wrote to Baroness von Heldburg that he would bring the clarinet pieces (Trio and Quintet) to Meiningen for rehearsals and performance there in late November. Joachim's quartet (with Hausmann also for the Trio) were essential for the enterprise, and they both asked Brahms not to worry about getting them engagements with the orchestra, for instance the Double Concerto, assuring him that coming for the chamber music was reward enough. Brahms had described the pieces to the Baroness—'your pieces' he called them—as decidedly difficult, and for once he was accurate, not teasing, in his choice of adjective.

Before this rendez-vous took place there had been a written altercation with Clara, about the publication of the first version of Schumann's D minor Symphony. He had thought he had secured Clara's agreement that the first version and the later re-scoring should be published side by side. Brahms's musical judgement was entirely correct, namely that the re-scoring was a safety-first, thick affair, brought about by the mediocre standards of the then Düsseldorf orchestra. To Brahms the obvious corollary was publication of the orchestral parts as well. Either impatiently or carelessly, or because he genuinely thought Clara had agreed, he gave the matter to his friend Wüllner, with a view to securing early publication and performance. It is hard to believe Clara's angry protestations that he had proceeded in the whole matter without any reference to her. (One must gather this from Brahms's reply, her letter of protest not having survived.) If Clara had thought her financial interests had been disregarded, Brahms replied rather trenchantly: 'The fact that I did not take your interests into consideration, you will surely easily forgive, when you realise you could have gotten very little out of it anyhow.' The letter breathes more defiance than comfort. A two-month silence was broken by a conciliatory Christmas greeting from Brahms, reciprocated by Clara, and achieving a truce soon to be broken.

Meanwhile things had gone so well at Meiningen that Joachim had there and then proposed, and Brahms accepted, that the works should figure in the Berlin chamber concert season in the Singakademie, at the concert on 12 December. Brahms wrote to both Simrock and Hanslick of the coming loss of virginity of the Joachim Quartet by the irruption of piano and clarinet on the string scene. The adagio of the quintet was an enormous success, with its muted strings and Hungarianisms. Brahms had for once been sanguine and pleased in anticipation, for he had written to Clara in July, again not over-tactfully:

> It is a pity that owing to the need of so much transposition [of the clarinet part] you cannot read the pieces. For there are some that you would certainly want to repeat at once!? (I am thinking of a very soft adagio).

While in Berlin Brahms stayed with the Simrocks, but he hurried back with Joachim to Vienna for what had been an annual event since 1887, a musicians' dinner on Beethoven's birthday, 16 December.[1] Just before his death on 18 November, 1887, Marxsen had given enough money 'to add a glass of champagne', but that meant he died before he himself had had a single such dinner. On 17 December the Clarinet Trio had its first Vienna performance, given by the clarinettist Syrinek, Hellmesberger and Brahms.

The beginning of 1892 was marked by pleasure and immediate sorrow. On 5 January the first Vienna performance of the Clarinet Quintet was given by Steiner and the Rosé Quartet, a success celebrated at supper afterwards in the 'Red Hedgehog'. On the 7 January Brahms received a telegram from San Remo to say that Elisabet was dead. Her weak heart had succumbed to the strains not so much of promoting her husband as of nursing him while her 'queen-bee' life slipped away from her. Heinrich was shattered, but so was Brahms. In his condolence letter he truly said:

> It is vain to attempt any expression of the feelings that absorb me so completely. And you will be sitting alone in your dumb misery, speechless yourself and not desirous of speech from others . . . You know how unutterably I myself suffer by the loss of your beloved wife, and can gauge accordingly my emotions in thinking of you, who were associated with her by the closest possible human ties.

Brahms's resilience must have been helped by another performance in Vienna of the Clarinet Quintet, this time by Mühlfeld and the Joachim Quartet on 19 January, only a fortnight after the previous one. Joachim and Mühlfeld then took the work to England. For the Quintet they added Straus, Ries and Piatti, and for the trio used the pianist Fanny Davies, making a successful career with Joachim's frequent encouragement. She had in fact been Clara's pupil at the Frankfurt Conservatoire. Mühlfeld being unknown in England, the concert agent Samuel Chappell had been unable to get the engagements requested by him to justify the expense of getting him there. The 'angel' who put his hand in his pocket was that same Adolph Behrens, now an invalid, who long ago had offered to pay for copying and performance costs of the *Requiem*. Joachim's letter from London of 5 April tells of three performances of the Quintet, the last completely sold out. Miss Davies had played a splendid part in the Trio, which had two performances.

Meanwhile Clara on 1 February had a severe inflammation of the lungs. This on top of other recent illnesses caused her to send her resignation, from her sickbed, of her post at the Frankfurt Conservatoire. Apart from the tendency to rheumatism which sometimes precluded her from playing for any length of time—and sometimes stopped her writing—she had an almost incessant buzzing in her ears.

In the course of this year Brahms developed a close friendship with the mezzo-soprano singer Alice Barbi, set in train by her public performances of some of his songs—and one of them, 'Vor dem Fenster', the first of op.14 came to be particularly associated with her. Although Italian, she was not an opera singer. She was then 28 years old, and already well-travelled, having had considerable success in London before Brahms came to know her. As was the way with some mezzo-sopranos, she captivated him with both voice and person. She was flattered by his flirtations and was kind to him.

In April Brahms was earnestly begged by Spitta to join the committee responsible for the newly started series of *Denkmäler Deutscher Tonkunst* (Monuments of German Music). Its first volume, received with delight, was quite sufficient to persuade him. It was the collection of keyboard pieces, mainly for organ, called *Tablatura nova*, by Samuel Scheidt, dating from 1624. His happy summer in Ischl was spent with this and the latest volume of Schütz flanking the treasure of many years' seeking, at last secured by Simrock's efforts, the full score of Bizet's *Carmen*. He went to Ischl on 21 May, but earlier in the month at Karlsgasse 'in spite of all my protestations they have installed electric light in my rooms'. His Ischl happiness, 'all in blue and green', was darkened by the death of his sister Elise in Hamburg on 11 June. He told Clara that Elise 'lay desperately ill the whole winter . . . We who were watching could not help wishing for the end long ago.' Clara was quick to sympathise, from Interlaken, where she had gone to recuperate with her daughter Marie. She alluded to what probably no-one else except Simrock knew: 'You have the great comfort of knowing that you made her life easy and sunny both through your brotherly help and your art.'

Such composition as there was reverted to piano solo music. The one certainty is that the two sets ultimately called Fantasias (op.116) and Intermezzi (op.117), totalling ten pieces, were published by Simrock in November of this year (1892), but as usual we have to remember that this sort of short work, like songs, was sometimes kept unissued for a long time. The letters serve to confuse the issue, because at the beginning of the year Brahms sent Clara what he called 'a little further instalment, assuming that it will not be regarded with less favour than the first'. But there is no acknowledgement extant by which we might identify what is referred to. On the other hand in mid-October she acknowledges 'wonderfully original pianoforte pieces', which certainly was a fitting phrase, but it does not sound as though those she now mentions correspond to the January 'instalment'. The explanation must lie in Brahms having after all decided that some, perhaps a good number, of the earlier pieces sent to Clara were not fit to publish at the final consideration. At any rate the consummate artistry in the terse forms, the imaginative but never unpianistic fingerwork required, and the constant variety of colour and mood, make them, in retrospect, a huge step in an unpredictable direction. As soon as Simrock saw the first of op.117 with its superscription 'Schlaf sanft, mein Kind' ('Sleep soft, my child') he could compare it to the 'Wiegenlied' for Frau Faber of more than 20 years before (in the same key) and knew he had a winner on his hands. Brahms had given Mandyczewski a typical reason for turning to the piano: 'here there are many lady pianists, and you reckon that they like mouths full and fingers full'.

Brahms returned to Vienna in mid-September and the verbal altercation flared up again with further recriminations from Clara about the Schumann edition, supposedly put to rest long ago. According to the extant letters (no very secure guide in matters like this) Brahms strikes first in a letter purporting to celebrate her birthday:

> Please allow a poor pariah to tell you today that he always thinks of you with the same respect . . . Alas, to you more than to any other I am a pariah; this has, for a long time, been my painful conviction, but I never expected it to be so harshly expressed . . . In my dealings with my friends I am aware of only one fault—my lack of tact. For years now you have been kind enough to treat this leniently. If only you could have done so for a few years more! After 40 years of faithful service (or whatever you care to call my relationship with you) it is very hard to be 'another unhappy experience'.

To which Clara replies (27 September):

> You reproach me with having shown you too little consideration in connection with the Schumann edition . . . If I offended you, you should have told me openly and not have given free rein to the base suspicion that I did not like to see your name connected with Robert's. Such a thought could only have occurred to you in an evil hour.

At the beginning of October Brahms sent as a peace offering 'a volume of piano pieces' but having apologised for his tongue he could not resist worrying away like a dog at the 'Schumann altercation'. On 13 October Clara thanked him for the wonderful pieces, and also could not resist worrying away like a dog at the 'Schumann altercation'. Only with the Christmas exchange of letters was peace declared.

It is in the letters to Simrock, as ever, that we return to the world of business, of jokes and of ordinary life. We learn for instance that Hamburg suffered harshly from cholera in the autumn, and that Brahms ascertaining that his fellow-Freeman Bismarck had given 1000 Marks to the fund, gave

500 keeping a respectful distance, but dealing handsomely all the same. Later, it transpires that the honorary doctorate was again offered from Cambridge—and to Verdi at the same time. Verdi refused as being too old; Brahms told Simrock with intentional ambiguity that the honorarium (Simrock's?) was too small for the expense of the journey. The doctorate fell to Max Bruch.

Brahms had one more honorific concert engagement this year. A new Bechstein Hall had been built in Berlin and was opened with three consecutive concerts, the first on 4 October being given by Bülow, the second by Brahms and Joachim, the third by Rubinstein. Joachim brought colleagues to the joint concert and the programme was the Sextet op.18, the D minor Violin Sonata op.108 and the Clarinet Quintet op.115. Brahms and Joachim attended Bülow's recital, but he was in such a state of nervous exhaustion that he could not meet them.

Through Simrock's kind offices (kind offices were his *forte*) Frau Truxa's boys received at Christmas a copy of Grimm's *Fairy Tales*.

By 1893 the easing out of concert life had become conspicuous. Brahms paid a visit to Meiningen at the end of January, but its main object was not music, but to attend a performance of his friend Widmann's comedy (full of scenic tricks) *Jenseits von Gut und Böse* ('Beyond good and evil'). The title had been used by Nietzsche some eight years before, and obviously lent itself to the lampooning of a philosopher almost universally regarded as a dangerous iconoclast. True, he had fallen out of love with Wagner, but had also been rude about Brahms. There was of course some music at Meiningen as well, nothing less than the Clarinet Quintet with Mühlfeld, 'my prima donna' as Brahms called him.

The next call was on Clara at Frankfurt, made expressly to get back on the old terms of affection and mutual respect. Clara viewed the prospect with some misgiving. Her diary for 31 January records:

> Brahms comes today. How anxious I feel at heart! If only we could frankly discuss all that has happened during the past year, and that has distressed me so much, but with him this is impossible, he gets so violent that one is reduced to silence.

However, this is the last critical or unfriendly word for the whole year 1893, whether in diary or correspondence. Much was due to the solicitous and flattering sending to her of the manuscripts, sometimes one by one, of the new piano pieces, and to Clara's realisation that her health and her technique were improving enough for her to master them, though she could only manage, on most days, two half-hour bursts of practice. In March Clara at last heard a live performance of the Clarinet Quintet, with Mühlfeld, at Frankfurt, and was bowled over. This time Brahms did not neglect a letter of thanks, and ingratiated himself thanks to poor Bruckner, referring to the constant sounds in Clara's ears:

How many in these days would not find pleasure in what to you is insupportable agony. Our great Bruckner would be only too delighted to have your odious hummings in his ears. We should then get them on Sundays in the form of symphonies, and Heyse and Levi would write appreciative criticisms about them!

From Frankfurt Brahms had gone to Hamburg to set family matters in order after his sister's death, any home-sickness he might have felt being completely washed away by 'genuine Hamburg weather'. He then went on a social visit to Berlin, meeting among others Herzogenberg and Marie Soldat. He was saddened by the death in February of Hermine Spies in Wiesbaden.

In April, with the usual instructions to his friend about 'Caporal' cigarettes, Brahms met Widmann and two musicians from Zürich, Robert Freund (pianist) and Friedrich Hegar (conductor) for a tour in Italy. It was his eighth and last visit, and this time Sicily was achieved. Having described the long railway journey down Italy as a torture, Brahms when confronted with the alternative by sea elected for the lesser torture by land, thereby supporting the supposition that it was the English Channel which came between him and his Cambridge doctorate. They visited Genoa, Naples, Sorrento, Palermo, Girgenti, Catania, Syracuse, Taormina and Messina. There Widmann came within an inch of his life. On a ship which was to take them to Naples he was almost knocked into the hold by a load swinging from a crane, but was saved from a death-fall by being trapped, swinging between life and death, by an iron ring, which, however, broke his left leg. He went to Naples nonetheless, and Brahms contentedly nursed him there while the other two went on the excursion to Pompeii. When Widmann was fit enough, Hegar escorted him back to Berne, while Freund and Brahms went to Venice on the way back. Having succeeded in being away for his actual sixtieth birthday Brahms found waiting for him in Vienna the congratulations of the Mayor, the City and the University, and 'many more than 50 telegrams and countless letters'. The Gesellschaft der Musikfreunde had a gold medal struck for him with replicas for him to give his friends. Clara refused his offer of exchanging his gold for her replica. But he did manage to give a birthday present to her, marking *his* birthday, when he was settled in Ischl again in mid-May.

> I am tempted to have a short piece of music copied for you, as I should very much like to know how you get on with it. It teems with discords . . . It is exceptionally melancholy, and to say 'to be played very slowly' is not sufficient. Every bar and every note must be played as if *ritardando* were indicated, and one wished to draw the melancholy out of each one of them, and voluptuous joy and comfort out of the discords. My God, how this description will whet your appetite!

He did send it, and Clara loved it. 'One actually revels in the discords, and, when playing them, wonders how the composer ever brought them to birth.' Pianists thus have a precious and authoritative lesson in how to play op.119

no.1. It does not sound in the least like 'all passion spent'. Clara eloquently called it 'a grey pearl'. She also enjoyed and mastered the E flat Rhapsody, Brahms's last piano solo work, commenting on its 'Hungarian' five-bar phrases.

Later in the summer Brahms teasingly compared himself in Ischl with Clara in Interlaken. 'The only thing to be said [in his favour] is that on the whole the accessories to be landscape are more pleasant. Instead of Swiss people and Englishmen I have Austrians.' As with the previous year, the published fruits of this summer's completions were two sets of keyboard pieces opp.118 and 119. Each of the ten pieces has its individual title, but for a designation of each set Brahms could not, or would not, think of anything more exciting than 'Six Pieces' and 'Four Pieces' respectively. There was one other keyboard publication during the year, the set of 51 keyboard Exercises (*Übungen*). They had no opus number, because they were not pieces of music, not even to the extent implied by study or étude. They are pieces for mechanics, some of them very demanding. Brahms was amused and appreciative when he heard from Clara that she had ticked those which her pupils should play, and thus identified what they should *not* attempt. Another 'publication' greatly to whet the appetite were some proof copies of some of the extraordinary suite of pictures called 'Brahms Fantasies' which the artist Klinger had sent to Brahms at the year's end. But nearly a year more elapsed before the whole work was finally printed.

Just before Christmas Brahms surprisingly emerged on to the public stage in Vienna. Alice Barbi gave a farewell concert (before leaving the profession on her marriage) on 21 December. Her programme included four of Brahms's best songs: 'An die Nachtigall' ('To the nightingale') op.46 no.4, 'Der Tod, das ist die kühle Nacht' ('Death, that is the cool night') op.96 no.1, 'Ich muss hinaus' ('I must away') op.3 no.3, and 'Meine Liebe is grün' ('My love is green') op.63 no.7. Unannounced, Brahms came on to the platform and played for the whole recital.

Throughout 1894 there is little or no concert work directly involving Brahms to report. With most musical administration out of the way his many other interests show through in the correspondence. These interests were always there, of course, but now books, theatres, paintings, history and *belles lettres* seize the vacant places. Widmann and Simrock are the chief suppliers, the former with surprises out of the blue which always seem to judge to a nicety what will stimulate his friend, the latter more often the patient researcher and provider of old books and music at Brahms's own instigation. If it is a case of finding a seemingly out-of-print book or piece Brahms almost always is able to behave like an efficient modern scholar, with the correct title and author, the date and original publisher. As might be expected, he is repelled by the meretricious; a cause cannot be a good one helped thus. Writing to Widmann from Vienna on 6 January he expresses his disgust at seeing the famous *ingenue* actress Stella Hohenfels simpering her way through 'a travesty of the old sincere Christmas plays, done in our concert-hall with electric-light effects'.

He must have felt himself suddenly more lonely when in February he suffered the deaths of Billroth, on 6 February at Abbazia, on the Adriatic south of Trieste, and of Bülow, on 12 February at Cairo. Billroth was the perfect friend and tireless supporter, his mind brimful of eternal things. It is hard to gauge by this yardstick whether Bülow was a friend at all. A self-tormented genius of the baton and the keyboard, he had, at a crucial time, ensured Brahms's first-class ranking by first-class performances, yet in the years immediately before Bülow's death the unsettling of his mind had driven him away to Egypt in a fruitless search the purpose of which entirely eluded Brahms and his friends. In these years Brahms did not know how or whether to approach him. A funeral wreath seemed an inadequate formality, and Brahms, who did not wish to impose himself on the funeral, got Simrock to make handsome donations 'from J.B.' to the pension funds of the two regular orchestras, excluding the private Meiningen one, with which Bülow had been mainly associated, the Philharmonics of Hamburg and Vienna. Characteristically he wanted the widow to know this, in his absence, but for the press not to know: he did not want a story made of the deed. Needless to say, the contortions of Brahms's instructions meant that though the donations occurred, the semi-secrecy was unachievable, as might have been realised at the outset, when all that was required was a straightforward letter to the widow.

On 20 March Brahms heard in Vienna his *Requiem*, conducted by Wilhelm Gericke, for what turned out to be the last time, and was greatly moved by it. Nor was Death's obtrusive presence ready yet to withdraw, for on 13 April the great music historian and editor Spitta died, almost at the moment when a parcel from Brahms, asking for comments, arrived at his house in Berlin. At Brahms's request to Hausmann, through Simrock, the packet was retrieved and sent to Clara. The contents, which Simrock already had sampled, were either then or shortly afterwards no less than 49 German folksongs collected at various dates, all supplied with economical but most telling piano accompaniments. Brahms arranged them for publication in seven volumes each of seven songs. The first 42 are for single voice, but the last seven add *ad lib* four-part choruses. The last song of all, 'Verstohlen geht der Mond auf' is the very song which was the basis of the slow movement of the Piano Sonata op.1. This, as Brahms pointed out, to Clara as well as Simrock, could well be a symbol, like the serpent biting its own tail, 'that the tale is told, the circle is closed'. But he has not been to Ischl yet this year and furthermore a letter to Clara shows him still in Vienna on 6 May: 'Hausmann and Mühlfeld are here and we are getting a good deal of recreation.' Therefore, it is not a surprise to learn from Ischl that the tale is not yet told. 'I know what good resolutions are, and I only think of them and do not say them aloud to myself.'

What the recreations of Vienna were, beside music, can be glimpsed, together with the picture of his bachelor home, in a charming account preserved for us in the memoirs of George Henschel:

> My wife and I travelled to Vienna, in 1894, for the sole purpose of spending a few days in Brahms's company . . . On our arrival rather late in the evening of 23 April, we found a note awaiting us at our hotel: 'If not too tired after your journey, do come to us, quite close by, at the restaurant of the Musikverein; just as you are, informally, in your travelling clothes.' Who could resist the temptation? Arrived at the indicated place, we found a little party of men and women, mostly members of the Musikverein (Musicians' Society) gathered together in a social way, as usual, after one of their weekly concerts. Brahms, surrounded, as always on such occasions, by a host of admiring ladies, young and elderly, in regard to those charms and homage his susceptibilities had not by any means lessened with the advancing years, was in excellent spirits and gave us a most cordial welcome.

One thinks of Bach, having scaled his heights, relaxing with university students at Leipzig beside the Pleisse River. The domestic scene speaks of Frau Truxa without mentioning her:

> Early the following morning we went to his rooms. He received us, as was his wont with friends, irrespective of sex, attired in a short jacket of which the lowest button only was put to its proper use; without waistcoat or shirt collar, and in slippers. The coffee-machine—he always made his own coffee in the morning—was still standing on the table; the air of the large, yet cosy room was filled with the delicious fragrance peculiar to Viennese coffee; the sun shone brightly through the large windows and the whole atmosphere was one of quiet, inward happiness, contentment and ease.

Lest this feels altogether too Elysian, there was opportunity for a malicious glint of the blue eyes:

> Smilingly and with mock ceremony, he opened a large portfolio and read to us, with great gusto, the famous letters of Richard Wagner to the milliner. He had brought the collection recently and seemed very proud of the precious possession, chuckling with amusement as he went from one amazing letter to another.

Before going to Ischl in mid-May, Brahms was offered the conductorship of the Hamburg Philharmonic concerts on the retirement of Bernuth. What might this not have meant 30 years before! But now Brahms could be polite and clear-sighted, telling them 'You want some-one of younger powers, and not an intermezzo!'

The two Clarinet Sonatas op.120 were both completed in Ischl this summer. Mühlfeld was unable to come there for a try-out of them but was lured to Berchtesgaden instead on 19 September, Brahms adding a sense of solicitude by requesting only his B flat instrument, not the clarinet in A. From Ischl came Brahms and the Steinbachs, and from Gastein came Princess Marie and others of the Meiningen court. Through this organised overhearing

Brahms's last two chamber works were heard for the first time. An Indian summer of composition this may be, as long as it is recognised as a quick relighting of fires. 'All passion spent' is a travesty of a description. Indeed both sonatas have movements marked *allegro appassionato*, and explicit calls for passion are only to be found before this in two of the great range of chamber works. The calm of mind which Milton links with spent passion may also be doubted here. The mental excitement of the intense and unifying motive-work of the second sonata must rub off on any listener who is minded to penetrate below its lyrical surface.

A letter to Simrock from Ischl (17 September) floats an idea which came to nothing. 'I have thought now and then of putting together several piano pieces to make a sort of larger rhapsody for orchestra.' The mind in charge of the structure of the clarinet sonatas altogether rules out the possibility that the orchestral works, if proceeded with, would be *pot-pourri* or rehashes. Clearly Brahms was even now willing to bring new forms to life. Having again said, or rather asked whether Simrock has realised, that he has clearly made his farewell as a composer, he cannot resist another tease: 'You do not want two clarinet sonatas . . . I could well give them to Dr Abraham [of Peters] as a parting gift. After all you have seven volumes which can and will appear in 77 arrangements.'

Clara did not get an advance copy of the sonatas 'because the constant transposition [of the clarinet part] would make it difficult for you'. But increasingly deaf though she was, she was to have the joy of a command performance at Frankfurt which she had not commanded. But before that Brahms returned on 25 September to Vienna and there joined tirelessly in the festivities celebrating Johann Strauss and his golden jubilee of public appearance. The festival lasted from 12 to 29 October, no less. The performance for Clara took place in her house—four performances indeed, according to her diary. Mühlfeld had sent his tuning-fork in advance, as neither he nor his clarinet tolerated the increasingly high pitches then becoming common. She 'could only hear parts of the sonatas; I could only follow the simplest combinations; as soon as the harmonies became complicated I heard nothing but chaos. You can fancy that this made me very sad. But I know enough to realise that they are once more masterpieces.' Joachim was also at these trial performances, having played the Violin Concerto at an all-Brahms concert in the Museum series in Frankfurt. Clara's letter to her friend Rosalie Leser (dated 17 November) implies that the programme became all-Brahms, conducted by Gustav Kogel, when it was known that he would be there. Brahms sat by her and at the end he was called to the platform with great enthusiasm. In the course of the visit 'Joachim gave another chamber concert, but I did not hear it as I wished to spare myself the [mis-hearing] tortures— but it made my heart ache to stay at home.' After the visit Mühlfeld and Brahms went for a happy week to the country seat of the rulers of Meiningen, Schloss Altenstein in the Thüringer Wald. Here they gave the command performances promised after Princess Marie had heard them at Berchtesga-den in September. In a letter to Simrock (19 November) Brahms speaks of the delightful walks in the forest, accompanied by pheasants, fallow deer and red deer. He returned to Vienna on 21 November, and the year-end was much enlivened for him by the brilliance of Dvořák's 'Carnival' Overture, played at a Vienna Philharmonic concert on 9 December.

Though the clarinet sonatas were published in score in the following year, with alternative parts for viola (and indeed as violin sonatas a month later) string players will get little comfort out of Brahms's clear words to Joachim (17 October, 1894): 'I fear that as viola sonatas both pieces are very awkward and unenjoyable.'

Brahms and Mühlfeld took the sonatas on their travels at the beginning of 1895. They were both given their first public performances in Vienna in the chamber concerts organised by Rosé, the E flat on 8 January and the F minor on 11 January. On 20 January Brahms was cheered by an excellent perform-ance of the Third Symphony, under Richter with the Vienna Philharmonic, and then set out for Berlin where the clarinet sonatas were due. However, Mühlfeld had to telegraph that he had 'lost his lip'. Brahms was persuaded to carry out the visit nevertheless, and earned great applause when his op.111 Quintet was substituted. Mühlfeld had recovered in time for both sonatas to be introduced to Leipzig on 27 January. However, perhaps the greater pleasure for Brahms was an extraordinary concert, of which he had fore-warned Clara:

> I must go to Leipzig at the end of January and—show your indignation!-conduct my two concertos for d'Albert on the same evening. I do not think it is in very good taste, but the programme is fixed, and, in good mood, I thought it would be better to give myself the pleasure—which would certainly be none to Reinecke [the regular conductor].

Another letter to Clara afterwards shows a happy man—even, at last, being happy with some lionisation. It was

> one of the most pleasant concert adventures that I have ever had . . . Herr Kraft (of the Hôtel-de-Prusse) treated me like a prince but charged me as he would a poor peasant . . . d'Albert received 200 Marks more than he usually gets from the directors, and I who had only counted on a round sum for my travelling expenses received 2000 Marks!

Not only that, but he also received an orchestral fanfare and a laurel wreath. Two concertos were not the end of it. There was the Academic Festival as the 'final overture' and also 'intermediate items' by the singer, 'a really most delightful young girl who sang them excellently'. At a Leipzig party he encountered a banjo played by a lively young American girl. 'Now he knew' (says Kalbeck) 'where friend Dvořák got his American tunes from.'

Brahms was back in Clara's house on 13 February 'in a very amiable mood' which was not disturbed when Mühlfeld did not arrive for a rehearsal because no one had told him. Instead he rehearsed the G minor Piano Quartet, which was given the next day at Mannheim. He came back 'laden with laurels, favours and poems'. On 15 February there was the Museum concert at Frankfurt, with the Quartet again and both Clarinet Sonatas, and a 'very lively' supper at Clara's afterwards. Mühlfeld added to the gaiety the following night with Weber's F minor Concerto. On the next day, Sunday 17 February, she let herself be persuaded by Brahms to go to the Symphony concert. It was almost not a 'symphony' concert as far as Brahms was concerned, for he miscalculated the time and slipped in late for his Second Symphony. But 'at the conclusion he conducted his Academic Overture magnificently, and the enthusiasm was great'. The next day Brahms spent at the home of Frau von Beckerath at Rüdesheim, the next at Clara's for a very jovial dinner with some men, and then on the 20 February he went to Meiningen for further celebrations in his honour, including a special performance of *Fidelio*. He so enjoyed this that he went to all three performances. There were two more launches of the clarinet sonatas, at Merseburg on 21 February and at Meiningen on 25 February, then Mühlfeld took the sonatas with him (but without Brahms) to tours of Switzerland, the Netherlands and England. A grateful composer gave him the original autographs, inscribed 'to Herr Richard Mühlfeld, the master of his beautiful instrument, in cordial and thankful memory'. It was only now, having given Mühlfeld a sole use of the works hitherto, that Brahms gave a fair copy to Simrock for printing.

On three successive nights the Berlin Philharmonic gave concerts in Vienna. For some reason Brahms viewed the prospect with foreboding. On the 2 April the symphony was Beethoven's Seventh, conducted by Richard Strauss, then 30 years old. On the 6 April Felix Mottl, 39 years old, conducted the 'Eroica'. But the middle concert was conducted by Felix Weingartner, then 32 but still bearing the reputation of an *enfant terrible* thanks to a tearaway youth spent on the excitements of Liszt, Berlioz and Wagner. His symphony was Brahms's Second, and he won Brahms's heart by delivering it with warmth and passion, the explicit display of which qualities worried those who set Brahms up as a model of praiseworthy restraint. Brahms wrote to tell Simrock that the orchestra was made to stand to acknowledge applause after the first movement, and that the third movement was encored. The delighted agent, Guttman, threw them all a party breakfast at Schönbrunn afterwards.

What turned out to be Brahms's last appearance as a conductor in Vienna was at a concert by Conservatoire students on 18 March, the Academic Festival Overture very suitably bridging the one-and-a-half-generation gap.

Brahms went to Ischl in mid-May. Unless another heap of manuscript paper which we do not know about was thrown into the Traun, there is no composition to record—apart from the possibility of some of the Chorale Preludes op.122. He did, however, spend time and energy on getting manuscripts from Clara into a publishable state. She had contracted with Novello to produce a selection of Robert's *Studies and Sketches*, originally for pedal piano, arranged for ordinary piano. Clara was very disconcerted to realise her own inadequacies as a mistake-spotter, but Brahms set to work with a good will, and rejoiced to think of the money she would get from his work. He might for once have been writing the truth about composition in a letter to her in June. Talking of still-born (or nearly so) works by Rubinstein (*Christ*), Bruch (*Moses*) and Herzogenberg (*Birth of Christ*) he writes:

> The only pleasant feature of it all is if one can, as I think I can, thank God from having saved me from the sin, the vice, or the bad habit, of merely covering paper with notes.

Another Ischl activity was helping his friend Viktor von Miller zu Aichholtz[2] to organise a seventieth birthday feast at Gumunden for Hanslick on 11 September. In a letter to Simrock shortly afterwards Brahms, himself no slouch in such matters, found Hanslick's 'consumption capacity astounding'.

Then he went to his own celebration at Meiningen at the end of September, with five concerts in three days organised and conducted by Steinbach. The 'three Bs' were the sole composers represented. Steinbach had assembled 346 in the main choir, 40 semi-chorus, 75 in the boys' choir, and 91 in the orchestra. Among the audiences drawn from all over Europe was a friend of Brahms, Joachim and Clara, Edward Speyer, now an English businessman who did much for the dissemination of Brahms's music. On 3 October with the Speyers and others Brahms made a happy visit (which turned out to be the last) to Clara at Frankfurt. The last recorded dialogue between them, was, according to Kalbeck:

> Clara: 'What are you going to do with all that tobacco?'
> Brahms: 'Smuggle it.'

After a brief spell in Vienna Brahms left on 15 October for the music festival in Zürich. He was the guest of the conductor, Friedrich Hegar, but in effect also guest of honour to the festival, which had been arranged to celebrate the opening of a new concert hall. This festal opening took place on 20 October, and the first notes heard in public were the 'Triumphlied' conducted by Brahms himself. Brahms could, to his mind, have no greater honour than that his piece should be the overture, so to speak, to Beethoven's Choral Symphony, conducted by Hegar. Widmann was there, for some time now a victim of severe rheumatism, which came between Brahms and a further joint expedition to Italy, which he wistfully contemplated several times, but was not willing to undertake by himself.

Brahms went to Berlin for his last appearance as a conductor, presenting on 10 January the same double bill of d'Albert playing both Piano Concertos. Joachim celebrated the occasion with a dinner for them. Curiously enough, the conductor Nikisch persuaded Brahms to come to Leipzig on 16 January to hear his Fourth Symphony. Brahms found the performance 'exemplary; one could not hear it better played'. However, in the same letter (to Simrock, 27 January) he says how all cellists can be grateful to Dvořák for writing so great and capable (*tüchtig*) a concerto for them. (They certainly are.) We can draw on Henschel[3] again for a happy picture:

> In January 1896 Brahms, Edvard Grieg, Arthur Nikisch and myself spent a delightful evening together at one of the favourite restaurants of Leipzig. Brahms, rather stouter, it seemed to me, than I had ever seen him before, was in the merriest of moods and did ample justice to the excellent beer of Munich brew, of which he consumed an astounding quantity before we parted, long after midnight.

Back in Vienna Brahms and Dvořák sat in the same box at the Vienna Philharmonic concert on 16 February which included the first performance of the 'New World' Symphony. To add to Simrock's happiness Brahms told him that the symphony was 'enormously successful'. Another happy event was the furore caused by the 13-year-old Bronislav Hubermann playing the Violin Concerto. He played the cadenza—presumably Joachim's—so beautifully that the audience went on clapping during the soft music at its end.

However, a cloud abruptly descended. Clara suffered a slight stroke at her home in Frankfurt on 26 March, having felt ill for most of the month. Brahms wrote to her daughter Marie:

> Although at a time like this I should like to do everything possible to spare your feelings, it cannot be helped, and with a heavy heart I must ask you, if you think the worst is to be expected, to be so good as to let me know, so that I may come while those dear eyes are still open; for when they close so much will end for me!

However, there was an improvement, for some five weeks. Clara's last words to Brahms were written on his birthday, 7 May, after her grandchild Ferdinand had reminded her what day it was. Her greetings, in pencilled scrawl, read in literal translation thus: 'Heartiest good wishes from your affectionate and devoted Clara Schumann. I cannot very well do any more yet, but or soon—'. Brahms's last letter to her (8 May) begins: 'The last was the best—never has this maxim been brought home to me more beautifully than it has today when the dearest thing of all, your wishes for the 7th, arrived.' He is buoying her up in taking seriously her notion that she might be going to beloved Baden-Baden, and ends thus:

> You can have no idea how much you are in the thoughts of numberless people here! At all events I hope you will believe that none of them send you heartier greetings than your Johannes.

On that day Clara felt better and went out in her wheelchair to enjoy her summer garden. But on the night of 10 May she had suffered a more severe stroke, and died on the afternoon of the 20th. Brahms was by then in Ischl. He

Brahms's birthplace in Hamburg. Exactly which part of the tenement was Jakob Brahms's is uncertain, but Kalbeck had reason to suppose it was half of the first floor—on the viewer's left (*reproduced from* Ein Brahms Bilderbuch).

The beautiful 'young eagle' as the Schumanns first encountered him. The photograph (of a silverpoint drawing by the artist Laurens) was given by Brahms to Sir George Grove and wistfully inscribed '40 years later!'. *(The Royal College of Music)*

Brahms and a trusted interpreter, the singer Julius Stockhausen. *(The Royal College of Music)*

Clara Schumann, taken on one of her many English concert tours. *(The Royal College of Music)*

Robert Schumann, a drawing done by E. J. F. Bendemann in 1859, after a daguerrotype of 1850. *(The Royal College of Music)*

Joseph Joachim, violinist, composer and friend, as portrayed by E. J. F. Bendemann in 1870. *(The Royal College of Music)*

Brahms before the beard. *(The Royal College of Music)*

Two views of Brahms's music room in Karlsgasse. In the upper picture can be seen the table with its coffee-machine. On the wall opposite the piano is a bust of Beethoven and a bronze of Bismarck surrounded with a laurel wreath (earned and discarded by Brahms and put there by Frau Truxa). In the lower picture is Brahms's writing-desk and the piano whose lid, always shut, served as a surface both for everyday necessaries such as keys and spectacles and for occasional displays of mementos for lucky visitors. *(Reproduced from* Ein Brahms Bilderbuch*)*.

Brahms as an old man. *(The Royal College of Music)*

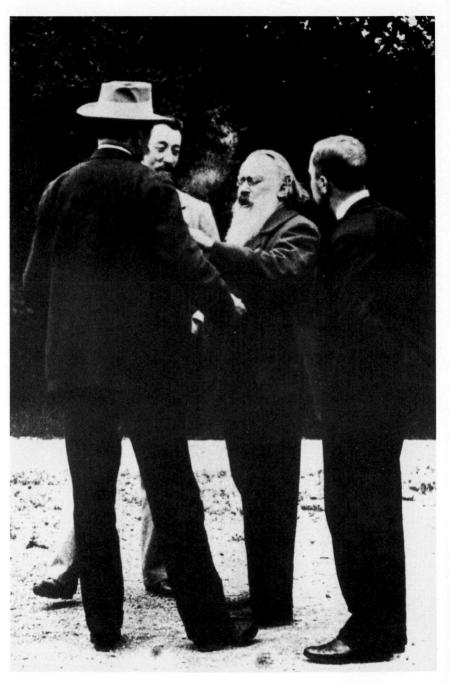

Brahms adding his voice to the sung tributes at Clara Schumann's funeral. *(The Royal College of Music)*

thus got the telegram late, and rushed off to make the awkward overnight journey to the Rhineland. The journey took on a nightmarish quality when Brahms somehow found out *en route* that the burial was not at Frankfurt but at Bonn, with Robert. He arrived just in time to join the family mourners and to cast in his three handfuls of earth.

Some premonitions—possibly a sudden sense of lassitude in his own body—had already turned his musical thoughts to death once more. On his birthday he had shown Kalbeck the manuscript of his *Four Serious Songs* and within a week he had offered them to Simrock for publication, calling them his 'Alpine Songs [*Schnadehüpfl*] of 7 May'. They are thus certainly not memorial songs to Clara, who at the time seemed to be getting better. It has been suggested that the last song, which sets part of St Paul's celebration of faith, hope and love in I Corinthians Chapter 13, was written some time before the other three. Its manuscript is on a different paper, printed with ten staves instead of nine. At first glance it is not closely related in key (E flat) to the other three (D minor, G minor/major, E minor/major) and its words do not relate to death as such, but are an answer to those who are looking through a glass darkly at the question 'why?'. If it were indeed written earlier, the fact remains that Brahms published it as an answer to the almost comfortless musings of the first three.

There seems no compelling reason to go beyond what Brahms himself had to say to Marie (7 July) in the last letter in Litzmann's collection, in a paragraph which takes us perhaps as far as Brahms himself ever got in expressing his thoughts on the well-springs of composition:

> If you should receive a volume of 'serious songs' in a few days' time, do not misunderstand it. Quite apart from my dear old habit of always writing your name first in such cases, these songs really concern you very closely. I wrote them in the first week of May. [N.B.] Some such words as these have long been in my mind, and I did not think that worse news about your mother was to be expected—but deep in the heart of man something often whispers and stirs, quite unconsciously perhaps, which in time may ring out in the form of poetry or music. You will not be able to play the songs yet, because the words would affect you too much, but I beg you to regard them and to lay them aside merely as a death offering to the memory of your dear mother.

The songs were therefore not a particular memorial, as for example they could have been, when they were written, to Elisabet. They could be thought of, perhaps, as a memorial in advance to himself.

However, organists in particular will have one further opus to point to, which truly can be thought of in this way, because it was published only after Brahms's death: the eleven Chorale Preludes op. 122. A letter to Simrock from Ischl on 30 June almost certainly connects this summer with the composition or re-composition of some of them. He asks to be sent his organ fugue on 'O Traurigkeit'. This work dates back to the years of contrapuntal study, probably to 1858, though it did not appear in print till 1882 in the magazine

Musikalisches Wochenblatt, with no opus number. Brahms in the letter simply calls it a fugue, but the latter is preceded by a choral prelude very much in keeping with some of those in op.122.

Brahms's health was already deteriorating. The exertions of Clara's funeral, and a chill which he fancied he caught there, caused symptoms which would not go away, notably a yellowing of his usually ruddy face. This was apparent to his friends the Fellingers, when he journeyed back to Vienna in mid-June for their silver wedding. Back in Ischl the 'jaundice' was again noticed but nothing was said. Eventually his friend Richard Heuberger on a visit from his summer lodging in Hallstatt nearby noticed that the yellowing had spread to his eyes, and plucked up courage to advise him to see a doctor. Brahms felt sufficiently ill to heed his friend, and saw Dr Hertzka, who ran a cold-water cure in Ischl; he confirmed jaundice. However, Brahms got himself thoroughly examined by a Dr Schrötter, a Vienna specialist summering nearby. Although Brahms thought himself reassured, Schrötter had not recommended a particular cure for what he deemed incurable. Brahms returned to Vienna at the end of August, then overnight on 3 September to Karlsbad into the care of Dr Grünberger; but he too recognised the incurable worst in the inflammation and swelling of the liver. He kept it from Brahms, who quickly came to like Karlsbad. He may even have done more work on the Chorale Preludes. The 'cure' at Karlsbad could naturally do nothing, and he returned to Vienna, to his own doctor, on 2 October. His diagnosis was certain, but not told to his patient—cancer, now eating away at the liver. He even put Brahms on a diet, but allowed a remission of it for Christmas. Frau Truxa, unknown to him, had altered his clothing so as to make it seem he was filling out. This made a special cause for rejoicing at Christmas at the Fellingers. He proposed a toast 'to our meeting in the New Year' but after an alarming and touching hesitation, he pointed downwards in an afterthought: 'But I shall soon be there.'

His letters of 1897 to Simrock continued to ask for books and to comment on politics in their old vein, and he tried, in spite of pain and lassitude, to give an impression of living his old life. He attended concerts by the Joachim Quartet on 1 and 2 January, the second containing a moving performance of the Quintet op.111. As late as mid-February Joachim, whom he was not to see again, sent a letter full of plans for a chamber music festival in May, and even asking, though not sanguinely, whether Brahms would consider playing in the Piano Quintet. Brahms's refusal was kindly; he still had the beautiful sound of op.111 in his ears, but he confessed to tiredness and feebleness (*Mattigkeit*), the same terms as he used to Simrock on 4 March.

On the 18 February a slight stroke had stiffened the left side of his face, but this had passed off early in March sufficiently for him to attend his last Philharmonic concert, at which Richter conducted the Fourth Symphony, to arouse an enormous demonstration of public affection. On 27 March Brahms put himself to bed. Other friends came and went, but Frau Truxa was his real confidante. In April his bowels bled, and in moments of delirium he had to be held down in his bed. His new doctor, Josef Breuer, relieved some of the pain as best he could with morphia. Breuer's son Robert, also a doctor, passed Brahms's last night with him. To Robert he said 'That tastes good', having drained a glass of hock in two gulps. His last words of all were to Frau Truxa: 'Thank you, thank you.' He died in the morning on 3 April.

By the time Henschel had arrived that afternoon, silver crosses, black velvet, brass candelabra and tall wax candles lent an inappropriate air to the scene, mitigated by hundreds of flowers. An enormous mass of silent people thronged the streets for the funeral on 6 April. A standard-bearer in old Spanish costume, riding on a black horse, headed the cortège. Henschel says that 'the sun, which had come out gloriusly by that time, shone, as it were, on a moving garden'. At the building of the Gesellschaft der Musikfreunde the Singverein took their leave with the simple haunting part-song, op.93a no.4, 'Fahr wohl' ('Fare well', or 'Safe journey'). There was a short service in the Protestant church in the Dorotheengasse. Then with Dvořák, Weingartner and Busoni amongst the mourners they took the body to the cemetery. Brahms had wanted to rest near Beethoven and Schubert, and he did.

NOTES

1.   One puts it thus, because this seems to be the Viennese dinner date, but strictly speaking the only certain date is that of baptism (17 December).

2.   He published the only comprehensive set of pictures relative to Brahms: *Ein Brahms Bilderbuch* (Vienna, 1905).

3.   G. Henschel, *Musings and Memories of a Musician* (Dent, London, 1918), p. 126.

CHAPTER SIX

The Sum of Brahms

The annotated catalogue which follows this chapter amounts to a large and wide-ranging corpus in every medium of the day except stage music. If we make a guess as to works written or part written and then destroyed we can hazard that Brahms put enough notes down on paper to have run up a second century of opus numbers for Simrock. Brahms whimsically complained of the altered times and of his inadequate powers in comparison with the great ones. Certainly his four symphonies and three string quartets do not occupy the space in a dictionary catalogue that do those of Haydn. However, there are crucial differences to invalidate the comparison. Only 18 of Haydn's symphonies are written for 'the public' in the sense that we and Brahms would understand it, and these, six for Paris, twelve for London, were composed for specific occasions. There is hardly one piece by Brahms (certainly no major one) which is occasional; all were thrown upon the water; they were not addressed to posterity, but to his contemporaries. A few short periods apart, Brahms never earned a salary. He had to sell his work to a publisher and the whole operation would fall to the ground, without a safety-net, if the publisher could not sell the works to the public. The only means of propaganda for the works apart from live performance were publishers' advertisements and press reviews. A finite number of performing outlets and concerts, even in so happily diversified a milieu as Germany, meant that Brahms, until thoroughly established, had to spend time and energy—not usually unhappily, it must be said—on playing, conducting or at least presiding at, concerts of his works. We have seen him as his own agent in the world of dates, fees and railway timetables. To write the equivalent of some 200 opuses when, as we have seen, uninterrupted periods of composition could be as short as three months out of twelve shows him to have been remarkably fertile, especially considering how little inconsequential music there is.

There is an obvious sense in which Brahms's music *had* to be music of consequence. The point is probably sufficiently made, but another crucial difference between Haydn and Brahms as symphonists was that between stood a colossal shadow, Beethoven, who with his nine had made 'the symphony' into the grand apex of instrumental music addressing Mankind with a capital M—indeed sending Mankind messages, literally in the Ninth Symphony by means of Schiller's words, 'O ye Millions, I embrace you'.

In this free-lance world, the veriest hack of a composer would be in Brahms's position as far as propagating his works went, and would have to make time and jealously guard it. How much more would a 'possessed' composer, such as the narrative shows Brahms to be, have to insist on his precious solitudes, at whatever cost in imagined or actual anti-social words and actions. In her memoirs[1] the Schumanns' seventh child, Eugenie, puts it sentimentally but clearly:

> [The creative artist's] life is one of eternal stress and strain; he is the slave of the elusive goddess of inspiration, she never lets him rest . . . No sooner has he laboured to produce one work, than new ideas for the next are beginning to stir and urgently demand to be brought to light. And when hours of doubt of his own genius come to an artist—and Brahms was spared these no more than others—life may become a veritable hell . . . He may sometimes have relieved his feelings momentarily by an outburst, but it did not make him happy. His ruggedness was a perpetual state of defiance against suspected attacks of others on his independence and the privacy of his existence.

Nevertheless, Eugenie recognised him as 'warmhearted, but usually hiding his deeply passionate nature under an appearance of ruggedness'. Since the word 'possessed' has inevitably entered into the discussion, this may be the place for a short intermezzo on Brahms's relations with women, or rather the lack of them, so far as we know. Nowadays permanent bachelorhood is apt to be taken as a sign that something is drastically—even infamously—wrong. Hugo Wolf's sneer to the effect that Brahms's music was a celebration of impotence is well known. It has been a lasting revenge for Brahms's advice— perhaps even well-intentioned—to the young composer to study counter- point. If we credit Wolf's remark with any meaning, the implication—that more (or even some) sexual activity might have led to better music—cannot bear serious examination, let alone rest on an iota of evidence. Brahms and the circle he lived in would on sexual matters have been reticent to the point of taboo. To raise an inane question, whether marriage would have made any difference to his music in quantity or quality, Brahms's repeated and only half-jocular law—'no opera, no marriage'—makes his answer clear, without our needing to suppose, as some writers have done, that working as a lad as pianist in Hamburg's waterfront 'dives' caused him to have inhibitions stemming from disgust. His patronising attitude to the opposite sex would have had present-day feminists frothing at the mouth, and was obviously too much for Ethel Smyth. But it was not notably different from the male ethos of the whole of German society, starting with the highest in the land. His almost reverential affection and devotion towards Clara and Elisabet forbids us to think of him as tarring all women with the same brush, and his loving relationships with his father and others do not suggest psychological quirks. The whole relationship between sexual passion and a passion for composition is a trap for the sentimental. For instance, to regard Mathilde Wesen-donk as in any real sense the 'cause' of *Tristan* is to ignore the gross disproportion between Wagner's spasms of requited love for her and the months of cool, calculating all-excluding effort that went with conceiving and writing down that enormous score.

There is no reason to suppose that Brahms did not put all his creative passions into his music, that he 'sublimated' them, to use an imprecise and unfashionable word. Whether he was, to 20th-century eyes, foolish or mistaken, is of no consequence. He thought the way he did, and we cannot even assume that his passion for composition allowed him any option in the matter.

There is plenty of evidence for what Eugenie Schumann calls Brahms's 'ruggedness'. He could be uncouth and unkind, and rarely brought himself to an apology. But he was always ready to admire, and to help if need be, a real talent. He had little opportunity to redress a superficial impression, shared by many of the German-speaking world, of the works and nature of Berlioz, and both Clara and Elisabet encouraged his blind spot over Bruckner. But his kindness to Dvořák, even to correcting his music for the printer, is well documented. Indeed, towards the end of his life, he overwhelmed Dvořák by offering financial support to help feed Dvořák's children, since he had none of his own. He was also on friendly and respectful terms with Grieg and Tchaikovsky, though scarcely on the same symphonic wavelength as the latter.

Brahms could never have achieved his purposes without speaking (and insisting on speaking without woolliness) a language which his audience understood or at least came to understand. It is a critical truism to categorise and contrast composers as between those who by and large build new roads and erect their own signposts along them—shall we say Monteverdi, Berlioz and Varèse?—and those who use the roads to give access to their highest thoughts—shall we say, with every fear of contradiction, Palestrina, Bach, Brahms and Shostakovitch? We quickly find ourselves begging several questions. Is the notion of a main road of any use in evaluating music, as opposed to tabulating it in a history book? Are we supposed to enjoy say Delius and Janáček less because on this notion they are dead-end composers?

Brahms in his lifetime was used against his will as a symbol and figurehead of the classical proprieties as opposed to the 'music of the future' of the Wagnerian camp, and hence of course as an 'Aunt Sally' by its more narrow-minded advocates. He might well have looked back not in anger but in irony, at the fact that in his youth he had been hailed by Schumann as a 'young eagle'. It is as well constantly to remember the 'young eagle' in Brahms's music of whatever date. Restraint is not a praiseworthy quality if it is a 'classical' mask for inhibition or impotence. The formal restraint, of his mature music as some tend to see it, is much more a case of making a channel than of erecting a dam. To write a passacaglia-cum-chaconne for symphony orchestra can be made to sound like an impossibly pedantic piece of misplaced antiquarianism. The final movement of the Fourth Symphony does indeed lend itself to the sort of description which tempts the reader to ask the question put to Ezekiel: 'Can these bones live?' And the ease with which Brahms's structural procedures (as opposed to Wagner's) can be described by using an analytical vocabulary which could be applied to Mozart, Haydn and Beethoven in itself makes his music easier to approach academically. But the magnificent sweep and force of the movement in question is neither enhanced nor diminished by the ease with which its form can be described. To speak of Brahms's music as new wine in old bottles is a mistaken but frequent critical cliché. But the taste of the wine is not to be deduced from a description of the bottle.

A variety of factors caused a severe depreciation of Brahms's reputation in the 1920s and 1930s. There was strong feeling in non-German countries that Teutonic hegemony in music had gone far enough, a view powerfully reinforced in the political field by the Franco-Prussian War, World War I and the prospect of another. In French eyes the anti-French Brahms (so far as he carried any weight) was lumped in with Wagner, who in Debussy's *mot* was a 'glorious sunset that was mistaken for a dawn'. The satisfying of middle-class taste was itself held to be a derogation of art, and 'Biedermeier' and 'Victorian' were equated as derisive terms. The anti-Romantic tide was running strongly. In England St Pancras Station was a monumental folly (it is now a grade one listed monument) and the Albert Memorial raised many an easy laugh. Those who permitted themselves to think there was still a place for the symphony in the twentieth century found a Messiah in Sibelius who was truly symphonic because motivic whereas Brahms was 'too lyrical'. One hopes that such false comparisons and specious assertions are a thing of the past. Poor Brahms contributed to his own downfall by writing integrated music whose workmanship enabled him to match what was said with the manner of its saying—and what is more, in a manner which disdained false mysteries. He paid the price for being understood by too many ordinary people.

He might still be paying that price had not Schoenberg devoted a lengthy chapter (dating from 1947) in *Style and Idea* to 'Brahms the Progressive' which particularly recalled the critical world to the realisation of Brahms's mastery of harmony, of phrase lengths and of pervasive motivic work, leading to unique designs. By 'unique designs' is meant something which will surprise the casual listener. Brahms used sonata form usually in two movements, in the vast majority of his extended works. The extent of the misnomer in using a word like 'form' is obvious since this is where his unique designs are principally to be found, no two being alike but each arising from the original idea, the 'gift of grace', worked out to its limits.

However, the one genre of music which he practised all his life was songs.

159

These contain adventurous harmonies, and subtleties of form and texture which, when his imagination is at full stretch, are truly remarkable. The tired images of mainly second-rank German lyric poetry may make for twentieth-century yawns. Brahms confronted them anew all his composing life, and he made them new time and time again. The key to his richness, and to his passion, lies here.

NOTE

1.   E. Schumann, *Errinerungen* (Stuttgart 1925); Eng. translation by Marie Busch as *Memoirs of Eugenie Schumann* (London, 1927; repr. Eulenburg, London, 1985), p. 155.

An autographed suite of sketches of Brahms conducting, by W. von Beckerath of Hamburg (The Royal College of Music)

PART TWO

PART TWO

CHAPTER SEVEN

Catalogue

This catalogue includes all the works with opus numbers and a selection of those without (werke ohne Opuszaw).

Orchestral Music

This category includes the four concertos as well as the symphonies, serenades and single-movement works. The obvious trait of the concertos is the sheer variety and richness of their subjects. In a sense the concertos hark back to the classical forms of Mozart and Beethoven, though it is a far cry from the punctual riches of, say K. 467 in C to the unprecedented—and still unique—grandeurs of the B-flat piano concerto. Of necessity, Brahms came to the orchestra via the piano, in marked contrast to the non-pianist Berlioz. But his orchestration was honed by the precious opportunities of Detmold and, particularly, Meiningen. There is certainly a penchant for the lower end of the spectrum, but a very Brahmsian sound consists of all the first violins playing high. Colours there certainly are but the tone is more of Rembrandt than Cézanne.

Op.11 *Serenade no.1 in D for full orchestra*

Allegro molto
Scherzo (*Allegro non troppo*)
Adagio non troppo
Menuetto 1 and Menuetto 2
Scherzo (*Allegro*)
Rondo (*Allegro*)

First publication: Brietkopf and Härtel, December 1860.

With its cheerful rustic sounds—wind solos and bagpipe basses—Brahms's first published work for orchestra takes over where Haydn's last ends. However, its multiple internal movements, consisting of two scherzos and a minuet 'sandwich', place it firmly in the classical serenade tradition of

Mozart. The exposition appears orthodox enough, with its formal repeat and its secondary subjects in A, but the transition to the latter is very abrupt, and the subsequent modulations cover much distant ground in a very short time, at one point going as far as the five-flat signature of D flat. When after prolonged hovering the recapitulation begins, the *pp* chord below the horn is not the straight D major, but a C natural is added with a delightful effect of added calm. The movement is made to peter out with silences, *pizzicati*, and a fragmented flute solo.

The first scherzo is a foretaste of Brahms's shadowy type in the minor key; its opening is tempestuously recalled in the Second Piano Concerto. On the other hand the faster trio is richly scored with plenty of sixths. The only slow movement in the six becomes a centre-piece by Brahms's unusual deployment of fully-rounded sonata form. The main second theme is signposted by a horn solo, and, indeed, the movement as a whole is notable for its wind writing. The tail-piece is particularly beautiful as the two clarinets, surmounted by a flute, give the second subject an extended dying fall. The two minuets initially contrast major and minor and wind and strings but mix them as the music proceeds. The main body of the second scherzo is like an affectionate parody of that of Beethoven's Second Symphony. The final rondo uses contrapuntal tricks in the service of its quick-moving wit—running accompaniments which go above or below their themes, and very close imitations, and there are again noteworthy wind solos, especially for horn and bassoon.

Op.15 *Piano Concerto no.1 in D minor*

Maestoso
Adagio
Rondo (*Allegro non troppo*)

First publication: Rieter-Biedermann, December 1874.

The classical function of the opening orchestral paragraph of a concerto is to deploy some, but not all, of the materials of the first movement while preserving a sense of expectation, to be satisfied when the soloist begins or emerges at what one might call the exposition proper. Beethoven's Fourth and Fifth concertos both have this feature in spite of the piano being allowed in momentarily at the beginning. The scope of this concerto is quickly apparent in that Brahms at the most conservative count introduces five themes before the soloist plays anything, and they are five different themes, certainly not incongruous with each other, but also without obvious motivic relationship. As to key, the work begins with a unison D for one bar after which 23 bars elapse, and with them the whole first theme, before a chord of D minor makes an appearance, and the introduction is ample enough to allow an excursion to B flat minor before being thunderously recalled to D. There is even time to mute the violins and unmute them again. What the music conspicuously does not do is to move as in a symphony towards an orthodox 'second subject' key or paragraph. This is reserved for the soloist, and in this work the importance of the soloist to the form is made very plain at this juncture in the design. He plays a big tune solo, in F, and at a slower tempo. What is more, he does the same in the recapitulation but in D major. These two pillars of orthodoxy permit wide, and seemingly wild, bursts of fancy elsewhere, perhaps most notably at the recapitulation when the D unison bar recurs and the piano crashes in above with a chord of E. Almost immediately there is another surprise: the rather dreamy passage with which the piano introduced itself is now thundered out by the whole orchestra to bring it within the family in the most emphatic way. For the pianist there is *bravura* writing in strings of octaves and thirds.

Violin mutes return for the slow movement. The piano responds to the phrases of the chorale-like theme with phrases beginning like variations but generating unpredictable fantasy as though they were being extemporised, as doubtless they originally were. There is a written-out cadenza towards the end.

With such a start to round off it is perhaps not surprising that the final rondo caused some anxieties, as can be seen in the Joachim letters. Going by themes and keys it is in the full A B A C A B A form, without short-cuts. Obviously, if as here C is a proper theme and not a development of the others, there is a danger that it will be too episodic and isolated. Brahms avoids this difficulty by elongating it with a quiet fugal treatment. At first it is dismayingly schoolmasterly, but then becomes amusingly tangled up with the main rondo theme. In any case, after another fantastic cadenza (in which for a moment one fancies one hears the vocal cadenza in the 'Choral Symphony') the C theme brings the concerto homewards on the horn. But the true homecoming is enshrined as it must be in the main subject with further glitter from the piano.

Op.16 *Serenade no.2 in A for Small Orchestra*

Allegro moderato
Scherzo (*Vivace*)
Adagio non troppo
Quasi menuetto
Rondo (*Allegro*)

First publication: Simrock, November 1860.

The orchestra as ultimately deployed is not particularly small. It uses two each of the woodwinds of the classical symphony—flutes, oboes, clarinet, bassoons—and adds for the last movement a piccolo which plays a full part.

165

There are two horns but no other brass or drums. The most notable absentees are violins. A viola-led string band makes for a tone more plangent and veiled. Brahms had already used it as the beginning of the slow movement of the First Serenade, albeit with the two top voices doubled by the bassoons, and he was to use it most strikingly in the first movement of the *Requiem*. However, as Tovey observed[1], the main purpose of the reduced strings

> is to throw the winds into high relief. Thus the Serenade is a work mainly for wind instruments, which are treated with the utmost fullness and variety of tone, while they are at the same time relieved from the burden of applying their own background.

The warmth of the wind band contributes much to the feeling of the happy spaciousness in the first movement, though this latter also springs from the readiness of the music to sit for some time on bass pedal notes, often gently energised with *pizzicato*. However, there are also quick and wide-ranging modulations in the development at whose close comes the long A in the bass which so puzzled Clara, but which means that although there is a feeling of homecoming in the recapitulation of the first tune we also have the surprise and gratification of realising that, key-wise, we have been at home for some time. The first of the subsidiary themes nonchalantly swaying on two clarinets has the last say in the movement. Whether using the upper or the lower neighbouring note, it is very much a fingerprint of Brahms:

The main

rhythm of the short scherzo carries on as the bass of the even shorter trio, using the bottom Cs of violas and cellos. The slow movement, though in a basic A B A shape, is full of sophisticated and unusual detail. Tonally one must notice that the basic A minor key is contrasted with a middle section mostly in A flat major, a quite spectacular change of horizons. The opening material is deployed over a recurrent bass which however is allowed to modulate. Nor is this *ostinato* confined to the bass of the beginning. It recurs in various forms in the middle and top of the texture, and in the A flat section it is heard, roughly upside down, on the oboe above the clarinet in a reminiscence of the slow movement in that same key in op.5.

(Bass throughout, a low E ♭.)

The first clarinet dominates the middle of this section, marked *molto espressivo* and using a high register (for Brahms) to express its passion. There is no other such example until the Mühlfeld works.

The two other movements are both very individual as well, the Quasi menuetto for its sometimes mysterious and fragmentary textures, and the last for its childlike gaiety, greatly enhanced by the long-awaited piccolo.

Op.56a *Variations for orchestra on a theme of Joseph Haydn*

This is the title as published. The theme is found in a wind-suite, ascribed to Pleyel, and is there headed 'Chorale St. Antoni'; hence the modern title of 'St. Antony Variations'. For an analysis of this piece, see under Keyboard Music, pages 237–9, as this was originally composed as a work for two pianos.

Op.68 *Symphony no.1 in C minor*

Un poco sostenuto, leading to Allegro
Andante sostenuto
Un poco allogretto e grazioso
Adagio, leading to Allegro non troppo, ma concerto brio

First publication: Simrock, October 1877.

This long-pondered, long-awaited symphony is a grand statement of the Brahmsian paradox, a deeply original work defiantly making clear its claims to its lineage. Bear in mind that Wagner completed *Tristan* in 1859 and examine the first 90 bars of Brahms's first-trumpet part. The instrument is used in 27 of these bars and uses the notes C, G and D, all playable on a natural trumpet pitched in C, as though valves had not been invented. Put in another way Brahms's first-trumpet part could have been played with ease on

167

a C trumpet by Bach's third trumpeter. In these circumstances 'highlights' are relative (for instance a crescendo from *pp* to a high G *ff* in two slow bars of the introduction). For most of the rest of the first movement the trumpets are treated as higher-pitched, punctuating drums, which, considering that the insistent rhythm of the repeated-note punctuations is

♪♪♪⸍♩

and the key is C minor, means that Brahms has at last accepted the challenge of Beethoven's famous Fifth Symphony in the most brazen fashion.[2] Of this remark one can imagine him saying, as he impatiently said of the last movement's reminiscence of Beethoven's grand Choral-Symphony tune, '*das bemerkt ja schon jeder Esel*' ('every ass sees this'). The symphony as the ultimate in public utterance, is there for everyone, including every ass, to 'see'. This stark clarity of thought, insisted upon to the smallest detail, but with every excrescence tracked down and removed, makes Brahms's music a gift for analysts. The more familiar the music becomes, the greater the danger of an academicism which cannot see the 'wood' of what overwhelms the ears and emotions for the 'trees' of what strikes the analytical eye. This very integrity of the musical construction, when it is compared with the less obviously penetrable work of his contemporaries, leads to a symptomatic phrase such as 'and then Brahms gets on with his knitting'. It is indeed hard on a composer to make his integrity of workmanship a source of criticism.

The introductory bars (1–37) of the Symphony were not in the first draft of the first movement which Brahms sent to Clara as early as the summer of 1862, four years before the Symphony was complete. Brahms's covering letter no longer exists, but she quoted the first four bars (i.e. starting at what is now the *Allegro* in a letter to Joachim dated 1 June 1862. The slower introduction was thus an afterthought to what would have been a strikingly abrupt beginning, though Brahms's skill ensures that the audience would not suspect it. Why did he feel he had to write a musical prelude as a mental postscript? The answer must lie in the ultimate shape of the drama as it became clear to him, which will be apparent when we arrive at the last movement. Suffice it to say that the attentive listener feels relentlessly pushed by pounding drum and *pesante* double bass and contra-bassoon through a great and gloomy portal. One is put in mind of a portentously opening door by the widening of the wedge-shaped pair of principal subjects whose shapes are shown here as they first appear. However, it must be remembered that both the upper lines are thickened out by each also being duplicated at the octave above *and* the octave below, so that already by the fourth bar there is a truly Brahmsian growl and opacity.

168

By the time the string tune has reached the sixth bar we encounter again Brahms's penchant for the melodic arpeggio in which there is a gap of a sixth (see also op.10). For instance, as here:

the harmony is the C minor chord but the G is omitted from the melody. This gapped melodic figure foreshadows a principal motif of the coming *allegro*. However, Brahms is not the man to let an effect like this rest on the impression on an uninstructed ear of two semiquavers. On the contrary, the premonition is soon expressed thus:

He hopes that anyone can hear that, especially as it is marked by (1) the first *pp* of the symphony (2) the 'open-string' sound of the lowest note of the violins (3) the *pianissimo* resumption of the pounding of the drum. This is one of so many 'correlations made audible' in Brahms's work as to justify the corollary: that any cross-reference which is not truly audible to a reasonably attentive and experienced ear does not exist. In the ninth bar the repeated *pizzicato* notes to the rhythm are borne out as a preliminary airing (composed afterwards, remember) to bars 51 plus of the *allegro*, but also perhaps of the middle of the third movement, without contradicting our audibility axiom?

So to the *allegro*. The integrity of the thematic workmanship can be sufficiently expressed in a diagram of the exposition; the fact that the diagram is easily made admittedly says nothing for the intrinsic quality of the themes but much for the enduring quality of the symphonic thought: theme B is

Themes A1 and A2 are the upward and downward shapes of the first-subject 'wedge'.

Bar 38   42

$\begin{cases} \text{A1} & \text{B} \\ \text{A2} & \text{A1} \end{cases}$ (this combination twice) leading to

70   78

$\begin{cases} \text{B} & \text{A2, then} \\ \text{A2} & \text{B} \quad \text{modulations to} \end{cases}$

new major key (E flat) traditionally related to
  C minor

bar121   125

$\begin{cases} \text{A1} \\ \text{B} \end{cases}$ $\begin{cases} \text{B} \\ \text{A1} \quad \text{interrupted by} \\ \text{A2} \end{cases}$

157

subject (C), immediately turning into

161

$\begin{cases} \text{C with A1's rising shape} \\ \text{B upside down} \end{cases}$

169

$\begin{cases} \text{B upside down, leading to the final } \textit{ff} \text{ paragraph of the exposition with C both ways} \\ \text{C} \qquad\qquad\quad \text{up, } \textit{agitato}, \text{ followed by hammered minor-key 'cuckoos' consisting} \end{cases}$
of the first two notes of upside-down B.

It may be as well to promise not to do this sort of thing again, but even so the diagram takes no account of the other unities of rhythm which to most ears make for the most convincing propulsion of all.

This sort of writing is truly symphonic, not only in the sense of coherent onward-sweeping drama which the great classics have led us to expect, but also in the more limited literal sense of 'sounding together'. The elementary diagram shows a texture of never less than two simultaneous ideas. (Shades of the contrapuntal exercises-cum-competitions with Joachim now brought to full orchestral apotheosis in the service of passion.) In this context the moments of unanimous chordal writing, whether sledge-hammer-like or hymn-like, fall into all the greater relief. Here is the 'hymn' from the middle of the development of this movement, as it first appears:

Is it reminiscent of Beethoven's lead into the hymn of thanksgiving after the 'Pastoral' Symphony's storm? *Das bemerkt jeder Esel*? Every ass is also likely to note that Brahms's hymn is unfailingly punctuated by the fateful

on horns or trumpets. Beethoven's peasants celebrate the end of the storm, but Brahms's captives pray in vain for the tempest to cease. On the contrary the hymn brings on the paroxysm which leads into the recapitulation, and the ultimate cessation of the storm seems only to lead to a tired and still leaden sky as the music slows to *meno allegro* for the last 17 bars.

As to the key structure, this is bound up with the obvious darkness-to-light emotional scenario of the whole symphony. The gleams of a major key are few. Brahms could easily have made the E flat major paragraph (bars 121 plus of the diagram) a good deal longer, and also the corresponding place in the recapitulation. The final *meno allegro* of the movement does indeed end in the major, but has persistent inflections of the minor, and its very brevity as a tail-piece leaves the listener far from any sense of dénouement. He has been through a satisfactory structural experience, and been party to a strikingly expressed emotional storm, but the clouds are as grey and opaque as before.

This feeling of being hemmed in is induced by the insistence on a limited range of motifs and by their being confined (as far as basic structure is concerned) to the classical expected key relationship of C minor and E flat major—and not much of the latter either. But the incidental modulations are very free. For instance, in the early stages of the *allegro*, when the music is merely moving from one statement to another of the same subjects in the same C minor key the harmony touches on such exotic keys as C flat (bars 60–61) and A (bars 64–65), to name only two in close proximity. These quick excursions while the music is getting under way are more akin to Schubert than Beethoven, as is the slightly distant choice of E major—most of its scale contradicting C minor—for the second movement. But this is no whimsicality, as there is the same interval (a major third) between the key centres of all four movements: I,C; II, E; III, A flat ; IV, C. One is tempted onto dangerous ground in wondering whether the key of E major itself had an intrinsic quality of Brahms—perhaps of luxurious quietude at some remove from the everyday? One thinks of the slow movements of the A major Piano Quartet op.26, and of the Fourth Symphony, and of Schubert's almost stationary ecstasy in the E major parts of the slow movements of the String Quintet and the last Piano Sonata. However, there is no disputing the physical effect of E major in the context of C minor, the two most important notes of the latter, C and G, being raised to C sharp and G sharp.

In 1981 some manuscript violin and viola parts of this symphony were discovered in Vienna; they had been used before the definitive published materials came out in October 1877, and they largely confirm a hypothesis made by Sidney Newman[3] based on English programme notes for performances in the UK (Cambridge 7 March 1877, London 31 March and 16 April). The matter is closely examined by Robert Pascall[4] and it is clear the slow movement was a rondo from its first performance, under Dessoff at Karlsruhe, 4 November 1876, until at least its English performances. That is, the first themes returned in the original key, albeit in reverse order, in the middle of the movement (in bar 47 out of 125 bars in all). The experience of hearing the early non-English performances, and of conducting the work in Leipzig (18 January 1877) and Breslau (23 January 1877) led Brahms to a recasting. It must have become evident to him that the modest length did not lend itself to a rondo shape, and while using all but four bars of the original music he arrived at the definitive version which uses a simple ternary design with the middle episode ushered in by the oboe solo at the end of bar 38. The point of such detail is to show the sure-footedness of genius in finding its way at the last moment. Brahms reckons that this *andante* is the right length, ultimately 128 bars instead of 125, by elongating the last chord; but he uses the extra elbow-room of the simplified design to make a richer first paragraph of 27 bars instead of 15. The chief enrichment is a most significant one: instead of 'answering' the first symmetrical, slightly Mendelssohnian phrases, Brahms unmistakably alludes to the wedge-shaped motto of the first movement, a clear indication that four comparatively serene bars do not dispose of the matter (*see opposite, top*).

This episode evokes, indeed necessitates, a very typical lengthening so that there is no cadence till the seventeenth bar and even then not a full close on to the tonic chord, but only a half close on to the dominant; this leads in turn to an *espressivo* oboe rounding off the now much extended paragraph. It is by such means that we recognise by ear that we are still listening to a symphony movement, not the nocturne that the beginning might suggest. But there is another sidelight available into the workshop which Brahms usually pro-

tected so jealously from the public gaze: this same inter-movement motto
(bars 4 and 5 of the above example) *does* exist in a sketch pre-dating those
first performances which lacked it.[5] To catalogue the many beauties of this
movement—the soft and seemingly conservative trumpets and drums at the
recapitulation, its rich variations of the motto, the concluding violin solos—is
to succumb to bar-by-bar description.

If one uses the Beethovenian hallmarks of a scherzo—ebullient fast triple
rhythms, often irregular, and a clear-cut compartmented distinction between
scherzo materials and those of the 'trio'—then there are no scherzos in any of
the Brahms symphonies. This scherzo substitute uses whimsicalities and
playful pedantries, but is very short on ebullience. The first two phrases, on
the clarinet, are five bars long, and the second is an exact inversion of the first.
Soon a varied repeat of the opening, now on the violins, substitutes a new
irregularity for the first; the phrases are now seven bars long (determined not
to be four or eight) and the extra length comes from incorporating falling and
rising chromatic phrases which hark back to the motto (not the only such
reference either—see bars 146–49). The contrasting material—6/8 time,

rhythm—slides in as though it were a transition, not a tune, and when the
clarinet resumes the opening tune the middle material remains in the picture
for a moment as a delayed parting guest. Thus this movement, like the

andante, has been rendered plastic and rich in 'symphonic' cross-references. In Tovey's words 'five minutes, a small orchestra, and quiet climaxes may suffice for a very large movement indeed.'[6]

In the second half of the eighteenth century the last movements of sonatas or symphonies were often of a chirpy lightness to offset earlier rigours, notwithstanding examples to the contrary by Haydn and Mozart. But symphonic life could never be the same again after Beethoven, notably the *Fidelio*-like release into the grand sunlight in his Fifth Symphony and the all-embracing joy of the choral finale of his Ninth. For better or worse, the symphony had become a drama for which audience as well as composer girded up their loins. Explicitly programmed or not, this drama needed a *dénouement*, and emotions were brought to a head; the joy of their resolution necessarily involved an increase both of the momentum of the work and of its weight towards the last movement. Paradoxically the word 'joy' holds good, as the Greeks knew, even in a tragic end, such as that of Brahms's Fourth Symphony, or for that matter of Tchaikovsky's 'Pathetique', if the performance is good enough to turn ostensible self-pity into universal catharsis. A large contribution to this 'end-weight' in this First Symphony is the portentous, dramatic and almost fantastically diverse introduction to the last movement (60 bars, all but half *adagio*, and the rest not much faster). Brahms did not use this particular device again, and its two predecessors were the last-movement introductions of the F sharp minor Piano Sonata op.2, and the Piano Quintet op.34. The former of these was undoubtedly one of the works which Schumann hailed as 'veiled symphonies' and the latter was a symphonic work which suffered changes of media before its eventual form. The long period of gestation of the symphony means that some ideas are coloured, to say the least, by the passionate rhapsodising still sometimes evident in the music of the 1860s. Of course, such words as 'fantasy' and 'rhapsodising' are relative, but coming after the close-knit previous movements this introduction has the air of an unrelated succession of ideas only held together, at this stage, by their proximity, and with even this succession disturbed by sudden changes of tempo. The feeling induced is of an almost lost soul trying to escape from the glooms of the first movement which were only held in abeyance by the relief of the two intervening intermezzos. The gloom resumes thus:

The middle of this texture, delivered as before in thirds and in three octaves, drives us immediately back to the parallel opening of the Symphony. Now we see it, but seemingly Brahms did not when he began. But though we do not know it yet the seeds of relief are already there: the bass of our example is the repeated low carillon accompanying the main second subject, and the top, again in three octaves, hints at the great tune which leads out the main part of the movement in the major key. But in fact, and very surprisingly, the major key steals over the scene earlier than this. For once, 'picturesque' seems a permissible word: the accompaniment is muted swaying violins, *pianissimo* chords from the trombones now heard for the first time, and a string bass reinforced by *pianissimo* drumrolls. Above, *forte sempre e passionato* the horn rings out with the melody posted to Clara as a birthday greeting from Switzerland in September 1868. The words, presumably Brahms's, begin 'Hoch auf'm Berg'; a non-fitting literal English is here given beneath the tune.

Students of orchestration may note how the second horn is called in aid in the second, fourth and sixth bars of this tune to hold out the full four-beat length of the note while the first takes a breath on the last crotchet. Thus the tune should emerge as a long, rich and continuous sound. After the flute has repeated the tune (again with the second flute ensuring continuity) a solemn gleam of a trombone-led hymn-like phrase completes this striking procession of apparently unrelated fragments. The instruments of the hymn are the three trombones, two horns, the two bassoons and the contra-bassoon forming an organ-like bass an octave below the bass trombone (to the exlusion, in this symphony, of the fatter sound of the bass tuba).

This symphony was completed no less than 70 years after Beethoven's Fifth, and in the meantime, particularly in opera, trombones were fairly indiscriminately used as the principal noise-makers below the trumpets. Brahms's historical and instrumental sense combined to preserve for them the solemnising function that Mozart used them for. Skilled orchestration also subsists in the non-use of instruments. To hold the trombones in reserve until the fourth movement of a symphony in C minor/major is another Beethovenism for every ass to notice. But whereas in the Fifth Symphony they launch the movement *fortissimo*, here their first two entries are *pp* and *p dolce*; they rise momentarily to *mf* under a third delivery of the Alpine tune than relapse into silence for *the* tune when the last movement 'proper' begins. This third delivery has a crucial one-note difference, however. Instead of ending D E C as in the example on page 175 it ends, or rather stops, thus: D E D^7, making us want the coming C, and providing Brahms with a small building-block like the ensuing, and opposite, C B C shape in the tune:

Note the launching-pad effect of the open-string sound of the bottom note of all the violins of the orchestra.

The exposition knits together some of the introduction's motifs, now in purposeful onward dialogue. The trombones are silent, and the extremely conservative trumpet parts give the impression that they are trying to recall the natural modulations of the material to the starting point of C. And this does in fact happen, to such an extent (16 bars of the original tune) that the listener might think Brahms was making the time-honoured repeat of the exposition. This feint however is part of the process of transferring climactic weight to the end. Instead of the return of the first theme being the climax of the development, as in classical works, we now find the horn theme used to recall C major after hectic excursions, and leading in the second group of themes. We are to hear only derivations from the main theme, and then the *più allegro* whisks us up to the true climax: the *fortissimo* declamation of the 'hymn' phrase with the trombones at their long-awaited loudest, this being the only part of the introduction not used for any subsequent purpose.[8] How can a climax be made after this climax? By short and shattering silences, which had their effect on Sibelius's Fifth as well.

Op.73 *Symphony no.2 in D*

Allegro non troppo
Adagio non troppo
Allegretto grazioso (*Quasi andantino*) alternating with
Presto ma non assai
Allegro con spirito

First publication: Simrock, August 1878.

The first nine bars of the symphony, a bland eight-bar melody with an 'upbeat' bar on the bottom strings, sound, as intended, like a carefree euphonious song—in short, everything that the beginning of the first symphony was not intended to convey. Yet they also contain the materials of the whole movement to an astonishing degree, which is why the quotation is bespattered with letters:

A careful reading of the structural methods of the First Symphony will save the reader (and the printer) from exemplifying this work at similar length. So far from being a mere lead-in, or joiner of phrases, as above, (*a*) turns out to be the initiator of 'new' phrases, and not only in this movement, the interval being a semitone or a tone and the notes sometimes doubled, sometimes halved in length. Similarly (*b*) can initiate 'new' phrases (indeed one may ask what is new in this context) and be used as an accompaniment. The phrase (*c*) is (*a*) reversed; it too is plucked out of its melody to serve another purpose. The same is true of (*d*), the often-observed fingerprint of Brahmsian melody with its three ascending notes leading to a longer one. It would only have taken five more bars to have found (*d*) beginning a phrase downwards, and not long after that solemnly elongated by the first phrase of trombones and tuba, piano, ushered in by a *pp* roll and the timpani—a first utterance again. There is a new key and a new tune 82 bars into the piece—cellos characteristically above the violas—but it is grafted on to the body by (*b*) on the violins. (A pianist playing the example will need a colleague or imagination for the bass.)

The music can stir itself strenuously from such idylls. Two examples must suffice: from the exposition:

and from the development, a fugal altercation starting with (*d*). Note how in the second bar of this example one of the counter-rhythms reproduces that of the 'left-hand' (including the final accented tied note) of the previous example:

At the end of the movement the horn sums up the idyllic features of the music in a heart-easing meditation on (*c*). The thrill of hearing at this late stage the poetic mill being served by such initially unpromising grist is one which Brahms was intent on giving his audiences once they had penetrated beyond initial impressions, and he was content to put his heart on his sleeve for the purpose.

The outline of the slow movement is a very simple one, a long theme given first to the cellos alternating with a graceful tune, mainly for wind, in 12/8 time but with the beats anticipated by tied chords. However, this contains some contrapuntal discussion begun with a rising scalewise phrase (see the previous example) and furthermore the lead-back to the reprise features, of all things, second trombone and tuba in a quiet dialogue on (*a*), both ways up. The scherzo substitute is a sandwich, of a graceful tune, like a minuet with some third-beat accents, together with two faster variations of itself, the second at a greater distance from the original theme.

The reference back to the first movement is unmistakable at the start of the last:

The four notes of this first bar are as omnipresent in this movement as bar one was in the first, including as before the accompaniment of the 'big tune' second subject. The latter is used quietly on the trombones (reverting momentarily to their historical solemn functions) to begin the final climax, which is enhanced by two short and shattering silences. The first and last movements have much in common, then, as to compositional method. This enforces unity but also helps proclaim the contrast between purring and unbuttoned exhilaration.

Op.77 *Violin Concerto in D*

Allegro non troppo
Adagio
Allegro giocoso, ma non troppo vivace

First publication: Simrock, October 1879
Dedication: Joseph Joachim

Some of this work's history figures in the narrative. As to how to regard the two precautionary marks of *non troppo*, the Brahms/Joachim timing of 35 minutes is significant. What Brahms disarmingly called his 'poor Adagio' has little effect or function if it occurs after a lengthy slow allegro.

Whereas the second symphony, this concerto's sister-work, propounds a variety of colours and moods united by motifs, the concerto's orchestral procession is of a succession of strongly characterised, greatly differing themes, thus representing Brahms's different notions of symphony and concerto—the differences being accentuated by the similarities of their opening themes, in D major, triple time, and arpeggio shape. The first theme's first eight bars are:

The next chord, *piano* without transition, is of C major as the tune continues. The other themes of the introductory procession—five more, at a conservative count—take care not quite to contradict D nor yet to suggest the A major normal to a 'second subject group'. For instance:

This becomes, in outline:

Note the first *pianissimo*, and the way the five-crotchet phrases contradict—without accents—the three-crotchet bars, as in the slow movement of op.115. Now there is a playing with classical expectations: a winding phrase of four bars on actual or implied dominant harmony after these excursions must surely lead to an important subject, perhaps to the soloist's entry:

180

But this leads to neither of these satisfactions, only to a repeat of the five-crotchet enigma with different notes, in outline thus:

Note the punning use, in the bass, of the first bar of (c).

It is a different postman's knock altogether which leads in the soloist, at last unequivocally in D, but in D minor.

The soloist makes a violent start to an accompanied strict-time cadenza with a timpani accompaniment almost throughout. Needless to say, the quoted examples are by no means all the materials in this rich movement. In spite of all that has happened so far, the soloist has to establish himself in the music's form. It by no means suffices for him to perform elegant arabesques on what the orchestra has proposed. The crucial moment in this process occurs when the music moves round to the 'right' key for A for the purpose and example (d) winds upwards not to cheat us again but to lead into a melting tune which does not need quotation. In the recapitulation this lead-in occurs again but in the 'wrong' key of F sharp and it is deliciously corrected not by the soloist, though he could easily have done so, but by the sudden warmth of all the first violins.

The slow movement contains beautiful examples of variation by elongation. The theme is first given to the oboe, supported by the wind band. At the soloist's entry the oboe's first four-bar phrase is expanded to six, almost as though time were standing still for the purpose, and the next four-bar phrase is expanded to no fewer than eight. Thus a basically simple ternary form grows under the mind's ear without vying with the luxuriant growth of the first movement.

The Hungarianisms of the main rondo theme call for double-stopping and *élan*. There is a short cut in the scheme, often taken by Mozart, after the middle theme denoted by C in the scheme A B A C B A, but this throws into relief the final escapade of A played as if on hunting horns, *poco più presto*.

Op.80 *Academic Festival Overture*

First publication: Simrock, July 1881.

Most of the melodic materials are student songs, or Brahms's manipulations of them. The *pianissimo* minor key beginning is a surprise in the designated festival, though listeners versed in Brahms, especially C minor Brahms, will smell a rat at the immediate introduction of cymbals and bass drum. The solemnities are at once relieved and added to by the change to C major and the three quiet trumpets singing 'Wir haben gebauet ein stattliches Haus' ('We have built a stately house'). After this the design begins again, so to speak, as an overture in C major. At the mid-point there is not so much a development as a *mélange* of student songs. The famous 'Gaudeamus igitur' is given a once-only full-blast rendering by way of coda.

Op.81 *'Tragic' Overture*

First publication: Simrock, July 1881.

The two first chords are far more than an introductory gesture. they immediately attach themselves to the end of the main subject's opening phrases:

Either with its harmony or melodically with its falling fourth this 'motto' permeates the piece. Naturally one can find falling fourths in any tonal piece, but Brahms is so persistent that one even comes to feel that the rhythm and its

182

elongations, even without the fourth, are a continuing thread. The trombones are used to contribute a special aura of solemnity, in long soft notes with even a mark of *ppp*. They rise above p only twice, first in a

$$p <$$

(the top is not specified, but there are muted violins above) at a consoling elongation of the main theme in the major, and for their one and only *forte* contribution to its final statement in the minor. Though the work ends *fortissimo* the trombones' individual task is done and they are silent. Of particular note is the delivery of most of the development as a slow—twice as slow—march on the dotted theme at the end of our quotation. Tovey, writing at least half a century ago[9] said of this piece, but of Brahms in general too:

> It is an unfortunate fact that Brahms's profoundest . . . developments . . . are inevitably woven in a close contrapuntal texture which is very interesting to analyse. Experience has taught me to withhold the analysis of such passages altogether so long as the view prevails that all such things are inherently pedantic. It is, of course, foolish to suppose ingenuity to be more than a practical necessity for the construction of such passages. But is is worse than childish to suppose that the necessary ingenuity is a sign of pedantry.

Some of this problem remains today.

Op.83 *Piano Concerto no.2 in B flat*

Allegro non troppo
Allegro appassionato
Andante
Allegretto grazioso

First publication: Simrock, July 1882.
Dedication: Eduard Marxsen

The basics of the classical concerto first movement have been discussed in the notes to op.15 and op.77, and are not altered by the fact that, as in Beethoven's two last examples, the piano is here heard before the orchestral prelude, making elaborate echoes to the solo horn's statement of the principal subject and then leading by a powerful written-out cadenza to the *tutti*.

An irregularity threatens, when in the course of this the music appears to be going to the dominant, as it might in a symphony, but swerves aside to a new subject indeed, but for the time in D minor. This turns out to be the first of the secondary themes in the solo-and-orchestra exposition, so that the first individualised subject for the piano is a hammer-and-tongs tail-piece which is emphatically its own property. The three rising opening notes of the main subject are never far from the scene, however, and bring cohesion to the very adventurous modulations both long-term and transient. These bring for example a substantial stretch of B natural minor into a B flat movement (the spectacular semitonal shift again). There are passages of quiet, for instance when the piano trickles down over the horn's recapitulation, but the 'big' sounds and gestures are much to the fore. Nor is Brahms sated, for the piano now hurls itself into a full-blown scherzo equivalent. If it has anything to do with the abandoned scherzo for the Violin Concerto it can only be at a very great remove, so thoroughly does it explore the *martellato* of the piano. It does have at its opening a passing and inconsequential similarity to the first scherzo of the First Serenade op.11. The trio is a horn tune to which the pianist must answer in leaping double octaves marked *pp, sotto voce* and *legato*.

The slow movement is similar to that of the First Concerto at its start, but different in colour with its opening cello solo above the lower strings. The piano, after its exertions, takes its time to rejoin and uses a vein of quasi-extempore fantasy which now seems to grow from the theme, now leaves it entirely. There is a passage of remote stillness above clarinets marked *ppp docissimo*, in F sharp—not consistent with restraint, unless it is hardly daring to breathe.

The final rondo uses the full A B A C A B A form, or almost does so. But C is more a development (including B minor again) than a centre-piece tune. The B of the scheme, on the other hand, contains three subjects, one of them decidedly Hungarian in tone. As in the Violin Concerto the final statement of the main theme is speeded up into a 6/8 version.

This is the biggest concerto of the nineteenth century, in all senses.

Op.90 *Symphony no.3 in F*

Allegro con brio
Andante
Poco allegretto
Allegro

First publication: Simrock, May 1884.

The opening of the symphony, in outline, shows both the pervasive motto (*m*) and the first theme:

The cross rhythms of this theme have caused commentators to link it to the slightly more explicit ones in Schumann's 'Rhenish' Symphony:

In both cases there is something of an ennobled Viennese waltz, but with Brahms's leaps the effect is the more heroic. The exposition is somewhat more relaxed than in the first two symphonies because there is not the over-riding concentration of a few motifs, and, indeed, the first of the second subjects is sharply distinguished by a different time signature (9/4) and by the slightly unorthodox key of A. Furthermore, it is delivered by the clarinet in a teasing repetitious way over a pastoral accompaniment of A (bass) and E:

The music is continued in a very typical new-yet-old manner by a string phrase which uses the same rhythm as the quoted subject, but not the same tune. One encounters again the combination of intellectual play and *esspressivo* marking. But the exposition ends with a vigorous A minor, growing out of the motto (m), its A-C-A[1] serving as a pivot (again the intellectual play) equally at home in F major as in A minor.

The quoted second subject might well have struck the hearer as charming but symphonically unpromising, which is what Brahms probably intended, the more to surprise his audience, for the development storms along *agitato* in a discussion of it. Instead of propelling us in one sweep to the recapitulation Brahms introduces another of his horn solos this time making the motto the basis of a theme and slowing down the music to a ghostly rendering of the first subject, deepened by the contra-bassoon, and made more solemn by *pp* trombones. Suddenly the recapitulation is in full swing, but the end is not heroic, the first theme descending as though at sunset. It is worth noting how the quoted second subject is given the first time in A, a third *above* the home key, and reappears (at any rate to start with) in D in the recapitulation, a third *below*.

The beginning of the andante is deliberately simple and plain, on the woodwind—mainly clarinets and bassoons—with the vibrant contrast of divided violas and cellos taking up the ends of the phrases. The tune of the first four bars is

The last phrase is altered to

and the gapped arpeggio motto is immediately apparent.

The secondary materials are short and diverse but include a passage of almost disconnected harmonies spread mainly two notes at a time over a wide compass. The combination of austerity and mystery makes us the more ready for the movement's—indeed the symphony's—great erotic moment, the passage where the tune-starved violins take over and expand to bursting-point the motto at the end of the main theme:

Even were it possible to put in the harmony the piano could give next to no impression of this long-awaited place. All right-minded people should begin to tremble when they see the violins getting ready to play it.

A leisurely triple time is all that remains of the minuet or scherzo element in the third movement, in C minor. The increasingly luxurious rescorings of the principal theme, without any compositional reconstruction, notably the horn solo at the reprise, are the essence of lyricism, and the relaxation this engenders makes us ready for the heroics of the last movement, whose effect on Joachim has already been described in the narrative. But another fairly unusual effect (though not entirely unprecedented) is to choose a tonic minor

186

for the main body of the movement when the first was unequivocally major. Brahms must have deliberately recalled the Second Symphony in electing to start thus:

This 'motto' appears in many guises through the movement, and is the mainspring of the oboe's turning the music to the home major at last in a *poco sostenuto*, which brings the music to another sunset close like that of the first movement, but naturally longer. The Symphony ends as quietly as it can given that the whole orchestra, including trombones, play the last chord and the first flute is on top F. This dying fall is similar to that of the *Requiem*, which is perhaps what Brahms meant when he described the work to Simrock as 'some jottings from my youth'.

Op.98   *Symphony no.4 in E minor*

Allegro non troppo
Andante moderato
Allegro giocoso
Allegro energico e passionato

First publication: Simrock, October 1886.

By starting immediately with the first subject Brahms abandoned the preliminary 'motto' idea of the Second and Third Symphonies. However, it was a close decision. At the end of the first movement, in the autograph score he added the following beginning, then crossed it out.[10] (For ease of playing it is written on two staves, and the player or reader must add in his imagination a *pizzicato* reinforcement of the wind chords at bars one and three with top E on the first.)

Thinking chordally, this motto is most obviously to be seen in the final cadence of the first movement, hammered home by four timpani strokes, and

in the A minor chord starting the last movement which is the first utterance of
the trombones. One writes 'A minor' but the trombones, the loudest
instruments, play only

although it would have been perfectly possible to add the A. Thus there is in
the bottom of the chord a strong foundation of C, which leads us to a melodic
consideration of the motto, its fall from C to B. Now, every piece in the minor
is bound to feature its most characteristic sound, the fall of a semitone from
the sixth note of the scale to the fifth. But the way the first subject is expressed
in the first movement draws attention to the B C B alternation. We have
already had examples of falling thirds of Brahms's melodies. This one calls
our attention by reverting upwards to the C, and to its resolution, the B:

At the end of the exposition the music leads gently back to E minor and the
listener hears, as though *de capo*, a repeat of the opening eight bars, identical
in scoring as well. Then the music diverges into masterly variations and
fragmentations in the usual wide range of keys, settled in or momentarily
implied. Having used his first subject twice identically, Brahms might well
have referred to it obliquely, or not at all, at the point of recapitulation.
Instead we have two elongations, *pp* but spectacular:

This throws into much greater relief the B to C to B shape of the previous
example.

As far as tonality is concerned, the C emphasis has two obvious effects. At
the beginning of the slow movement the key of C is strongly implied by the
horns' lead-in:

Or perhaps, with the key of the first movement ringing in our ears, we might think of the key as still E with a flattened second note, which a learned few among Brahms's audience might have called Phrygian, or the harmony students Neapolitan. Brahms could easily have resolved the ambiguity but instead slips straight into the first subject, in E, with its ecstatic implications. The main second subject, showing once again the scale-wise rise at its start, occurs in the regular sonata-form keys, the second time in a luscious harmonic dress of divided strings. At the end the horns' opening motif recurs, and the key is now E but even now there is a teasing modulation into C which is resolved back to E at the last moment.

The long-term planning means that beneath the shock of the boisterous onslaught of the third movement there is the feeling that its C major had to be. The trombones are still being saved, but piccolo, contra-bassoon and triangle are called in as reinforcements with nothing particularly sparing about their parts. The piece is in two time, and Scherzo is not mentioned, but *giocoso* is the direction, and for the most part ebullience is the order of the day. If one feels there is something frenetic here this is from foreknowledge of the tragedy to come, rather as in the march of Tchaikovsky's 'Pathetique' symphony. Even so, a mainly quiet paragraph in C sharp minor/D flat major shows a reversion to the semitonal relationship with the main key.

In the last movement the F natural in E is still heard from time to time, for instance in the seventh bar of the opening when it reinforces the A minor tendency of the motto.

The chromatic A sharp in the sixth bar, not in the original 'Bach' (Church Cantata No. 150; 'Nach Dir, Herr, verlanget mich'), is powerfully marked by the entry of trumpets and timpani. Counting from the first bar there are twelve versions of this theme-cum-harmony, in some of which the full close is avoided which would otherwise divide the whole into eight-bar sections. The thirteenth limb is still in E minor, a pathetic broken solo for the flute, but in 3/2 time to make the transition to the four sarabande-like middle statements in the major key (the equivalent in time to eight statements in the original sequence). There are many C naturals in the E major, so that we are able to resume the E minor with a chord of A minor. There are 15 limbs before the coda, but there are references back in the ninth and tenth of them to give an effect of recapitulation. It is not only a case of recapitulation within this movement, for the falling thirds of the first movement make their way back in, culminating in this canon:

The coda, più allegro, sticks on the A sharp/B flat of the ascent, making masterly harmony to clinch the tragedy.

Op.102 *Concerto for Violin, Cello and Orchestra in A minor*

Allegro
Andante
Vivace non troppo

First publication: Simrock, May and June 1888.

There is no published dedication, but when Brahms sent a printed score to Joachim he wtote on it 'to him, for whom it is written'.

With this last orchestral work Brahms embarked also on his last Concerto, and with a mind still restlessly enquiring. If he needed a fillip to his imagination it was the prospect of two soloists, and the necessity for equal shares when one of them—the cello—is naturally less likely to be audible. Apart from the expertise gained by having more than a century of opus numbers behind him, he had practical experience of multiple concertos, having played Beethoven's Triple Concerto at Meiningen.

He carried further the technique of introduction in the Second Piano Concerto by delivering just four bars of the first subject *tutti* whereupon the cello establishes itself with a strict-time cadenza carrying it further. Then in the major key the clarinet leads in the beginning of the main second subject, taken up by the violin. Thus at two strokes we have the main themes (there are few others) and the masculine and feminine characterisation of the soloists. The violin solo becomes a cadenza for two; there is none other in the work. Then the full-dress orchestral *tutti* begins. However, having already introduced the beginning at least of the second tune, there is no point in withholding it until the soloists' re-entry, so the orchestra plays it fully; thereby Brahms consciously breaks with the classical externals, but allows the soloists to make impact with it all the same by a very typical manipulation of the tonality. In the *tutti* the tune is in F, stepping a third down from the basic A; in the solo exposition it is 'corrected' to the orthodox key of the

190

relative major, C, namely a third up from the original tonic. It is given here in the form the cello gives it, and its likeness in rhythm to a leading theme in the Clarinet Trio op.114 is apparent. For the reply by the solo violin read the example an octave higher and prolong the top C to make it four beats, a small but very telling illustration of the variation-by-prolongation technique:

The comparative terseness of the rest of the movement permits a minor-key coda of 44 bars. Indeed tail-piece hardly seems the word when the orchestral *tutti* of the opening only amount to 55.

The steep contours of the main theme of the slow movement have been fancifully compared to the view south from Thun, the rising octave, one supposes, deriving from the spectacular triangle made by the Niesen. The shape is a simple ternary with coda, but the shift from a home key of D to (mainly) F in the middle section shows the relationship of a third again. At the reprise there is a beautiful example of the orchestra making three bars when there were two before.

The main theme of the rondo is announced by the cello in the tone of whimsical complaint which specially befits it and which is a little reminiscent of the last movement of the Piano Quintet. Interestingly Joachim said that Brahms's bowing for both soloists (top of example)

was only fit for 'complete masters of the bow' and suggested the bowing shown below the example. Brahms was content to let matters stand, entrusting himself to masters of the bow. The movement uses the full rondo scheme of ABACABA without short cuts, and to avoid the danger of the 'C' being lonely, this paragraph is a substantial one. Yet in spite of this, and the necessity of catering for two soloists, Brahms is sufficiently economical of our time to make room for a happy ending.

Chamber Music

The crucial importance of Brahms's contribution to this genre can hardly be exaggerated, and the matter is discussed in Chapter Two. The deliberately 'classical', non-commital titles of the works and the seeming ease with which, thanks to their clarity, they can be described, is apt to obscure that fact that with very few exceptions the details of their forms are thought out *de novo* on each occasion. It is noteworthy that a very large proportion of the whole corpus can be said to be frequently played.

Op.8 *Piano Trio no.1 in B major (First Version)*

Allegro con moto
Scherzo (*Allegro molto*)
Adagio non troppo
Finale (*Allegro molto agitato*)

First publication: Breitkopf and Härtel, November, 1854.

Brahms immediately shows his individuality in the choice of basic key; as far as his Viennese classical forebears are concerned, B major is almost unprecedented. What is more, all four movements are in B, major or minor. The long-breathed tune with its accented top-note dissonance (*x*) is a trait of Brahms form first to last; it is first heard on the piano alone:

The rising and falling phrases (*a*, *b*) each side of *x* are used as motifs in much of the material of the movement. Its expansiveness is soon evident, for there are restarts in the home key of the main theme, but slightly modified, in the twentieth bar and again the thirty-fifth, and no less than 62 bars in B before any real diversion. Instead of going to the orthodox secondary key (F sharp) the music turns to G sharp minor, sign-posted by two bars of *sostenuto*

and a printed double-bar. Thus the music is sectionalised, in spite of obvious affinities with the initial theme, when the piano leads out the following theme without harmony:

This looks momentarily as though it might begin a fugue, and it is played by the strings in canon before giving way to a euphonious derivation in the major key of E (even now not F sharp) before the music slips back to end the exposition in G sharp minor again. The rest of the movement continues the pattern of surprises by way of quick changes of mood and texture and sudden new accompanying motifs with a compensatory insistence on the original materials from time to time. The fugue threatened in the exposition appears for a while in the recapitulation, and there is a very large peroration in orchestral style, as in the piano sonatas.

Op.4 and the scherzos of the three piano sonatas showed this to be the genre in which the young Brahms was most certain and individual, as was recognised by Schumann and Dietrich when they allotted him this movement in the 'committee' sonata welcoming Joachim back to Düsseldorf. Whether it is Mendelssohnian gossamer or the Beethovenian sledge-hammer that is called for, echoes of orchestral sound are actual ingredients, and here the French horns, more than once imitated in the first movement, are in constant play, as often as not in some quirkish elf-land. The hurtling energy is relaxed for the trio, a big diatonic tune delivered mainly in sixths, with a high orchestral climax employing, of all non-chamber effects, a *fortissimo tremolando* in octaves on the solitary violin. The quiet ghostly coda, marked *pianissimo possible*, ends on a chord of identical compass to that of the piano which like a hymn-tune opens the slow movement. This opening subject may be held to refer to the first movement again—any three or four notes going up or down a scale are bound to do so! The main secondary theme seems so unmistakably to refer to Schubert[11] as deliberately to enshrine a message which is not ours to decipher:

Not only does this melody begin identically with the song 'Am Meer', but the expansion into a five-bar phrase is typically Schubertain. Heine's words speak of the lonely lovers sitting dumbly by the sea, she weeping and he poisoned by her tears. The movement was certainly written before Schumann's leap into the Rhine, but there were occasions for Clara's tears well before then.

The finale resumes in B minor, so that the movement maintains the major-minor alternation. The rhythm of the main subject

is never far away, though its momentum, and that of the movement as a whole, is interrupted curiously often, no fewer than ten slowings being marked. The 'quotation of a quotation' second theme has been cited in the narrative. However, there is one truly Brahmsian modification of the expected shape of the movement: at the moment when his audience would expect either the beginning of the development or a repeat of the exposition the first subject does indeed re-appear in its original key but then loses itself in a discursive development, leaving the sense of dénouement, *forte* in the tonic major, to the secondary theme, with the first theme contradicting it in the minor key by way of turbulent close.

Op.8 *Piano Trio no.1 in B major (Second Version)*

Allegro con brio
Scherzo (*Allegro molto*)
Adagio
Allegro

First publication: Simrock, February 1891.

The effect of the tightening up of compositional procedures is to shorten the whole piece, and this intention is evident before the first note. *Allegro con moto* is replaced by *allegro con brio* and C by ₵. Brahms allows the youthful ardour of his first theme for fully 60 bars with almost no alteration. However, a typical detail is the omission of the violin's first contribution which was a punctuating phrase, now deemed unnecessary, above the cello's first theme. The violin's entry is now the main theme, which grows in dynamics from then onward. But now not only is the erstwhile secondary-theme nexus to be entirely abandoned, but so is the means of getting there. The mature Brahms uses only 13 bars of transition to get to a new secondary subject—new also in the sense of using no re-quoted elements of the first. We must beware of using hindsight to say that the youthful Brahms was incompetent. The kind of movement whose interest and coherence depended on following the adventures of a theme in its various guises (like Faust in his different situations) was very much 'in the air' in the mid-century. For a splendid example, close to Brahms, one need look no further than Schumann's Fantasia for Piano and Orchestra which became his Piano Concerto. It could even be that the uncertainties of direction and key relationships noted in the trio's first version also expressed what Brahms expected the listener to experience as part of his journey through the movement. All we can say is that Brahms did not care for them a composing life-time later. The miraculous unification of motifs in say the Second Clarinet Sonata is a different matter altogether from that of the *appliqué* transformations in op.8. The new exposition is so much tighter that Brahms now writes in a repeat of the whole, obviously not optional since he has composed three 'first-time' bars to make the lead back. After some moments of stillness the development unites old and new in a straight-through sweep of powerful modulations. The recapitulation occurs with both strings in unison, but at first subtly harmonised in the 'second subject' key of G sharp minor, before swinging into the home key. Mindful of the retained ample beginning of the movement Brahms has an ample coda, made of both subjects.

Brahms has left his first-love scherzo virtually unaltered except for tightening up the coda. The orchestral climax of the trio is retained for old times' sake.

The 'Am Meer' theme in the slow movement is completely replaced by a new middle section. One could say that the only Schubertism remaining is the extension of the phrases by re-harmonised 'echoes', but this is a technique Brahms has long made his own. Brahms the plastic surgeon has retained almost exactly the notes, and quietly spectacular modulations of the restatement, of the hymn-like theme on the piano, but has ruthlessly cut out an *allegro* episode from the earlier version.

In the revision the word 'Finale' is dropped from the heading of the last movement probably because by then the word had come to connote something more extrovert than this movement's turbulent agitation. Brahms suppressed the secondary theme not for any lack of beauty but simply because it seemed too lengthy and self-sufficient to be treated with enough plasticity and resource in a more tightly-argued structure. Not only the theme itself but the portentous and dramatic transition leading to it has to go. The new secondary theme which Clara found so repellent is indeed distressingly blunt in contrast, couched in a succession of four-bar phrases rare in Brahms and accompanied by off-beat quavers thudding (*pesante*) on the cello and piano at both entries. However, this very concision leaves room for a coda rising from a long *pianissimo* to a large climax which is the more telling for the almost exclusive use of the main subject.

195

At first sight this clarifying technique may, among other things, make the music easier to analyse at the blackboard with the usual technical terms, a process which cannot improve or detract from the quality of the music by one jot. However, a study of the tonality reveals unusual choices, yet balancing ones, in the secondary areas, now sharply defined. For instance, in the first and third movements B major moves down through a minor third interval to G sharp minor; in the second and fourth B minor moves up through a minor third interval to D major. If, like the sun in the psalm, the composer 'rejoiceth as a giant to run his course', he is all the happier for knowing what course he has set himself.

Op.18 *String Sextet no.1 in B flat*

Allegro ma non troppo
Andante ma moderato
Scherzo (*Allegro molto*)
Rondo (*Poco allegretto e grazioso*)

First publication: Simrock, January 1862.

Simrock also published at the same time as the score and parts an arrangement made by Brahms for four hands on one piano. This was not a substitute medium for concert performance but a means of domestic pleasure before the days of the gramophone.

In his first published chamber work without the piano it looks as though Brahms is finding compensatory 'safety in numbers', and it is significant that nearly a dozen years were to elapse before the op.51 quartets were published. The unusual medium is exploited immediately with sounds which no string quartet could make: an immediate statement of the main theme on the first cello with viola and second cello underneath.

As we have seen, it was Joachim's idea to start thus, so that the main theme was adumbrated twice, first by the cello, then by the violin. The work originally began with what is now the eleventh bar. There are only four bars in the entire work where just the four instruments of the string quartet are used, and even these are not typical, as double-stops make the harmony up to six parts. The euphonious triple-time writing in the first movement is typical of Brahms but in a way difficult to define. It is an amalgam of rising scalewise movement of three notes, of rising and falling melodic sixths, of underlinings of melodies in sixths, and of chromatics making transient modulations in the course of a theme. The most well-known instance of this sort of music is in the *Requiem* chorus 'How lovely are Thy Dwellings', which is pre-figured here in bars 77 to 80. Some of these traits can be illustrated from early in the first movement. The first subject paragraph ends thus (bar 39f):

At bar 61, with the music ostensibly making towards the key of F, the above phrase is turned into this:

Note how the doubling voices in the first two bars lend a really low C sharp in the chord of A—a very characteristic sound. Passages like these simply belie the accusation that Brahms is indifferent to colour, such indifference even being claimed as a virtue. The end of this movement contains two striking timbres: the viola as the top of the six-part ensemble at bars 370f, and the slow-waltz *pizzicato* by all six players, with double and treble stops, at the close. The variations also show a delight in different colours, this diversity being enhanced by their very strictness, with the tread of the spondee rhythm of the theme present almost everywhere. Unusually for Brahms, the scherzo continues its very animated *allegro* into the trio which indeed recurs even *più animato* as a coda, making a truly orchestral impression and using far more than six voices in its closing bars. After this the full-blown, leisurely rondo (A B A C A B A) can seem insufficiently cumulative, as indeed it did to Joachim. But Schubert is a very respectable example when it comes to relaxing finales. Brahms later solved this problem by drastically relaxing the scherzo instead, to the point of writing intermezzo-like substitutes.

Op.25 *Piano Quartet No.1 in G minor*

Allegro
Intermezzo (*Allegro ma non troppo*)
Andante con moto
Rondo alla zingarese (*Presto*)

First publication: Simrock, late summer 1863
Dedication: Baron Reinhard von Dalwigk

Unorthodox though its scoring was, the op.18 Sextet put its themes in exactly the places and keys that a listener versed in the classics expected—and in every movement. The puzzlement of both Joachim and Clara over the exposition of the first movement of op.25 shows how drastic were Brahms's thoughts on its design. In effect, they both complained that there was too much D and not enough G in the exposition. A modern listener, not used to the idea of taking one movement at a time, and applauding it or not, might well say that there is more than enough G in the last movement to balance things up tonally. There is perhaps some substance in the complaint, inasmuch as Brahms does indeed allow the 160-bar exposition to contain 111 bars in D minor or D major with only small deviations. But the pains taken to reinforce, by dwelling on its cadence themes, a key which is already obvious may be intended to set in relief the unorthodox treatment of the rest of the movement—of which, it must be remembered, Brahms's friends had had no previous experience. The opening shapes begin thus:

On the heels of this, after a silence instead of a transition, comes

As it happens, (*b*) is in the 'right' key and contrasting mood for a 'second subject', but too soon, and (*a*) returns *fortissimo* in a G minor tutti, making an A B A first paragraph. There is no printed repeat at the end of the exposition, but the listener hears one for ten bars, with the same silence before (*b*). It is when the latter occurs in a different, minor, key that it is evident that the development is beginning. This occurs in one fine sweep as Joachim acknowledged and at its climax there is another silence, followed now by (*b*)(*a*), not the first quiet (*a*) which we have heard already. So this middle limb is now behaving like a subject in its own right, and now in the home major key at last, though not for long dispossessing the *tutti* (A) resumed in the minor key. This is the place where Clara could feel she was on the right lines for the home run—but what she evidently thought of as the main secondary subject again upsets expectations by appearing in the 'wrong' key of E flat , leaving to others the task of getting home. One is only too conscious of how far this explanation is from giving any idea of the emotional sweep of the music. However, these calculated surprises are of the very essence of Brahms's originality. There may be a composing price for them. Joachim finds the invention (his underlining) of the first movement's theme not so pregnant as Brahms's best, and he also remarks that there is more *Kitt* (cement or putty) to be observed than in other compositions of Brahms—the development always excepted. What constitutes a worth-while theme is a subjective matter, but the mere manipulation of *Kitt* is an obvious danger which detractors will observe to a greater degree than friends.

The title 'Intermezzo' is a clear way of saying 'not a scherzo'. However, its whimsicalities, with the violin muted but apparently not the viola, and the overall shape, with trio and coda, make the relationship clear. The first entry of the piano could be held to be a reminiscence of (*b*). More certainly the trio and the coda are linked to the main intermezzo by the same starting rhythm. In the slow movement a very broad theme flanks a most unusual middle section—a dotted rhythm fanfare-cum-march (though still in triple time) first *pp* and then *ff*. One would think these materials too diverse to use in the same movement, but the transitions are masterly. The Gypsy rondo is the most sectional movement Brahms ever wrote. With its three-bar rhythms, piano cadenzas and a final speed of no less than *molto presto* it was obviously intended to bring the house down, and it did.

Op.26 *Piano Quartet no.2, in A*

Allegro non troppo
Poco Adagio
Scherzo (*Poco allegro*)
Finale (*Allegro*)

First publication: Simrock, June 1863.
Dedication: Frau Doktorin Elisabeth Rösing.

It is a commonplace, but true, that when Brahms embarked on new media (for instance, symphonies) he wrote a pair, as though the way has been cleared for the second by the birth-pangs of the first. This quartet is sunny almost throughout, and amiable in its abundance of hummable themes. In striking contrast to the G minor first movement the exposition of this one has a repeat and moves without mystery from A major to E major to deliver at least three second subjects, all fluently arising from each other as from the cornucopia which Clara was to evoke when discussing the riches of op.34. How hard-worn this apparent nonchalance is cannot be guessed, of course. As before, the development proceeds with a fine sweep, helped by strenuous work on the piano to balance which the strings mainly unite as if they were an orchestra. There is also a formal surprise: at the dénouement into A what is heard is not the first subject but the last of the second subjects, marked *appassionato* and delivered in the minor by the insistent piano. The original first subject quietly returns 17 bars later in the major, as though offering a balm after the contradictory outburst. From there onwards the order of themes is as before, making an undisturbed succession which winds naturally down to a lingering coda.

The slow movement begins with one of Brahms's most beautiful inspirations. To say that it is in E might seem unremarkable, E being the dominant of A. But there is a Brahms mood associated with the key. (See the discussion of op.68.) Luckily he is not here to pour scorn on adjectives, but one must risk calling it rapt, ecstatic, nocturnal. Brahms is content to mark it '*espressivo e dolce*', but he also mutes the strings for the first 83 bars. At the moment when one supposes that a leisurely A B A form has been accomplished there is a sudden impassioned return of the first of the B subjects in F minor, a surprise which necessitates another lingering coda, with mutes. This extreme contrast of key is to be found serving much the same emotional purpose in the slow movement of Schubert's String Quintet, which of course Brahms knew, just as he knew he was momentarily recreating the slow movement of Beethoven's 'Emperor' concerto at bars 75 to 77.

The next movement is indeed called scherzo but for most of its length it is exceedingly gentle. Its proportions are ample, however, the main body consisting of over 200 bars. The trio is interesting for its energetic canon, a bar apart, between the piano in three octaves, and the strings also in their three octaves. The contrasting material in the trio uses the rhythm, but not the notes, of the Scherzo's main subject, another and not infrequent aspect of Brahms's variation technique.

The way is thus cleared for the finale to burst in with a true allegro, having a highly rhythmic first subject and a plethora of complementary ones. Though there is much incidental modulation the key scheme does not depart form the standard expectations of sonata form. There is an interesting rhythmical trick which Brahms was to use on later occasions as well. It gives the effect of a dislocating acceleration by contracting the original rhythms of a tune to shorter ones, with the bar-lines momentarily forgotten:

See indeed the closing allegro of Brahms's last chamber work, the clarinet Sonata, op.120 no.2.

Op.34   *Piano quintet in F minor*

Allegro non troppo
Andante, un poco Adagio
Scherzo (*Allegro*)
Finale (*Poco sostenuto* leading to *Allegro non toppo*)

First publication: Rieter-Biedermann, December 1865.

Op.34   *bis Sonata for two Pianos in F minor*

First publication: Rieter-Biedermann, December 1871.
Dedication (both versions): Princess Anna of Hesse.

Obviously the version of this work for two pianos has some validity as Brahms allowed it to be published, whereas the string quintet version is conspicuous by its absence. In July 1864 Clara played it through very thoroughly with Rubinstein at her house in Baden-Baden and wrote a very interesting verdict to Brahms:

> It is not a sonata, but a work whose ideas you might—and must—scatter as from a horn of plenty, over an entire orchestra. A host of beautiful thoughts are lost on the piano, and recognisable only to a musician, the public would never enjoy them at all. The first time I played it, I felt as if it were a work arranged for the piano.

Clara put her finger unerringly on the symphonic scope and complexity of the work, but Brahms was not prepared to be a symphonist yet. The rich arpeggiations, and sometimes the *martellato* style of the piano writing, which cannot have been present in the string quintet version, would not lend themselves to a symphony orchestra either, without yet another drastic rescoring of the long-suffering work. A comparison shows that for much of the length of the work the piano part of op.34 is allotted as it stands to one or other of the two pianos in op.34 *bis*. It is rarely shared out between them at any one time. This means that the other piano adds all the string parts. This bears out the piano-versus-the-rest scoring of much of the quintet (as also of Schumann's example). This priority certainly extended to the title-page of the first edition which mentions the piano first.

As to the symphonic thought, examples abound from the very start of the way the materials change and grow before the mind's ear, and in an explicitly 'public' way, but always serving an emotional scenario which is itself deliberately constructed. Working on these lines there is everything to be said for a stark unison opening without the distraction of harmony—compositional common sense indeed, but the gaunt sound means more to the listener as an emotional signpost that the comforts and consolations are far off, if indeed they are going to be heard:

Any idea that this is merely introductory is immediately dispelled by the *tutti*. The *x* and *y* speak for themselves; so shortly will the violin's falling semitone *z*.

Even at the first restatement of the opening the elongations and other variations begin, and *z* is marked with accents. More tentative *z*'s could also have been placed between the D flat of the first bar and the C of the second. The eye sees an F in between, but the shape of the theme and its natural accentuations count for more. One could add the G to G flat in the third bar for better measure:

Almost immediately the falling semitone has become a melodic connecting tissue and the erstwhile first subject has become an accompaniment:

203

The falling semitone began within, or as the tail of, the first theme. Now it is the head of another, making it new and yet not new.

At bar 57 the viola varies this theme while the *xy* reappears as an accompaniment:

The key signature at this point does not tally with the key of the example, which is F sharp minor, albeit temporarily. Most of the secondary material in the exposition is in C sharp minor. Whichever of these keys is our concern they are a semitone (that semitone again!) away from the orthodoxies of F or its dominant C—a very short way on the keyboard, but very remote (ostentatiously remote, one might say) in the tonal spectrum. It is of course imperative to make the exposition repeat to make audible the effect of shifting back down the semitone to C and then to the home of F minor. It also ought to weigh that to do otherwise is to omit five bars that Brahms wrote.

To carry on in this manner would mean printing the entire first movement in a host of annotated music examples. The point is that it would be possible, and for the sake of an intelligent composition student, justifiable to do so. But Brahms did not regard his public as composition students. Even if they were, he would expect to approach them by ear. His processes, fascinating though they are, do not in themselves guarantee masterpieces. On the other hand, the attention of the most devoted listener to a work of this length is bound to retire if he cannot attain any sense of its coherence, consciously or otherwise.

As to the larger emotional design, the storm and stress is hardly relieved by anything more than plaintive sounds. There is a brief moment of major key near the end of the exposition, and this is repeated in the recapitulation. Only in the slower tailpiece does it appear that the music may end calmly in the major, and here there is a brief passage (the only one in the whole movement) where the quartet plays without the piano. But at this moment the minor key inflections are creeping in again, and the allegro returns to insist on the minor key with no fewer than twelve *fortissimo* bars in succession.

The relaxation is postponed till the next movement, where it is achieved in a number of ways. The overall shape is a simple A B A, where the reprise is luxuriously rescored rather than recomposed. The phrase lengths are symmetrical and almost all four bars at a time, and the harmony deals in thirds and sixths in more than 100 of the 126 bars—truly an indulgence. In the coda the semitone oscillates on the first violin to cause one striking modulation.

The ample design of the piece affords room for a scherzo which begins in a shadowy way over the pizzicato bottom C of the cello. There follow two more phrases abruptly contrasting in dynamics but obviously connected:

However, a reference back to the music example on page 204 will show yet another connection with the first movement, a migration which is not so common in Brahms as not to be noteworthy. The trio uses a 'big' major key tune which could be described (like a good many others in Brahms at this juncture) as heavy relief. The scherzo proper ends with a very vehement falling semitone, D flat to C, which cannot escape comment as a defiant re-use of the same notes as the end of Schubert's String Quintet. But is is equally obvious that a composer who hammers home a

rhythm in C minor—see also Brahms's First Symphony—is adopting a 'so-what' attitude to borrowing from the great ones.

By now the work is on a scale which threatens to make any last movement anticlimactic, an option which Brahms did not feel was open to him. But one hammer and tongs cannot lead to another, so the music reverts to a slow tempo and a quiet, groping mood for a long introduction, from which comes not a real allegro, but a jog-trotting complaint very characteristic of the cello in certain moods. The music has a straightforward sonata shape and seems to be dying of inanition when it is rescued by a presto of notable length and energy. In the final agitato the technique of anticipating the beat with tied chords (see op.33) is much in evidence, and the work ends with a drastic epigram.

Op.36 *String Sextet no.2 in G*

Allegro non troppo
Scherzo (*Allegro non troppo* with *Presto giocoso*)
Adagio
Poco allegro

First publication: Simrock, April 1866.

Agathe von Siebold's signature tune, enshrined in the first movement, already occurs in the narrative. As the second in a pair, this work contrives to be masterly in technique and easy-going in effect at one and the same time. The most important elements in the first movement are heard in the first six bars (*shown opposite, top*). The alternating semitones are never far away, nor are the rising fifths of the theme. Note the leisurely changes of the harmony, and the changing colours caused by adding the inflections of the minor scale. Note also how in the sixth bar the first cello answers by (roughly) inverting the theme, giving the effect of an assent at the end of a sentence. The development

is almost entirely concerned with using these materials through a beautiful string of modulations. The alternating quavers have a simple but magical hand in one of these. In the exposition the upper notes are part of the harmony, as in the opening quotation. However, if the lower note is now the harmony note and the upper note ornamental (and dissonant) what a beautiful glide to another key ensues (A to C sharp minor):

Here is the familiar Brahmsian paradox: one describes a piece of sheer poetry, and it sounds like a knitting pattern!

To give the title of Scherzo to a plaintive *allegro non troppo* (again) in duple time leads one to expect an anti-scherzo. But the middle section, a fast and mainly loud *Ländler* in the major key and in triple time, reverts to almost more than the 'real thing'. It is not called a trio, nor does it sound in the least like one.

One distant wellspring of the work is indicated by a letter to Clara (already mentioned) dating from as far back as 7 February 1855, in which he quotes without any explanatory comment the first four bars of what becomes the theme of the variations which constititute the third movement. The first two bars are quoted thus:

In the finished work the second violin plays the chromatic notes of the viola's triplets, but as quavers—two against three—thereby increasing the sense of an angular strain beneath the tune. Here then is another paradox. The gaunt passage, bereft of any other harmony, and making a great contrast to the two preceding movements, is marked *molto espressivo*. The whole movement defeated Hanslick who called it, perversely, 'a kind of free variation on *no* theme.' Perhaps needless to say the five variations *are* strict, to such an extent that Brahms feels no need to hammer home the theme. Indeed he does not even describe the movement as variations. The last movement has twin first themes: fluttering semiquavers with many repeated notes and a tranquil diatonic theme, beginning as so many do with three scalewise upward notes. The middle section uses the semiquavers to such an extent that it is the tranquil theme which starts the recapitulations. Otherwise it is plain sailing.

Op.38 *Sonata no.1 for Piano and Cello, in E minor*

Allegro non troppo
Allegretto quasi Menuetto
Allegro

First publication: Simrock, June 1866.
Dedication: Josef Gänsbacher.

Brahms's liking for the lower end of the instrumental spectrum has already been seen in his lowering of the string quartet's centre of gravity by adding a ballast of another viola and cello. His first published duo sonata is for cello, rather than violin, and the first thing to be heard is the cello's bottom E, beginning a noble but sombre theme, to be immediately continued on the singing top string so as to impress on us the cello's main characteristics of gravity and tenor song. The piano does not retain for long its accompanying role of off-beat sighs but becomes, at least, an equal partner. Some of the piano writing both in this movement and the least makes one suppose that Gänsbacher had a big tone. In any case the gruffness which sometimes results from the cello's efforts to retain its share, with a mainly low compass, is part of the instrument's character, to say nothing of Brahms's. As usual in minor-key movements, there is a 'consolation' theme in the major, to mark the end of the exposition and of the movement; with the piano and cello joining in a gently pulsating drone, this has a pastoral air. There are again some very low thirds supplied by the cello.

There was a slow movement at one stage, but Brahms removed it. However, the next movement serves as an intermezzo, rather than a weighty centre-piece. What appears to be a mere 'lead-in' phrase turns out to be part and parcel of the the 'minuet', and from it are derived the hesitating phrases which begin and punctuate the subdued passion of the otherwise perpetual motion of the 'trio'.

Taking a cue from Beethoven's last Cello Sonata Brahms begins the last movement fugally, but the texture is intermittent; what began life as a counter-subject becomes a sonata-style subject in its own right. A considered effect of the movement is one of struggle. (Not many pianists can spare overmuch thought for the cellist in confronting trills, double thirds and fast octaves!) As we have seen in other chamber works, the first subject, having been much used already, does not appear at the deemed moment of recapitulation, but is used instead to storm home in a coda, *più presto*.

Op.40 *Horn Trio (Horn, violin, piano) in E flat*

Andante, alternating with Poco più animato
Scherzo (*Allegro*) with Trio (*Molto meno allegro*)
Adagio mesto
Finale (*Allegro con brio*)

First publication: Simrock, November 1866.

Kalbeck says that Brahms showed his friend Dietrich the exact spot in the woods above Baden-Baden where the first theme of the work came to him—a most unusual thing for the secretive composer to do. But then the whole concept is unusual, the trio being unique among the chamber works in not having a sonata-form first movement. Indeed the first two andantes begin and end in the home key, making the very antithesis of the forward-moving sonata procedure. The faster alternating sections are not vigorous enough really to disturb the woodland scene, so that the way is clear for exploiting the more robust side of the horn's nature in a real scherzo. The proportions are big enough for excursions to be made. For instance, the main theme (*a*, below) becoming (*b*):

So far from adopting a more popular tone, the central section turns to the seven-flats depths of A flat minor keeping the violin below the horn almost completely. The sadness explicitly called for in the slow movement's *mesto* is relieved towards the end by a molto *p* pre-echo in the major key of the subject of the last movement. The consolatory horn calls—major in a minor context—are one of Brahms's fingerprints. Here he is able to incorporate the right instrument. So at last the six-eight allegro permits full rein to the 'hunting-we-will-go' aspect of the horn, with a full sonata form making a natural climactic weight. It is exhilarating, especially for the pianist, to have Brahms going at full gallop over an extended distance.

Op.51   *Two String Quartets*

No.1 in C minor
No.2 in A minor

First publication: Simrock, November 1873.
Dedication: Theodor Billroth.

Brahms wrote to Simrock in June 1869: 'Seeing that Mozart took exceptional trouble to write six beautiful quartets, so we want to use our utmost exertions to make one or two passable ones.'

Quartet no.1

Allegro
Romanze (*Poco adagio*)
Allegretto molto moderato e comodo
Allegro

Some of the integrations in this unrelenting battle with the shades of Mozart and Beethoven can be seen in quoting the beginning of each movement:

At first sight, melodically speaking, (*c*) is the odd one out, though the slurred pairs are evident in (*b*) and (*d*). But tonally its apparently whimsical playing at being in a Neapolitan C minor matches (*d*)'s outright statement of F minor as a preludial motto to C minor. One is forced to take this line if one puts oneself in the shoes of the audience who have not seen a key signature but who have just heard (*c*)'s unambiguous close in F minor (albeit the last-moment chord is F major).[12]

In the first movement it is soon apparent that the drama and density of the motivic work is what is foremost in Brahms's mind as matter for the listener, as a high proportion of the movement is devoted to what can most kindly be

211

called non-melodic work, combined with a good deal of sheer ungainliness. It is difficult to suppose that an experienced composer, having waited so long to publish, would have spent the time and trouble to make petulant gestures to a public who would, some of them, buy quartets to play them at home. Nevertheless the viola player must have wondered what he had done to deserve his part,[13] consisting of a high proportion of harmonic in-fill with remorseless quavers and exposed moments when he must sustain fp octaves and court comparison with the couple of horns who could (?should) have done the job naturally and easily.

Some more easily transcribed horn calls are the main subject of the Romanze. The title for Brahms seems simply to imply a mood—indeed a loosely 'romantic' one—rather than the melodic simplicities one could look for in Mozart or Beethoven. But the form is simple enough, an alternation of paragraphs (A B A B) almost without transitions. The melodies are sophisticated in their phrase-lengths, and the repeat of A is a beautiful example of wide-ranging melodic variation, its feet retaining contact with the ground so to speak by the strictness with which the original harmonies are retained. The secondary material exploits the sighing effect caused by omitting, on successive beats, the first chord of a triplet figure.

In the third movement Brahms marks the first violin's opening *semplice*. The tune may be simple but is key is not. Indeed it is 79 bars before, for a moment, the key of F is unambiguously heard, to be instantly undermined again. However, there is in the 'trio' what in this context must pass for a straightforward tune in quite a lot of F major, accompanied for much of its length by an alternation of A's on open string and stopped string on the second violin.

The opening phrase of the last movement has been described above as a 'preludial motto', but it is soon apparent that it is far more than that, quite dwarfing the first subject, if that is what it is, in bar 3. This motto launches the development at the top of a climax rising out of the exposition. But in less than a minute's playing time the music comes back to a quite long stretch of secondary subject material unaltered from the exposition except for transposition back into C major. On the heels of this comes the motto in C minor as though to make a coda (a procedure Brahms has used several times before). But now, at last, so much of the exposiiton is requoted as to make 'coda' seem an inadequate word. Whittall's outright pairings, development/recapitulation and recapitulation/coda seem exactly to describe the case.

Quartet no.2

Allegro non troppo
Andante moderato
Quasi minuetto (*Moderato*, alternating with *Allegretto vivace*)
Finale (*Allegro non assai*)

Though this second work of a pair is still in the minor mode as to most of its length it is more relaxed as to its procedures. In the first movement the secondary subjects not only begin in the expected key (C major) and at the expected place, but are signposted by a *ritardando* lead-in by the solo violin (as also in the recapitulation). What is more, 66 consecutive bars, almost half the exposition, reappear virtually unaltered, except for transposition, in the recapitulation. There is one small but beautiful example of Brahms's variation technique at the moment of recapitulation. One could almost be surprised that the first subject occurs here; it is not a dénouement, but rather slips in, in the course of a sequence, with at one point a delicious reharmonisation. The second subject is quoted as it occurs in the recapitulation, partly for its reference back to the fingerprint in op.16, but partly to show how Brahms's penchant for conflicting rhythms can have an unsettling effect in a medium which has no sustaining pedal:

There is even a three-fold conflict of rhythms in the coda (bars 315f). The emotional curve in the slow movement consists in the gradual melting down of the main theme's presentations from angular two-part counterpoint to a full-blown Brahmsian harmony. This relaxation is interrupted by a spectacular top-and-bottom canon with *tremolando* accompaniment, but confirmed by a *molto dolce* cadence theme which must have haunted Richard Strauss when he wrote *Don Juan*.

The third movement (akin to the middle movement of the Cello Sonata op.38) is twice interrupted in the major key by faster music whose affinities to the minuet emerge towards the end of their sections.

Some of the third movement rubs off on to the finale in the shape of the main subject—presented in energetic three-bar phrases. Whittall has pointed out how the secondary paragraph, though including no fewer than three full closes in C, mainly inhabits its own dominant:

It is hard to imagine that Brahms cared whether this movement was called a rondo (A B A C A B A) or not. There is enough A in the orthodox places to do so. But whereas in classical orthodoxy the C is either marked mainly (or wholly) by development, or by a new tune—see for instance Beethoven's Violin concerto—here Brahms occupies a half-way position between the alternatives. There is a tune indeed, but it is a statement of the main secondary theme (see the above example) but beginning on C, making it outline the dominant of F, which key it never succeeds in arriving at. Perhaps needless to say, the coda makes the quartet end in the A minor from which it has never strayed far. But its effect is now of a rather pugnacious exuberance rather than the fabricated gloom of the sister quartet.

Op.60   *Piano Quartet no.3 in C minor*

Allegro non troppo
Scherzo (*Allegro*)
Andante
Finale (*Allegro comodo*)

First publication: Simrock, November 1875

The complex history of the composition of this work, beginning life as early as 1855 in C sharp minor, has been unravelled by James Webster.[14] The first two movements, the earliest in their conception, reveal the young man of *Sturm und Drang*, mentally clothed in his Werther outfit. However, this by no means implies he has left his restless form-probing mind behind. One can hardly talk of an opening subject in any thematic sense. After a loud unison C on the piano the strings play a downward-groping figure to the rhythm in 3/4

which permeates much of the movement. The next step is the downward one to B flat , evoking echoes of op.1, but in gloom instead of ebullience. Although it is preceded by much chromatic harmony, the final lead-in to the second subject is quite devoid of any surprises, leading in a very leisurely way to the expected key of E flat mjor. What is surprising is the unique way Brahms handles this subject, once arrived. It is a diatonic eight-bar phrase; instead of leading to a nexus of other contrasitng themes the eight bars expand to forty, occupying almost all the rest of the exposition by being couched as theme and variations; indeed one could count one further 8-bar variation, but its material is

though implying harmony of the second subject. With so long a stretch based on E flat behind it, the development ranges very widely, becoming very orchestral in its sound with the piano greatly dominant. At the recapitulation there are more second-subject variations but in G major, not C. But there is never a real possibility, formally or emotionally, that the movement will escape its ineluctable C minor. Brahms has not done with this key yet, for the scherzo pounds along in his best abrupt style, with a more equitable distribution of the interest of the parts. But the insistent thrust of the music is not relieved by anything that could be called a 'trio', so that the time is ripe for the quite foreign key and comparative repose of the E major andante. Here at last the strings, led by the cello, can sing to the accompaniment of the piano. Webster has shown that there is nothing in Kalbeck's assertion that the movement represented a covert declaration of love for Clara. Nor does it appear to be anything to do with the C sharp minor original work. However, it obviously expresses the same mood as the slow movement of op.26.

The most notable feature of the finale is the almost perpetual motion of the piano's rainfall, see the previous opus. The plaintive main theme, with a falling third made prominent, is given to the violin in a long solo. The other notable subject has hymn-like five-bar phrases which are almost the only occasions when the accompaniment stops. The recapitulation brings some C major, though far from triumphantly. The major is not battered down into the minor as before; instead the minor insinuates itself into a passage marked *tranquillo*. However, there is no escape, all the same.

Op.67   *String Quartet no.3 in B flat*

Vivace
Andante
Agitato (*Allegro non troppo*)
Poco allegretto con variazioni

First publication: Simrock, November 1876.
Dedication: Theodor Wilhelm Englemann.

After the stern, minor-key concentration of the first pair of string quartets, this third and last one, published in 1876, is much more relaxed both in mood and in construction. The first movement, perhaps with Mozart's 'Hunt' Quartet in mind, starts with an imitation of horn calls, but later the 6/8 rhythm is mingled with the 2/4 of Czech dances. Some of the transitions are by silences rather than by notes, and the general mood is what Beethoven would call 'unbuttoned'. The slow movement has a serenity caused by balancing eight-bar phrases, but the central section modulates widely with greater rhythmic freedom leading to a varied reprise which begins in a foreign key and which gradually loses its elaboration as it comes home. The third movement is a *tour de force* inasmuch as it is led by the viola, the other three instruments being muted. In those places where the viola does not have the tune it uses its inevitable prominence to hold the harmony together as a French horn would. The 'trio' section does indeed begin as a trio with the viola omitted. By a lively touch of compositional skill, what the trio have played, though individual enough to stand on its own, becomes a background for yet another viola tune. The last movement uses a theme made quirky by its middle modulation and comically shortened return to the home key. As the variations proceed a kinship with the horn-call subject of the first movement emerges, to wrap up a happy conclusion. The example shows the combination:

Variation theme

1st movement

Op.78 *Violin sonata no.1 in G*

Vivace ma non troppo
Adagio
Allegro molto moderato

First publication: Simrock, November 1879.

The heights to which Brahms aspired in this work are indicated by Imogen Fellinger:

> In his inscription of a copy of the original edition . . . to the designer Heinrich Groeber, he referred to Mozart as well as to Beethoven by writing on it the incipits of the violin Sonatas in G major of both masters [Beethoven, op.96], setting above them the words spoken by the *Himmelskönigin* ['Queen of Heaven'] from Faust's *Verklärung* ('Transfiguration') in Goethe's *Faust-* . . . 'Come, rise to higher spheres!'[15]

Although in his duos Brahms is perfectly prepared to make the violin accompany the piano, as his classical pedecessors did, in this work he balances perfectly the natural *cantabile* of the violin and the natural but quite different sonority of the piano. Sharing between them a truly limpid flow of varied but cognate ideas. From the first bar the music is haunted by the Viennese-waltz cross-rhythm

and with the rests removed it begins both the subsidiary subjects. At the beginning of the development there is a pseudo-recapitulation. We know that it cannot be an actual one, because we hear as accompaniment *pizzicato* for the first time. However, when the moment of recapitulation comes, the violin twice makes as if to start the main theme, but each time the harmonies are not ready, so to speak. When the tempo and the key are truly at home, the violin resumes in the second bar of the main theme. The key of the slow movements (E flat) certainly follows in Beethoven's footsteps, but the violin's song flowers into sophisticated figuration. The basic shape is A B A B A, and in the B the waltz like rest occurs, but more in the nature of a funeral march. The last movement arises from the 'Rain' in op.59 no.3, and is suffused with again.

The music seems to propose a regular rondo, but then reverts to the theme, but not the tempo, of the slow movement. The 'rain' returns but at last the tonic major is heard; the adagio's theme again returns, and the most beautiful close hints at the harmonies of the first movement. Clara hoped, but in vain, that this last movement would accompany her in her journey to the next world.

Op.87 *Piano Trio no.2 in C*

Allegro
Andante con moto
Scherzo (*Presto*)
Finale (*Allegro giocoso*)

First publication: Simrock, December 1882.

Apart from op.1 this is the only extended work of Brahms which he chose to write 'in C'. It is thoroughly in that key, too, as to both the outside movements and the substantial 'trio' of the scherzo. This makes it more in C major than the beloved Schubert String Quintet. To enter the realms of Gluck's *Elysium*, Haydn's *Light* and Mozart's 'Jupiter' for a man like Brahms was, to say the least, a significant decision. Faced with a piece of manuscript paper one of the first things to be written (before the twentieth century at any rate) was a key signature. One supposes that the imagined music calls out for its key, but it is not impossible for the key to evoke the music. At all events the Olympian connotations of C (its grand sonorities in chamber music building up from the bottom note of the cello) evoke a large style and an ample procession of themes. The first subject is delivered by the two strings in octaves, and the richness and athleticism of the piano part means that, to hold their own in the matter of balance, the strings play together for much of the first movement. Indeed, it is not until a string phrase winds elegantly downwards to the beginning of the second group that violin and cello are heard separately—in a downward version of the upward phrase in the Violin Concerto which serves the same lead-in function. There are, at a conservative count, three strongly differentiated second-subject themes, which in themselves cause a different kind of music from the concentrated and closely-knit motif-work of which Brahms was so capable. The development is comparatively short, considering what is available for the purpose, and it begins, once again, with a very short 'false reprise' in the home key, which, however, is not long enough to prevent a real recapitulation at the expected place. Quite a large amount of the development discusses an elongation of the first subject in dialogue between the strings, but a reversion to this dialogue in the coda, after a perfectly normal recapitulation, brings it into proportion. It is significant that a 'perfectly normal recapitulation' has become a matter of comment.

The slow movement is a theme and five variations, very wide-ranging in style but rigorous as to shape. The statement of the theme is by the strings two octaves apart, on which Clara approvingly commented. A quirk of the theme is that its last seven bars consist of a four-bar phrase and its inversion telescoped thus into seven bars.

This reads very academically, no doubt, but it serves two purposes: first, to help the listener with a signpost to the end of each variation, but second, and more poetically, to throw into relief the moment when in the fifth variation the shape is not observed, but the music expands lovingly to its dying fall. The movement is in A minor but the fourth variation is in A major with piano harmonies in syncopated 6/8 time which are euphonious even by Brahms's standard. It is linked sweetness, but not drawn out.

The unconditional *presto* mark of the scherzo is in itself rare and calls for dexterity since much of the swiftly altering texture is soft as well. There is relief in the slower C major tune of the middle. (Not called a 'trio', perhaps because it is one.) The title 'Finale' and the overall *giocoso* direction proclaim an unbuttoned mood, and as in the first movement there is an outpouring of many themes. They become more closely knit as the work proceeds to its completely extrovert conclusion.

Op.88 *String Quintet no.1 in F*

Allegro non troppo ma con brio
Grave ed appassionato alternating with Allegretto
Vivace and Presto
Allegro energico

First publication: Simrock, November/December 1882.

Elisabet's remark about the 'bald, prosaic fashion' in which the framework is exposed is certainly true of the first movement. However, Brahms called the work a 'product of spring' and 'probably one of my finest works'—not in any defensive way. The opening tune lacks conviction and fire, beginning *poco f* and *non troppo allegro* to eliminate all danger of being carried away. The inversion, chromaticisms and contradictory rhythms that follow by way of transition do not sit well on the medium and the lead into the secondary subjects is by way of a bald dominant seventh followed by a silence, a rather startling baldness. But the change of key from F to A at this juncture has the same brightening effect as in the almost contemporary Third Symphony, because the new key involves sharpening both the principal notes (tonic and dominant) of the old. The new tune, whose swinging triplets also anticipate the Third Symphony, is given *con anima* to the first viola, but it is overlaid, both here and at the recapitulation, with contradictory rhythms: three against four and two against three. The feeling of manipulation remains in the contrapuntal discussions in the development, but clarity breaks out in a large climax before the reprise, liberally using the bottom Cs of the three lower instruments.

On the other hand, the second movement shows Brahms at his most imaginative. It is a sandwich of slower and faster tempi. The opening *grave* is taken from a sarabande for piano written as an essay in baroque pastiche probably as early as 1854. It begins in C sharp major with the cello playing the tune above the other four. At the fifth bar it is C sharp minor, and thus it remains till the first alternative, a vivacious pastorale in A major, 6/8 time. This ends in silence on an ambiguous harmony, and the music reverts, but more elaborately than before, to the sarabande. The next element in the sandwich is a presto, again in A, which is a greatly accelerated version of a gavotte probably dating back to 1855. Brahms has made its first paragraph exactly the same shape of that of the allegretto. After beginning in the key of the presto (A) the sarabande makes its way back to C sharp . The music subsides on to alternations of the two basic keys, then surprises us by choosing to end in A after all.

This use of A, arrived at by coming down from C sharp, balances the arrival of the first movement there by coming up from F. It is to be the first destination again in the last movement. The dashing fugal opening is reminiscent of Smetana's *Bartered Bride* overture, which all Europe knew soon after it was first heard in 1866. The initiating hammer strokes are put to very untragic use in comparison with op.81, with the second amusingly failing to appear when expected. The end is quite unbuttoned, *presto*.

Op.99   *Cello Sonata no.2, in F*

Allegro vivace
Adagio affettuoso
Allegro passionato
Allegro molto

First publication: Simrock, April 1887.

This sonata, from its trumpet-like opening, employs on the whole a higher cello range than the first, and is also, with its four movements including a true adagio, bigger and more profuse in its total effect. Curiously, when there is so much to choose from, Brahms bases much of the texture of the first movement on the *tremolandi* with which the pianist accompanies the opening. These are more effective on the piano than on the cello, and in the middle of the movement are developed into a shadowy episode in a distant key, greatly in contrast to the exuberant style of much of the rest. As with the Fourth Symphony, the recapitulation is marked by a soft return of the first subject in longer notes. Kalbeck surmised that the slow movement was the one originally intended for the First Cello Sonata, but there is no evidence. Its tonal surprises tempt one to doubt the earlier date. It adopts the very distant key of F sharp major, in keeping perhaps with the tonal manipulations of the Fourth Symphony. However, perhaps even more surprising after this leap, after only 19 bars the cello is announcing a second theme in F minor, of all unlikely things. Considerable use is made of *pizzicato*, to an extent unusual in a Brahms duo, and not only in the easy sonority of the bottom of the instrument, but high and loud as well.

Reverting to F minor and to his intermittently stormy style Brahms writes a substantial scherzo equivalent, its difficulties for the pianist greatly increased by the necessity to keep quiet for much of the time. For instance, to quote only the first two bars for the right hand:

After three such movements, large in every sense, the last movement seems disconcertingly short, at *allegro molto* and two in a bar. There is, however, a moment when the cello reverts to some of the passion and material of the slow movement. In its light surroundings it could sound parodistic, but it is hard to imagine Brahms parodying himself.

Op.100   *Violin Sonata no.2, in A*

Allegro amabile
Andante tranquillo alternating with Vivace
Allegretto grazioso (*Quasi andante*)

First publication: Simrock, April 1887.

The work begins with a series of five-bar phrases, each instrument adding a one-bar echo to his partner's four-bar phrases. The second subject begins with an adaptation of the song 'Wie Melodien' op.105 no.1, written before but published after the sonata. But structurally more important is its pendant

whose first notes made into a sarabande rhythm signpost the end of the very gentle development and of the whole movement. The second movement is the familiar sandwich of lyrical and scherzo elements. If we discount the brief vivace at the end where the music shrugs its shoulders, the other two 'scherzo' passages are identical in structure, harmony and key, but the second moves faster than the first, of which it is a strict and witty variation. The *andante* parts are of seamless melody, fluctuating between the tonal poles of D and F, and leaving the settling of the issue until the last moment.

Lyricism still predominates in the last movement, and formally it is unconventional. After 30 bars of flowing tune the rhythms and harmonies are disturbed by a cloud of piano-arpeggios. Brahms's friends—'we pedants' as Heinrich Herzogenberg called himself and them—were puzzled by this cloud sounding like a transition but not leading to another subject. Instead it clears away, and the first subject is repeated. With hindsight we seem to be hearing a rondo of sorts with the 'cloud' as the first episode—or subject in itself. There is more definite shape in a further episode, an impulsive melody (by the standard of this piece) in the minor. However, the coda is still sunny and lyrical. Elisabet was justified in calling the whole work 'one caress'.

Op.101   *Piano Trio no.3 in C minor*

Allegro energico
Presto non assai
Andante grazioso
Allegro molto

First publication: Simrock, April 1887.

The main interest of the first movement lies in the tautness with which it is knit together, making it shorter than the examples in the other trios. The themes in themselves have no particular individuality, being representatives of the 'fierce' and the 'consoling-noble' respectively, complete with the three rising crotchets yet again, and all in the expected keys. At the end of the exposition the extension of the first theme is counterpointed by the rising crotchets of the second. This 'false reprise' begins in C minor, but only 17 bars later the music, at its first *dolce* mark, is in C sharp minor with the rising figure of the second subject expressed in the triplets which are the main feature of the first. The short development leads to a recapitulation, not of the first theme (which is not swallowed up *en passant*; it simply is not there), but of a passage which was a pendant to it, leading straight on to the large second theme scored as before, but in the major. This major however, cannot withstand the vehemence of the minor for long.

The second movement is another example of the shadowy C minor type, with muted strings. In keeping with the general terseness this scherzo movement (if it is one) does not have a formal 'trio' though Brahms's two double-bars suggest such a ternary shape. The main reason is that the main limb is only 30 bars long and is not repeated *da capo*, but rescored. The middle of the movement is itself ternary, so that the following sophisticated structure emerges: A B C B (identical, with a little coda) A (identical tune, much varied scoring, with a coda as long as A was). Thus the restless mind is able to think each form anew, even when the melodic materials are not striking in themselves.

The third movement arranges its main theme so that most of its phrases are seven crotchets long. It is exposed (the right word, one feels) by the two strings alone alternating with the piano for the most part. The fact that the cello has no sustaining pedal makes the repeats and echoes of the piano sound like a demonstration to the strings of what their phrases ought to have sounded like.

After the gentle third movement the piece comes to violent life with the main impulses coming from the piano in big leaps and handfuls of chords and arpeggios which are a physical pleasure to play. It is interesting from the marketing point of view that evidently Brahms and Simrock felt that music like this, issued as ever in score and parts, was not outside the scope of enough amateur music-lovers to make publication worthwhile.

Herzogenberg relished the trio with the apposite remark 'Smaller men will hardly trust themselves to proceed so laconically without forfeiting some of what they want to say.' However, he then addresses the writing in the finale, on behalf of an amateur wife:

> Your big paw comes down heavily with the very opening of the Finale, however, and one sees stars, and begins to count the slain; at least it nearly proved the death of my wife, that stormy semiquaver passage in particular . . . and finally the tremendous jubilations where the rhythm would not come right—not that it matters!

It may be paradoxical to speak of controlled abandon, but we have Brahms's words to the Herzogenbergs about this very movement to vouch for it: 'I should think that the Trio's Finale requires, first very careful handling, then the reverse!' From the professional viewpoint, Clara, having at first bewailed the fact that the trio was beyond her strength, played it in London in March 1888, on the occasion of her nineteenth and last English tour:

> Yesterday I had the joy of playing your Trio at the 'Popular Concerts' accompanied [sic] very beautifully by Max Neruda and Piatti . . . Neruda played with great warmth and beauty. One has to sweep Piatti along with one, which I succeeded in doing, and once again enjoyed your magnificent piece more than anybody else. I make so bold as to say that my feelings while playing could only be equalled by yours when composing it!!!

Op.108   *Violin Sonata no.3, in D minor*

Allegro
Adagio
Un poco presto e con sentimento
Presto agitato

First publication: Simrock, April 1889.
Dedication: Hans von Bülow

This, the last of the violin sonatas, is on a larger scale than the other two, not only in having four movements but also in the variety and (especially in the outer movements) the vehemence of its emotions. For instance, although the violin launches without preliminaries into song it is *sotto voce* and rendered restless by the syncopations of the piano, soon to burst into *forte* eruptions.

The central 'development' is a *tour de force*, reverting to *sotto voce* for the whole of its 46-bar length, during which the piano like a soft insistent drum strikes an A on every one of the 184 crotchets. This is balanced, by way of coda, by using the same technique on D. As if to compensate for the turbulence and mystery of much of the allegro, the adagio allows a full lyrical flowering to both instruments, with some reminscences of the Violin Concerto. The third movement is far lighter in style but, as often in Brahms, entirely avoids the boisterous connotations of the 'Scherzo'. Its whimsicality lies in the contrasts with which its falling third is treated: usually hesitant, even stuttering in effect, but sometimes abrupt and boldly modulating. The last movement unleashes an energy without precedent in the violin sonatas in an alternation of galloping 6/8 rhythms with a chorale-style second subject. At the end of the exposition there is, it seems, an immediate recapitulation, but this is broken off into a development of ever more insistent syncopations. Then with typically Brahmsian control the recapitulation is taken up not at the beginning but at the very point where it was broken off 64 bars before. The virtuoso piano writing of the final page bears out the old-fashioned order of instruments in Brahms's titling of the Sonata, used in the first edition: for Pianoforte and Violin.

Op.111 *String Quintet no.2 in G*

Allegro non troppo, ma con brio
Adagio
Un poco allegretto
Vivace, non troppo presto

First publication: Simrock, February 1891.

The cello leaps in to deliver the ardent first subject, making his way as best it can through the luxurious scoring, a richness which is a feature of the whole movement with rests few and far between. Particularly striking is the presentation of the first of the secondary themes, starting as a viola duet and sometimes employing a charming division of the nine quavers in a bar thus: 1 2 3 4 5 6 7 8 9 (the underlinings mark the accents). The slow movement is a minor-key march, full of variety yet not employing any contrasting themes. Its close is marked by a soaring cadenza-like phrase on the first viola. The third movement is a relaxed intermezzo, whose contrasting major-key section features alternating duets for violins and violas. Its easy-going style must have reinforced Kalbeck's opinion that the work owes its origins to the Prater. The vivacious last movement makes witty use of a main subject which begins softly in the 'wrong' key (*à la* Haydn) but which is loudly corrected into the right one. There is a final animato which uses a 'Gypsy-Hungarian' style in five-bar phrases.

Op.114   *Clarinet Trio in A minor*

Allegro
Adagio
Andantino grazioso
Allegro

First publication: Simrock, March 1892.

Simrock's title page still gives the piano priority, with the second instrument as clarinet (or viola). A viola part was available in print from the outset and was tried out by Joachim at the Meiningen rehearsals in November 1891. But so strongly is the trio redolent of the clarinet's individuality, particularly in the adagio, that we can assume that the alternative was for increasing the market by domestic use.

The problem of pairing the cello with an instrument more likely to catch the ear had already been addressed in the Double Concerto op.102. This leads to the cello starting both first and second subjects in the first movement. The *fortissimo* pendant to the first subject is also in the

rhythm of a prominent theme in the Double Concerto, but whereas the Concerto sounded joyful at this point, the trio uses it almost entirely in the minor, and rather overshadowing the C major secondary material. It usurps the place of the first subject at the recapitulation, and also begins the coda, whose final scales and arpeggios, *pp sempre*, make the cellist's life difficult by requiring him to match something which is far easier on the clarinet.

Brahms *prima donna* comes into her own in the adagio, leading out the main theme and exploiting the wide range of the compass and of the dynamics. It is a *locus classicus* of the combination of fantasy and passion within a coherent whole of only 54 bars. The next movement to some extent echoes the mood of the gentler 'Liebeslieder' Waltzes, though in a paler version. The scale of the movement is larger than its unassuming start would suggest. The last movement reverts to A minor with the beats sometimes divided into twos and fours, sometimes into three. The cello has the first say in both the principal themes. The clarinet, as an instrument, does not suggest the open-air ebullience of the horn, but Brahms shows without staleness that there is life in the old dog yet.

Op.115 *Clarinet Quintet in B minor*

Allegro
Adagio
Andantino, with Presto non assai
Con moto

First publication: Simrock, March 1892.

As with op.114 the viola is the published alternative to the clarinet. In this closely integrated work there is a wonderful plasticity of theme: an element of one can become a growth-point of another, yet all without the monotony which a description of such features can all too easily suggest. Indeed one of the connecting threads in the work is an ambiguity as between major and relative minor; the opening theme is in its third bar before it veers definitively to B minor from what could until then be heard as D major.

Brahms is not content simply to let the entry of the clarinet make its effect by the difference in tone colour. It immediately gives the opening theme a calm, delicious elongation. (Compare the elongations of the violin in the slow movement of op.77.)

The development falls into two distinct parts, both showing their subject material in a new light. The plaintive semiquavers of the opening theme are the basis of a passage of sustained energy; whereas the very rhythmical chordal passage which previously succeeded that opening theme becomes ever more smooth and meditative, unwinding the music before the recapitulation.

The adagio presents a theme of rapt calm over undulations of muted strings. The three first notes of the melody

are the basis of the contrasting *più lento* section, in which the clarinet plays a disciplined Hungarian rhapsody using, for Brahms, a wide range of compass. The lingering sweetness of this movement makes a trance-like stillness, a stepping out of the world. Particularly lovely is the way the main phrase, by the addition of one note, makes four-beat phrases extend across three-beat bars.

The next movement begins as a gentle hovering between D major and B minor again, with the major having the last word. But the next faster section, though obviously beginning as a varied form of the andantino, almost takes on the dimensions of a movement in its own right more obviously in B minor but teasingly going back to D at the end.

The last movement is a set of variations on another gentle theme, yet again hovering between D and B minor. However, this becomes permeated towards the end with the original theme of the whole work which rounds off the whole. (However, note how the second note of the scale is flattened to C natural as though it has lost the energy to raise itself further.) The piece is so bound up with the queenly qualities of the noble instrument that one is justified in nick-naming it 'the clarinet quintessence'.

Op.120 *Two Sonatas for Piano and Clarinet (or Viola)*

No. 1 in F minor
Allegro appassionato
Andante un poco adagio
Allegretto grazioso
Vivace

No.2 in E flat
Allegro amabile
Allegro appassionato
Andante con moto, with Allegro

First publication (in two books): Simrock, June 1895.

The two Clarinet Sonatas are Brahms's final chamber works. Composers and composition students rightly find in them an astonishing integrity of construction caused by supreme skill in shaping short motifs so that they serve in both themes and accompaniments, and flow into and out of one another with no 'spare' material. This may sound rather gaunt, and indeed old age, in these sonatas especially, reinforced Brahms's predisposition not to write two notes where one would do. But it is also noteworthy, before we think of 'all passion spent', that each of these sonatas contains an *allegro appassionato*, and, as Pamela Weston says in the *New Grove*, Mühlfield's interpretations were reckoned to be dramatic and very moving.

In the F minor Sonata the first movement, although held together by its related motifs, explores a wide variety of rhythms, keys and moods, and the last page, marked *sostenuto ed espressivo*, summarises the movement in concentrated emotion, yet even at this point the music is still growing out of earlier material. The gentle fantasy which is one of the hallmarks of the clarinet informs the slow movement which, although hints of sonata shape can just be discerned, gives the impression of uninterrupted song. The third movement is gentle again, at a far remove from the ebullience of a scherzo, yet playful in its slight ambiguity of key in the principal subject. There are hints of a *Ländler* in it as well, and the middle section exploits the 'hollow' sound of the lower notes of the clarinet. The final movement releases the extrovert energy which has been mostly abstained from hitherto in an ebullient rondo in the shape of A B A C B A. The C in the scheme is in the minor, standing rather apart from the rest. The principal subject is signposted by three repeated notes.

The first movement of the E flat Sonata represents Brahms's final essay in sonata form. It is an unsurpassed example of plastic variation of material, both in melody and accompaniment, so as to integrate the whole by innumerable cross-references. A few explosions apart, the general effect of the movement is of unbroken song, itself a departure from the normal terms in which sonata form is expressed. In this context the 'scherzo' needs to come second. It has most of the features: a triple rhythm, a ternary shape and a large *sostenuto* tune in the major largely clothed in thirds and sixths. But it is also in F flat minor (again!) as to its main paragraphs, and is explicitly passionate. Instead of forming a scherzo-sandwich the andante movement becomes the last movement, so to speak, It is a set of variations on a gentle but sophisticated tune, which characteristically ends with a six-bar rather than a four- or eight-bar phrase. A feeling of 'acceleration' is achieved by using the old technique of successively shortening the ruling note lengths. There is indeed an allegro in the minor key before the tail-piece of the variation theme gains the centre of the stage, after which a final burst of rhythmic energy brings to an end what remains, and is likely to remain, a unique corpus of chamber music.

Keyboard Music (Piano and Organ)

This falls into three groups: opp. 1 to 35 representing the young-eagle-cum-concert-pianist, then opp. 76 and 79, the latter particularly if played together representing one of Brahms's most passionate utterances, and opp. 116 to 119 making a unique body of mainly short works of a quite exceptional richness of harmony and rhythmic device, calling for an intimate fusion of fingers and brain.

Op.1   *Sonata for Piano, in C*

Allegro; Andante; Scherzo (*Allegro molto e con fuoco*); Finale (*Allegro con fuoco*)

First publication: Breitkopf and Härtel, December 1853. *Dedication*: Joachim.

Although the work begins with an unmistakable reference to the rhythm of Beethoven's 'Hammerklavier' Sonata, two traits can be ascribed to his 'Waldstein' Sonata, also in C, which we know was in Brahms's concert-standard repertoire just before his sixteenth birthday. It is a common procedure in major-key movements for the opening phrase to be answered one tone up (in the minor). See for instance the first allegros in Beethoven's first two symphonies: C major to D minor and D major to E minor respectively. In the 'Waldstein' on the contrary the 'answer' to the first four bars is a tone down, in B flat . However, whereas Beethoven's is a muttering effect, Brahms makes a climax of his modulation at the top of a *crescendo* run. Brahms had fairly frequent recourse to this modulatory way of starting, but none more beautiful and striking, because immediate, quiet and unprepared, than in the opening orchestral statement of the violin concerto, in the fifth bar where the D major drops to C. The 'Waldstein' would also have encouraged Brahms to be unorthodox in the key(s) of his secondary material. In a classical exposition the music would move from C to G major; in the 'Waldstein' it moves to E major (initially at any rate); in this sonata it moves to A minor after suggesting it is going to E, and Brahms also gives us suggestions of E flat and D minor. What is more, these excursions are in moods far indeed from the martial robustness of the opening, involving changes of tempo, use of soft pedal, and (later very uncommon!) *sospirando* ('sighing'). One can imagine the young man intent on making himself clear through the precious opportunity of publication. As to the daring harmonic excursions, one has to be confident of one's powers, and perhaps fired by Schubert's example, to defy so early the advice later put so tellingly by Hilaire Belloc: 'Always keep a-hold of Nurse.' At the end of the movement, and common to all three sonatas, is climactic writing with handfuls of notes in both hands covering a very large top-to-bottom range—perhaps part of what Schumann meant by 'veiled symphonies'.

The slow movement, written before the others, is 'after an old German love-song', and its opening, published complete with words, is laid out as though for *Vorsänger* ('leader-soloist') and chorus, all at male-voice pitch. 'The moon steals upwards', sings the *Vorsänger*, to which the refrain could not be more folky and Romantic: 'blue, blue, little bloom'—which sounds, in English, a good deal more stilted than the alliteration of the original: 'blau, blau Blümelein'. The last bars of the movement foreshadow the immediate onset of the Scherzo, but a more striking migration of themes is the transformation of the subject of the first movement into the beginning of the Finale. This technique was very much 'in the air' at this date, but Brahms never came near bringing it to its logical conclusion as in the single-movement sonata of Liszt which Brahms heard at Weimar—or half-heard depending on what one believes. The technical difficulties of the music are not so much in the passage-work like that of the Weber *moto-perpetuo* as in harmonic sure-footedness enabling the pianist to grasp handfuls of notes in a jump at a moment's notice, for instance the right hand's task *allegro con fuoco*, at the beginning of the Finale:

Brahms never grew out of this 'handfuls-by-jump' technique, as pianists will know from his very last sonata: bars 15–17 of the Clarinet Sonata op.120 no.2.

To complete the folksong picture, the slow movement's original was arranged no fewer than three times by Brahms, the last example being at the end of the set of 49 brought together in 1893–4. Brahms wrote to Clara from Ischl in August 1894: 'Has it occurred to you that the last of my songs comes in my opus 1 . . . It might represent the snake which bites its own tail, that is to say, to express symbolically that the tale is told, the circle closed . . .' Luckily, it was not so. One of the episodes in the Finale, Brahms told Dietrich, hovered (*vorgeschwebt*) before his mind to the Burns poem 'My heart's in the Highlands'.

Op.2 *Sonata for Piano, in F sharp minor*

Allegro non troppo ma energico; Andante con espressione; Scherzo (*Allegro*); Introduzione (*Sostenuto*) and Finale (*Allegro non troppo e rubato*).

First publication: Breitkopf and Härtel, February, 1854.
Dedication: Clara Schumann. Brahms asked Robert Schumann's permission (letter of 29 November 1853) to dedicate the work to her as a 'small mark of esteem and gratitude'.

The quasi-extempore effect of some of the showy piano writing in the first movement, and its tendency to sectionalise itself with pauses and silences, make for problems of continuity, though Brahms does allow a rising-bass motif to permeate the movement, e.g.:

and its inversion to being a sweeping and still passionate secondary theme:

As with op.1, the slow movement is based on a folksong, as Brahms told Dietrich. The tune appears to be the composer's own. It does not figure in subsequent arrangements, but it initially fits the words 'Mir ist leide' ascribed to the *Minnesänger* Kraft von Toggenburg. Here again the variations range widely, in incidental modulations and in rich pianistic device, and lead straight into the Scherzo which uses the same opening. There is here a foreshadowing of the *fortissimo* trills which feature in the First Piano Concerto. Though perhaps the introduction, and the balancing tail-piece (at last in the major key) of the last movement are too cadenza-like for their purpose, it is interesting to see Brahms intent on giving weight and length by these means, taking a cue from Beethoven's Fifth Symphony, whose first movement rhythm is alluded to *fortissimo*.

Op.4   *Scherzo for Piano, in E flat minor*

First publication: Breiktkopf and Härtel, February 1854.
Dedication: Ernst Ferdinand Wenzel, a foundation teacher at Leipzig Conservatoire, whom Brahms met in November 1853. (See the narrative.)

Op.5   *Sonata for Piano, in F minor*

Allegro maestoso; Andante espressivo; Scherzo (*Allegro energico*); Intermezzo (Rückblick—Andante molto); Finale (*Allegro moderato, ma rubato*)

First publication: Senff, February 1854.
Dedication: Countess Ida von Hohental. Kalbeck suggests it was a thank-offering for hospitality.

The composition of this climax of the sonata trilogy probably goes back to late 1852 with again the slow movement written first together with its Intermezzo aftermath—Rückblick means 'backward glance'.

The opening subject is as rhetorical as ever, with big contrasts of compass and dynamics, and the rhythm

much in evidence, in C minor yet again at its first appearance, what is more. The general effect of the movement is less sprawling than in the earlier sonatas because the themes, though individual, are less heterogeneous and the technique of deriving them from each other is much more subtle. It is clear evidence of the early mastery of the technique of making one thing lead to another which Brahms and Wagner were at one in regarding as the essential element of larger-scale composition. But the survival of the heart on the sleeve is also the essence of the matter, as is here conspicuously the case.

Three lines from the minor poet Sternau are quoted above the Andante.[16] It is not a 'song without words' insomuch as Brahms's tune does not fit them, and they speak, rather unremarkably, of the gloaming, of the moon and of two hearts united in love and encircled in bliss. There is a formal surprise, in that the alternative theme in what seems to be a slow rondo develops to such a climactic extent that neither the first theme nor its key returns at the end of the movement. After the Scherzo which is still virtuosic but taut, with one Trio, the Intermezzo harks back to the slow movement, but in the minor with funeral drums much in evidence. The clue lies in Sternau again. Brahms carried around with him for years a book into which he wrote poems which struck him as suitable for songs, though often it was a very long time, if at all, before the poems got their musical clothing. In this book are the three lines preceding the slow movement. But the succeeding stanza is also in the book: 'If you knew how soon, how soon the trees are withered and the wood is bare, how soon comes the dreary day when the heart's beat is dumb.' In effect it is a much more sombre and leaden-footed 'Gather ye rosebuds while ye may.' Assuredly Sternau is no Herrick! But, as with many a Brahms song, commonplace words are sufficient to spark off the music. The finale gradually, and somewhat whimsically—note the *rubato* direction—cheers itself up from F minor, and the process is begun by a lyrical tune beginning F–A–E. The three sonatas course with red blood. Brahms later admitted that he 'stormed away' (*tobte*), but there is no evidence that he repented of any of them.

Op.9 *Sixteen Variations for Piano on a theme by Robert Schumann*

First publication: Breitkopf and Härtel, November 1854.
Dedication: Clara Schumann.

The epigrammatic nature of Schumann's theme, with its contrasting and climactic middle and its subtly balanced harmonic destinations, make it an ideal springboard for the young man's fancy, yet also when he wills it a means of holding it in shape:

There are many harmonic surprises, some of a teasing, spectacular kind, some arising from the theme being put in the bass or the middle (variations 1 and 3). There are abrupt contractions of the length of the phrases (variations 2 and 7). There are swift contrasts of the capricious, the virtuosic and the nocturne-like. Salient Schumannisms and emotional counterpoint are noted in the narrative, to which should be added the very beautiful top-and-bottom canon at the sixth below (a difficult interval to work) in variation 15. As if seeking to ensure the unsuitability of the work for ordinary concert life, the last variation is mainly soft; it puts Schumann's bass into the major key beneath a minimal right hand.

Op.10   *Four Ballades for Piano*

1. After the Scottish Ballade 'Edward' in Herder's 'Voices of the Peoples'
2. Andante
3. Intermezzo (*Allegro*)
4. Andante con moto

First publication: Breitkopf and Härtel, February 1856. *Dedication*: J.O. Grimm, a student of the Leipzig Conservatoire six years older than Brahms. They met in Leipzig in 1853, and both stood by Clara in 1854 in Düsseldorf.

The pieces are discussed in some detail in the narrative (see pages 20–21). The Ballade 'Edward' is also set as an original song (op.75, no.1).

Op.21   *Variations for piano*

No.1 on an original theme
No.2 on a Hungarian song

First publication: Simrock, March 1862.

Though the sets were published together No.2 is probably earlier in date (certainly as regards the notation of the theme). The theme of the first set is a binary one of two phrases of equal lengths of four plus five bars, that is, with the middle and final cadences each elongated. Each variation has a consistent texture, often using wide extensions of the hands, which the pedal makes into rich, indeed luxurious harmonies. As with op.9, the most 'learned' variation—no.5 including a canon in contrary motion—is an emotional centre, with three markings in the course of the first three bars: *molto dolce, teneramente, molto espressivo*. The eighth variation, after much previous quiet music, explodes into the minor, and at its climactic second part makes a truly powerful effect by using ten bars instead of nine. The last variation begins with varied repeats, making 36 bars above non-stop left hand trills, but the ensuing long dying fall guarantees that the audience will not experience what it would expect in 'piano-recital' variations in the 1860s.

The Hungarian song, the basis of the second set, uses alternations of three and four in a bar, an irregularity which attracted Brahms. Compared with the first set the variations are less ruminative and are sometimes brash and orchestral. The final Allegro is ample enough to swallow a considerable section in a foreign key, but the peroration is a re-statement, *ff*, of the theme.

Op.23 *Variations for Piano four Hands on a a Theme of Robert Schumann*

First publication: Rieter-Biedermann, April 1863.
Dedication: Julie Schumann.

The theme, which Schumann fancied was at Schubert's and Mendelssohn's dictation, occurs in the slow movement of his Violin Concerto. Brahms thought of calling it in print 'Schumann's last musical thought' but Clara dissuaded him. Brahms relaxes some of the strictness mooted to Joachim by allowing three of the ten to be in other keys than the original E flat. The first three use the baroque technique of dividing the beats into successively shorter notes. The fourth is noteworthy for gaunt two-part counterpoint, each voice expressed in octaves. Most of the piece is appropriately elegiac and the last is a solemn march over which by way of coda parts of the original theme recur.

Op.24 *Variations for Piano on a Theme of Handel*

First publication: Breitkopf and Härtel, July 1862.

The domestic intimacy of Clara and Julie playing op.23 is abruptly replaced by the distinctly public style of this large and sometimes spectacular work. Here the symmetrical phrase-lengths of Handel's tune (which he himself constructed for variations) are rigorously adhered to, except that one extra bar occurs in the fifteenth of the 25 variations, and all are in B flat major or minor except no.21 which although in G minor carries the original tune, by harmonic sleight-of-hand, in grace-notes without transposing it. Within these constraints, or rather because of them, a great variety of timbres and idioms are employed, sometimes orchestral as with horns in variation 7 or horns and flute (variation 12). Moods vary from 'Hungarian' funeral march (variation 13) to Sicilian pastoral (variation 19) and there is even a musical box *à la musette* in variation 22. The final fugue at last breaks into longer paragraphs with wide modulations and towards the end cascades of octaves and thirds accompanied by 'pedal' notes first at the top, then at the bottom.

Op.35 *Studies for Piano*

Variations on a theme of Paganini

First publication (in two books): Rieter-Biedermann, January 1866.

The first edition gives 'Studien' as the first and sole word in the top line, and Variations etc. as the subtitle. But the use of an opus number shows that the work was regarded, as it had every right to be, as a piece of music. Kalbeck suggests, with reason, that Brahms's friendship with Tausig over op.34 *bis* inspired it. Its *bravura* demands caused Clara to call them 'witches' variations, and generations of perspiring pianists have reckoned that Brahms was intent on writing something as difficult for the piano as Paganini's original Caprices were for the violin. Schumann had written two sets of studies after Paganini Caprices (op.3 and op.10) but they did not include this, the last of Paganini's set. The theme has been a favourite variation subject ever since it appeared, and rightly so, because of its brusque clarity, its straight-forward destinations and the interesting 'acceleration' of its phrase-lengths, beginning with two-bar cadences:

(Brahms's grace-notes are omitted.)

So strictly is the basic phrase-shape preserved (until the final movements in each book) that analysis is hardly necessary. Brahms himself played the first performance, presumably of the whole. If the books are played separately one has to reckon with being plunged into a whirl of modulations and double thirds in the very first variation in the second book.

Op.39 *Waltzes for Piano four Hands*

> *First publication*: Rieter-Biedermann, September 1866.
> *Dedication*: Eduard Hanslick.

Brahms also supplied the publisher with two versions for piano solo, one for 'clever hands and one—perhaps for more beautiful hands'. The waltzes are all the same shape—binary with repeats—and do not need analysis. But it is interesting that after the winning no.15 in A (A flat in the standard solo version) he ends the set with the gentle melancholy of no.16 in D minor. This propensity for a ruminative end, certain not to bring the house down, may spring from Schumann's example, for instance in the Phantasiestücke op.12, the *Scenes of Childhood* op.15 and the *Forest Scenes* op.82.

Op.52a *Waltzes for Piano Duet without Voices*

> Texts from various languages, all in Daumer's German translations in his *Polydora*.
>
> *First publication*: Simrock, October 1869 (op.52); December 1874 (op.52a)
>
> (See the narrative, page 64.)

Op.56b *Variations for two Pianos on a Theme of Joseph Haydn*

> (see also pages 71–2, and 167)
>
> *First publication*: Simrock, January 1874 (op.56a); November/December 1873 (op.56b)

One can gather from Brahms's not unambiguous correspondence with Simrock that he regarded both the orchestral and two-piano versions as valid works; he particularly did not want op.56b the two-piano version, to be regarded as an arrangement. It was in any case written first.

The theme, with its preponderance of five-bar phrases, is set out for orchestra much as it appeared in the original, with the bass reinforced by the *pizzicato* cellos and double basses, and with the contra-bassoon standing in for the serpent. The repeated B flats, enclosing a seven-bar coda at the end of the theme, become the central support of the first variation which deploys a two-against-three between the upper and lower strings, mainly in contrary motion. Unusually the second variation plunges immediately and at a faster speed into the minor key with trumpets and drums marking the beginning of the phrases. Variation 3 reverts to the major, and a third different tempo, and varies the scoring for the two 'repeats'. In variation 4 an overt use of learned counterpoint is a feature: invertible counterpoint at the twelfth. That is to say that the countertheme will fit both below and above the other, but instead of being transposed one or two octaves, which is easier, it is transposed a twelfth which is a good deal harder. The variation begins thus (bass omitted):

At the repeat of this phrase it becomes:

In variation 8, a mysterious *presto non troppo* in the minor again, the opening phrase on muted violas and cellos is answered upside-down by the wind at the same interval of the twelfth, thus:

followed by:

What Brahms calls the Finale begins as a passacaglia above a five-bar ground-bass which has obvious affinities with the theme. Its actual emergence begins *pp* but is highlighted by the arrival at last of the triangle.

Colourful and worthy of its ovations as the orchestral version is, op.56*b* is a very effective recital piece, especially if the *staccato* brilliance of the fifth variation can be tossed off (and kept together!). Though variation 6 highlights the horns, the crisp *martellato* of the piano makes the music sound exceptionally well.

Op.65*a* *(same title as op.65)*

(Subtitle: Arrangements for Piano Duet without Song.) Texts from various languages, all in Daumer's German translations in his *Polydora*.

First publication: Simrock, op.65, September 1875; op. 65*a*, April 1877.

See the narrative. These differ from op.52 in that seven of the 15 items are solos and one is a duet.

Op.76 *Eight Piano Pieces*

Book 1
1. Capriccio (in F sharp minor)
2. Capriccio (in B minor)
3. Intermezzo (in A flat)
4. Intermezzo (in B flat)

Book 2
5. Capriccio (in C sharp minor)
6. Intermezzo (in A)
7. Intermezzo (in A minor)
8. Capriccio (in C)

First publication: Simrock, March 1879.

Both Clara and Elisabet made comments on some of these pieces, with which Brahms broke a long silence as regards piano solos. Elisabet roundly declared the first to be her favourite, now and for ever, but she also got Ethel Smyth to copy out the second for her. This is a quirky rondo with syncopations and a nimble dancing lilt in the manner which has been found reminiscent of Schubert's Moment Musicale no.3. Elisabet made an amusing offer to the composer (letter of 13 December 1878): 'If you want to see something beautiful look at the last eight bars.' Brahms asked Clara for an appraisal of all the pieces and in particular whether she agreed he should omit no.8. She replied (letter of 7 November 1878):

> A great favourite of mine is the C major, and yet you want to leave it out. If you omit any at all I should prefer it to be the A major, for though its middle movement is charming, it is too reminiscent of Chopin, and the beginning is too insignificant for Brahms.

This harsh opinion is a compliment, as the piece is only commonplace to the extent of taking breath on the dominant after a regular eight-bar phrase. This intermezzo and its successor are true to their names (as some are not) in that they relax the player and listener between two caprices which are highly sophisticated both in their layout for the piano and in their subtleties of chromatic harmony. Clara initially found them 'terribly difficult'. However, the difficulties are nothing like those of say the Handel or Paganini Variations. They consist of following the quick turns of chromatic language and acquiring the knack of going where Brahms's exploratory fingers had gone. In the C major it is notable (in view of op.79 no.2 to come) that a straight root position chord of C is not to be found until almost the end. It is certainly nowhere to be found in exposition or middle.

Op.79 *Two Rhapsodies for Piano*

No.1 in B minor
No.2 in G minor

First publication: Simrock, July 1880.
Dedication: Elisabet von Herzogenberg.

Taken together, as they usually were in Brahms's lifetime, these two pieces represent the most substantial of the mature solo piano works. Brahms had intended to dedicate to his friend in succession op.75 (the duets containing 'Edward') and op.78 (on the face of it highly suitable) but eventually decided on these pieces. One can read what one pleases into it, but they certainly deploy a grand passion with no punches pulled. The manuscript which he gave her heads them respectively *Capriccio* (*presto agitato*) and *Molto passionato*. The programme at Brahms's first performance of them (20 January 1880 at Krefeld) called them both 'Caprices'. Elisabet was surely correct in observing that 'the clearly defined form of both pieces seems somewhat at variance with one's conception of a rhapsody'. The first makes much of the contrast between the obstreperous main subject and the sad repeated

♩ ♩ ♩

of the second. The surprise is that the middle of the piece is devoted to the extension of this in the tonic major, a key very unexpected in that position. Similarly in the Second Rhapsody, in which the sonata form shape is easily apparent, the middle has a long patch in the tonic minor. But this balances the conspicuous lack of a 'proper' G minor in the exposition. The insistent triplets in the G minor give the piece some affinity with 'Edward', but to less melodramatic ends.

Op.116 *Seven Fantasies for Piano*

First publication: Simrock, November 1892.

Brahms had evidently expended his imagination on the pieces, rather than their titles, for they were published as 'Capriccio' as to nos.1, 3 and 7, and 'Intermezzo' (nos.2, 4, 5 and 6), the former being the loud and fast ones. (However, the autograph gives the title 'Notturno' to no.4.) Jonathan Dunsby[17] has made a case for the musical inter-relationship of the entire set, citing among other things the falling thirds adding up to a seventh chord:

in no.1 and

in no.3.

This is borne out by Brahms advising Simrock that if the pieces were to be published in two books 'the first three and the last two go together'. Nevertheless the set was published in two books without Brahms suggesting they must be an integral whole. There is no record, among the early first performances, of the set being brought before the public as a whole, but we do know that Brüll played the first three at a Vienna concert in January 1893, thereby bearing out Brahms. None of this disproves Dunsby, of course. We are on slightly vaguer ground in seeing an overt connection between nos.6 and 7, if indeed these are the 'last two' to which Brahms was referring. But the connection of the rising chromatics between the two beautiful E major intermezzos is palpable enough:

Op.117 *Three Intermezzi for Piano*

First publication: Simrock, November 1892.

Kalbeck records that Brahms described these pieces to Rudolf von der Leyen as 'three cradle songs for my sorrows' (*Drei Wiegenlieder meiner Schmerzen*), but this was a phrase he used fairly often at the time. Simrock wanted to call the famous first intermezzo 'Cradle song' referring back to the famous 'Wiegenlied' op.49 no.4. However, Brahms wanted any such title, if used (it was not, eventually) to be amplified to 'Cradle song of an unhappy mother', because in the autograph he had written a motto: the words, which fit the beginning of the tune which, translated, run 'Sleep soft my child, sleep soft and well; it grieves me sore to see thee weep.' Where the word *Weinen* comes in the German there is a realistic grace-note in the music. The words were in Herder's German translation of a piece called 'Lady Anne Bothwell's Lament', coming in turn from Bishop Percy's *Reliques of Ancient English* [sic] *Poetry*. There is an enclosed calm in the use of tonic pedals both above and below the main tune, and a further relaxing when the six quavers in the bar are dissolved by quiet chords into the accentuation

instead of

The use of the tune within the texture is also exploited in the 'Wiegenlied's' companions.

Op.118 *Six Piano Pieces*

First publication: Simrock, November 1893 (with op.119).

Brahms is very slightly more adventurous in his titles, calling nos.3 and 5 Ballade and Romanze respectively. On the other hand the rest are all called Intermezzos in spite of the fact that nos.1 and 6, in the nature of the case, are not between anything. In the second intermezzo the inconspicuous technical mastery is evidenced by such things as the climax, *dolce*, of the first limb being the inversion of the opening

to

and by the canons and near-canons in the middle section. The middle of the Romanze uses a pedal bass and, unusually for Brahms, more than a touch of the modal by raising the fourth note of the major scale at the phrase-ends—a possibly Scandinavian touch with Grieg in mind? The last intermezzo exploits the darker tones of the instrument while allowing a rise to a big climax which could hardly have been foreseen from the opening paragraph.

Op.119 *Four Piano Pieces*

First publication: Simrock, November 1893 (with op.118).

The pieces are three intermezzos, followed by a rhapsody, the first so titled since op.79. For Brahms's views, to Clara, on how to play no.1, see the narrative. No.2 is a wistful yet playful piece, an excellent example of the late variation style, with a central variation partly looking back to the most ingratiating of the waltzes. There follows a true, quick-silver intermezzo (only 1½ minutes) beginning with the tune at the bottom of the right hand. Note the teasing cross-accent implications shown by the brackets:

The Rhapsody is the last published piano solo. It begins very robustly with the five-bar *martellato* phrases of Brahms's youth, then becomes for a while a sectional mosaic; but it is pulled together with a real 'hammer and tongs' ending. The piece having begun in E flat major ends with triplets in E flat minor, coming in a sense full circle back to the athleticism of the op.4 Scherzo.

Op.122 *Eleven Chorale Preludes for Organ*

1. Mein Jesu, der du mich
2. Herzliebster Jesu
3. O Welt, ich muss dich lassen
4. Herzlich tut mich erfreuen
5. Schmücke dich, o liebe Seele
6. O wie selig seid ihr doch, ihr Frommen
7. O Gott, du frommer Gott
8. Es ist ein Ros entsprungen
9. Herzlich tut mich verlangen
10. Herzlich tut mich verlangen
11. O Welt, ich muss dich lassen

First publication: Simrock, April 1902.

The Protestant German tradition of the prelude on a chorale faltered, to say the least, with the death of Bach. In his lifetime chill winds of rationalism and of new fashions in worship had been blowing upon, and freezing out, the 'high' view of church music's function which he reckoned he had inherited from Luther. This, coupled with the manifest impossibility of emulating Bach in this field, meant that these few mature organ works of Brahms represent the only chorale preludes in the nineteenth century by a great composer. Consequently there is a risk of over-valuing them, but most of them show a poised beauty of counterpoint and harmony suffused with emotion which would make them outstanding in a world of competitors.

At first sight the opening prelude is the most antiquarian, using the traditional technique of fugal discussion of each successive line of the tune, leading up to its presentation in longer notes. (The German single word for the process is *Vorimitation*.) But the chromaticisms and the subtle variety of the textures bring it into a world where 'ancient' and 'modern' lose much of their relevance. The pairs of settings, nos.3 and 11, and nos.9 and 10, call for particular mention. The tune of the first pair was early notated by Brahms and its setting by Heinrich Isaac (*c*1450–1517) figured in his choral concerts. Its secular words were 'Innsbruck I must leave thee' but spiritualised at an early date they became the gentle leave-taking of the world which Brahms expresses here. The first puts to individual use the slurred pairs of neighbouring notes which Bach often uses, for instance in the chorus (itself a huge chorale prelude) which ends the first half of the *St Matthew Passion*. Brahms's farewell (no.11) treats the tune in successive lines of five-part harmony of great richness, each followed by a double echo with the last touchingly elongated. No.9 takes the 'Passion Chorale' and gives a four-part setting, straight through but with spectacular chromatics. No.10 is the jewel of the whole. The tune, on the pedals, is enclosed above and below. The right hand plays a constant run of semiquavers, the left adds a heart-throb of repeated quavers. The first two bars show this texture. Note how the throbbing bass imitates in advance the first phrase of the tune, and also the very beautiful and entirely Brahmsian sophistication whereby the 24 semiquavers in the second bar are arranged in eight groups of three:

Fugue in A flat minor for Organ

(unnumbered work, Werk ohne Opuszahl)

First publication: Breitkopf and Härtel, July 1864.

See the narrative for the genesis of this work in 1856. It seems to have had a prelude, now lost, at one stage. The subject of the fugue seems to have a likeness to a theme from Schumann's *Manfred* quoted by Kalbeck. The answer to the subject proceeds by inversion, and there are also augmentations and diminutions. In spite of this scholasticism the effect of the piece is powerfully emotional. The way it is printed makes it uncertain whether, and if so by how much, it ends more loudly than the penultimate *pp* on another manual.

Choral Music

In view of the Requiem one can only regret that there is no other work of comparable size in this category. All show the experienced hand of a well-versed choral conductor. Particularly noteworthy are the extraordinary modulations of op.89 and, for skilled singers, the gloom and consolation expressed in op.74.

Op.12 *Ave Maria for Women's Choir with Orchestral or Organ Accompaniment.*

First publication: Rieter-Biedermann, December 1860 or January 1861.

See the narrative.

Op.13 *Begräbnisgesang ('Burial song') for Choir and Wind.*

First publication: Rieter-Biedermann, December 1860 or January 1861.

See the narrative, but note also how Brahms partly reverts to the movement's opening shapes in the first of the 'Four Serious Songs', op.121.

Op.17 *Four Songs for Women's Choir, two Horns and Harp*

1. Es tönt ein voller Harfenklang (Ruperti)
2. Lied von Shakespeare (trans. by Schlegel)
3. Der Gartner (Eichendorff)
4. Gesang aus Ossian (trans. by Herder)

First publication: Simrock, January 1861.

With their three-part (S S A) voices in close harmony and their 'bardic' choice of instruments these songs represent, as the 'Ave Maria' does, Brahms as a deliberate exploiter of colour and euphony. The Shakespeare text is 'Come away, come away, death', the clown's song in *Twelfth Night*, Act 2 Scene 4. 'Ossian', a shadowy figure at best, was not so much translated as invented by the Scottish eighteenth-century poet James Macpherson. Young Brahms could have researched this, but was in distinguished company, for instance that of Goethe, in preferring to believe in the romantic prototype of the innocent and noble savage.

Op.22 *Seven Mary-songs for unaccompanied Mixed Choir (SATB)*

1. Der englische Gruss
2. Marias Kirchgang (SSATB)
3. Marias Wallfahrt
4. Der Jäger
5. Ruf zur Maria
6. Magdalena
7. Marias Lob

First publication: Rieter-Biedermann, October 1862.

The texts of all these short pieces have folksong origins. It is interesting to note that Brahms composed anew although he knew the original tunes of three of them (as is also to be seen in the case of some solo songs). The style is mainly homophonic, but the vocal lines are so melodic that a hymn-like effect is avoided. No.6 appertains to Easter, the rest to Christmas.

Op.27 *The 13th Psalm, for three-part Women's Choir (SSA) with Organ or Piano*

First publication: Spina, May 1864?

As early as September 1859 Brahms wrote to Clara about his 'Psalm 13 for female choir and small orchestra, and he conducted a performance in Vienna (2 April 1876) with organ and orchestra. The surviving parts show that the orchestration is for strings alone. For practical purposes it may be noted that the string parts contain no note that is not in the organ part. There are some additional notes in the organ part but these double the voices, whose parts though very effective are not by any means difficult. One must accept that there is no overt unification of the piece by musical motifs, since like its Renaissance and Baroque predecessors it proceeds on the principle of 'new words, new motifs'.

Op.29 *Two Motets for five-part Mixed Choir (unaccompanied)*

1. Es ist das Heil uns kommen her
2. Schaffe in mir, Gott, ein rein Herz

First publication: Breitkopf and Härtel, July 1864.

The layout is SATBB except that there is a one-bar division of the tenor at the end of no.1 and a short division of the alto in the third movement of no.2. The two motets are musically independent and were indeed published separately. However, they are obviously linked by their affinities to the techniques of Bach and his predecessors. The words and tune of the first motet date back to the beginnings of the Protestant church in the sixteenth century, and the words are the first verse of a hymn by Paul Speratus. The impulse to use them could well arise from Brahms's possession of Bach's Church Cantata no.9 in the first volume of the Bachgesellschaft. The stanza is first set as a chorale, but with striking harmonies, and then proceeds to a contrapuntal discussion of a type very frequent in baroque chorale preludes for the organ, in which each line of the tune is treated by a fugal exposition culminating in its delivery by one voice in longer notes, in this case the first bass. Brahms allows some very characteristic chromaticisms for the final entry.

The second motet sets verses 12–14 of the penitential Psalm 51, beginning at 'Make me a clean heart, O God'. The art conceals art in the euphonious canons of the first movement and the beginning of the third, but elsewhere the reverse is the case in rhetorical imitations and inversions of the subjects.

Op.30 *Sacred Song for four-part Choir (SATB) and Organ or Piano*

First publication: Breitkopf and Härtel, July 1864.

The text of this work is by Paul Flemming (seventeenth century) and it dates back to the contrapuntal studies shared with Joachim in 1856. Brahms accurately describes it on the autograph as 'double canon at the ninth', that is to say (in this case) that, until the final 'Amen' section the tenor follows the soprano exactly, a bar later and a ninth lower, while the bass similarly follows the alto. A *tour de force* certainly, but dextrously smoothed by the figuration and harmonies of the organ. Joachim made some criticisms of the counterpoint when he received it, but we do not know whether Brahms heeded these before he published the piece eight years later.

Op.37 Three sacred Choruses for female Choir (SSAA) unaccompanied

O bone Jesu
Adoramus
Regina Coeli

First publication: Rieter-Biedermann, September 1865.

The first two numbers, at least, were written for the Hamburg Ladies Choir. The intricacies of these studies in canon make for some ungainly patches. The texts and motifs are of Renaissance-style music, which make for discomfort where the rules of the style are flouted by such things as unprepared second inversions.

Op.41 Four Songs for male Choir (TTBB) unaccompanied

1. Ich schwing mein Horn (Old German)
2. Freiwillige her! (Lemcke)
3. Geleit (Lemcke)
4. Marschieren (Lemcke)
5. Gebt Acht! (Lemcke)

First publication: Rieter-Biedermann, November 1867.

These are occasional, mainly chordal pieces, all except the first being soldiers' songs uttering conventional sentiments. The more interesting harmonies and colours are to be found in the fifth song. The first song reappears in op.43 as a solo.

Op.42 Three Songs for six-part (SAATBB) Choir unaccompanied

1. Abendständchen (Brentano)
2. Vineta (Wilhelm Müller)
3. Darthulas Grabgesang (James Macpherson trans. Herder)

First publication: Cranz (Hamburg), 1868?

These songs are altogether more extended and interesting than op.41. Brahms shows a fine sense of colour in the grouping and part-writing of the six parts, and is assured in expressing his adventurous harmonies in a way which sits comfortably on the voices. The charming melody of 'Vineta' sets it above the others, and rightly, in popular esteem.

Op.44 *Twelve Songs and Romances for Women's Choir, with Piano ad lib*

1. Minnelied (Hölty)
2. Der Bräutigam (Eichendorff)
3. Barcarolle (Italian, trans. Witte)
4. Fragen (Slavonic, trans. Grün)
5. Die Müllerin (Chamisso)
6. Die Nonne (Uhland)
7–10. Four songs from Heyse's 'Jungbrunnen'
11. Die Braut (Müller)
12. Märznacht (Uhland)

First publication: Rieter-Biedermann, October 1866.

All twelve of these songs were in the repertoire of the Hamburg Ladies Choir. The piano part, though sparing, does more than merely support the voices, and often adds the bass an octave below the women's compass. It is especially effective in what is in any case the song—no. 12—of most musical substance, a gentle chromatic storm preluding the spring. The assured vocal writing, even with a minimum of counterpoint, shows how well and quickly Brahms had learnt this aspect of his art, since some of the songs were certainly at least six years old when they were published.

Op.45 *A German Requiem according to the Words from the Holy Scriptures, for Soli (Soprano and Bass) Choir and Orchestra (organ ad lib.)*

First Publication: Rieter-Biedermann, 1869.

The title of the work means simply that is it not the Latin Requiem Mass which Brahms has set. Indeed it is not a liturgical work at all, but a series of texts connected with death drawn by Brahms from the bible in the German vernacular. It makes it difficult to know what to call the work when it is not sung in German. 'Brahms's Requiem' is as good a title as any in that circumstance.

The first chorus has words from the Beatitudes—'Blessed are they that mourn' (*St Matthew* V. 4) and from Psalm 126 verses 5 and 6, beginning with 'They that sow in tears shall reap in joy'. In the whole chorus the violins are silent, but the effect is very different from the Second Serenade, being now one of a different and darker-coloured string orchestra surmounted by wind instruments and choir. The austere effect (austere for Brahms, that is) also springs from the absence of clarinets, and the centre of gravity of the brass is lowered by the absence of trumpets while permitting the solemnities of soft trombones. On the other hand though there is only one harp part Brahms asked for it to be played by at least two harps. The main key is F, but the psalm is introduced in D flat, and this relationship of a major third down from the tonic, often episodic in Schubert, is a persistent long-term element of tonality in the *Requiem*. It is noteworthy that at the return to F for the recapitulation the woodwind changes places with the voices for several phrases, establishing an equality of partnerships between orchestra and choir which, except in the set-piece fugues, is a distinguishing mark of the work. Just before the harps resume at the end of the movement, a climax is made by spreading the phase

through the voices. It is no more than a cadence phrase at this juncture, beautiful though it is.

The full orchestra is used for the second movement, but in a sense the strings are still led by the violas, as their slow triple-time funereal march is either in their hands alone, or is doubled by muted violins. The chorus sings with unison conviction the words from I Peter 1 verse 24 that all flesh is grass. In this section, in B flat minor, the piccolo plays like a chill wind adding intimations of mortality. Few of its notes here would be inaccessible to an ordinary flute; what is clearly sought is its hollower, bleaker tone. For the next section the husbandman's patience is recalled, waiting for the rain. The key is now G flat (again the major third down). The piccolo could perfectly well assist the flute with the raindrops, but its characterisation is established and it is silent, as also for the bright fugal procession of the ransomed going into Zion. The soft choral cadence with the sopranos falling from the third to the tonic, echoes the same interval at the end of the first movement.

The third movement begins with the bass soloist's prayer (Psalm 39 verse 5) 'Lord, make me to know mine end, and the measure of my days', with the strings reverting to a sonority without violins, who enter unobtrusively with the chorus, but quickly take over as the pessimism takes on a more despairing tone. The first modulation is out of D minor to B flat —a major third down again. Ultimately with the onset of more hopeful texts two very surprising things occur: first a strict-time cadenza for choir, *crescendo molto,* then the considerable fugue in D major on D whose unhappy fate in Vienna is described in the narrative. The expressive reason for this *tour de force* is that it shows the righteous secure in the hand of God (Wisdom of Solomon 3 verse 1).

The possible connection between the next chorus, 'How lovely are Thy Dwellings' (Psalm 84 verse 1) and Schubert's Mass in E flat is mentioned in the narrative. To use, by way of introduction the inversion of the main theme may seem a mere pedantry:

but it returns to add a sense of benediction at the end. This feeling is reinforced by the great beauty of the soprano solo, with chorus, 'Ye now are sorrowful' (John 16 verse 22) with its promise of comfort, like that of a mother. There are sublime modulations, and the reprise is marked, most unusually, by a small cello solo.

However, the next chorus sets 'Here we have no abiding place' (Hebrews 13 verse 14) very graphically, the *pizzicato* bass restlessly tramping through very vague tonal country. There is a splendid depiction of the last trump. The German being *Posaune* it is given to the trombones, marked *ff* for the first time in Brahms's music. This crisis is resolved by a big C major fugue with episodes, and time-honoured strettos. The first two intervals of the subject, formed by the notes C B G are ultimately inverted and stride through the whole texture from bottom to top. This ending does not ring as true as the serene last chorus 'Blessed are the dead which die in the Lord' (Revelation 14 verse 13). This reverts to the tempo and key (F mayor) of the first chorus, but the first choral phrase is a proclamation derived from its end:

The first conspicuous modulation is up a major third to A, thereby balancing the previous falls with a gleaming effect caused by sharpening the principal notes of the tonic, F and C. The violins are now in full flow from the beginning of the movement, contributing a spectacularly high entry from this A:

The first outright quotation from the 'Selig sind' of the first movement is in D flat (again) on the flute, but gradually the work comes fully home to end as the first movement did, with harps but without trumpets.

Op.50 *Rinaldo, a Cantata by Goethe for Tenor Solo, Male Choir and Orchestra*

First publication: Simrock, August 1869.

To twentieth-century eyes, the main disadvantage of this work is simply that it is a cantata by Goethe, not set to a libretto by, say, Quinault. Armida's garden without Armida, and remembered infatuation without seduction, is a curious state of affairs, but if Brahms is to blame it is only for choosing Goethe. But another difficulty in imagining the piece as a living work is that it was written in the hey-day of large male-voice choirs (see the narrative), and its effect is partly dependent on this sound which is very difficult to arrive at in the late twentieth century. The chorus are the heroes—not Rinaldo obviously—and must sound heroic and needing a symphony orchestra to match them. Indeed, otherwise the extended last chorus, over which Brahms took much trouble, has little point when, if one looks at the piece as drama, the work is by then all over bar the shouting.

However, there is much interesting detail. The clean-limbed chorus is interrupted by a Rinaldo still bewitched and, amusingly, somewhat Wagnerian for a moment. The *poco adagio* in A flat in which he is unable to renounce the 'golden days' contains elaborate and beautiful wind writing, which continues into the somewhat Mendelssohnian E major with which the chorus pleads with him to ignore the doves and nightingale. Muted violins and a long oboe solo accompany Rinaldo's last backward glance before the final destructions of the accursed palace. In short, Brahms gives fascinating glimpses of a Venusberg of his own—which can, of course, be enjoyed because reason and duty are the winners.

Op.53 *Rhapsody for Alto Solo, Male Choir (TTBB) and Orchestra (A fragment from Goethe's 'Harzreise im Winter')*

First publication: Simrock, January 1870.

It is evident that Goethe speaks directly to Brahms with the figure of the misanthrope who has lost his way and drunk hatred out of the cup of love. The sense of being lost is powerfully, but of course not arbitrarily, evoked in an orchestral introduction beneath muted *tremolando* violins, the C minor tonic chord only being heard on the last beat of the first bar. Much play is made with the lower alto compass, most spectacular being the word-painting of the desert (Oede). The following example gives every note of the score at that point:

The music turns to a consolatory major as the choir enters to second the prayer to the Father of Love to open the sufferer's eyes to the wellsprings in his wilderness. The pizzicato triplets of the cello reinforce Goethe's prayer that the Father's psaltery may be heard to begin the deliverance. There is a solemn and soft cadence, *tutti,* as of some cosmic 'Amen'.

Op.54 *Schicksalslied, by Friedrich Hölderlin for Choir and Orchestra*

First publication: Simrock, December 1871.

The poem contrasts in starkest terms, without a hint of reconciliation, the gods above in gleaming light with heavenly zephyrs playing upon them, like the fingers of the artist playing the sacred strings, and below them man with no continuing place, thrown by circumstance like water from one cliff to another, ever downwards.

The orchestral introduction, 'slow and longing' clothes a luxurious tune on the muted violins with soft harmonies, but with a persistent

on the timpani. Typically, there is no harp for the fingers of the heavenly artist, but *pizzicato* lower strings. The drum triplets, however, can be read as a distant, and disregarded, allusion to the tumultuous depiction of man's blind struggles in a C minor 3/4 time, with jagged cross rhythms, and adding the full force of trumpets and trombones to two climaxes, each made the more shattering by a sudden silent bar before them. When this vision has disappeared, the orchestra resumes in C major, but slower than before, the music of the prelude, now with the addition of soft brass, and ending entirely serenely. Some critics, perhaps with wishful thinking, have seen this melting music as a 'correction' of Hölderlin's bleak antithesis, as though beautiful music can make the reconciliation. Brahms wrote to Reinthaler (October 1871): 'I even say something that the poet does not say, and clearly it would be better if what is unsaid had become for him the principal matter'. However, this does not necessarily mean that the postlude is some sort of reconciliation, but that the gods' luxuriating disregard of man continues (see also 'Iphigenia's Song' in op. 89). There is a sketch, quoted in Kalbeck, of the C major ending incorporating the chorus very quietly reverting to the opening words describing the light-filled bliss of the gods, which seems conclusive. It is hardly possible that someone of Brahms's beliefs—and disbeliefs particularly—should attempt to utter in music words of comfort which would never have passed his lips.

Op.55 Triumphlied for eight-part Choir and Orchestra (organ ad lib)

First publication: Simrock, November 1872.
Dedication: Kaiser Wilhelm I.

Brahms deploys the big forces with a very sure, if inevitably somewhat impersonal, touch. The many Hallelujahs and the broad sweep of the ceremonial music are bound to evoke Handel, but three trumpets in D also add a touch of Bach. Brahms only otherwise used three trumpets in the Academic Festival Overture. If listeners fancy they hear snatches of 'God save the King' at the opening they are assuredly wrong; the tune is that of 'Heil Dir im Siegerkranz'. The second movement begins in gentler style in triple rhythm in G, but retaining Handelian dotted notes. After another outburst of Hallelujahs the choirs are more particularly antiphonal, one in common time, the other in 12/8 for a movement woven round the opening phrases of "Now thank we all our God'. A short baritone solo begins the third movement with the passage from Revelations 19.11: 'And I saw the heaven opened, and I saw a white horse, and him that sat thereon.' The chorus completes the sentence: 'called faithful and true; in righteousness he doth judge and make war'. The King of Kings and Lord of Lords is finally greeted with more Hallelujahs. But the music is not mere pastiche, and despite the massive lines it is written on, it contains some adventurous patches of swiftly modulating harmony.

Op.62 *Seven Songs for mixed Choir unaccompanied*

1. Rosmarin (SATB) (from *Das Knaben Wunderhorn;* Arnim and Brentano)
2. Von alten Liebesliedern (SSAATTBB) (from *Das Knaben Wunderhorn;* Arnim and Brentano)
3. Waldesnacht (SATBB) (Paul Heyse)
4. Dein Herzlein mild (SATB) (Paul Heyse)
5. All meine Herzgedanken (SAATBB) (Paul Heyse)
6. Es gehet ein Wehen (Paul Heyse)
7. Vergangen ist mir Glück und Heil (Old German)

First publication: Simrock, September 1874.

These are unpretentious part-songs almost entirely homophonic but with considerable variety of mood. Most are strophic, but no. 6 uses imaginative vocal scoring and a minor/major contrast.

Op.74 *Two Motets for mixed Choir unaccompanied*

1. Warum ist das Licht gegeben
2. O Heiland, reiss die Himmel auf

First publication: Simrock, December 1878.
Dedication: Philipp Spitta.

Though there are unmistakable allusions to the techniques of Renaissance music in these works, Brahms in calling them 'motets' is using the word in the sense that Bach used it, namely as a suite of religious meditations whose texts are held together by their subject matter and whose music embodies a chorale. Brahms clearly also regarded Bach's motets as unaccompanied, as did scholars of his day.[18]

Op.74 *no. 1*

The text was assembled with skill and pride. The four movements set the following (*a*) Job Chapter 3 verses 20–23, desparingly asking why life is given to groping unhappy man; (*b*) Lamentations of Jeremiah Chapter 3 verse 41: not an explanation but an admonition to lift heart and hands up to God; (*c*) James Chapter 5 verse 11: we praise the enduring ones, for their Lord is merciful; (d) Luther's versification of Nunc Dimittis: Lord now lettest Thou Thy servant depart in peace. Pascall has shown in detail how much of the music is derived from a Canonic Mass in C begun in 1856 as part of the famous contrapuntal studies with Joachim. The surviving parts of the Mass—'Sanctus'. 'Benedictus', Agnus Dei' with 'Dona Nobis', were published by Doblinger in 1984, edited by Otto Biba. Brahms used the 'Agnus Dei', much expanded, for (a), the 'Benedictus' for (b) and the 'Dona Nobis' for (c). The final chorale used Luther's first verse set to what is traditionally regarded as Luther's tune. But the harmony is by Brahms, as striking as Bach in his best vein. The question 'Why' punctuates some highly chromatic writing sufficiently dangerous and taxing, then as now, for Joachim to comment on a student performance at his *Hochschule* in 1879 that the pitch did not sag by even as much as a comma. Musical and didactic impulses are both served at once by relating the end of (c)—'for the Lord is merciful'—to the beginning of (b)—'Let us raise heart and and hands to God', much as a preacher might do before announcing the relative hymn to reinforce his sermon.

Op.74 *no. 2*

Here Brahms has used five verses and the tune of a German setting of 'Rorate coeli desuper', asking for heaven to be opened and for the quickening dews of mercy to be shed on suffering man. The shape is thus that of chorale variations, such as Brahms knew well from having rehearsed and conducted Bach's Church Cantata No. 4. The progress towards this consummation is vividly portrayed in music by the slow beginning with verses ending on bare fifths leading through various sufferings to the climax of the 'Amens' in quick-moving canons.

Op.82 *Nänie by Friedrich Schiller for Choir and Orchestra (harp ad lib)*

First publication: Peters, December 1881.
Dedication: Frau Henriette Feuerbach.

Schiller's poem catalogues famous classical examples of the powerlessness of the immortals to save mortal beauty and ripeness from death, and concludes that nevertheless it is good to sing a funeral song for the loved ones since the common fate is to go songless to the grave. Schiller even uses the traditional classical metre of elegiac couplets for the purpose.

   In spite of the 'optional harp' of the title page, Brahms hopes for more than one harp where possible, and in any case uses loud *pizzicato* in the upper strings to add to the imagined voices of Thetis, Aphrodite, and the other gods in the central section (F sharp major in D). Significantly trombones add their voices—more often soft than loud—but not trumpets. The gentle counterpoint embodies harmonies which are rich and diverse, often expressed in falling sequences. Webern used the final page in teaching advanced harmony.

Op.89 *Gesang der Parzen, by Goethe, for six-part Choir and Orchestra*

First publication: Simrock, February 1883.
Dedication: Duke George of Sachsen-Meiningen.

The six parts of the choir are typically SAATBB, since Brahms is always more ready to lower the centre of gravity. In the play Goethe puts the words into the mouth of Iphigenia as she remembers them from her youth. Brahms uses no solo voice and treats the matter as though a chorus of a Greek drama is singing it, using indeed the traditional anapaest rhythm of such chorus entries in the accompaniment. Brahms explains his intentions in a letter to Billroth (6 August 1882) in which he says he will not mention Iphigenia in case critics judge the music by how near it is to her character (or to Goethe's play for that matter). 'It would never have occurred to Goethe that later generations would regard Iphigenia with that kind of reverence [*Ehrfurcht*]'. The sentiments of the 'Schicksalslied' are heard again, but the chorus address man in a baleful D minor vehemently expressed: 'Let man fear the gods who hold in their immortal hands, for their own satisifactions, the fate of all'. The outer darkness of waiting in vain is depicted in a startling and abrupt range of modulations (remember Elisabet's remarks about intonation). The late D major section brings not solace but a description of heedless serenity. The D minor descends again in muted strings as the Fates end their song and the despairing listener shakes his head. It is a short vivid, modern cry of despair.

Op.93a *Six Songs and Romances for four-part mixed Choir unaccompanied*

1. Der bucklichte Fiedler (Folksong from the Rhine)
2. Das Mädchen (Kapper, from the Serbian)
3. O süsser Mai (Arnim)
4. Fahr wohl (Rückert)
5. Der Falke (Kapper, from the Serbian)
6. Beherzigung (Goethe)

First publication: Simrock, December 1884.

These are cosy part-songs, not without a sentimental tinge. The fourth song is at once the simplest and the most effective. Its farewells resounded at Brahms's funeral.

Op.93b   *Table Song, Dank der Damen by Eichendorff*

First publication: Simrock, January 1885.
Dedication: to the friends in Crefeld, on 28 January 1885.

See narrative, page 117

Op.104   *Five Songs for mixed Choir unaccompanied*

1. Nachtwache I (Rückert)
2. Nachtwache II (Rückert)
3. Letztes Glück (Kalbeck)
4. Verlorene Jugend (Wenzig, from the Bohemian)
5. Im Herbst (Groth)

First publication: Simrock, October 1888.

The first three songs are for SAATBB; nos. 4 and 5 require SATBB. Chamber choirs would find these songs a taxing but rewarding experience. A mastery of counterpoint and harmony will go without saying, but what is most striking is the sense of vocal scoring which Elisabet commented on, perhaps adversely in the case of no. 4, 'the little string quartet in D minor'.

Op.109   *Fest und Gedenksprüche, for eight-part unaccompanied Choir*

First publication: Simrock, February 1890.
Dedication: His Magnificence the Lord Bürgermeister of Hamburg, Dr Carl Petersen

See the narrative.

Op.110 *Three Motets for four- and eight-part unaccompanied Choir*

1. Ich aber bin elend
2. Ach arme Welt
3. Wenn wir in höchsten Nöthen sein

First publication: Simrock, February 1890.

The striking ancient-and-modern flavour of this music can be heard in the opening seven bars, quoted in short score:

Palestrina, for one, would not have approved the unprepared dissonances at * (seventh above the bass) and ** (ninth above) and would have blanched at the entry of a new voice on a sharp dissonance at ***. Of course these are the places to savour. (See also the narrative.)

Op.113 *Thirteen Canons for Female Voices*

First publication: Peters, November 1891.

These canons, some of them easy 'rounds', some with quite dense musical content, represent a lifetime's interest beginning with works for the Hamburg Ladies Choir. The texts range from Goethe to folksong translations. The last is for six voices, two altos making a canonic drone while four sopranos discuss an adaptation of Schubert's music for the hurdy-gurdy man in the last song of '*Winterreise*'.

Songs

This is the category to which Brahms contributed all his composing life. The fact that so many of the songs are strophic, or nearly so, and use folk-song words and a matching (not original) folk-song style, tends to lessen their incidence in non-German programming. But the melodies are a key to Brahms's style, and it will be evident from the catalogue what treasures reside in such songs as op. 96.

Op.3 *Six Songs for Tenor or Soprano with Piano Accompaniment.*

1. Liebestreu (Robert Reinick)
2. Liebe und Frühling I (Hoffmann von Fallersleben)
3. Liebe und Frühling II (Hoffmann von Fallersleben)
4. Lied aus dem Gedicht 'Ivan' (Bodenstedt)
5. In der Fremde (Eichendorff)
6. Lied (Eichendorff)

First publication: Breitkopf and Härtel, December 1853.
Dedication: Bettina von Arnim.

The most noteworthy of these songs, deliberately chosen as the first published song, is discussed in the narrative. The key of the third song (B major) and the rising chromatics make it sound like an anticipation, not proceeded with, of Wagner.[19]

Op.6 *Six Songs for Soprano or Tenor and Piano*

1. Spanisches Lied (Trans. by Paul Heyse)
2. Der Frühling (Rousseau)
3. Nachwirkung (Meissner)
4. Juchhe (Reinick)
5. Wie die Wolke nach der Sonne (Hoffman von Fallersleben)
6. Nachtigallen schwingen lustig (Hoffmann von Fallersleben)

First publication: Senff, December 1853.
Dedication: Luisa and Minna Japha.

For the first song, see the narrative. When Simrock wanted to buy the set from Senff in 1885 to make a complete holding of Brahms, the composer did not value it highly, suggesting instead that Simrock saved his money and bought for him Burckhardt's *Cicerone* (guide). The songs in comparison with later ones fall into conventionality in their usually extended cadences.

The Rousseau words, though set strophically (i.e. with the same music for each verse) use an amount of modulatory sequence and word repetition which would have much displeased their author. In 'Juchhe' the first two verses are strophic, to permit interesting climactic modulations later (a frequent device of Brahms). The last vocal phrases, rather long drawn out, seem to refer to the introduction to 'Der Frühling'. As to interference with Rousseau's 'back to nature' simplicities, there is a fairly clear distinction which emerges as Brahms's songs proliferate, between folksong texts set as folksong equivalents, and art songs which do not 'set' the words at all in a mechanical sense. In the latter case one suspects that Brahms would concur heartily with Susanne Langer: 'Song is not a compromise between poetry and music . . . Song is music . . . when a composer puts a poem to music he annihilates the poem and makes a song.'[20]

Op.7 *Six Songs for Voice and Piano*

1. Treue Liebe (Ferrand, pseudonym for Eduard Schulz)
2. Parole (Eichendorff)
3. Anklänge (Eichendorff)
4. Volkslied (from Scherer's collection)
5. Die Trauernde (from Scherer's collection)
6. Heimkehr (Uhland)

First publication: Breitkopf and Härtel, November 1854.
Dedication: Albert Dietrich.

The first song has already been noted. The most Brahmsian of the others is no. 3 with its austere harmonies, one telling modulation and low thirds in the left hand darkening the texture.

Op.14 *Eight Songs and Romances for Voice and Piano*

1. Vor dem Fenster (Folksong)
2. Vom verwundeten Knaben (Folksong)
3. Murrays Ermordung (Scottish, in Herder's *Voices of the Peoples*)

4. Ein Sonett (Thirteenth-century French, in *Voices of the Peoples)*
5. Trennung (Folksong, in Kretschmer–Zuccalmaglio collection)
6. Gang zur Liebsten (Folksong, in Kretschmer–Zuccalmaglio collection)
7. Ständchen (Folksong, in Kretschmer–Zuccalmaglio collection)
8. Sehnsucht (Folksong, in Kretschmer–Zuccalmaglio collection)

First publication: Rieter-Biedermann, December 1860 or January 1861.

This is the first set of songs wholly given over to the folksong type as to texts and music, this particular 'sonnet' hardly being an exception. Since there are examples throughout his working life, we must suppose that Brahms was fascinated by meeting the challenge of inventing and honing melodies of sufficient beauty, simplicity and memorability to stand comparison with 'real' folk melodies. It is significant of his attitude to the task that he already knew two of the original folk melodies of this set, those of nos. 1 and 6. Indeed, they meant enough to him for him to arrange them for his Hamburg Ladies Choir. He is no mere scientific collector content once he has established authenticity. Some of the accompaniments are fairly elaborate for all the simplicity of the basic harmony. The fact that the style requires that divergences from the 'strophic' setting of the same tune for each verse are kept to a minimum is a constraint that Brahms meets with ease, but which tends to remove the songs from what one would expect at a modern Lieder recital. Nevertheless Alice Barbi made herself a particular favourite with the first song of the set.

Op.19 *Five Songs for Voice and Piano*

1. Der Kuss (Hölty)
2. Scheiden und Meiden (Uhland)
3. In der Ferne (Uhland)
4. Der Schmied (Uhland)
5. An eine Aeolsharfe (Mörike)

First publication: Simrock, March 1862.

Clara commented on some of these songs on 20 December 1858, and the song she liked best was 'Scheiden und Meiden': 'I constantly had to look at the title because I could not help thinking it must be a folksong, I mean a popular melody.' This must have been music indeed to Brahms's ears, and it is the prominent B natural in the D minor that gives the song its modal, Dorian feel. The next song, also praised by Clara, begins with the same phrase, but then turns luxuriously to the major key whose musings die away with a dreamy horn call. 'Der Schmied' with its hammering and sparks-flying accompaniment and gapped-arpeggio melody is a famous and very characteristic short strophic song. There are, most unusually, two passages marked *recit* in the last song, but the ensuing passages of song though they have the harmonic waywardness suggested by the romantic image, are not particularly grateful as melody. Wolf does it better in the *Mörike-Lieder*.

Op.20 *Three Duets for Soprano and Alto with Piano*

1. Weg der Liebe I (from the English, trans. in Herder's *Voices of the Peoples*)
2. Weg der Liebe II (from the English, trans. in Herder's *Voices of the Peoples*)
3. Die Meere (Wilhelm Müller, from the Italian)

First publication: Simrock, March 1862.

Kalbeck rather harshly calls all three songs 'routine Biedermeier products with Mendelssohnian trimmings'. Papa Biedermeier was a cartoon character, a solid bourgeois citizen, unimaginative to the point of philistinism as regards the deeper and higher things, but with a taste, which he could afford to indulge, for domestic comfort and sentimental art. In England Mr Pooter would be a kindred spirit. Musical evenings among the aspidistras may still provoke smiles, but those who will, on balance, rue their loss will also feel that young Brahms and Mendelssohn are praiseworthy for devoting some of their energies to this influential amateur public.

The first two songs of the set are devoted to the cliché that love will find the way, but they both have some harmonic subtlety as well as simplicity. The sad barcarolle of the third song is quite a long way from what one supposes Kalbeck meant by his adjective *gewöhnlich* ('commonplace'?).

Op.28 *Four Duets for Alto and Baritone with Piano*

1. Die Nonne und der Ritter (Eichendorff)
2. Vor der Tür (Old German)
3. Es rauschet das Wasser (Goethe)

4. Der Jäger und sein Liebchen (Hoffmann von Fallersleben)

First publication: Spina, December 1863.
Dedication: Amalie Joachim.

Brahms, while sending the published songs to Amalie as a Christmas present in 1863, was perhaps not using false modesty when he described the offering as a thin one. Certainly her name does not figure in the first public performances. But as 'musical evening' domestic pieces they are successful, three of them being of the 'frustrated serenade' variety. The first is the most characteristic with its evocation of a passion more or less extinguished by a parting for the crusades.

Op.31 *Three Quartets for four solo Voices (SATB) with Piano*

1. Wechsellied zum Tanze (Goethe)
2. Neckereien (Moravian)
3. Der Gang zum Liebchen (Bohemian)

First publication: Breitkopf and Härtel, July 1864.

The exchanges of the first title are between those who are indifferent to the claims of love against dancing (alto and bass) and the other pair who feel the opposite. The voices come together at the end, but not in agreement. The teasings of the second movement are between the male and female pairs, again with a short-lived, lively and unresolved quartet at the end. Brahms gave his own description of the third piece to Schubring: 'The Way to the Beloved goes like a pleasant waltz of middling tempo. I can't describe it any more closely.' However, we can describe the background dance as having the same tune as the fifth of the op.39 Waltzes. All three quartets could be described as mellifluous party-pieces.

Op.32 *Nine Songs for Voice and Piano*

1. Wie rafft ich mich auf in der Nacht (von Platen)
2. Nicht mehr zu dir zu gehen (Daumer, from the Moravian)
3. Ich schleich umher betrübt und stumm (von Platen)
4. Der Strom, der neben mir verrauschte (von Platen)
5. Wehe, so willst du mich wieder (von Platen)
6. Du sprichts, dass ich mich täuschte (von Platen)

7. Bitteres zu sagen denkst du (Daumer, after Hafis)
8. So stehn wir ... (Daumer, after Hafis)
9. Wie bist du, meine Königin (Daumer, after Hafis)

First publication: Rieter-Biedermann, January 1865.

There being no individual titles, only the opening words are given. Kalbeck found strong Schubertian influence in some of these songs. If he meant that they were derivative he was quite wrong. But they are, as to most of them, on a level of powerful inspiration which only Schubert equalled in the depiction of love betrayed or denied. Some of the harmonies and twists of tonality are truly astonishing, for instance this passage in the first song. To get a notion of the writhing intensity of its line, one might try singing it unaccompanied:

Note how greatly the desperate feeling that the lover's world is teetering in the soul's night is enhanced by the sinking G to F sharp parallel between voice and bass at the star(*)!

The wonderful harmonic and melodic beauty of the last song (in a sense Brahms's 'Liebestod') gains enormously by being preceded by some or all of the set.

Op.33 *Romances from Tieck's Magelone for Voice and Piano*

First publications: Songs 1-6 in two books of 3 each, Rieter-Biedermann, September 1865; Songs 7-15 in three books of 3 each, Rieter-Biedermann, December 1869. *Dedication:* Julius Stockhausen

All the texts come from *The wonderful Love Story of the beautiful Magelone and Count Peter from Provence* by 'Peter Leberecht', a pseudonym for the poet Ludwig Tieck (1773–1853). Thus the title 'Romances' is Brahms's, not Tieck's. Stockhausen won Brahms's admiration for, among other things, his commanding performances of classical song cycles, but we must note that although this is the nearest Brahms comes to a song cycle himself, he was content initially to leave the number at six. In a letter to Schubring (March 1870) he is explicit:

> In the case of the Magelone Romances one does not need many at one go, and should not pay any attention to narrative at all. It was only a touch of German thoroughness which led me to compose them through to the last number.

Thus the singer as well as the commentator is warned.

However, it would be easier to avoid unjustly blaming Brahms for failing to achieve what he did not set out to do if one could be sure what his intentions were. It appears that the poems were never in themselves meant to constitute a narrative; viewed as separate works of art a number of the songs show dismaying commonplace turns of phrase for both singer and player, resulting perhaps from indecision between bardic naivety and the artistry and deep explorations of the previous opus. Only two songs are given titles. One of them is 'Sulima', who appears late on the scene and who is clearly not intended to be the sharer of the homely domestic bliss which is evoked by the anticlimactic last song.

Nevertheless, the rapture of successful love is captured with much élan in the fifth song—'so willst du des Armen'—which relives the sentiments of Schubert's 'Mein!' in a different but just as successful manner (with a taxing two-against-three piano part). The beautiful beginning of the love lullaby which is the ninth song is often quoted. Truly Brahmsian is the left hand part with its anticipations of the beat and its seventh chords reduced to two neighbouring notes. Note also the soft clash of the chromaticism D natural against the established D flat.

A similar technique, urging the music on instead of sending the lover to sleep, is used in the first movement of the Second Symphony.

Op.43 *Four Songs for Voice and Piano*

1. Von ewiger Liebe (Leopold Haupt, from the Wendisch)
2. Die Mainacht (Hölty)
3. Ich schall mein Horn (Old German)
4. Das Lied vom Herrn von Falkenstein (Westphalian)

First publication: Rieter-Biedermann, December 1868.

The first song is well-known but rather obvious in its responses, with horn calls in the minor for the young man's speech about the worries of love, and horn calls in the major about the girl's certainties. There is a fine climax, for a mezzo voice. On the other hand, 'Die Mainacht' must have meant much to Brahms, since he quoted its theme to Henschel when confiding his ideas on letting compositions mature. The Asclepiad rhythms naturally integrate the song, which seems to contain a reminiscence from 'Ich grolle nicht' by Schumann. If so, it is a reference to lost love at the very moment when the singer hears the happy sound of the pair of doves. The long cadences require considerable breath control, as so often in the slower songs of Brahms. The third song is a solo setting, entirely chordal, of op. 41 no. 1. The fourth song uses a forthright folksong style—strophic with deviations—and much depends on telling the tale.

Op.46 *Four Songs for Voice and Piano*

1. Die Kränze (Daumer, from the Greek)
2. Magyarish (Daumer, from the Hungarian)
3. Die Schale der Vergessenheit (Hölty)
4. An die Nachtigall (Hölty)

First publication: Simrock, October 1868.

The fourth song is of a high musical quality, not only for its memorable beauty of line and sublety of variation, but for the way the metre of the poetry forms a springboard to Brahms's thoughts. Each verse is an alternation of lines of eleven and only four syllables. To establish the latter Brahms at first simply doubles their length (minims after crotchets); then he elongates them by repetition (two bars followed by three); at the end, following and enhancing Hölty's own repetition—'*entfleuch, entfleuch*'—he allows a rest between the two minim pairs to suggest the sighing silence of the musing poet. In comparison with Schumann or Wolf, it is not so often that Brahms, as here, puts an interrupted cadence below the last notes of the singer, so that the postlude of the piano must wind down the harmony as well as the song.

Op.47 *Five Songs for Voice and Piano*

1. Botschaft (Daumer, after Hafis)
2. Liebesglut (Daumer, after Hafis)
3. Sonntag (Uhland's German Folksongs)
4. O liebliche Wangen (Flemming)
5. Die Liebende schreibt (Goethe)

First publication: Simrock, October 1868.

With the famous 'Sonntag' Brahms achieved a folksong of his own composition. By its recognition the world has proved this. But the fourth song deserves the same success—it requires slightly more technique from both performers. The Goethe setting is a subtle study in line and modulation, with three-bar phrase lengths matching the poetry.

Op.48 *Seven Songs for Voice and Piano*

1. Der Gang um Liebchen (Wenzig, from the Bohemian)
2. Der Überlaufer (*Des Knaben Wunderhorn,* Arnim and Brentano)
3. Liebesklage des Mädchen (*Des Knaben Wunderhorn,* Arnim and Brentano)
4. Gold überwiegt die Liebe (Wenzig from the Bohemian)
5. Trost in Tränen (Goethe)
6. Bergangen ist mein Glück und Heil (Old German)
7. Herbstgefühl (von Schack)

First publication: Simrock, November 1868.

The text of no. 1 appears to different music in op. 31 no. 3. This is a strophic song, again to a waltz background, with a nimble accompaniment reminiscent of Chopin. The second song, a forlorn ditty of bereft love, was apparently first sung by Hermine Spies. A much more sophisticated rendering of the same sentiments is no. 3. Interestingly among the chromatic harmony, the only vocal phrase to fall straight on to the tonic is the very first one. 'Trost in Tränen' affords a direct comparison with the 17-year-old Schubert. Both composers adopt the strophic style for the question-and-answer poem, with the minor key for the lover's sad answers, but Schubert not only repeats the last two lines of each verse, but also, to achieve his beloved minor-major change repeats the last line yet again—a process which would surely not have pleased Goethe. Brahms is a good deal more clever in this respect achieving the sense of finality without any repeats at all by continuing the vocal line downwards on the piano:

No. 6 is a strophic tune imitating old German homophonic song. Its lover's complaint is set to a good vocal shape, but it is hardly exportable. A curiosity of the piece is that each syllable has its own root-position chord, with no exceptions. A mixed-choir version appears as op. 62 no. 7. As before, the last song of the set is the most individual and substantial in musical interest. The powerful portrayal of the chill of autumn could hardly be a matter of fewer notes.

Note the subtlety with which the eerie entrance of the left hand is first an 'echo', and then occurs with the last note of the voice, because it is a near-echo of the previous bar.

Op.49 *Five Songs for Voice and Piano*

1. Am Sonntag Morgen (Paul Heyse, *Italian Song Book*)
2. An ein Veilchen (Hölty)
3. Sehnsucht (Wenzig, from the Bohemian)
4. Wiegenlied (*Des Knaben Wunderhorn*, Arnim and Brentano)
5. Abenddämmerung (von Schack)

First publication: Simrock, November 1868.

The famous 'Wiegenlied' excepted, these songs have more intricate piano parts than the previous three sets, especially the quiet thirds in 'Abenddämmerung'. In the middle of this song there is a truly Brahmsian dislocation when for the whole stanza the twelve semiquavers are continuously employed in four groups of three (with a change of chord at the beginning of each group) against the normal three beats of the vocal line. Nos. 2 and 3 do not rise far above their commonplace sentiments, but the first song is epigrammatic and powerful; the jilted lover brave in public, weeping in private would have suited Wolf well in his *Italian Song Book* settings, but his failure to use it might be an unspoken compliment to Brahms.

Op.52 *Leibeslieder Waltzes for Voices and Piano Duet*

See pp. 64 and 237.

Op.57 *Eight Songs for Voice and Piano*

These having no titles, the opening words are given.
1. Von Waldbekränzte Höhe (Daumer)
2. Wenn du nur zuweilen lächelst (Hafis, trans. Daumer)
3. Es träumte mir (Spanish, from Daumer's *Polydora)*
4. Ach, wende diesen Blick (Daumer)
5. In meiner Nächter Sehnen (Daumer)
6. Strahlt zuweilen auch ein mildes Licht (Daumer)
7. Die Schnur, die Perl an Perle (Indian, from Daumer's *Polydora)*
8. Unbewegte laue Luft (Daumer)

First publication: Rieter-Biedermann, December 1871.

These songs are redolent of yearning love and some give themselves over to a striking sensuality. None of the songs is strophic, though one, no.2, is written as it were in one verse and one sweep without any sense of beginning again. The sense of quiet luxuriating is particularly strong in the dreamlike B major of no.3. The substantial last song is rich in the imagery of love, and its first vocal phrase is a telling example of the chromaticism Brahms indulges; note how the 'Neapolitanism' combines to decorate both the first and fifth notes of the scale, the former making something highly scented of an otherwise ordinary dominant chord:

Op.58 *Eight Songs for Voice and Piano*

1. Blinde Kuh (Kopisch, from Sicily)
2. Während des Regens (Kopisch)
3. Die Spröde (Kopisch, from Calabria)
4. O komme, holde Sommernacht (Grohe)
5. Schwermut (Candidus)

6. In der Gasse (Hebbel)
7. Vorüber (Hebbel)
8. Serenade (von Schack)

First publication: Rieter-Biedermann, December 1871.

The first four songs show Brahms nimbly addressing light sentiments of love, with the piano having to contribute almost more than the singer. The second song is a rain-song far less known than the one enshrined in the First Violin Sonata, but it is notable for its soaring phrases, all to be encompassed in a short time. The fourth song is a soft, fast nocturne, published with Brahms's fingerings for the rippling accompaniment. The next three songs are most unusual in that the second part of the poem may be a consequence of the first, but of a kind which forbids the musical shaping by reprises. Brahms has allowed the piano a recurrent rhythmical motif in the short and bitter sixth song, but in the fifth and seventh he allows the words to take their course to the musical shape A B, and holds attention throughout this risky procedure by the modulations and an unusual intensity of utterance. The Serenade reverts to the A B A form but, ironically, the shape is not so convincing because the middle section seems not to fit the rest.

Op.59 *Eight Songs for Voice and Piano*

1. Dämmerung senkte sich von oben (Goethe)
2. Auf dem See (Karl Simrock)
3. Regenlied (Groth)
4. Nachklang (Groth)
5. Agnes (Mörike)
6. Eine gute, gute Nacht (Daumer, from the Russian)
7. Mein wundes Herz (Groth)
8. Dein blaues Auge (Groth)

First publication: Rieter-Biedermann, December 1873.

The Goethe song is problematical. The twilight's falling begins low in the compass and ends lower still, and the music seems hampered by the many four-bar phrases, and the occasional breaking up of the pattern by lengthening seems rather routinely done. The second song comes far more naturally, to a shapely tune, but not, apparently, aiming for anything deeper. The famous rain song suffers from too long and incongruous a middle. The fourth song, as its name implies, is an echo of 'Regenlied' and does in fact contain the 'Violin Sonata' subject matter, and in a more economical shape. 'Agnes' sings a sad ditty of lost love, its main interest being the irregular lengths of the phrases brought about by mixing three with two crotchets per bar. The final three songs show more artifice, especially the counterpoint in no. 7, but cannot escape a lightweight impression.

Op.61 *Four Duets for Soprano, Alto and Piano*

1. Die Schwestern (Mörike)
2. Klosterfräulein (Kerner)
3. Phänomen (Goethe)
4. Die Boten der Liebe (Wenzig, from the Bohemian)

First publication: Simrock, September 1874.

The third duet is the B major piece which so haunted Levi on his lonely Christmas at the Tegernsee (see the narrative). The other three are well polished pieces for domestic music-making.

Op.63 *Nine Songs for Voice and Piano*

1. Frühlingstrost (Schenkendorf)
2. Erinnerung (Schenkendorf)
3. An ein Bild (Schenkendorf)
4. An die Tauben (Schenkendorf)
5. Junge Lieder I (Felix Schumann)
6. Junge Lieder II (Felix Schumann)
7. Heimwen I (Groth)
8. Heimweh II (Groth)
9. Heimweh III (Groth)

First publication: Peters, November 1874 in two books: 1–4 and 5–9.

The first six are heart-on-sleeve love-songs. There is most musical artifice in the first song where a persistent left hand figure is given ever-changing harmonies, though the change in and out of the contrasting key is rather perfunctory by Brahms's standards. The next three songs, though well shaped, would need a good deal of carrying off in the face of their rather commonplace vocal lines. Both of Felix Schumann's songs are treated strophically, but they are altogether more imaginative. Brahms obviously meant to please him and his mother, and we know he did. The second of the Groth songs has always been a favourite through the indefinable beauty of its melody, in spite of its banal sentiments, but the last of the set has again a charming tune, with a well-balanced contribution from the piano in its diverse textures and occasional counterpoint.

Op.64 *Three Quartets for Voices (SATB) and Piano*

1. An die Heimat (Sternau)
2. Der Abend (Schiller)
3. Fragen (Daumer, from the Turkish)

First publication: Peters, November 1874.

Brahms himself suggested to Peters (letter of October 1874) that the quartets could also be sung by small choirs. The sentimental verses about home, nightfall and falling in love (questions to, and ardent responses from, a tenor of course) are given music of substance and resource, with wide and apt modulations. As the melting and pleasing phrases follow each other, one feels that the drawing-room composer more than compensates for the deficiencies of the drawing-room man.

Op.65 *New Liebeslieder Waltzes for Voices and Piano duet*

(see page 239 for opus 65*a*)

Op.66 *Five Duets for Soprano, Alto and Piano*

1. Klänge I (Groth)
2. Klänge II (Groth)
3. Am Strande (Hölty)
4. Jägerlied (Candidus)
5. Hüt du dich! (from *Des Knaben Wunderhorn*, Arnim and Brentano)

First publication: Simrock, October/November 1875.

Both the Groth songs have a decided individuality. In the first there is a beautifully-tailored canon, the alto imitating the soprano's plaint a fifth away and by inversion, with no hint of the academic in its sound. The second begins

275

with a reminiscence of the beginning of the slow movement from op. 2, but with arching lines and well-contrived collisions. 'Jägerlied' is a question-and-answer song; the soprano's questions have virtually identical phrases but with variations from the piano; the alto huntsman is ever more morose and varied. As in many of Brahms's songs, the folk-like beginning suddenly becomes altogether more knowing and resourceful. However, the last song has five strophic verses of folk-wisdom.

Op.69 *Nine Songs for Voice and Piano*

1. Klage I (Wenzig, from the Bohemian)
2. Klage II (Wenzig, from the Slovakian)
3. Abschied (Wenzig, from the Bohemian)
4. Des Liebsten Schwur (Wenzig, from the Bohemian)
5. Tambourliedchen (Candidus)
6. Vom Strande (Eichendorff, from the Spanish)
7. Über die See (Lemcke)
8. Salome (Keller)
9. Mädchenfluch (Kapper, from the Serbian)

First publication: Simrock, July/August 1877

In April 1877 Brahms sent the manuscript of most (perhaps all) of the songs that were to be published as opp. 69 to 72 inclusive to the Herzogenbergs, calling them 'greenstuff', but with a request a few days later to forward them to Clara. Their detailed replies constitute verdicts for good or ill from the more musically skilled of Brahms's prospective public. The texts of seven of op.69 are folksongs and the other two have the same flavour of short lines, pat rhymes and home-spun sentiments. Some of Brahms's settings add only a minimum of artifice, while others are tricky for both performers. Both Elisabet and Clara felt that Brahms had not found the right balance between art and artlessness in Klage I, with its fussy accompaniment and convoluted refrain. But the next two songs, though in each the three verses are musically identical, make their brief points limpidly and gracefully. The palm was given to 'Des Liebsten Schwur'; it is set to a deftly invented Bohemian dance, in the last verse of which the piano introduction turns into the accompaniment of a new snatch of tune. The pleasure of this surprise resides in the identical settings of the previous three verses. Brahms, the master of variation, is unwilling to use it for mere adjustments to, say, verbal rhythms altering from verse to verse—an obvious point of criticism when comparing him to Wolf. Luckily the last lines of each of the four verses of the song allow him a delicious syncopation that Wolf would have been proud of. Neither lady cared for the drummer's song, Clara finding it too reminiscent of Schubert.

There are many Schubert traits in Brahms's works, which are none the worse for them. This is an effective song for a tenor of boyish timbre and impetuosity, but it is an odd man out amongst women's songs.

'Vom Strande' is a vivid piece, calling in vain from the shore for lost love, with the only answer a bravura depiction of wind and wave. The ladies were for omitting the next two songs, which indeed have much less musical individuality. The sentiments of 'Mädchenfluch' did not appeal—'Mother, help me curse him. Let him hang, but upon my neck'—being too Serbian for Leipzig drawing-rooms—but the music certainly did appeal. Elisabet found it 'glorious'. Like much more Brahms than some expect, it needs to be delivered with passionate bravado.

Op.70 *Four Songs for Voice and Piano*

1. Im Garten am Seegestade (Lemcke)
2. Lerchengesang (Candidus)
3. Serenade (Goethe)
4. Abendregen (Keller)

First publication: Simrock, July/August 1877. No. 4 in *Blätter für Hausmusik* ed. Fritzsch, October 1875.

The three images in three short verses—the high trees, the sounds of waves and unseen birds, the lost love—are expressed with such economy and feeling as to set the first song somewhat apart from the other three. The combined achievement of variation and coherence within a mere 38 bars is extraordinary. The song is introduced and punctuated by the melodic falling thirds of which the prime example is the Fourth Symphony. The piano part of the next song evokes the spring twilight. The voice for the most part sings a triplet rhythm against the quavers of the piano. The resulting three against four looks, and can sound, laboured unless the tempo flows and the voice floats. In 'Serenade' the rapid rhymes and verbal sleight-of-hand of Goethe are hardly to be matched, and Brahms, as Clara noticed, feels obliged to elongate and repeat words at the end, severely militating against the lyric's punctuality. In the otherwise rather laboured 'Abendregen' there is another example of the falling thirds which is even closer to the Fourth Symphony, particularly if the singer takes the alternative to the top A. Brahms is so intent on the rhythm of the rain that he countenances an obvious misaccentuation of the very first word:

Lang - sam   und schimmernd fiel   ein   Re - gen

Op.71 *Five Songs for Voice and Piano*

1. Es liebt sich so lieblich im Lenze! (Heine)
2. An den Mond (Karl Simrock)
3. Geheimnis (Candidus)
4. Willst du, dass ich geh? (Lemcke)
5. Minnelied (Hölty)

First publication: Simrock, July/August 1877.

The Heine song has a spring-like tune with dextrous small alterations as the story proceeds. It is very difficult to catch in music the ironies within Heine's dangerous appearance of naivety, and this is what may have underlain Clara's slight uncertainties about the ending. Both ladies gave the next two songs unqualified approval. 'An den Mond', partly serenade, partly plaint, is distinguished by three-bar phrases which persist until the postlude. In correspondence with Heinrich Herzogenberg about the tempo of 'Geheimnis', which Heinrich wanted slower, Brahms professed to have lost interest in it. He may have felt it lent itself to an easy-going sentimentality—hence the opening mark *Belebt und heimlich* ('lively and secretly'). In the next song the young lover is inviting himself to stay the night, because of the icy blasts outside (with vivid work from the piano). Both ladies draw their skirts round them, finding the suggestions too suggestive for an art song. Their notion that such words were only suitable for a folksong style was duly met with Brahmsian scorn. The final love-song anchors a 'gapped-arpeggio' tune to a bass with many repeated notes, but becomes rather prosaic towards the end, as Clara justly felt.

Op.72 *Five Songs for Voice and Piano*

1. Alte Liebe (Candidus)
2. Sommerfäden (Candidus)
3. O kühler Wald (Brentano)
4. Verzagen (Lemcke)
5. Unüberwindlich (Goethe)

First publication: Simrock, July/August 1877.

Clara's comments (letter of 2 May 1877) put this set firmly above the other three of 1877 in consistency of quality, and rightly. The modulations in 'Alte Liebe' are wide, and all the more striking for the economy of length and texture with which they are expressed. The gossamer threads of the second song are expressed in a striking run of two parts, one in each hand. The second verse begins as though to repeat the music of the first, making more striking the sudden depth of new harmonies and the abrupt transitions from *pp* to *f* and down again. Again the effect is given of a passion, hardly hinted at, suddenly coming to the boil. 'O kühler Wald' is the romantic core of the set, evoking in a perfectly-timed fusion of voice and throbbing accompaniment the lost love, the lost songs and their lost echoes. 'Verzagen' ('Despair') is one of the several songs in which the bereft one standing on a beach seeks a sort of solace in the buffeting of wind and waves. It is a common, indeed common-place, image, but here it evokes not only a spectacular piano part but also a vocal line that can ride the storm with rhetorical power. 'Unüberwindlich' ('Unconquerable') ending the set on a truly flamboyant note, makes use of a Domenico Scarlatti motif about which Brahms consulted Henschel. It is indeed acknowledged, but its authorship is immaterial, put beside the use Brahms makes of it. These five songs suit a lower voice, mezzo-soprano or baritone, but the texts preclude their being sung as a set by one singer. As far as first performances were concerned singers simply chose what suited them. For instance Amalie Joachim was the first performer of nos. 1 and 4, and Stockhausen the first with no. 5.

Op.75 *Ballads and Romances, for two Voices and Piano*

1. Edward (Herder, from the Scottish)
2. Guter Rat (From *Das Knaben Wunderhorn*, Arnim and Brentano)
3. So lass uns wandern! (Wenzig, from the Bohemian)
4. Walpurgisnacht (Alexis)

First publication: Simrock, November/December 1878.
Dedication: Julius Allgeyer.

The duets are for different combinations: nos. 1 and 3 for soprano and tenor, no. 2 for soprano and alto, no. 4 for two sopranos. For 'Edward' Brahms reverts to the blood-thirsty Scottish song whose words prefaced the first of the op. 10 Ballades for Piano. From the beginning 'why is your sword so red?' to the final cursing of the mother the movement runs in a continuous sweep of changing shapes and figurations—the non-stop, ever-developing piano part is a *tour de force*. Clara thought the words horrible, their setting wonderful. The middle songs lack musical distinction but the question and answer of the final song—'Mother, where was your broom last night?'—is a rare and effective presto. Clara trembled happily at the noises in the chimney, and pitied those who could only giggle. It is difficult to imagine her giggling at anything.

Op.84 *Five Romances and Songs for one or two Voices and Piano*

1. Sommerabend (Hans Schmidt)
2. Der Kranz (Hans Schmidt)
3. In den Beeren (Hans Schmidt)
4. Vergebliches Ständchen (Folksong from the Lower Rhine, Kretzschmer–Zuccalmaglio collection)
5. Spannung (Folksong from the Lower Rhine, Kretzschmer–Zuccalmaglio collection)

First publication: Simrock, July 1882.

The first three, presumably the 'romances' of the title, are mother-and-daughter duets; the other two are for would-be lovers and achieving lovers respectively. Only at the end of the last song is an optional second voice-part given, to achieve the singing in sixths which is a traditional rendering of hand-in-hand love. In this case the man must be a tenor. The minor-major alternations of mother's warnings and daughter's blitheness are rather conventional in the first song, but a good deal more individual in the second, which has taxing but satisfying ripples for the piano, as though a stream were, as usual, near at hand. In the third song the contrast is between the keys of mother and daughter, the latter's second verse subtly changing to accommodate the all-important kisses. The last two make a pair, the well-known love-shut-out the more obvious, the eventual happiness of released 'Spannung' ('Tension') the more satisfying. Elisabet called it 'strangely touching'. The folk song to its original tune was also a favourite of Brahms's, occurring in an arrangement for his Hamburg ladies' choir, as well as in the published collection op.49 (No.4).

Op.85 *Six Songs for Voice and Piano*

1. Sommerabend (Heine)
2. Mondenschein (Heine)
3. Mädchenlied (Kapper, from the Serbian)
4. Ade! (Kapper, from the Bohemian)
5. Frühlingslied (Geibel)
6. In Waldeinsamkeit (Lemcke)

First publication: Simrock, July 1882.

The Heine songs are a pair. In the first the summer moonlight reveals to the singer shapes real and fanciful; in the second, later at night, it comforts his suffering heart and tired limbs, and brings him to healing tears. The musical *tour de force* consists in making both songs, different in effect as they are, out of substantially the same materials. Apart from small but telling cross-references in prologue, postludes and interludes, Brahms achieves masterly migrations of the piano's countermelody through three different pitches while the voice is unchanged, saving itself for a final modulation as the sorrows and the tears begin to flow away. 'Mädchenlied' uses five beats to a bar until the very end, when the expansion to six is used to underline the fact that the beloved is gone over the water. The sense of being bereft is conveyed by using the piano's extra beats not for more notes but for silence. The quiet farewell of 'Ade!' is delivered in three identical stanzas to a trickling accompaniment which only allows one small accent in each verse; each time the final farewells, in Schubertian style, leave the prevailing minor key for the major. The spring song that follows makes a contrast, with a A B A shape permitting swift modulations in the middle and a slight elongation as the singer realises that the old heart could bloom once more. The last song, slow and in B major, is a perfect specimen of a genre dear to Brahms, the entranced night piece, in which the lovers in bitter-sweet pleasure hear at last the nightingale. The bird is of course not imitated, as the music is itself listening.

Apart from the first two songs, there is no particular coherence of key and text to suggest the singing of op.85 as a set, but all the same the songs are all of good quality, and are crowned with one, of which Elisabet was moved to write: 'The man who can listen to it dry-eyed is surely past saving!'

Op.86 *Six Songs for a deeper Voice and Piano*

1. Therese (Keller)
2. Feldeinsamkeit (Allmers)
3. Nachtwandler (Kalbeck)
4. Über die Heide (Storm)
5. Versunken (Felix Schumann)
6. Todessehnen (Schenkendorf)

First publication: Simrock, July 1882.

A quick wit is needed for 'Therese'. The first part of the song poses in folksong style a question about a glance. The second part does not answer the question but teasingly suggests that the questioner listens to a seashell. This 'answer' has no vocal tune, only a quiet declamation over the piano's expansion of its prologue, beginning in a foreign key. The singer cannot or will not do any more. Thirty-nine bars must suffice.

The famous 'Feldeinsamkeit' is another of Brahms's slow contemplative trances, but now lying in the still sunlight looking upwards at the blue sky.

The feeling of calm security is reinforced by the harmonies being enclosed, from time to time, between pedal notes at top and bottom. The beautiful white clouds travelling through the blue make the singer imagine he has died and is travelling with them through eternal space—a harmless enough conceit, but the very notion is enough to send Brahms on a downward-thirds plunge without harmonies.

The poet of 'Nachtwandler' is Max Kalbeck, the tireless biographer without whom many details would have been unconsidered trifles. The tune is unremarkable, but a major-minor figure in the accompaniment out-Schuberts Schubert:

Two vivid and taxing songs follow, the first tramping, even thumping, through the autumn of life and love, the second drowning, not unwillingly, in Love's strong sea. This song is marked 'very passionately, but not too fast'. This is where the passions are to be found which have no real-life consummations. The heading is an apter banner than the problematical 'free but happy'. In the final song the longing for the release of death is more powerfully expressed in the initial minor key than the prayer in the major key for it to be granted. This is again a Brahmsian trait, perhaps inevitable when one does not know to whom one is praying.

The succession of keys and moods, and the specification of 'lower voice' makes this into a true set rather than a repertoire.

Op.91 *Two songs for alto Voice, Viola and Piano*

1. Gestillte Sehnsucht (Rückert)
2. Geistliches Wiegenlied (Geibel, from Lope de Vega)

First publication: Simrock, December 1884.

'In the golden evening the winds and birds whisper the world to sleep. When does my longing heart obtain its rest? When the winds and birds whisper my life to sleep.' This simple ternary design is greatly enriched by Brahms. He writes a mainly low-lying theme for viola, as though beginning a sonata movement, but this turns out to be a counter-theme when the voice begins. The obvious parallelisms of the poet's design evoke far from obvious variants towards the end of the final stanza, with elongation, syncopations and a very remarkable passage of harmony in which the viola arpeggiates mild dissonances and the piano supplies their resolutions.

The prelude to the second song is the old Christmas song 'Josef, lieber Josef mein', to which the first vocal phrase stands in close relationship:

The middle section is a contrast in the minor key, changing the time to 3/4 and with the viola not only making plaintive dissonances, but also adding a subdued conflict with the piano in very typical two-against-three rhythms.

Op.92 *Four Quartets for Soprano, Alto, Tenor, Bass and Piano*

1. O schöne Nacht (Daumer)
2. Spätherbst (Almers)
3. Abendlied (Hebbel)
4 Warum? (Goethe)

First publication: Simrock, December 1884.

The first two songs are nature pictures. The Daumer song is an E major Nocturne, itself a second version, with imaginative spacing of the piano part. The second song, an evocation of autumn in rather naïve words, employs sophisticated counterpoint to lend it the most elaborate music of the four.

Op.94 *Five Songs for a deep Voice and Piano*

1. Mit vierzig Jahren (Rückert)
2. Steig auf, geliebter Schatten (Halm)
3. Mein Herz ist schwer (Geibel)
4. Sapphische Ode (Hans Schmidt)
5. Kein Haus, keine Heimat (Halm)

First publication: Simrock, December 1884.

These songs specify a deep voice, and indeed the first one, but not the others, is given the bass clef. But this need not weigh heavily since Brahms consented to a simultaneous publication of an upward transposition. What is more, the keys for a higher voice (d, f, b, F, f sharp) do not use transpositions by a consistent interval.

The first song uses a posthumous poem first published a year before. Its sentiments seem to chime oddly with a hale and harty composer just past his fiftieth birthday: 'With 40 years of effort we stand and look back from the mountain . . . No need to waste breath climbing further . . . You will be in port before you think.' The composer has not seemingly exerted himself much to mitigate the obviousness of the poem. On the other hand the next two songs express the longings for lost youth, and lost past generally, with graphic and surprising harmonies; in comparison with the 'Sapphic Ode' they are hardly ever sung. The two stanzas of the latter, echoing the parallels of dew and tears, are a beautiful example of the subtlest use of variation. The harmonies are essentially the same both times; the upward stems mark the first verse, the lower the second:

The last song is a vivid codetta, a song of a man of straw, too tiny to be sung by itself, but making an extraordinary whimsical effect after 'Sapphic Ode'.

Op.95 *Seven Songs for Voice and Piano*

1. Das Mädchen (Kapper, from the Serbian)
2. Bei dir sind meine Gedanken (Halm)
3. Beim Abschied (Halm)
4. Der Jäger (Halm)
5. Vorschneller Schwur (Kapper, from the Serbian)
6. Mädchenlied (Heyse, form the Italian)
7. Schön war, dass ich dir weihte (Daumer, from the Turkish)

First publication: Simrock, December 1884.

All the songs are of the folksong type, and from the female viewpoint. In the first, the pert maiden will wash her face in wormwood if it appears that an old man will kiss it; if a young man, it will be rose-water. This leads Brahms to a mixture of three and four time, usually alternately to make seven-beat phrases. The three almost identical stanzas of the second song depict with a dexterously-timed modulation and fleeting piano writing the thoughts hovering, enchanted, round the loved one. The third song is unusually marked 'impatiently' (*ungeduldig*). When the song was first published Brahms made this effect by changing to a 2/4 accompaniment of the 3/8 song towards the end, but subsequently he used this unusual (but not difficult) contradiction throughout. The homespun but pointed sentiments of the remainder use good tunes and are vehicles for a good actress, who does not mind mocking herself. The last song, which ruefully feels that kindnesses deserved a better reward, is a masterly and seamless weaving of a few simple strands, unobtrusively serving words and mood.

Op.96 *Four Songs for Voice and Piano*

1. Der Tod, das ist die kühle Nacht (Heine)
2. Wir wandelten (Daumer, from the Hungarian)
3. Es schauen die Blumen (Heine)
4. Meerfahrt (Heine)

First publication: Simrock, March 1886.

It seems, from Kalbeck, that a severe criticism of a manuscript setting of a Heine song dissuaded Brahms from an all-Heine volume. We are indeed compensated by the substitute. Daumer's original may be Hungarian, but Brahms treats it as a full-blown art song; it would not, for example, fit happily in op.95. Its beauty of melody and elasticity of form ensure its fame. The Heine songs capture his economically expressed mood-pictures. In the first the singer dreamily hovering between life and death's sleep hears the nightingale, but again the song itself is listening, and it is the obsessive rhythm whether below or above which can represent the knell or the quiet breathing. In the second the rippling three-against-two accompaniment bears away the unrewarded love-songs on its stream, and the last song is a slow and mournful barcarolle of very Heinean lovers journeying sadly past a ghostly, mist-shrouded island. The harmonies are as striking as any Brahms wrote in the songs, and the eerie chromatics are set off by a rising two-note cry as of some despairing gondolier. A downward transposition of this set was simultaneously published; this time the transposing interval is the same throughout.

Op.97 *Six Songs for Voice and Piano*

1. Nachtigall (Reinhold)
2. Auf dem Schiffe (Reinhold)
3. Entführung (Alexis)
4. Dort in den Weiden (Lower Rhine folksong)
5. Komm bald (Groth)
6. Trennung (Swabian folksong, from the Kretz-schmer–Zuccalmaglio collection)

First publication: Simrock, March 1886.

Not surprisingly the nightingale's song is not to be heard (except, inexplicably, by Clara) but only the poet's reaction. The song in its daring varieties of texture and note-lengths, its whimsical, almost mocking, expression and, yes, its exact verbal accentuation make this the nearest Brahms comes to Hugo Wolf, though chronology makes this an inexact and unjust thing to say. Wolf might not, perhaps, have allowed the final vocal phrase, but left it to the pianist to shrug off the song. On the other hand the next song does give a feel of the bird's free darting over the head of the passenger in the morning brightness on the Rhine, one of Brahms's favourite sights. (But we must remember that to Elisabet it represented sail-flapping). The forceful, and difficult, gallop of the following abduction shows what Brahms can do by way of direct representation. Most elopements are with willing partners; this stirring song is not long enough to show whether the lady becomes complaisant. Brahms knew the original tunes of both nos.4 and 6. They both appear arranged by him in the repertoires of the Hamburg ladies and of the Vienna Singakademie and in his published '49'. It is significant that here he accepts the challenge of writing another two memorable tunes for them without expanding them into true art songs. The key and the pervasive rhythm of "Komm bald', (A major and

$$\quad \text{♩ ♩ ♩} \mid \text{♩. ♪♫)}$$

have obvious links with the Violin Sonata op.100. The tenor Gustav Walter is credited with the first public performances of five of the songs, but again there was simultaeous publication of the set for lower voice, though not by a consistent interval. 'Reinhold' is the pseudonym of a Tübingen professor, Christian Köstlin, who was Maria Fellinger's father.

Op.103 *Zigeunerlieder ('Gypsy songs') for four Voices and Piano*

First publication: (eleven numbers in all): Simrock, October 1888. A version supplied by Brahms for solo voice and piano comprised numbers one to seven and eleven from the original, and was published by Simrock in April/May 1889.

The texts come from a publication of 25 Hungarian folksongs—words and music—by Zoltán Nagy, with German translations by Hugo Conrat. Not surprisingly we look in vain for any undigested Hungarianisms in Brahms's music. There is little here that Bartók or Koadály would have regarded as authentic, whether Hungarian or Gypsy. Even the accented short/long rhythm familiarised by Korbay's song arrangements and by Liszt's Rhapsodies is conspicuously absent. But the unbuttoned rhythmic *élan* of most of the songs is outstanding, usually avoiding the regularity of four-bar phrases, either by writing them in fives or sixes or by adding echo or interlude bars. The final song has always proved irresistible both in its swing and its modulation.

Op.105 *Five Songs for a deeper Voice and Piano*

1. Wie Melodien zieht es mir (Groth)
2. Immer leiser wird mein Schlummer (Lingg)
3. Klage (From the Lower Rhine)
4. Auf dem Kirchhofe (von Liliencron)
5. Verrat (Lemcke)

First publication: Simrock, October 1888.

The arching 'Wie Melodien' which Brahms incorporated in the Second Violin Sonata is a touchstone in considering his melodic art in songs in other than folksong style. To play or sing its first phrase unaccompanied (in comparison with, say, many of Schubert's):

reveals immediately how much it depends on its harmony. In particular it is crucial that there is a C sharp below the first D, a D below the first G sharp and a clothing to the fourth bar (reading upwards) of D, B flat and F natural. This is not an invitation to think of the harmony as added to the tune. On the contrary the whole conception is simultaneous, for voice and piano, not with piano. The overall direction is *Zart* ('sweetly') and at this point the piano has it in Italian too (*sempre dolce*), but for a moment lasting only a quaver's length Brahms puts his first dissonance quite starkly to make the point, his C sharp under the D being

with nothing between.

With a masterpiece like 'Immer leiser' one feels the only helpful course is to print the whole song and get someone like Hermine Spies to sing it. On her death-bed the bereft girl dreams that her lover is at the door. Awake and weeping she begs for his return before it is too late. To compare the second verse with the first reveals Brahms at his most sensitive and overpowering. The second verse begins with the piano playing the first phrase, as though the singer can sing no more; then she finds the strength to join in the second phrase. Put baldly like this can give the reader no idea of how touching is the 'ja' with which she re-enters. The other variation that cries out for mention is the rising-third phrases which end each stanza. The first time, they are heard in a descending sequence of three; the second time, as the girl desperately uses her last breath the sequences rise, making a top F, *forte*, as the quite overwhelming climax.

The next song could hardly cap that, and uses three simple strophic verses, but with the quirk that beginning in F the voice ends in D minor, leaving the little postlude to bring us back to F. The churchyard song quotes, as Brahms said, the opening of the chorale tune, originally by Hassler, used by Bach five times in the *St Matthew Passion*. The fifth song, melodramatic but powerful, is a tale of overheard infidelity and murderous revenge. It is printed in the bass clef, and is as certainly a man's song as 'Immer leiser' is a woman's so that the question of op.105 being a set does not arise, unless with two singers.

Op.106   *Five Songs for Voice and Piano*

1. Ständchen (Kugler)
2. Auf dem See (Reinhold)
3. Es hing der Reif (Groth)
4. Meine Lieder (Frey)
5. Ein Wanderer (Reinhold)

First publication: Simrock, October 1888.

In the serenade there are artful and abrupt modulations: G to E to G in the flanking verses of a ternary shape. The middle section mentions three students with flute and fiddle and zither, and it is just possible to detect a reference to the Academic Festival Overture. Elisabet found in the second song a discrepancy between its vocal line and an 'array of obstacles in the harmony', but this perhaps refers to the sophistications of rhythm with which they are expressed in this unusual combination of barcarolle and contented love. The third song is a study in an obsessive dream marked by the constant

$$\text{♩ ♩ ♩ ♩}$$

rhythm of both voice and piano. The text is a hoary cliché, the imagined love in the reality of winter, but the song in the right hands has the potential power of a 'Winterreise' cameo. The delicate harmony, 'like fine gold tracery', of 'Meine Lieder' made it Elisabet's favourite of the set, to be offset immediately by the short but powerful glooms of Brahms's 'Wanderer'.

Op.107 *Five Songs for Voice and Piano*

1. An die Stolze (Flemming)
2. Salamander (Lemcke)
3. Das Mädchen spricht (Gruppe)
4. Maienkätzchen (Von Liliencron)
5. Mädchenlied (Heyse)

First publication: Simrock, October 1888.

Elisabet discussed this set in a long letter of 28 October 1888. She could not reconcile words and music in the first song, which goes on its lively way in spite of the man's sentiments, veering from 'have a heart' to 'but you have none'. Elisabet evidently did not always recognise irony when she saw it. Small wonder, perhaps, that she also detested Lemcke's 'skim-milk' in 'Salamander', another whistling in the dark, or rather in the fire, male piece, which goes well as a tail-piece to the first. The third song expresses a succinct female irony in what Elisabet calls 'a pretty enough piano piece', and the yet shorter 'Maienkätzchen' ('The catkin') she describes as 'sure to be popular'. One learns much about Elisabet, and some of Brahms's audience, from this letter. On the other hand, the last plaintive spinning song—for what purpose? for what man?—draws the bitter-sweet with a master hand, and is a worthy last published solo song before the Serious Songs of eight years hence.

Op.112 *Six Quartets for solo Voice and Piano*

1. Sehnsucht (Kugler)
2. Nächtens (Kugler)
3–6. Four Gypsy songs (Conrat, from the Hungarian)

First publication: Peters, November 1891.

The first two of the set rise well above the merely domestic in their imaginative construction and atmosphere. 'Sehnsucht' in particular has something of the combination of rich harmony and economical expression to be found in the First Clarinet Sonata, in the same key. 'Nächtens' is a night-piece, but certainly no nocturne with its five-four time, unusual vocal scoring, and shuddering piano part. The Gypsy songs are an acceptable appendix to the others.

Op.121 *Four Serious Songs for Bass and Piano*

First publication: Simrock, July 1896.
Dedication: Max Klinger.

The narrative records what Brahms told Marie Schumann about this work. Brahms also told Kalbeck that the songs were a birthday present to himself [Brahms] and to himself alone.[21]

The texts lead from the extreme pessimism of Ecclesiastes 3 verses 19–22 to St Paul's hymn to love in I Corinthians 13. Whittall has pointed out how in the music this is paralleled by the first song being wholly in the minor mode (D minor with some C sharp minor) the second being mostly in G minor but ending in G major, the third being roughly equally in E minor and E major, and the fourth being wholly in the majors (E flat with a B major middle).

The andante funeral march of the first song, with its frequent empty fifths, is contrasted with the hounding wind of the allegro which is the principal reason why not to orchestrate the song. All is vanity indeed. The second song takes up the final D of the first to begin a falling arpeggio

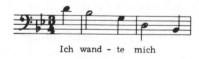

Ich wand - te mich

whose initial thirds spread further:

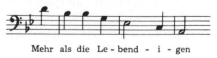

Mehr als die Le - bend - i - gen

290

so that when the song turns to G major, the accompaniment turns naturally into the comforting harmony of

and thereby foreshadows how the third song will grow from the second:

with its final welcoming of death by turning minor to major and the thirds to sixths thus

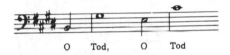

At first sight the E flat major of the final song is far removed, but the G sharp at the top of the last chord of no.3 leads by a pun (G sharp = A flat) through the abrupt but sufficient piano introduction to no.4 thus:

What is more, the E major key at the end of no.3 stands in that semi-tone-up 'Neapolitan' relationship to E flat which is a continuing thread in Brahms's tonal relationships.

On pages 292–3 will be found the last page of Brahms's manuscript to be published in his lifetime. Though the date is May 1896 the hand retains its clarity; there is no note on the page which would be ambiguous for an experienced musical draghtsman. In the third and fourth bars will be seen the big leaps for Faith and Hope, then the top climax extending Love to more than the one bar allotted to the others. Brahms's alternative to the top G (E natural) is not *faute de mieux*. The E natural is interesting musically because of its collision with the piano's E flats, nor is there any lapse of grammar, because the latter go down whilst the E natural goes up—Brahms is grammatical till the end. It can be seen in bar 15 of the facsimile that the right hand thumb was originally tied as in the previous bar, but then instead accommo-

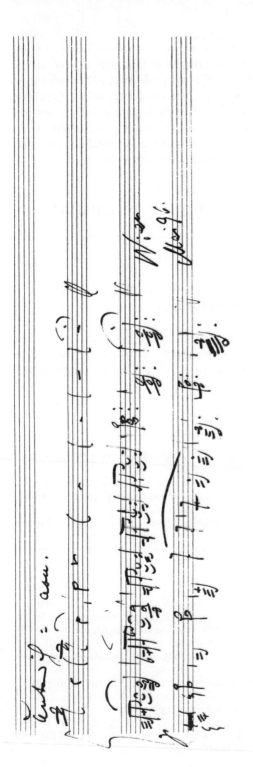

The last page of the Four Serious Songs, op.121.

dated the F sharp because there was nothing for an F natural to do that was logical. The last vocal phrase reverts to the blissful (*Wonnevoll*) passage from the end of the 'Wie bist du, meine Königin', also in the same key. One final typical detail may be noticed: the left hand at the beginning of the last line uses the bottom note only, one being enough. The octave is reserved for the keynote two bars later. We may not know what sort of love Brahms saw as his solace, but we do know him as a passionate craftsman to the end.

WoO21 *Mondnacht (Song for Voice and Piano)*

Text by Eichendorff

First publication: Wigand (of Göttingen), 1854, in a collection called *Albumblätter*.

This is a dreamy song with some striking modulations, well worth singing in a group, but inevitably suffering by comparison with the incomparable: Schumann's own setting of the words in the 'Liederkreis' op.39, which Brahms may not have known in 1853.

NOTES

1. D. Tovey, *Essays in Musical Analysis*, vol. 1 (Oxford University Press, London, 1935), p. 133.
2. This rhythm also permeates the first movement of another Beethoven successor, significantly described by Schumann as a 'veiled symphony', the Piano Sonata in F minor op.5, and is also very obvious in the trio of its scherzo.
3. S. Newman, 'The slow movement of Brahms's first symphony', *Music Review*, vol. ix (1948), p. 4
4. R. Pascall, 'Brahms's first symphony slow movement: the initial performing version', *Musical Times*, vol. 122 (1981), p. 664.
5. Ibid.
6. Tovey, *Essays*, vol. 1, p. 90.
7. An experiment with a piano, for instance, will show that D E D when C is expected will not only lead the ear to want C, but if D E D is persisted in, it can lead to an expectation of the key of G, which is what Brahms uses it for in preparation for the G major subject (first trumpet and first horn from bar 111).
8. The re-use of the introduction to the last movement as culmination is also Schubertian—see especially his Octet.
9. Tovey, A further note on Brahms's Tragic Overture', in *Essays* vol. 6, p. 55.
10. The matter, and its implications, are very thoroughly addressed by L. Litterick 'Brahms the indecisive', in Musgrave (ed.) *Brahms*, 2, pp. 223f.
11. I called this an 'unconscious' reminiscence in 1974 (see I. Keys, *Brahms Chamber Music*, BBC Music Guide (BBC, London), but cannot now believe it. Unconscious or not, Brahms excised it in his revision.

12. These and kindred matters are taken much further than our space permits in two essays in M. Musgrave (ed.), *Brahms,* 2 (CUP, Cambridge, 1987): A. Whittall, 'Two of a kind? Brahms's op.51 finales', and A. Forte, 'Motivic design and structural levels in the first movement of Brahms's string quartet in C minor'.

13. See A. Walker *An Anatomy of Musical Criticism* (Barrie and Rockliffe, London, 1966), p. 15, for a disparagement of the writing, but not the music.

14. J. Webster, 'The C sharp version of Brahms's op.60' *Musical Times*, vol. 121 (1980), pp. 89–93.

15. I. Fellinger, 'Brahms's view of Mozart', in Pascall (ed.), *Brahms*, p. 53.

16. The sonata must have been in Senff's hands, for publication at least by Christmas 1853, since there is a letter from Brahms dated 26 December quoting these words for printing.

17. J. Dunsby, 'The Multi-piece in Brahms', in R. Pascall (ed.), *Brahms: Biographical, Documentary and Analytical Studies* (CUP, Cambridge, 1983), pp. 257ff.

18. Essays particularly valuable to the further study of these works: (*a*) V. Hancock, 'Brahms's links with German Renaissance music' for background and detailed reference to op.74 no.2, and R. Pascall, 'Brahms's 'Missa Canonoica' and its recomposition in his motet 'Warum' op.74 no.1, in Musgrave (ed.) *Brahms*, 2; (*b*) V. Hancock, The growth of Brahms's interest in early choral music', in Pascall (ed.) *Brahms 5*.

19. I. Braus, 'Brahms's Liebe und Frühling II, op.3, no.3: A New Path to the Artwork of the Future?', *Nineteenth Century Music*, vol. 10 (University of California Press, Davis, California, 1986–7), pp. 135ff.

20. S. Langer, *Feeling and Form* (Routledge and Kegan Paul, London, 1953), quoted in D. Lindley, *Thomas Campion* (E. J. Brill, Leiden, 1986), p. 129.

21. For a detailed essay see A. Whittall, 'The vier ernste Gesänge op.121: enrichment and uniformity', in Pascall (ed.) *Brahms*.

Fingerprints: Brahms's Musical Style

T he imprint of Brahms's style covers so many facets that to summarise it suggests rewriting most of the book from a more particular viewpoint. But some may find this last chapter a temporarily useful alternative to re-reading the whole book immediately. The musical examples have been chosen, as far as possible, from the three piano pieces comprising op.117, in the hopes of facilitating hearing them instead of reading them. The summary is divided into fields which inevitably overlap, and are not in any order of importance.

For rhythm a very obvious trait, and one which arises from Baroque music, is what is nowadays called hemiola, that is the division of six beats (whether in one bar or two) which are normally accented 1 2 3 4 5 6 into 1 2 3 4 5 6. In Baroque music this is usually cadential, in the six units immediately preceding the final chord of the phrase. With Brahms the hemiola can occur anywhere in triple time or compound time, sometimes occupying the whole texture, sometimes in combination. In the fifth bar of this example from op.117 no.1 it lends a sense of yet more complete relaxation of the 'lullaby', to which the static tonic bass also contributes.

Example 1

Rhythmic dislocations are frequently caused by anticipating the main beats by tying in shorter notes in advance of them. There are very robust examples in the first of the two rhapsodies op. 79 for Piano, and a spectacular string of them in the D minor Violin Sonata, op. 108. This may be a case of altering the melody while the harmony remains on the beats, or it may be that the harmony is also dislocated. This kind of syncopation is a trait of Schumann as well, particularly in the piano music (see for instance the March movement of his Fantaisie, op. 17, a work which Brahms knew intimately), but Brahms is much more systematic and intellectually controlled. The beginning of the middle section of op.117 no.3 shows a half-way house between the two versions; the theme is not 'against' the harmony, but the harmony is not *en bloc*; it emerges. Note the cloudy, and decorated, diminished seventh beginning in bar four and elongated so that the phrase becomes five bars long. Note also that the sense of the second five bars answering the first, is achieved not only by enlarging the intervals of the melody but duplicating the rhythm of the first five bars exactly.

Example 2

297

Eugenie Schumann[1] has an amusing tale about one such 'distressing' accompaniment, when Atnonia Kufferath was singing in the Schumann house with Brahms as her partner.

> At the end we all asked for our favourite, 'In stiller Nacht' [no.42 of the 49 folksong settings]. Brahms has enhanced by a wonderful accompaniment with strange rhythmic device the appeal of this haunting, touching plaint . . . For the greater part the piano is a quaver in advance of the voice . . .'Can you sing that in time?' Brahms asked her. ' I think I can' she said with a mischievous smile, 'if you can play it in time.'

Elongations and diminutions of melodies are in the arsenal of any contrapuntist; of the former there is a straightforward example in the closing bars of op.117 no.3. The splendid climax of the Tragic Overture op.81 is achieved simply by the exact doubling in length, on wind and brass, of the phrase which immediately precedes it on the strings. This example of diminution from the last movement of the Second Clarinet Sonata is a teasing and drastic one.

Example 3

A penchant for unusual phrase lengths—of three, five, or seven bars rather than four or eight—needs no further examples. See the notes on op.87 for a seven-bar phrase made by telescoping.

In the field of *harmony* Bach left very little for the nineteenth century to invent. The diminished seventh, electrifying for shouting 'Barabbas' in the *St Matthew Passion*, had borne as much as it could in Beethoven's 'Appassionata' Sonata, and been done to death in Liszt's Praeludium and Fugue on BACH. This would not prevent Brahms using it plain if it suited his purposes, but here are two beautiful sophistications from op.117 no. 2. In the second bar of the first the ear hears nothing but a gentle descent of a minor chord (G flat or F sharp). At the bottom of the diminuendo the E flat appears and the left hand comes up with at length a diminished seventh—that is, it would be one were the D flat not still there. At the last possible moment there is release as the D flat falls to C to restart the melody over such of the chord as remains in the minds' ear.

Example 4

The next example is of a later *pianissimo* descent. Here because Brahms is preparing, apparently, another reprise, the left hand plays the arpeggiated chord fairly straight-forwardly. But see (bar two of the example) how the right hand uses, with extraordinary effect but perfectly logically, notes which are not of the harmony: the first D flat out of the blue, and the passing-note A flat which leads to the diminished octave A flat/A natural on two successive notes in a *legato* phrase. At the end of third bar the main theme is expected to start again. It stops and 'corrects' itself as though it has just thought of a charming variation-C flat for C natural, coming back to the 'right' recapitulatory course at the end of the example.

Example 5

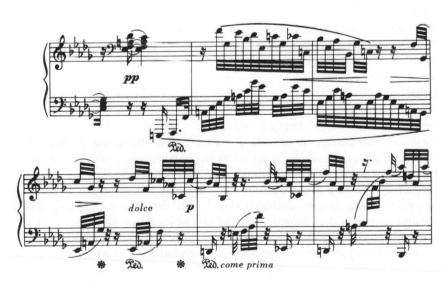

299

The planning of long-range tonal balance is the very essence of Brahms's designs large and small, and is referred to many times in the notes. But a particularly beautiful example is to be found in op.117 no.2. The secondary material turns out to be a version in fairly straight harmony of the arpeggiated first subject. Given that the tonic of the piece is B flat minor, it is not surprising to find this variant in the relative major, D flat.

Example 6

At the end of this piece's ternary scheme A B A, composing decisions have to be made. Brahms doubtless made them in a flash—they may be said to have 'come to him'—but we will proceed by question and answer.

Shall we leave it at A B A?

No, the momentum we have built up requires a coda.

Shall we use B or A (yes, we know they are closely related) or something else?

I want to end slower, so we shall use B, but *più adagio*.

B is, or was, in the major. Do we want to end the piece in the major? Certainly not!

Are we then to repeat B in the coda in B flat minor?

Not immediately, because the second A already uses B flat minor at some length.

What shall you do then?

I shall bring back B in B flat major, then elongate it by sequence using D flat major again for the next step.

But this will prolong the major, will it not?

Yes and no; putting it into D flat major will stress the D flat which paradoxically will give a B flat minor feeling as it is the minor third note of the B flat minor we all have in our mind's ear, and I shall help the conclusive feel by persisting with F in the bass. In the hopes that you will not ask any more questions I invite you to admire the right hand's first note in the elongation, E natural—a pretty dissonance to remind you of Example 5.

Surely this right-hand addition is somehow akin to the left-hand fill-up figure in much of the piece, for instance the last two bars of Example 5?

Clever; I never thought of that.

Here is the beginning of that *più adagio*:

Example 7

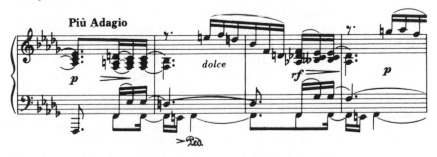

A master of harmony will not hesitate to employ, where suitable, what one might call come-what-may sequences, that is sequences by precise transposition of all the intervals, for he will be confident that he can get out of any tonal labyrinth this may lead him into. Here is an example from 'Immer leiser wird mein Schlummer', op.105 no.2; by the momentary predominance of interval over tonality it was just the thing to appeal to Schoenberg:

Example 8

An advantage of speaking a language understood, by and large, by the people he was addressing, was that Brahms thus had the opportunity of surprising them. Each extended piece is potentially a unique experience, with multiple choices on offer. One of the areas around which surprises and questions cluster are the recapitulation—where is it? What theme will be used? What variations will there be? Will it come in like a lion, or take us by surprise? Another area is tonality. What is the key of the second group? Has it a new subject or an altered old one? In such works as the Piano Quintet tonal surprises abound as though Brahms was intent on being spectacular. Here he could take his cue, if he needed one, from Schubert, whose last, great, Piano Sonata is in B flat. When the moment is ripe, orthodoxy suggests that the second subject begins in F major. He adopts the furthest remove: instead of F natural major, F sharp minor. Brahms's imagination leaps, but the results are not whimsical, nor ever arbitrary. There is a melodic component binding together the most outré of progressions.

Counterpoint we have seen as an omnipresent force. Almost every texture of Brahms is held together by logical interior melody. Op.117 no.1 offers two small but beautiful canons: bar seven, where the bass leads the treble, and the quiet climax, characteristically marked *dolce*, eight bars before the end.

But there is more to counterpoint than the erudite display of traditional resources, prominent though these are in the piano variations and the early organ pieces. The ability to make a melodic line of a bass is what gives the characteristic flow and push of Brahms's music, to say nothing of its incidental modulations. The songs (op. 32 for instance) abound in wonderful parts for the left hand. The polarity, and the exchange of top and bottom in the 'St. Antoni Variations' are so well known as to be in danger of being unremarked.

It has often been said, and as far as we know may be true, that Brahms was 'the end of the line'; so too was Bach. Brahms would not for a moment wish to be compared with Bach, but he could be, on various grounds. Before we allot him to a *cul-de-sac* we should remember that his integrity and industry helped ensure that in the twentieth century there were quartets for Bartók to write, and symphonies as living forms for Shostakovitch. Composers are opportunists, though many are not fraudulent. If they find themselves unable to surpass Brahms's use of musical language they go on to persuade themselves, innocently enough, that the language is a dead one. The process of obsolescence took longer with Wagner, but if Brahms is on the end of the line, so too is Wagner. Luckily the audience whom Brahms addressed, and still addresses, cares nothing about these things.

NOTE

1. *Ibid.*, p. 172.

Indices

NOTE: *References to Clara Schumann, Joachim, Simrock and Elisabet von Herzogenberg are found throughout the narrative. Certain of the musical works have been listed under their title in the name index above, but all the works may be found under opus numbers in the index of compositions below.*

General Index

303

Index of compositions

309